DRIVEN
an elegy to cars, roads and motorsport

Our life is not our life, merely the stories we have told about our life. Told to others but – mainly – to ourselves

Julian Barnes, *The Sense Of An Ending*

More from Veloce Publishing

A Chequered Life – Graham Warner and the Chequered Flag (Hesletine)
A Life Awheel – The 'auto' biography of W de Forte (Skelton)
Amédée Gordini ... a true racing legend (Smith)
André Lefebvre, and the cars he created at Voisin and Citroën (Beck)
Bunty – Remembering a gentleman of noble Scottish-Irish descent (Schrader)
Chris Carter at Large – Stories from a lifetime in motorcycle racing (Carter & Skelton)
Cliff Allison, The Official Biography of – From the Fells to Ferrari (Gauld)
Edward Turner – The Man Behind the Motorcycles (Clew)
Driven by Desire – The Desiré Wilson Story
First Principles – The Official Biography of Keith Duckworth (Burr)
Inspired to Design – F1 cars, Indycars & racing tyres: the autobiography of Nigel Bennett (Bennett)
Jack Sears, The Official Biography of – Gentleman Jack (Gauld)
Jim Redman – 6 Times World Motorcycle Champion: The Autobiography (Redman)
John Chatham – 'Mr Big Healey' – The Official Biography (Burr)
The Lee Noble Story (Wilkins)
Mason's Motoring Mayhem – Tony Mason's hectic life in motorsport and television (Mason)
Raymond Mays' Magnificent Obsession (Apps)
Pat Moss Carlsson Story, The – Harnessing Horsepower (Turner)
'Sox' – Gary Hocking – the forgotten World Motorcycle Champion (Hughes)
Tony Robinson – The biography of a race mechanic (Wagstaff)
Virgil Exner – Visioneer: The Official Biography of Virgil M Exner Designer Extraordinaire (Grist)

www.veloce.co.uk

First published in July 2019 by Veloce Publishing Limited, Veloce House, Parkway Farm Business Park, Middle Farm Way, Poundbury, Dorchester DT1 3AR, England. Tel +44 (0)1305 260068 / Fax 01305 250479 / e-mail info@veloce.co.uk / web www.veloce.co.uk or www.velocebooks.com.
ISBN: 978-1-787114-39-5; UPC: 6-36847-01439-1.

DRIVEN

an elegy to cars, roads and motorsport

John Aston

VELOCE PUBLISHING
THE PUBLISHER OF FINE AUTOMOTIVE BOOKS

CONTENTS

Introduction   5

Foreword by Simon Arron   9

1   Cold War Cool   10

2   The Little Red Book   16

3   Marshal Arts   23

4   Oversteer – A Victim Speaks   32

5   Escape From Krakatoa   39

6   Seven, The Magic Number   49

7   Tracks 'n' Hills 'n' Hole Shots   59

8   Refuge Of The Roads   69

9   La Mucca Chi Ride   80

10 The Glittering Prizes   90

11 Supping With The Devil   107

12 Southern Comfort   122

13 Seasonal Variation   130

14 The Way It Was   236

15 A Reader Writes   251

Afterword The Scottish Playlist   263

Index   268

INTRODUCTION

Most of life, maybe, is only time served

Graham Swift, *The Light of Day*

It's a grand thing to get leave to live

Nan Shepherd, *The Quarry Wood*

If writing a book is an ego trip, then the trip that I have taken in *Driven* is a much longer one than I had anticipated. In mitigation, I have a lot to say, as you might expect from someone who has been fascinated by cars, driving, and motorsport since 1967 – the year when I realised that Ford's Le Mans winning GT40 Mark IV was even sexier than Sandie Shaw, if equally unattainable. I have two consuming interests, angling and driving, and as I have already written two books about the former, it was time to indulge in the latter again. Does any author ever write the introduction to a book before they write the book itself, I wonder? Perhaps a writer with more self-discipline than I have might do so, but I believe that the best journeys don't need a map and so, when I started writing on 1 January, 2017, all I had was a single sheet of A4 with some scribbled ideas on chapter themes. I wanted to be able to ad lib down a side road whenever I felt tempted, which, with my not-so-iron willpower, turned out to be rather often. I was not surprised that the trip turned out to be longer than I had expected, and what the hell if some of those turnings were culs-de-sac?

This is a very personal book, as I wanted to reflect what Barack Obama called "the messy, contradictory details of our experience," and to include my own biased, infuriatingly inconsistent, and subjective opinions rather than bombarding you with too much of the sort of information you could find out on your iPhone in seconds. The 15 chapters have three broad themes: autobiographical stuff about cars and driving; opinion pieces on topics including Ferrari, motoring journalism, and motorsport; and finally, a series of accounts of the motorsport events I attended between April 2017 and March 2018. I bemoan the fact that what used to be called Grand Prix racing (which then became 'Formula 1' before the almost universally abbreviated 'F1') is assumed by the man on the Clapham omnibus to be a synonym for motorsport in general; it really isn't anything of the kind, as my year-long odyssey embraced not only circuit racing contested by cars as diverse as Thirties' Bugattis and this year's model BTCC racers, but also drag racing, speed hill climbs, rallying, rallycross, sporting trials, autograss, Time Attack, and banger racing. The spectacle varied from the thunderous brevity of Top Fuel dragsters at Santa Pod to the slo-mo scrabble of Austin Seven Specials on the Lakeland Trial, the venues ranged from Goodwood's top table to York Raceway's rebel cool, and the people I encountered ranged from the 'hail fellow well met' old stagers of Shelsley Walsh to the tattooed lads and lasses in Autograss. My accounts of events were not meant to be the sort of detail-heavy reports you would find in the specialist press, so you'll look in vain for fastest laps and qualifying times, but instead I have described the look and feel of the day, even its smell and taste, those things which you might first mention to the friend who asked how it was. That's why I can remember the red kites soaring over Harewood, the opening lap of a Formula Ford race through Coppice Bend, the spooky howl of a Williams Renault FW 14B at Village, and the flat white and bacon sandwich at an early morning Silverstone, with a whole summer day ahead of me.

My favourite Niki Lauda quote came in his crisp reply to the journalist who had told him that the German Grand Prix of 1976, in which Lauda's near fatal accident occurred, had not actually taken place at all, as its running order had not counted at the race's restart.

"Okay then, so tell me, what the fuck happened to my ear?" Lauda replied.

In Chapter 10 and Chapter 11, I wonder about what the fuck happened to my sport, and I then suggest how Grand Prix racing (I don't answer calls from Mr F1) might change direction in future. Yeah, it's a vain hope and not everybody will listen, and God knows I have been out of step for years with some of the F1 demographic (as they probably call themselves). I can't identify strongly with a fanbase which, on one website, devoted 60 pages to 'the great grid girl debate' but only two pages to marking the death of Le Mans and Grand Prix winner, team owner, technical innovator, and all round good American, Dan Gurney. For all that, Grand Prix racing is still the greatest show on earth, even if I argue that it was even better during the years between 1985 and 1995.

You will learn from this book that my admiration for Lotus founder, engineering genius, and out of the box thinker Colin Chapman knows few boundaries, and I am not alone, as two of the most gifted racing car designers of all, Gordon Murray and Adrian Newey, are also disciples, as well as being Elan owners, as I once aspired to become. Their adherence to Chapman's gospel has been exemplified in the succession of designs that have dominated Grand Prix racing since the early Seventies, the time when, at 18, I first saw a Formula 1 car in action. As a result, my life underwent a seismic change and, nearly 50 years later, I am delighted to report that I still haven't recovered and am still enjoying the aftershocks. Chapman's 'added lightness' mantra is not only the reason why I still regard the 1962 Lotus Elan as the definitive small sports car, but also why I owned Caterham Sevens from 1997 until last year, when my creaking back made a transition to an MX5 more of an urgent imperative than a choice. But even then, despite Mazda's funky Jinnba Ittai philosophy, it was Chapman's Elan that inspired the MX 5, and on the right road I can still sense the delicacy of touch and immediacy of response that makes up the Lotus DNA. If only my MX5's driver could add some lightness too ...

But even though I adore the giant killing antics of a lightweight Lotus, a full fat racer with a howling Ferrari V12 or a bellowing Chevy V8 can leave me speechless, breathless and, rather too often of late, embarrassingly close to tears. There is something elemental, almost atavistic about the appeal of the fast and noisy racing cars that have held me in their thrall for so long, and even at 65 (and how the hell did that happen?) my fever shows no signs of abating. Sevens apart, I am slightly more grown up in the road car arena, as my enthusiasm for steroid pumped 2-tonne SUVs and thuggish premium brand saloons is held well in check. Admit it, if a brute like a BMW M4 were in human form it would have a buzz cut, carry a baseball bat and almost certainly fail a drug test. Tell me I'm wrong, as Jeremy Clarkson has asked rhetorically, and rather more than once.

There are many memories in this book, and as that man Julian Barnes put it (that's twice I've quoted him already) I am "an unreliable witness to my own life, but can you claim to be different?" So don't be too surprised if my take on subjects as diverse as NASCAR, the prophet without honour that was the NSU Ro80, the tragic decline of rallying, and the masterpiece that is the Citroën 2CV does not coincide with your own view. If some readers don't disagree with me, or don't hold opinions or political views very different to my own, then I really have failed in what I set out to achieve. I don't want consensus, and listen, it's just fine if you shout "bollocks" when you think I am sounding like a limp-wristed liberal (again), or if you harrumph into your glass of Malbec that this daft bugger Aston is not actually in denial about climate change, and must therefore be part of a global conspiracy. All I want is for you to enjoy the reading as much as I enjoyed the writing, and if I can sound like Noel Gallagher's description of brother, Liam – "Like a man with a fork in a world of soup"– then why shouldn't you, too?

You know already that this book isn't short, and I hope its length is actually one of the reasons why you are reading it. Like everybody else, I spend far too much time on the internet, and I am a regular poster on various car and racing websites, sometimes as myself or, when the company is a little feral, under a pseudonym, if only to reduce the risk of my house being torched by the guy who doesn't share my view that objectors to noise from racing circuits don't actually deserve to be lynched. YouTube can be fun, too, and I take a special delight in reading comments on the driving technique of a Kenny Brack or a Tom Kristensen made by someone who keeps his fifth hand Civic Type R on his mum's drive but hasn't left his bedroom since Friday night. But website forums do bring people with common interests together better than any medium other than real life, or 'meat world' as it is termed by those who don't get to see much daylight. Forums do have one major shortcoming though, and it is embodied in the acronym that every poster dreads when it is made in response to his own finely argued points: TLDR (too long; didn't read). I think that some themes need space to thrive and can't be reduced to a quick-fire factoid with matching emoji. That is why this book, about a lifetime spent thinking and talking about cars, driving, and motorsport, does need a little more lebensraum than I can find in any place prefaced by www.

Music is important in my life, and there are more than a few musical references in this book. I have attributed some of them, others are so familiar that they don't need attribution and I will confess that there are some others that I have just secreted into the text. *Refuge of the Roads* is the title of a song composed and sung by Joni Mitchell, the woman who has provided the soundtrack to the key moments in my life. And not only is *Refuge of the Roads* a sublime song, but it's the perfect title for the chapter that describes the elemental joy of a long drive in the most uncompromising and purest sports car of them all, the Caterham (née Lotus) Seven.

I need to thank a lot of people, including my friends in motorsport, the members of the Lotus Seven community – whose encouragement and kind words have made me keep on keeping on writing – and the scores of people (including a Le Mans winner, a TV personality, a couple of former Grand Prix drivers, a BTCC battler, and the many weekend warriors in club racing and speed events) who kindly let me interview them for the book. My special thanks also are due to Sarah Standeven, who not only has a quite brilliant surname, but who has been of so much help in transforming my dreadful typing into something more legible.

I am deeply grateful to Simon Arron of *Motor Sport* magazine, who has written the foreword. Simon is the man whose enthusiasm for, and knowledge of, motor racing makes me feel like the dilettante I probably am.

My thanks to Steve Carter (www.stevecarter.com) and Richard Whittaker for allowing me to use their photographs as part of the cover illustration and also to Veloce Publishing for their support and encouragement.

My final and most heartfelt thanks are to my wife Joanne, for never complaining about my pre-dawn departures to race meetings, my weekends away at Silverstone, Cadwell, Santa Pod (and the rest ...), my mountain ranges of car magazines and motorsport books, my insistence that she must watch at least the start of every Grand Prix and, two hours later, listen to my penetrating analysis of the race. She gets her own back by making me watch productions of Aeschylus, but I still thank her from the bottom of my heart.

John Aston, Thirsk
www.refugeoftheroads.co.uk

Foreword

If you relied on evidence from many countries' mainstream media, you might form the impression that motor racing was something that happened 20-odd times a year – a travelling circus followed around the world by movie stars and celebrity chefs, plus an artillery of TV cameras that permit microanalysis of every manoeuvre, irrespective of significance. But there is rather more to the sport than just Formula 1 – or grand prix racing, to use a formal label that seems to have been lost during decades of marketing hype.

I should perhaps point out that I remain a fan of grand prix racing. I loved reading about it as a lad (the most reliable option back then, as it was very rarely on TV before the late 1970s) and had the wonderful experience of writing about it professionally for many years. The action was sometimes riveting and occasionally dreary, the way racing has always been, but it was an opportunity to engage with elite drivers in their prime and, better yet, experience myriad different cultures. As I write, I have covered events on every continent bar Antarctica – a privilege for which I will be ever grateful, and one that can never be taken away.

When weekends weren't consumed by grands prix, I would often frequent other motorsport venues, the kind of which the wider public remains largely unaware: a hillclimb at Prescott, a Vintage Sports Car Club meeting at Oulton Park, or perhaps Citroën 2CV racing at Cadwell Park. This is motor racing in its purest, rawest form – a band of enthusiasts united by a common passion. Male or female, old or young, they love their sport and all that surrounds it … and have no need to bite their tongues for fear of upsetting a sponsor.

For the past few seasons this has been the world in which I've operated, principally as a writer and photographer for *Motor Sport* magazine, and it was here that I first encountered John Aston – at Silverstone, if memory serves, though our paths have since crossed at many locations, from Thruxton in Hampshire to Croft in his native Yorkshire.

In *Driven – An Elegy To Cars, Roads & Motorsport*, John's passion for the sport and all matters automotive are abundantly obvious, likewise his appreciation of the bigger picture. The competitive element of a sporting weekend is important, but so too are the journey, the car in which you make it (I once drove to the Belgian Grand Prix in a Caterham Seven and thoroughly recommend it), the surrounding landscape … and the standard of the catering. He hasn't mentioned that Wiscombe Park in Devon serves a very fine portion of chips with curry sauce for £3.50, but perhaps such details are being saved for a future second volume.

Simon Arron, features editor, *Motor Sport*

1
COLD WAR COOL

I pressed the fire control ... and ahead of me rockets blazed through the sky ...
Roy Lichtenstein, Whaam!

Sometimes adjectives just aren't fit for purpose, they start to buckle under the strain until, eventually, they just give up, with not an ounce more meaning to impart. It was happening now, at home, in the kitchen, and I was marooned in that scary no man's land that lies between terror and exhilaration. It was early spring in 1967, I was 14, and home was Allerton Bywater, a mining village in the West Riding. The cause of the adjectival stress? The fact that the entire house was vibrating, that the flower vase on the window sill was shimmying a crazy little dance and, most of all, the fact that there was no room left in my brain to process anything apart from The Noise. The sky was full of it, the house had become possessed by it, and I was home alone.

You're thinking 'mining village, trouble at t'pit,' and why wouldn't you, with Aberfan still casting a long shadow from the previous October? And you'd be wrong, because this noise came from above, and an Avro Vulcan's four Olympus turbojets were to blame. We lived a ten-minute flight away from RAF Finningley, where the Vulcans were based and, although, on this occasion the pilot had moved the throttles to volume 11, our days were frequently interrupted by rumbles and howls from the sky. It was the binary era of the Cold War where the choice was simple and stark – either a thermonuclear holocaust with all life turned to radioactive dust in an eye-searing flash, or peace. Nothing in between: no asymmetric war perpetrated by bearded jihadis in Toyota Hilux pickups, no scary Somali pirates, no Boko Haram horror stories, and not even any pro-life nutjobs in the flyover states of the USA. And closer to home, in 1967 even the IRA had only historical footnote status, the killing wasn't to start again until 1969. Terrorism was on gardening leave in most of Western Europe, but all of us, from primary school kid to pensioner, knew that the attack would come from the sky, unannounced except by a flicker on the radar as the missiles were launched from somewhere unpronounceable east of the Urals.

I had been too young to fully understand the details of the Cuban Missile Crisis five years before, but I'd been old enough to see the worry and fear in my parents' eyes. I had heard the brittleness of their conversations as they watched Kennedy and Khrushchev play their mind games, and waited to see who would blink first. If I lay awake at night I would worry myself silly about a doomsday of mushroom clouds, an irradiated end to my world and all that inchoate adolescent stuff about never being able to grow up to see the 21st Century but, in daylight hours at least, 1967 was just the greatest of times for a teenage lad to grow up. Philip Larkin reckoned that sex "began in nineteen sixty-three (which was rather late for me) between the end of the Chatterley ban and the Beatles first LP," but I don't think the Sixties arrived in nearby Castleford until at least four or five years later. In our collective memory we think that what was happening in Carnaby Street in 1966 had to be happening everywhere else, with mini-skirted dolly birds easing their way into purple E-Type Jaguars driven by cravat wearing Simon Dee wannabes. It wasn't like that in the town which now ironically calls itself 'CasVegas,' and I am pretty sure it wasn't happening in Abergavenny or Arbroath either.

But you still just knew that "there's something happening here" (as Buffalo Springfield said in *For What It's Worth*), because all I had to do was listen to the music. For years I'd endured the stifling conformity of the BBC Light Programme, with its wilful ignorance of popular music, and its apparent mission to patronise an audience that they felt was too young, or insufficiently educated, to listen to the serious, grown-up stuff on the Home Service or the arias and symphonies on the Third. Radio 270 changed all that, Yorkshire's very own pirate station that pumped out the sort of music I would never hear Keith bloody Fordyce play on *Easy Beat* – songs like *Psychotic Reaction*, the only hit single made by Californian psychedelic band Count Five, The Byrds' *Eight Miles High*, or Jimi Hendrix's *Hey Joe*. But if revolution was in the air, it was still grey porridge austerity on the road.

You know those nostalgic programmes that TV schedulers love to give a passive audience on a Sunday night as a soft-focus distraction from Monday's imminence? The shows that can induce narcolepsy in their viewers, the cosy pap like *Heartbeat*, *Call the Midwife*, and *The Darling Buds of May*? They are invariably set in some half-remembered pastiche of the past, a televisual comfort blanket where the world was a better place because what wasn't there to like about infant mortality, rural poverty, and rickets? But the producers always get it wrong, and not just with the godawful attempts made at a Yorkshire accent by actresses from Epsom or Esher, but also with the choice of cars that litter every scene to add period atmosphere. Shining Anglias, gleaming Consuls, burnished Morris Minors, and the inevitable Jaguar Mk II driven by the caddish Terry Thomas lookalike who plays the villain. But this is an ersatz past, because the reality was very different; in the West Riding of the Sixties very few had the money to buy any car at all, and those who had scraped the cash to do so drove the most terrible old tut. The streetscape was just as likely to contain some tottering wreck of a Fifties Austin A90 or the wheezing three-speed penury of an E93 Prefect, as the gleaming MGAs and Healeys that populate TV's false televisual memories. Rusted horrors from prewar weren't uncommon in Allerton, and very few newer cars caught my uneducated eyes as just what, exactly, could anybody find interesting or attractive in a Hillman Minx?

My dad was the village doctor, and he had always assumed that I would share his interests with the same fanaticism he applied to them. He may have been well educated but he could be almost child-like, because, despite his medical training at University College he blithely assumed that his only son was more clone than successor, and thus would be pre-programmed to love model trains, horses, fox hunting, and gardening with the same passion as he did. What a disappointment I must have been; despite the inevitable 'one day all this could be yours' speech in the surgery, I dropped every science subject as soon as I could and developed a lifetime indifference to horses, gardening, DIY, and trains? Despite the massive trainset Dad had bought himself – ostensibly for me of course – I didn't know or care about the difference between a 4-4-2 and a 2-6-2, and if the Flying Scotsman's number was 4472 then so what? Poor man, he was utterly bemused that I adored fishing, literature, and rock music but that I was apparently immune to the thrill of the canter or to the simple reward of A Job Well Done.

Dad's cars were little more than white goods to him, a means to an end. There was the big one to pull his horsebox and the little one in which to make home visits to patients. The big car had originally been a Humber Hawk, an underpowered four-cylinder saloon which smelled of old leather (overlaid by a hint of something far more organic) but in 1967 he'd bought a 1964 Rover 3-litre, which was certainly a move upmarket from the parsimony of the Humber. The Rover P5 had a physically huge straight-six engine and a cabin that, although exquisitely made, was designed as conservatively as you'd expect from the firm that made cars for the Queen. God knows what she made of the cutting edge, cool-as-you-bloody-well-like, David Bache and Spen King designed Rover 2000. And the little car? Inevitably a Triumph Herald, chosen for its astonishingly tight turning circle, as Dad's rounds included miles of Council estates with roads that weren't ever designed for cars, for how could mere miners have afforded such luxuries? Heralds had underwhelming 1147cc engines, tight cockpits, and awful synchromesh; none of these were convincingly redeemed by the veneered dashboard, itself an attempt to bestow a dignity to which a painted metal dash Ford or Vauxhall could only aspire.

If the cars in my teenage world seemed too dull to notice, then the planes were impossibly glamorous and sky watching became a way of life. In the 21st Century, when a jet goes over my house, it's a Hawk if it isn't too noisy, and a Tornado or a Typhoon if it is. And if it's got a propeller it's always an irritating little Tucano from RAF Topcliffe with a learner at the controls. But in the Sixties? Such a long list to choose from as there were screaming Lightnings, Phantoms, Hunters, Voodoos, and Buccaneers; buzzing Gnats and Provosts; whirring Chipmunks; lumbering Hercules, Shackletons, and Blackburn Beverleys; whispering Canberras and, of course, the thundering majesty of the V bombers. Actually, nobody ever saw a Valiant, but when there was the sci-fi cool of the Victor, and the malevolence of the Vulcan to admire I didn't mourn the runt of the V bomber litter too much.

If medicine wasn't in my DNA, then planes were, and my two uncles were almost certainly to blame. My mother was Australian, and I am named after her younger brother, John, whom she adored but I never met: having survived a Wellington ditched in the North Sea, John died in 1944, shot down over Picardy in a Halifax bomber. We visited the simple but elegant war grave on the outskirts of the village of Méharicourt in the Nineties, and I have rarely been more moved than during this, my very own 'some corner of a foreign field' moment. The other Uncle was Dad's brother Freddy who, four years after escaping from Dunkirk, led his squadron of gliders into Normandy on D-Day and then did the same at Arnhem. Unlike so many of his comrades, he survived the war without a scratch, but if he had his nightmares then nobody would have been surprised, least of all his baby boomer nephew, who still feels humbled by men like him. Freddy was charming, wickedly funny, flirtatious, sometimes intimidating, and possessed of a natural authority – and all that's hard to deal with when you're 14. But he was a hedonist too: he loved a good cigar and an edgy claret, and he was also a man who just loved to drive – and fast. Unlike Dad, he invariably drove cars well out of the mainstream, such as an early Volkswagen Beetle (only ten years after he'd been killing Germans), a sexy Fiat Millecinquecento, followed by a twin-cam Fiat 125, and a very left-field Renault 16TS. I loved Freddy, and I found that John, the uncle I could never meet, became a constant companion in my thoughts. He still is, and his picture looks on as I type these words. I may be bemused at my country's near-hysterical obsession with the armed forces, where everybody who ever wore a uniform, ever, is elevated to hero status, but I will forever admire my two uncles who fought the good fight.

Dad spent most of the war in India, as an RAMC Major. He had an enjoyable war and he was not embarrassed to admit as much, even though hindsight makes me realise that there was more than a hint of sibling rivalry in his conversations with Freddy. Dad's wartime work involved training Force 136 personnel on how to survive Japanese-occupied Burma, and his service was distinguished by saving the life of an Indian prisoner suffering from terrible dysentery; some chap called Gandhi, apparently. Unlike Freddy, Dad often talked about the war and I guess there might be conclusions to be drawn from that alone. Dad and I were almost defined by our differences and, if father/son bonding wasn't invented in the buttoned-down Sixties, we did share one passion, and that was the annual air display at RAF Finningley or Lindholme.

Postwar Britain wasn't risk averse and neither were its citizens, thousands of whom would flock to the aerodromes (not a term you often hear now) near Doncaster to see and hear a flying circus of war machines. Planes were free to fly as low and as fast as their pilots would dare, and when you're 24 and given a Mach 2 fighter to play with, that's a few feet above the runway in a transonic flypast where you flew by in silence, towing the screaming thunder of your afterburning jets a 100 yards behind you. Watching a Lightning punching a hole in the clouds in a near supersonic vertical climb was thrilling, but little could compete with the apocalyptic sight and sound of four Vulcans being scrambled. You surrendered to the moment, reduced to slack faced joy and terror, incapable of any thought or awareness than this, now, here. But even the Vulcans couldn't overshadow my favourite, the plane that looked like an avenging angel of death, the McDonnell Douglas F4 Phantom. The Lightning was simple form defined by function, but the Phantom introduced a gratuitous air of malevolence. From its leering nose, via its stubby, multi-angled wings, to the sheer pornography of its tailpipes, it exuded menace in the same way as a Sixties Ferrari sports prototype can, not that I knew this at the time. What I did know was that if a Lightning moved in next door, sooner or later it would pick a fight with you and end up knocking you out cold. But if your new neighbour were a Phantom, it was inevitable that it would kill you, but only after it had seduced both your teenage daughter and your wife and then kicked your Labrador for good measure.

But hold on, this book is about cars, you're thinking, and I have talked about bloody planes when you really wanted to read about Lotus Elans and E-types, Cortinas and DB5s. Guilty as charged, but when your main exposure to cars was being given a lift to school in a friend's dad's wallowing, gutless, and tasteless Vauxhall Victor 101 it was hard to see the appeal of such cars when contrasted with the extraordinary planes I saw almost daily, or which I read about in my subscription copy of *Flight International*. Even the allegedly sporty Vauxhall VX 4/90, a car which aped US style but lacked any of its substance, wasn't ever going to thrill like a F105 Thunderchief or a B58 Hustler, an F100 Super Sabre or an F104 Starfighter, was it? Perhaps not, but everything was about to change in my teenage world ...

It was Friday afternoon, autumn term, and I was leaving my loathed Grammar School, Queen Elizabeth's in Wakefield, the school that behaved like a Poundland public school with its gratuitously gowned teaching staff and its absurd school song: *Floreas Wakefieldia* (sample lyric – 'quid-quid rectum'). I was en route to catch the bus for the hour-long trip home when a friend asked if I'd like a lift home with his mother, as they'd be passing through my village on the way to see some relatives. The car wasn't the expected stodgy Morris Oxford, but a gleaming gunmetal grey Jaguar Mark II 3.8 with red leather seats and a walnut dashboard, studded with white-on-black Smiths instruments. My friend's mum turned out to be a glamourous vision in fur, with an aura of expensive scent and a hint of menthol cigarettes. My parents would have sneered at 'her type,' especially the fags, but I was already awestruck as I slid into the warm (and possibly Freudian) embrace of the rear seat with my now-forgotten pal. She could drive too, confidently slicing through the traffic with an authority that entranced me. The Jaguar moved through the Minis and A40s like a shark through a school of baitfish, yet nothing prepared me for what happened when we hit the open road; I was curiously unsettled by what seemed to be somebody pushing my shoulder blades back into the red leather. The nose of the car had risen a degree or so, and a soul stirring howl came from somewhere up front. Heralds and Victor 101s, Humbers and

Rovers gained momentum over half a minute or so, soundtracked by mechanical wheezing and thrashing from the engine room, but the Jag (as I had to term it) was offering a real-time lesson in the physics of acceleration, and I loved it, I was captivated and beguiled, desperate to feel that sublime push again. And whilst a Vulcan's push would have been immeasurably greater, nobody was going to collect me from school in Avro's finest in the foreseeable future.

The Jag-induced nirvana was followed by another Damascene moment, this time at home. My oldest friend, then and now, is Alan Moore, who lived a short walk from home. He lived in a council house, and I lived in the doctor's big house, and we were the best of friends. My parents liked Alan, and he them, but I knew that, deep down, they felt that a middle-class boy like me should really only mix with vicars' and other doctors' sons and daughters – People Like Us. People who spoke with a long A, and who held a knife and fork 'properly.' Class could quicksand every encounter, every conversation in the not-very-liberated-at-all England of 1967, and thank God we have now moved on from that quagmire – haven't we? But back to Alan; he had always been practical, just like his father who worked as a Coal Board engineer, and (also like his dad) Alan knew about cars, adored them. For some reason he had brought round the previous copy of *Motor* with him. My father joined us, and Alan asked him: "So Doctor, who do you fancy for Le Mans this year?" Dad looked nonplussed, which in itself was unprecedented, and said he really didn't have the faintest idea, but, utterly unabashed, Alan reckoned that whilst the Ferrari P4s would be fast, they'd be fragile, and another Ford win was most likely. Alan, ever the patriot, added that he really wanted the Lola-Aston Martin to do well. I knew Le Mans was in France, and I knew what 'Vingt Quatre Heures' meant, but what I didn't know until then was what a Le Mans sports prototype looked like. Alan showed me the picture of the Ford Mk IV, asking if I wanted to borrow the magazine, and might I want next week's too, he'd drop it round? Suddenly *Flight International* looked a dull, serious, and technical read, and *Motor* was looking like pornography, and in quite the best of ways. The Ford, the bloody Ford! It looked like a spaceship, it had a V8 engine (whatever that meant) that was nearly seven times bigger than the Herald's and 12 times more powerful. It did 200mph! More! At night down the Mulsanne Straight! Everything changed in my world in five short minutes, and 50 years later I still get the shivers when I think about that Mark IV.

2
THE LITTLE RED BOOK

I want that line to have a duflunky, to come across, have a little hook in it and do a rashoom or a zong

Instructions given by Harvey Earl to stylists of
the 1959 Cadillac Eldorado Brougham Seville

The Lola-Aston Martins expired early at Le Mans in 1967, the best Ferrari P4 was runner-up, and the thundering big-block Ford Mk IV averaged 135mph (217km/h) in the hands of AJ Foyt and Dan Gurney. I knew all this from reading my own copy of *Autocar*, the weekly contemporary and rival to Alan's *Motor*. I guess that, since 1967, I must have read about 7000 car magazines, and I can still remember the first one I ever bought, and where I bought it from. I was in York railway station in spring 1967, a week or so after falling for the pornography of the Mk IV in my borrowed *Motor*, and I was looking for something to read on the train home. The then chief suspect would have been the deathless prose I'd find in *Angling Times* ('Huge bream caught by pensioner in Tring reservoir' might be the siren call headline) – but then I saw a copy of the current *Autocar*. It might have cost more than twice the *AT*'s shilling, but it did have a picture of a tyre smoking Sunbeam Tiger on the cover, with the headline 'Underrated Tiger.' The headline was staid enough, but the typography was bizarre as the word 'Under' was inverted; it was obviously a doomed attempt at getting in tune with the late Sixties' zeitgeist, which, given the magazine's pedestrian house style, must have prompted some serious harrumphing in the editorial conference earlier that week.

Autocar and *Motor* had been weekly contemporaries and rivals for decades, *Autocar* having been on the go since 1895, with the young upstart rival having started in 1903; the older magazine was published on Thursday and the newer on Wednesday, doubtless to give it an edge in the newsagent. Despite the imminence of the Summer of Love and the reputed prevalence of miniskirts and paisley, both magazines were written by serious men in ties for serious readers who often smoked pipes and probably loved to reminisce about their National Service. Both titles had huge circulations as they were quite literally the only shows in town, national newspapers rarely covering cars and driving, except at Motor Show time in

October, when free supplements would extol the virtues of some new sub-species of Morris 1300 in the best advertorial tradition, and with a side order of jingoism. My parents took *The Sunday Express* and it was one of the few papers that featured a weekly car review – even if to have entitled it a 'road test' would have been to endow it with a gravitas that was entirely unmerited. The byline was Robert Glenton, an assumed and fictitious name, I now suspect, employed to enable the paper to survive the indisposition of the journalist by the time-honoured expedient of declaring that 'Robert Glenton is dead, long live Robert Glenton.' The reviews were almost beyond parody as the virtues of each car featured would be extolled in tones of wonder at the unparalleled genius of British engineering prowess, which cars such as the new Ford Corsair so uniquely displayed. Even back then, I was cynical enough to suspect that our correspondent had been the beneficiary of one free lunch too many, and that his critical faculties had long since left the building. The rehash of the glowing press release the Ford PR girl had given him after the six-course dinner would somehow omit to mention that the said Corsair was powered by the throbby old nail of a V4 engine more commonly found in the engine room of a Transit.

But if *Autocar* and *Motor* had more editorial rigour, their journalists could be earnest and pernickety, and whilst the younger title showed signs of levity on occasion, *Autocar*'s grinding seriousness often made it a challenging read. But I read everything anyway, from the OCD detail of the weekly road test (where I could learn about the turning circle of a DAF Daffodil – to the inch) to the *Straight From The Grid* column by Eoin Young (typical story – what colour Bruce McLaren's new Can-Am car would be, and why), from Industry News (about when Mark Lucas-Tooth would be taking up his new position at Ferodo) to the classified ads (TVR Griffith V8 or Vauxhall Cresta for £995? Your call). I pored over the road test results with a diligence that would have got me a first, had I applied it a few years later to my law degree. Instead, I scraped an LLB, but I did obtain distinctions in my specialist subjects: the works of Pink Floyd and the Art of Talking Bollocks Whilst Discussing The Meaning Of Life In The Early Hours.

In my comparative studies of road test methodologies, I learned early on that the key metric in *Motor* was 0-50mph, but in *Autocar* the now universal 0-60mph was the key determinant in separating the merely quick from the fast, and the slow from the absolutely glacial. Discussions with Alan focussed on just how and why an E-Type Jaguar could be slower to 50mph than its costlier rival, the Aston Martin DB6, but somehow have 0.2 seconds advantage to 60mph. And why was it invariably the case that adding ten seconds to a car's 0-50 time would produce the same car's standing start quarter-mile time? And if Alfa Romeos had five-speed gearboxes, then why didn't Lotus Cortinas? And overdrive – sorry Alan, tell me again just how it works, and why is fuel-injection so good? All this stuff mattered (and it still does, half a century later) but not half as much as my practical field work did ...

Tell me this, do you know any bird watchers? Yes? Been for a walk with one, or driven with one? If you have, you know just what I'm going to say – they never, ever stop looking do they? Every distant speck is analysed and then dismissed, every 'little brown job' (those unremarkable small birds that punctuate every hedgerow) given a piercing appraisal and every chirp and trill instantly reviewed. It's the Twitcher's Imperative, they don't miss a thing and never, ever, confess to not knowing what you've just seen even, no especially, if it's the unexpected Siberian visitor and they never let their friends know that, just once, they got it wrong, even in poor light and with foggy binoculars. As an angler, I incline to a similar level of obsession, with every pond and stream appraised for piscatorial potential, every lake and drain identified as I speed west on the Transpennine Express or south on the A63 to the empty never-never land that is East Riding. But I've never been more observant than as a teenage pedestrian, when the makes and models of car I had read about in the magazines could be stalked and spotted in their natural habitat, which for me was the roads within a 12-mile radius of Allerton Bywater. Those 12 miles encompassed school in Wakefield, shopping in Leeds, fishing at Tadcaster, as well as shopping and socialising in the local towns of Castleford and Pontefract, aka 'Cas' and 'Pont.'

But it could be slim pickings; my home village had a pit and an opencast mine, the NCB workshops and offices, two working men's clubs (entitled t'top club and t'bottom club), the Alexander Rose sewing factory, the Aire and Calder Navigation Canal, a cobblers, and two petrol stations – one selling Cleveland Discol and the other selling Murco (about whose quality many harboured dark suspicions). Allerton Bywater, universally known as Allerton but pronounced 'Ollerton' was not the natural habitat of Le Jet Set, the closest to whom we got was hearing the late Peter Sarstedt warbling about the whereabouts of his lovely. Dad would get the odd visiting consultant to the surgery (which formed part of our house) but, as most consultants still wore pinstripes with many even sporting bowler hats, neither Maseratis nor Morgans were much in evidence. The consultants' P4 Rovers and Austin Westminsters were never able to bestow quite the level of gravitas that came from being called a Mister and not a Doctor. But one gynaecologist did deliver (sorry) in the form of a steel-grey Daimler Dart SP250, and the oh-so-sexy Reliant Scimitar driven by Dad's oldest friend, Doctor (not Mister) Neil Hamlin, graced our drive often. It wasn't the trendy GTE estate either, not the car so royally endorsed by Princess Anne, but the much rarer Coupé with straight-six Ford power, and in head-turning gold. Dad's flat white Herald looked like a supermodel's ugly friend in comparison. These exotic visitors apart, I saw very little else to drool over in Allerton: a metallic blue E-Type Jaguar howling out of the Murco garage, a white Lotus Elan Plus 2 was a frequent visitor to a house up the road ('Local Boy Graham Poulter Making It Big In The World of Advertising' was the headline about the Elan's owner in the Pontefract and Castleford Express), and the other car that really made an impact was a Ford Mustang. It was shocking pink (is there any other sort where cars are concerned?), and it was driven by a hard-faced woman with bleached blonde hair and attitude to spare. She was called Viv Nicholson, the legendary "Spend, Spend, Spend" pools winner, her fur coat and no knickers chutzpah and her frittering away of her £156,000 prize had ensured her notoriety throughout West Riding. She was one of Dad's patients and the 'Stang was the latest in a succession of pink hued cars from Detroit; parked outside the surgery between an AC invalid carriage and the inevitable Austin A35, it looked like a pastel pink UFO.

But the slightly less mean streets of Wakefield and Leeds offered far, far richer pickings for the young car obsessive, and with frequent reference to the back pages of *Autocar*, I soon learned to distinguish the brassy growl of an MGB's four-pot A Series from the bonnet-bulged MGC's six-cylinder whoomph. In traffic you'd hear the arrhythmic tickover of a Cooper S before you even saw it, and as you walked by you'd note the lowered steering column, tiny Speedwell or MotoLita steering wheel and the obligatory big bore central exhaust. Big Healeys and TR3s and 4s weren't uncommon, nor were XK 150 Jaguars, but all these traditional, Brit, fit-for-purpose sports cars – no nonsense but no clever ideas either – looked ludicrously old-fashioned next to the Emma Peel svelteness of Lotus Elans, invariably hued in Lotus Yellow or Old English White. My Latin teacher had his Bristol 401 permanently parked up at school and, whilst it remained motionless throughout my eight-year sentence, I never failed to admire its aerodynamic shape, so at odds with its square-rigged, late Forties contemporaries. Leeds, the Big City, offered the siren call of Arnold G Wilson, the Aston Martin dealer whose showroom windows Alan and I would often haunt, admiring the Savile Row brutishness of a DB6 or even (cue huge excitement) the one-off, Touring-bodied DB-SC show car. There'd sometimes be a Lagonda Rapide on display, the car that might have aspired to the grand routier status of a Facel Vega HK500, but instead of killing an Albert Camus, as the Facel so spectacularly managed to, the Rapide's unhappily resolved appearance meant that it was far more likely to have scalped a Keighley wool merchant than a French philosopher. As avid viewers of *Top of The Pops*, we were also quick to recognise the driver of the gold Rolls-Royce Silver Shadow Drophead, oozing his way along Briggate, cigar clamped between teeth and faux blond hair waving in the breeze. I heard about Jimmy Savile OBE, KCSG first-hand, 40 years later, from the woman rally driver who'd had to endure the odious Savile as a publicity stunt co-driver on the RAC Rally. What she told me about him was no surprise, and neither was the post mortem exposé in 2012 – you just couldn't look and sound like he did and have even a passing acquaintance with normality or conformity. Or decency …

Longer trips meant more car spotting opportunities, and whilst Eric Porter's *Doctor Faustus* in Stratford was spookily brilliant, it was the long, low red shape lurking in a private car park near the theatre that shone even brighter. Neither Paddy (my school friend and fellow obsessive Patrick Hanson), nor I had a clue what the exquisitely styled sports car could be. Closer inspection revealed it to be a Bizzarini Strada, which left us none the wiser, the marque being virtually unknown in the UK. But it had an allure, an aching sexiness that threatened to eclipse even the scantily clad Helen of Troy in the Christopher Marlowe play we were studying in the first year of Sixth Form. The Strada has recently had somewhat of a renaissance in historic racing, even though I suspect it enjoys far more success now than it did then, but racing success or not, back in the Sixties it truly seemed, just like Helen, to be "fairer than a thousand stars." Maybe I always did have a thing about European sports cars with Detroit V8 power; I clung to the memory of *Motor*'s road test of the Gordon Keeble GK1, the Bertone built car whose exquisite lines epitomised Giugario's genius. But unlike its near stablemate, the Alfa Romeo 2600 Sprint, the GK1 wasn't all mouth and no trousers, it packed 327 Cubic Inches (5.3 litres) of Corvette power. I only ever saw the one in period, again on a school trip, this time to London to see either *Pericles* or *The Winter's Tale*, I forget which but, be honest, both possibilities have the capacity to make the audience feel more punished than entertained. But the Gordon Keeble, sexy knock off wheels, V8 rumble from the lights, and my instant recall of its 60mph in 6.2 seconds potential, still made the trip worthwhile.

But if car spotting was fun, I knew my enthusiasm couldn't just stop there. I was 16 and therefore couldn't learn to drive for another year but surely there was more to see and do in the car world than just trying to spot another Sunbeam Tiger? Even if I was now diligent enough to analyse its stance to ensure it was the 260 V8 and not the wussy Alpine (another Anglo American V8 hybrid already, and I haven't even mentioned my Jensen CV8 and Bristol 409 thing yet …). The motoring world then had only two real choices of career arc for the enthusiast: either you developed a Swarfega and socket set habit, and spent happy hours decoking cylinder heads, grinding valves, and setting points, or you were drawn to the siren call of motorsport. If in the former camp, *Practical Motorist* became your choice of weekly read, featuring as it did advice on a 'Victor Engine Strip' and tempting you to buy a pair of Notek Blue Spot Fog lights or an SPQR tachometer cowl. Trouble is, after ten years of immersion in this stuff you'd be boring your friends into near catatonia as you recounted the virtues of the legendary Rootes 1725cc engine, "40,000 miles and I've never had the head off, I said I've never had the head off. Now Frank's bloody Renault … I could tell you a thing or two about French engineering … mind you, it's only what you'd expect from them in't it?" The other arc was equally inevitable; you'd read about a race meeting, gawp at the black and white photographs of Cortinas on three wheels and sideways Mustangs, wonder bemusedly what people with names like Sir Gawaine Baillie or Sir John Whitmore were actually like, decide to attend a race meeting, love it beyond words, join a motor club and within 18 months you'd find yourself wielding yellow flags and push starting pensioned off Formula 1 cars. This all happened to me with bewildering speed, and here's how …

Autocar previewed almost every single motorsport event in the UK and in September 1969 it had mentioned a club race meeting at Rufforth near York. I'd spent the week pulling peas for local farmers at 4/2 per full sack (okay, 21p if you must) and if my pea-pulling rate was only half that of the formidable women who worked alongside me in the fields, I still had enough cash to get to York from where – somehow – I'd get to Rufforth. Autumn term started the week afterwards and I needed anything to distract me from the long downward slide into winter afternoons, cross bloody country, and double Latin. It wouldn't be my first experience of live motorsport, but so mentally unprepared had I been for my first exposure, it may as well have been. It had been four years ago, when planes mattered and cars didn't, when my two cousins had taken me to Snetterton. I was spending a few weeks in Essex with Guy and Steve, where we were only 90 minutes away from the circuit in Uncle Freddy's Fiat 1500, but I spent most of my time at the circuit wondering, but not daring to ask, just what spectators were supposed to do when a driver was killed. My only knowledge of motor racing was its danger, and the sport only made the papers when yet another driver was killed or maimed. I'd been too young to remember the Le Mans carnage of 1955, but Stirling Moss's Goodwood accident had triggered banner headlines in the *Sunday Express*, with bad words like 'coma' and 'grave' littering the front page which was illustrated by a huge, if blurry, picture of what was left of the Lotus 18/21. It was obviously the case that bodies would be littering the track at Snetterton and all I really wanted to know was where I was supposed to look – I knew that 'the show must go on,' that was almost the law – but did one look away discreetly or did one admire the efficiency of the St John's ambulance staff by watching their handiwork on the victim, or at least his component parts? It wasn't necessary, to my relief, and once I twigged that not every race would claim a life I watched, half bemused and half amazed, as the Anglias and A40s slid through the corners at crazy speed, if not as quickly as Keith St John's race winning Elva BMW, sexily sponsored by Radio London, one of the first pirates. The smell of Castrol R is a cliché in itself and whilst it possibly belongs in the trash can brimming with worn out phrases like 'well-earned pint' and 'hearty breakfast' there's still an elemental truth somewhere; once that confection of hot metal and musky vegetable oil has been savoured it will haunt you for the rest of your life. It's a Proustian thing, and trust me, the perfumed reek of Castrol R on a hot afternoon resonates harder and longer than any bloody Madelaine cake ...

Rufforth wasn't quite as easy to get to as I had hoped; I'd already caught a bus to Castleford, another to Pontefract, walked a mile (1.6km) to the station, spent 20 minutes on the train to York and now I was still in the Acomb suburb having already walked for 30 minutes. It turned out to be a five mile walk (8km) to the old RAF base (which was converted to a race track on the morning of each event) and the last mile and a half (2.4km) had been almost frantically paced, as the distant buzz of unsilenced racing engines can exert a strong pull on an impressionable 16-year-old. Not only was the volume far higher than one would now hear at a club race meeting, the diversity of machinery made it far outshine our current diet of safely silenced spec formulae. The Formula Libre race even featured a Formula 1 car: John Scott Davies' tired old Cooper T86, whose BRM V12 may have misfired constantly but hell, a Grand Prix car! And I'm watching it, smelling it and hearing it, right there in front of me. Other sights and sounds competed to captivate me, such as Bill Wood's thundering Cobra 289, Harry Ratcliffe's snarly Mini, and best of all, the shrieking FVA engined Lotus Cortina of Brian Robinson as it streaked down the back straight, commentator Johnny Higham gleefully describing yet another piece of outbraking heroism. And how I loved it all.

Back at school I told Paddy all about it, but not until after he'd told me that his dad had taken him to the Oulton Park Gold Cup, won by Jackie Ickx, who, unlike John Scott Davies, was mentioned weekly in *Autocar* because this sublime driver drove a Brabham F1 car, and in real Grands Prix, not clubbies at Rufforth. We plotted, Paddy and I, and he showed me the magazine he was now buying, no longer the all things to all men *Autocar* but the weekly racing bible *Autosport*. And there was more too; Paddy showed me a news piece about the British Motor Racing Marshals Club, who were looking for new young members in the Leeds Bradford area. Free admission, an armband and the best view in the house ... bugger rugger, sod school, fuck French, our world was about to change, and very much for the better.

Oh, and the Little Red Book that gives this chapter its title? PM Taylor had a copy of Mao Tse Tung's eponymous book, quoting often from it, as befitted his coolest kid in school status. He had even been to Paris during the '68 riots and topped that by having hung out with Jean Paul Sartre. Bet he came to regret those initials later in life though. Anyway, my little red book featured little about the overthrow of capitalist running dogs because it was entitled *The Warner Medical Diary 1969* and it formed part of the endless tat with which GPs like Dad were bombarded to induce them to prescribe drug A in preference to drug B, almost certainly regardless of their respective pharmaceutical qualities. Pens, blotters, notepads, erasers, and staplers arrived in every post, supplemented by diaries and planners as Christmas approached. 1969 is the only year I have ever kept a diary and reading its contents in 2017 offers an only slightly disturbing insight into my teenage obsessions. I will allow that there's repeated reference to a girl called Sally who, in an only slightly crazy stalker way, I found delivering a lecture on YouTube last month. (You should note that I didn't leave a comment, as I was just a peripheral presence on the 8.05 bus to Wakefield, an occasional acquaintance on Saturday mornings in The Coffee Pot in Castleford, and now I'd just be a tragic old loser.) There's an account of the inaugural meeting of The Castleford Progressive Music Club, where po-faced, angst ridden teenage boys (no girls there, obviously) would discuss the unique genius of Savoy Brown, Blind Faith, and early Deep Purple. And there's also a note of every single interesting car I saw. Such as the white Oldsmobile Toronado that was gliding down Wakefield's Westgate on Wednesday 1 October; my note is juxtaposed with an advert for "Anusol-HC – for haemorrhoids and other ano-rectal conditions." And two days later, I struck gold with an Elan +2, a Daimler SP 250, an NSU Ro80 and, bloody hell, wait till I tell Paddy, it's only a Samantha: the Vignale styled Fiat 125S based coupé, whose Positano yellow curves made it glow like a film star against a background of grey Cortinas and flat green Oxfords.

But most notable of all, and footnoted by an advertisement for the "specifically acting vasodilator Opilon" was an account of my first experience of marshalling – the 1969 RAC Rally in Dalby Forest, when Hannu Mikkola and I had our first and only conversation ... so far.

3

MARSHAL ARTS

... and then, in dreaming,
the clouds methought would open, and show riches
ready to drop upon me; that, when I waked,
I cried to dream again

William Shakespeare, *The Tempest*

Paddy and I had responded to the BMRMC appeal in *Autosport* and turned up to the Roebuck Hotel, Greengates, where the marshals' club was holding its 'Noggin and Natter,' a term that made me cringe even back then. Do people still say this now? I suspect that the CSMA just might, unless they have switched to the racier, if even more outdated, Piston Broke model. Probably to be held in what they would so coyly term a hostelry too ...

We knew we were in the right pub as soon as we saw the spotlighted Cortina GT, the Cooper 1275S with Minilite wheels, and the weird looking old roadster we were soon to learn was a Dellow. And in the snug we immediately identified our tribe, easily distinguishable by the high incidence of yellow striped Dunlop rally jackets and by this week's *Motoring News* spread on the table and already soaking up the carelessly spilled mild and bitter. We sat next to the Dellow owner, a carbon copy of my Latin teacher – tweed jacketed, pipe smoking, and with a genial, if slightly detached, demeanour. There was no formality to our joining the marshals club, no application form nor parental consent required and, obviously no training or induction either. I did eventually receive some practical training at Oulton Park a year or so later, having already attended everything from Rallycross to Formula 3, but the day would have been slightly more useful if any of the fire extinguishers we were given had produced something more than a pathetic dribble of foam or the tiniest dusting of dry powder.

The RAC Rally 1969 started from London and had 160 entries, with cars ranging from the predictable Minis and Escort Twin Cams, to the rather less expected Wolseley Hornet and Fiat 124. It ran for five days and featured 73 special stages, all open to the public. Neither Paddy nor I had ever seen a rally, and so we were obviously uniquely placed to make our marshalling debut on what was then, in numbers of spectators and geographical reach, comfortably the UK's biggest sporting event. We had been instructed to make our own way to the New Inn in Thornton-le-Dale, on the edge of the vast Dalby Forest complex, and 50 miles (80km) from home. We had to be there by midday as our first job was to lay out the directional arrows and warning signage on the 20 mile (32km) long stages. Dalby South and North were the eighth and ninth stages, and were to start at 10.30pm, nearly 12 hours after the London start. Not very much resemblance to a modern WRC round, where a handful of stages are run by a smaller field of cars. But back in 1969, running 14 stages over 16 hours, punctuated by only three stops, was not at all unusual.

It took three bus rides to Pickering, and then an hour's walk to Thornton, but the atmosphere when we arrived justified the early start as I was to feel, for the first time, that electric buzz of anticipation, that urgent, feverish excitement that big time motorsport can generate. It's the beat your heart misses when you first hear that ripsaw bark of a race car as you park up at Silverstone or Santa Pod, Brands Hatch or Goodwood, it's the breathless catch in your chest as you are reminded yet again why this stuff isn't some lame weekend pastime but an addiction that can come close to defining you.

We were willing victims as we piled into the back of Dellow Man's only slightly more practical set of wheels, an early Fifties Ford Popular E93A. The Pop was no ball of fire up the long hill to the forest itself, its progress not helped by its 30bhp side-valve four and three speed gearbox, but its skinny tyres and generous ground clearance actually made it ideal transport along the empty forest rides. Dalby's a spooky place, even in daytime, and our fellow marshals entertained us with stories of burned out rally cars rotting away in inaccessible gullies, having crashed on earlier RACs, their disoriented crews having wandered miles through the trees before being rescued. Our work was simple enough, consisting of dragging fallen branches to block off junctions and nailing orange arrows to roadside pines to delineate the direction and severity of the next corner, this being long before pace notes and recces were allowed. Legally, anyway, and you've maybe heard the same stories as I have?

The first rally car wasn't due until 11.45pm and, having finished laying out the stage, we were back in the pub at dusk, drinking our halves of Sam Smiths like the grown-ups we weren't but realising that we were now insiders, part of the event, almost – crikey – important. And that was a good feeling for me to have as a teenager with shaky self-confidence and cursed, like all teenagers, by parents who just didn't understand. In my case, I was also suffering from a hitherto undiagnosed mental illness that struck me dumb in the presence of any girl, anywhere, and at any time – especially if she was called Sally. Worse still, I was the only victim and not even the Warner's Medical Diary had hinted at a cure.

Anticipation built as the first rally service cars arrived at Thornton-le- Dale, just as we were leaving en masse to man the stage. There were Transits and Cortina Estates, even the odd Abbott bodied Zodiac, all sitting low on their springs, burdened by cargoes of spare wheels, welding kit, and rows of jerry cans of five-star fuel for their thirsty charges. But one semiworks team had a far more streamlined and stylish approach to servicing – Porsche.

No lumbering VW van for them, instead they had just redeployed the factory rally cars from the Monte Carlo Rally by bolting on a roof rack to take a couple of spare tyres and filling the space behind the front seats with what few spares this notoriously reliable sports car would need on a five-day, 2000 (3200km) road mile, 500 (800km) stage mile, endurance rally. Each 911 had the trademark rank of Cibie Oscars across its low bonnet and even the drivers looked younger, fitter, and infinitely cooler than the Georges and Micks who were dragging hard on their Embassy Tippeds as they waited for their Mini and Escort drivers to arrive, doubtless with a catalogue of a complaints about high speed misfires and broken sump guards. If the 911 drivers weren't called Manfred and Rudolf then they really should have been, looking so Teutonically stylish in Porsche rally jackets and fur hats, and the way those two Männer drove out of Thornton Dale still makes me smile. Both cars, obviously exempt from tedious stuff like 30mph speed limits, accelerated away in unison, with their near unsilenced engines growling that unmistakeable flat-six drone, but what happened next was astonishing. Just when the growl was of a pitch that suggested a higher gear was urgently needed, as it would have been on a rattly old TR 4 or MGB, the Porsches' engine notes changed from growl to howl and the cars accelerated furiously into the November night, leaving a spine tingling, demonic wail hanging in the darkness. We were speechless and spellbound, and if this was just a service crew, on a public road, then what the hell would Björn Waldegård look like on the stage?

"Be not afeard, the isle is full of noises," quoted Paddy, as we heard the first distant bang of sumpguard on stone, and saw the brief flashes of spotlights on the forested hill to our east. Quoting Caliban's speech from *The Tempest* should have felt absurd in a North Riding forest but at midnight, with a million stars above, the smell of pines in the still air and the low murmur of excitement from the few spectators behind us, it felt more perceptive than pretentious. And, if the pace of the Rover 2000 course car was eye-opening, the speed of Waldegård's 911 was astonishing. For the second time that night we heard the song of a howling flat-six, but this time overlaid by the sound of gravel ricocheting off car and trees. As the dark red car slid downhill into view, daylighted briefly by flashbulbs, we could see the co-driver hunched low over his maps and to his left we saw the head down, busy handed stance of Waldegård at work. Gone in seconds but remembered for decades. Engine sound rising and falling, disappearing and reappearing, snatched gear changes, blipped down changes, revs flaring through endless pines, and then diminishing to just an echo in the cold emptiness of Dalby. We were speechless because, although the right words might have conveyed the speed, there was no vocabulary to translate our exhilaration.

More cars followed, twitching sideways on the downhill kink opposite our refuge on the high bank under the tall trees. All were quick, if not quite 911 paced, at least not until car 9, Hannu Mikkola's Escort, arrived, insanely sideways, hammering and barking that twin-cam song. He slid broadside, ran out of opposite lock and instantly went from ace to accident as the little white Ford rolled on its left side and disappeared into the trees, spotlights shining skywards, engine silent but branches snapping and crackling as the car crashed violently in front of our disbelieving eyes, the consequence of a maximum attack strategy. Suddenly we were no longer spectators but players, running over the forest road, somebody's whistle sounding, senior marshals shouting and torches flaring in the dark. Co-driver Mike Wood was lucid and calm but Mikkola was dazed and – yes – confused. We asked if he was okay, he mumbled incoherently – in Finnish, English, or a combination of the two – then he wandered back on to the stage, where older and wiser hands took charge, guiding him to the safety of a parked car and radioing for help.

But the show went on … and within 40 minutes of Mikkola's crash, on the bend that would enter rallying folklore as, you guessed, 'Mikkola's Bend,' Per Eklund's V4 Saab copied the earlier shunt but with an added dose of sheer chutzpah. The 96 rolled several times down the bank, snapping trees in its descent and came to rest inverted. Shouts came from within the car for help, but only to roll the Saab back on to its wheels. Much shouting and grunting, a hefty bang, and then the sound of a whirring starter quickly overlaid by the breathless backbeat of Ford's V4. Eklund carried on, of course, as Swedes do, speed apparently unabated but now with a mortally wounded car, which didn't last the night …

John Gierach is the most gifted author alive on the joys of fly fishing; he described how, when he bought his first fly rod and reel, he felt as though he "had been handed a big, jangling ring of keys to a new reality." I only read those words for the first time in the Nineties, but none could have better described my sheer elation after that long November night in 1969. I may have been awake for nearly 30 hours by the time I got to bed but I just knew that much of my life was now destined to be spent in and around motorsport and fast cars.

If winter meant time spent in the forests of the North York Moors, spring and summer meant speed hillclimbing, typically at Harewood but also at the now almost forgotten venues, such as Castle Howard. The venue compensated for being deficient in both the 'hill' and 'climb' departments by having a crazily fast straight in front of the house that, a decade later, would become Brideshead. I doubt there has ever been a larger engined single-seater than Martin Brain's Cooper T81, which packed 7.2 litres of Chrysler V8, and which, reputedly, was reaching over 150mph (240km/h) at Castle Howard as it bellowed past the cowering and exposed marshals. Our protection comprised only a couple of straw bales half way along the straight, and watching the Cooper and other big banger single-seaters at such dangerously close range was both addictive and idiotic. Oliver's Mount, the Scarborough track more famous for motorbike racing, was also used for speed events and we were told by Martin Brain that he was pulling an even more insane 170mph (275km/h) at one point. A racer as well as a hillclimber, Brain died later that year after crashing his Cooper BRM at Silverstone.

Harewood became my second home; the British Automobile Racing Club (BARC) Yorkshire Centre organising regular weekend events throughout the spring and summer. Occasionally I would be allocated the role of course marshal, which offered a good view but rarely involved much activity and so, after much lobbying on my part, I became a startline marshal. And it was just wonderful; days would pass in the hectic, noisy blur that you'd expect from managing up to 200 cars, each making at least four runs each up the hill. Entries would be gloriously diverse, and a typical meeting would include lots of road-going sports and saloon cars in varying states of tune – Minis, Escorts, Anglias, Elans, and Midgets – and progressively more specialised and powerful cars in the higher classes. It does now seem extraordinary that hotelier Jack Maurice would drive down to Harewood on the A1 from Newcastle in his wailing and whooping Ferrari 250LM, a car that now would be owned by a Silicon Valley billionaire, who had been happy to pay the Ferrari's $15m price to secure an entry to the Pebble Beach Concours D'Elegance. But back then it was just another old racing car being used for weekend fun, as was the Ford GT40 entered by Peter Blankstone. A pukka GT40 this, and not finished in the Gulf blue and orange that, thanks to the post mortem beatification of Steve McQueen, is now almost mandatory on replica GT40s, as well as 911s d'un certain âge. The Blankstone car was in metallic green, and if that wasn't sexy enough, the sight of driver Maggie made it a special treat; she was a gorgeous 30-something, wore a tightly fitting race suit, and was Emma Peel slim. And she drove the most brutally attractive Le Mans car of them all.

Most single-seater racing cars of the early Seventies were highly strung, temperamental beasts, much given to stalling at low-revs, backfiring exuberantly, and stuttering and shuddering at anything less than full throttle. Very few had batteries capable of starting the car more than once, and that meant our small team of startline marshals would spend most of the day pushing and pulling racers in three-point turns in the assembly area, and then push starting them, which was easy with a road-going Mini but much harder with a 5-litre small-block Chevy V8, as found in many of the F5000 cars then used, and even harder with a Formula 1 Cosworth DFV.

But there is something utterly addictive about being close to a big single-seater racing car as it prepares to launch itself off the startline; having pushed the brute into position after the driver had done a couple of burnouts to warm up the back tyres, I would slide the wheel chock to the back of the rear wheel, and I'd watch the lights with the same attention as the driver. It is intoxicating to be quite so close to a racing car, and you come to realise that it is an animate, almost organic, entity, as you smell that giddy cocktail of hot oil, petrol, and burning rubber, and then you see and feel the waves of heat shimmering from the exhausts, often rainbowed by heat. You watch individual screws and washers shudder and vibrate at each blip and bark of the engine; you watch the throttle slides opening and closing, and you savour the scream of a racing engine as it spikes to high revs in a heartbeat, the rev counter (often mechanical back then) moving to the vertical, dropping to nine o'clock, then spearing back up to midday with each twitch of the driver's right foot. The lights change and, starts being 'in your own time,' there'd be the calm before the storm as the driver let the revs drop and eased the stubby gearlever left and back into first, accompanied by a metal-to-metal graunch as cogs engaged and an almost sexual shudder from the car. Revs would build up, up, higher still, and then I'd see the driver's left leg move sharply back, instant wheelspin and suddenly, shockingly the car was gone, arrowing up to the first left hander. And only then would I remember to breathe again.

It was shatteringly, absurdly, exhilaratingly, and dangerously loud, as only road cars were properly silenced, with all but a handful of single-seaters having no silencing at all. My ears would ring after a day of this and, even though I'd take the ear defenders I used for clay pigeon shooting, I'd rarely wear them, seduced as I was by the addictive, brutal, all-consuming scream a racing car made when roused. I have paid the price and, even though I will admit that frequent exposure to bands such as Hawkwind; Emerson, Lake & Palmer; Groundhogs; and Deep Purple at university gigs didn't help, the fact that far too much birdsong is now quite inaudible is mainly due to happy days at Harewood, and to Ligier F1 pilot Pedro Diniz's Mugen V10, which pierced my left eardrum at Silverstone in 1996.

The other appeal of startline work was the chance to talk to the drivers; some would be visibly nervous and preoccupied, but others were happy to chat and joke until the serious stuff started. Most were polite and appreciative of our efforts, some even bringing us cold drinks and ice creams down from the paddock at the top of the hill, and one driver, David Good, would cheerfully dispense tubs of Ski Yoghurt from the cockpit of his McLaren M10B – it helped being sponsored by the firm (which I think he also owned). The odd driver could be rude and abrupt and whilst we'd give them the benefit of the doubt, laying the blame on pre-start nerves and sleepless nights' preparation, the occasional driver went well beyond the pale. The worst by far was a well-known driver who competed in the ex-Graham Hill, -Rolf Stommelen, and -Tim Schenken Brabham BT 33. Always aloof, uncommunicative, and scowling – even on a good day. He excelled himself at one meeting: having responded to his imperious gesturing for a push-start, we eventually got the DFV to fire up (but with not a wave of acknowledgement in return) whereupon the driver executed a burnout, and sat frowning in the car, waiting to be pushed to the start line. Two of us went to the back of the car and, just as we were reaching for the rear wing, he banged the car in reverse, popped the clutch, and shot backwards, knocking both of us to the ground. Our man had decided that another burnout was necessary, and obviously thought marshals were as consumable as his tyres – and gearbox too, as burn outs in reverse are almost unknown for a good reason. Remonstration having not worked (the driver taking the line that running marshals over was some sort of 'droit du seigneur' deal), none of us touched his car again that weekend ...

Marshalling at race meetings was a natural progression from speed events, but somehow it never exerted quite the hold on me that speed events had. But I loved the early morning starts, being collected from Leeds or Wakefield by the sort of time-served senior marshal, who would make me feel like the dilettante I undoubtedly was. I hadn't passed my driving test, and so all driving had to be an entirely vicarious experience. I would watch the driver's every move, learning exactly what was involved in the mysterious heel and toe technique I had read about in *Autocar*, it previously having been as unknowable, and therefore potentially almost as exotic, as Mrs Simpson's notorious 'Singapore Grip' – and I still don't know exactly what that involved. I travelled in the sort of cars that were unlikely to ever occupy Dad's garage: growling V6 Capris, up-for-larks Cortina GTs with fat wheels, ducking and diving Mini Coopers with bellicose Peco exhausts, a howling NSU TTS, and even a rare bird Cortina Savage. I was driven by people who took their driving seriously: a valued end in itself, not just the utilitarian means to an end it always had been before I entered this new world. Being a passenger in a car being pushed hard by a driver who was calm, chatty, and relaxed was a joy – and such a contrast to home. Dad abhorred unnecessary talking in cars and drove fast only out of anger, never for pleasure.

Derek Warwick once said that even after a lifetime in motorsport he still gets that tingle of excitement as he enters a circuit paddock, air thick with the familiar cocktail of bacon, coffee, oil, and petrol, and everywhere people in urgent conversation or bent over engine bays. It was all there to greet me as I arrived at Oulton Park, Croft, or Rufforth, but all too often I would find myself consigned to a marshal's post where nothing much ever happened, and where I would have to endure the endless telling and retelling of just how many pints Gerry Marshall had downed at Mallory last weekend, or of how Swiss F3 driver Jürg Dubler had tried to thump an over-eager marshal at Brands. I got to wave the odd yellow flag as somebody outbraked himself into the next corner, but the biggest appeal was the entirely passive one of being so close to the action. Later in the book I will describe in more detail just what an impression my first sighting of a Grand Prix car made, but I'll say now that being stationed at Oulton's Deer Leap as Pedro Rodriguez's P160 Yardley BRM howled by, lap after lap, just feet away in a great doppler smear of noise and colour was an experience that was near life-changing. And, less noisy, but nail-in-palm-of-hand scary was cowering in the flimsy marshal's post just inside the apex of Croft's Barcroft bend as Frank Gardner's Boss Mustang and Brian Muir's Camaro pointed straight at me at maybe 115mph (185km/h) and then bellowed past into Sunny.

Guantanamo Bay orange suits are now de rigueur for race marshals, and if I might cavil at marshals' elevation by circuit commentators, and sometimes even by themselves, to hero status I do admire their discipline and expertise. I didn't have a bloody clue about what I was expected to do and I was laughably ill equipped to do anything useful, let alone heroic. But I got in for nothing, felt and was made to feel part of the event, and I enjoyed the best view in the house.

I drifted back to Harewood, where my (real) name appeared in the programme along with such pseudonymous fellow marshals as Ivor Biggun and I Pokard, thus proving that male sophistication in the early Seventies was just as Neanderthal as the inexplicably popular *Confessions of* … films sought to portray; Mr Biggun probably thought they were documentaries. My picture would appear on the programme cover too, as startline shots, all smoking tyres and steely eyed drivers, portrayed speed much better even than a sideways slide out of Farmhouse. The meeting of the year was always the September Championship round, and in September 1972 I learned a new number – 38.47.

Numbers that may seem inconsequential to the layman can form part of the car guy's iconography. Nomenclature is a whole parallel universe, the one where 911 is far more important than the nominally superior 912, but which is itself crushed by 917 and eclipsed by 918. This is the world where 250 is nearly always more valuable than 275, 330 or even 365, and one where even its manufacturer termed 205 'le sacré numéro,' a label that could never, ever be applied to 206, but which just might be argued, especially in East Africa, as being appropriate to 404. Or it might be a capacity thing – 1558cc for the Lotus twin-cam, a homologation friendly 1601cc for the Ford BDA, 1275, 1071, and 997cc for the hottest of hot Minis, or, this time in cubic inches: 289 for a Mustang, 427 for a big block Cobra, or 428 for the eponymous AC that mirrored the Maserati Mistrale. It can be pure speed – perhaps the E-Type's dubious 150mph (240km/h) or the simple 'ton' that so many sports car owners once aspired to achieve – often in vain if they were driving the typical British sports car of the Fifties or Sixties. Or it might be the hit we all crave, acceleration, in which case it's the 0-60 metric, which is still the measure of acceleration that even a Green Party voter has heard of, or it might be the standing start quarter-mile whose elapsed time starts with a six, once the Holy Grail for any British drag racer. Racing's numbers tend to have more ephemeral heft, as last year's lap record can so often be this year's tenth row loser of a time, but two numbers remain high in my digital pantheon. The first one is 160.9mph (254km/h), the average speed set by Keke Rosberg's Williams FW 10 at Silverstone in 1985, which I describe in chapter ten.

The second number is the obsessive-compulsive precision of 38.47, which was the time (in seconds) that Richard Thwaites' McLaren M10A took to beat the Harewood hillclimb record in 1972. Thwaites was a genial, extravagantly-sideburned Yorkshireman who was battling with rivals such as Roy Lane, Mike McDowell, and the charming, chain-smoking Sir Nicholas Williamson for supremacy in the hillclimb championship. It was top ten run-off time at the end of an Indian Summer day, and the atmosphere was electric as each car juddered towards the start line in a series of high-rev burnouts. We had already seen the astonishing take off of David Hepworth's eponymous Hepworth Chevrolet, four-wheel drive traction bulleting the car up to the left-hand Country Corner, driver sitting high and straight armed, and looking as though he was a dour Yorkshire farmer just a little surprised suddenly to find himself subject to 1G+ acceleration. We'd watched hill record holder McDowell's 5-litre Brabham BT36 X Repco as it made its trademark aristocratic howl on the top straight, and now it was Thwaites' run. He rolled the car back as far as he dared and lit up the rear tyres again and again as he moved to the startline. Like many drivers of the era, he elected to use wet tyres, as they warmed up so much quicker than slicks – which back then were designed to run a full race length. Sometimes, especially when you are as close as you dare to a racing car, you just intuit that this lap, or this start, is closer to perfection than anything you've seen that day. It was like that at Harewood. Thwaites was always a contender, if rarely dominant, but today his stars aligned; hillclimb records are normally shaved by tenths, if not 100ths of a second, but Thwaites broke the two week old record by over half a second. And as we heard the time over the PA I felt almost as elated as if I'd driven the McLaren myself. Thwaites went on to race historics successfully but never did he triumph so exuberantly as that day when 38.47 became his own sacré numéro.

I haven't marshalled since the early Eighties, when I was volunteered into helping at a club race meeting at Snetterton. I lost count of the number of FF1600s and FF2000s that crashed into the scenery within our marshal post's territory, and whilst it was fun to help, what I really wanted was the ability to watch where I wanted, when I wanted, and with whom I wanted. I've been following that mantra ever since and je ne regrette rien. I'd look bloody stupid in orange overalls too ...

4
OVERSTEER – A VICTIM SPEAKS

Power is nothing without control
Young & Rubicam, Pirelli tyres advertisement strapline

"Just slip it into second," said Mr Tate, through a haze of Manikin cigar smoke as I slowed the Triumph Herald 13/60 for the junction somewhere deep in Pontefract's maze of back streets. It was my third driving lesson, and I had already learned that knowing the difference between a Lancia Flavia and a Fulvia, or an Alfa Romeo Giulia and a Giulietta was no help at all in enabling my left hand to describe precisely the correct arc between the narrow-gated Triumph gearbox's 3/4 and 1/2 planes. I knew all about H pattern gearboxes as *Autocar* featured the location of gears in every single road test, and I even knew that a Porsche 911's first gear was left and back in its five-speed box. But nobody had ever shown me a diagram of the erratic route from third gear (which was required to navigate a Herald's gearlever) to the safe haven of second without being marooned in the doldrums of neutral, or stranded in the badlands of a fourth gear stall. But at least it wasn't as bad as last week, when I had surprised even myself at the Olympic standard of cack-handedness I had demonstrated. At least I could blame *Autocar* again for its misleading graphics, and this time it was the immense challenge of getting from second to third. I knew it was a dogleg up and across, the diagram had confirmed that, but why the hell did the gearlever always end up in a baulking no man's land? Mr Tate, ever patient, reminded me that listening to him was more important than stuff I had read about, and he explained that thousands of hours of abuse by learner drivers (or, as I was later to learn about Triumph gearboxes, any type of use by anybody, ever) resulted in the selectors becoming badly worn and the gap between planes becoming so narrow that third was virtually a straight push forward from second. But I took 'virtual' to mean 'actual,' and the collateral damage of this etymological misunderstanding was the loud graunch of protest as I encountered the hostility of the non-synchromesh first gear to my inexperienced, questing hand on every single second-to-third change. Every single bloody one – no exceptions to the humiliation – in a lesson that, even though my watch suggested had only lasted for the usual hour, my great churning wave of embarrassment told me had actually lasted far longer. Teenagers would rarely complain of low self-esteem in 1971, but in my case it came close to self-loathing. How could I, who could recite road test extracts verbatim, be so completely hopeless, so bloody inept that I couldn't even push a stubby little gearlever in the right direction?

It's complicated; I was conflicted between being the head-in-the-clouds adolescent who loathed practical work of any description, who immersed himself in Thomas Hardy, Franz Kafka, Molière, Jean Anouilh, TS Eliot, Shakespeare, and the war poets for A-level English, German and French, and HP Lovecraft, Ian Fleming, F Scott Fitzgerald, and Graham Greene for fun but who spent just as much time reading about Ford Galaxies racing at Brands Hatch, and being the boy who thought that the all-white sci-fi cool of the Chaparral 2F made it the sexiest shape in history. I loved the sound of a Lotus twin-cam – I could even recognise it from two streets away – but I would have struggled to tell you just how a shock absorber worked, or the precise purpose of a Watts linkage, let alone the mystery of the Panhard rod. Or, as I had just found out, how to change gear in an unassuming little family saloon. It took me many years to realise that I am an empirical learner, which explains a mediocre law degree, a near total disinterest in the abstracts of the law, and a disinclination ever to speak in public, but a subsequent ability to negotiate the legals on multimillion deals involving ghastly terms like 'IPR indemnities' (which can only survive on the oxygen of conference room negotiations), as well as an almost unhealthy liking of hearing my own voice in public forums. Poundland psychology aside, what all this meant in 1970 was that there was a gaping ravine between my ambition to drive and my ability to learn how to do so. How was I ever to overcome my clod hopping inability to do anything that involved co-ordination between uneducated (and possibly ineducable) hands, feet, and eyes?

Dad had insisted I learn to ride a horse before there was any question of my riding a bike, and if I managed a vague competence to canter and trot, the extent of my abilities was sharply revealed by the first – and last – time I rode one of Dad's 'blood horses,' the term he applied to his prized, and highly temperamental, hunters. Used to the plodding progress made by cynical old riding school horses, I was unprepared for just how fast 17 hands and half a ton of horse flesh could move. I was used to horses that preferred to trot rather than canter, accustomed to riding nags that would only essay the latter gait under extreme provocation. As for galloping, that was the equivalent of Tesla's 'Insane Mode,' and therefore to be avoided at all times when a tyro like me was at the controls. The hunter, rather incongruously called Marcus, was the equine equivalent of a late Sixties Formula 2 car, and thus required only marginal encouragement to accelerate from gentle trot to the eye-watering speed of a full gallop. I know that even the quickest racehorse cannot exceed much more than 35mph (55km/h) but from my vantage point, eight feet above the unyielding ground, I can report that Marcus's V-Max, scenery blurring and hooves thundering, felt as though it was an equine bid to match a Saturn rocket's escape velocity. But unlike the aforementioned F2 car's slicks, wings, and big disc–enabled stopping power, bloody Marcus's powers of retardation were so lacking that even furiously yanked reins and involuntary yelps from the rider produced only the slightest diminution in speed, until the fast approaching fencing at the end of the field made the brute stop, if purely for his own self-preservation. As for bikes ... don't ask; the last time I essayed two wheels was on my sister Catherine's 50cc moped. I never did quite accept the gyroscopic alchemy that enabled two-wheeled conveyances to remain upright, and I harboured even greater doubts about how the things could turn almost by their rider's thought transference. This possibly explained the 'tank slapper' that resulted in a bent bike and a trip to the A&E department for lacerated knees and a sore head (as, of course, helmets were just for kid sisters) ...

I was thus uniquely unqualified to be allowed behind the wheel, and whilst I had done that Dad And Lad Bonding thing, where I sat on Dad's lap as an eight-year-old and helped steer the Humber Hawk over the field leading down to the beach, it hadn't ever developed from there. Now I was 17, Dad and I were engaged in the petty wars that rage when parental ambition collides with teenage obstinacy and, if peace only rarely broke out, there was at least a tacit acknowledgement that a Triumph Herald didn't have the luggage capacity to accommodate the amount of father/son baggage we had accrued. So Mr Tate it was, supplemented by ad hoc and off-road tomfoolery in a friend's Austin A40 – not the first ever hatchback, prophet without honour, Pininfarina styled A40, but its dull as ditch water, Fifties-austere predecessor: the four-door saloon with 1200cc, 42bhp, and the down the road graphics of a maiden aunt. My mate Rodney Gascoigne had towed the MOT reject to his grandparents' farm, five minutes' walk from home, and he'd drive it, with an abandon that was somewhere between enthusiasm and insanity, on the dirt tracks that criss-crossed the farm. Joined by our mutual friend Melvyn Bracewell, we'd smoke our illicit Embassy tippeds, ogle at Rodney's *Playboy*s and, in the parlance of the 21st Century Petrolhead, generally hoon about in the creaking, understeering Austin; Rodney at the wheel, deftly double declutching on the column change until the five bob's (25p) worth of fuel we'd bought from the Murco station ran out. Rodney drove superbly, and his road car Mini was tuned and tweaked with the mechanic's skill he'd inherited from his own father, a short-tempered firebrand with an uncanny resemblance to matinee idol Anthony Quayle. But even Homer nods, and one summer night Rodney's assault on a track, made slippery by an earlier shower, went awry as two wheels mounted the steep bank of one of the Victorian spoil heaps that littered the farm; gravity intervened and the ancient Austin rolled 360 degrees and stopped in a shuddering silence. Nobody was seriously hurt, but I was bruised by the contents of the toolbox raining down on me in a choking cloud of dust, fag ends, and the tattered *Playboy*s that had been stored under the seat squab. There's a metaphor here somewhere, but forgive me if I don't spend too much time searching it out.

Rodney was a decent guy and sometimes he'd let me drive, but purely out of the politeness he'd inherited from his mother, rather than any expectation I would be able to do it competently. So it proved, and it was only after he had painstakingly illustrated the workings of a clutch using the two redundant headlamp bowls of the Austin as visual aids, that I was able to make a rather less projectile take off. Steering was easy, even for me, but the co-ordination required for a second to third change was something I could not even hope to achieve, so arcane did the movement and timing seem to be. But I had learned one thing – and that was just what a good driver looked like in action (let the inversion be forgotten, okay?). Rodney was quick, smooth, could hold a slide for an eternity and his gear changing was sublime. And if your eyebrow was raised, incidentally, at friends who were called Rodney and Melvyn, let me just remind you that my Sixties mining village had a cornucopia of monikers that now seem more than a little quaint; it didn't seem unusual to go to school with a Bucktrout, an Oxtoby, or a Patricia Pygott (pronounced Piegott). 'The past is a foreign country' and all that …

Mr Tate introduced me to what passed as the open road in suburban Pontefract, and once I realised that working with a machine rather than forcing it to do stuff it really didn't want to do, my progress became smoother, my gear changes snappier, and even my hill starts became formalities, or at least they did until my first driving test, when my co-ordination was kidnapped by nerves and I failed. A few more lessons was all it took to pass, however, and even they were fun, as I found out that my instructor was a serious motor racing fan, and still remains the only person I have met who saw the legendary Silver Arrows and Auto Unions race at Donington in 1937 and '38. He grudgingly accepted my argument that his Golden Age might just be being played out all over again in 1970, as Porsche and Ferrari slugged it out in their mighty 5-litre sports prototypes, the 917 and the 512. History suggests I might just be right too, even though some of the glister might now shine as much from Steve McQueen's *Le Mans* as it does from the real thing.

There are certain rites of passage that most of us undergo in the magic decade between 14 and 24; that first effervescent hit of champagne, the shockingly grown up burn of a whisky, that head spinning hit of the first cigarette, and a whole load of other stuff that doesn't really belong in a book about cars. But perhaps just the one thing can compare to the sensation of the first mile you drive alone in a car. It feels so good that, despite the full licence you've just been awarded, driving feels almost illegally stimulating in its intensity and liberation. The fact that I only drove for 20 minutes on my debut solo didn't dilute the elation of knowing that I could have just driven and driven, free and unsupervised, to wherever I wanted – and having arrived there, nothing could stop me from driving some more …

The car was the 2-litre Triumph Vitesse that Dad had bought to replace the Herald – same packaging but double the power. Its modern-day equivalent would be something like a Focus ST or a warmer 1 Series BMW but unlike a 21st Century rocket shopper, its early Seventies' predecessor lacked the algorithmic caress of TCS, ABS, EBD, ESC, or any of the myriad safety systems that now ensure that even the most cack-handed driver is nannied away from harm. The 18cwt (920kg) Vitesse had a 95bhp six, 155 /13 Goodyear G800 radials, and swing axle rear suspension whose loss of grip under provocation was frequently the subject of pursed lip disapproval in *Autocar* and sneering derision in *Car*. For all these reasons it was obviously the best possible car in which to learn to drive solo, as the Vitesse would snap sideways at the slightest provocation from my right foot, at low to medium speeds in the dry and at almost any speed at all in the wet. But so benignly did it telegraph its intentions and so predictably did it slide that even I found that opposite lock correction was subliminally easy with its quick racked steering.

Or so it seemed. There was a Mr Hyde to the Vitesse's Dr Jekyll persona, and he would come bursting through your front door, murder and mayhem intent, if you dared to lift off the accelerator, even a fraction, whilst cornering with even the smallest helping of brio. Weight transfer would make the swing axle rear jack up, the massive positive camber which followed ensuring adhesion would be lost instantly and suddenly you'd become a passenger with a front row seat for your very own date with destiny. I found this out empirically, and I even had three witnesses. Dad had let me borrow the Vitesse for my first long drive in March 1971, which was the 120-mile (195km) journey to Mallory Park for the season opening Formula 2 race. I had never driven on the M1 before, and at 7am on a Sunday morning it was deserted. A friend, Ken, had reminded me that, even if all three lanes were free for as far as I could see, it was actually quite bad form to keep changing lane simply because I could. We settled for a brisk 80mph (130km/h) cruise in the deserted slow lane, and even though we were assailed by hurricane levels of wind noise from the frameless windows we didn't care, not with that lovely straight-six singing its brawny blare. Tipped off by our racing mad newsagent, we left the motorway illicitly by the Leicester Forest East service road in order to short cut to Mallory. I was in my element, confidence building by the mile and as we carved along the deserted country roads I was speed reading the road like a rally driver. Until, that is, I fluffed my lines and misread a key sentence, the one that I thought had said 'gentle left kink' actually read '90-degree right hander.' The Vitesse was still doing about 65mph (105km/h) as I was confronted with the consequences of my mistake and, whilst hindsight suggests that a straight on trajectory into the muddy field might have been more prudent, I somehow deluded myself that, in extremis, the Triumph could generate Lotus levels of adhesion and I turned the wheel a white-knuckled right whilst hitting the brakes as hard as I could. To nobody's surprise, not even my own, this turned out not to be quite the best strategy as the Triumph's grip quickly peaked, and the car described two 360 degree spins, with the flat-spotting G800s smoking long, black signatures on the road as we pirouetted onto the, hitherto unremarked, main road junction and shuddered to a standstill, the car rocking on its springs as it stopped next to a bus stop, at which stood two unmoving and unmoved middle-aged women. Not a word was spoken. I found a gear and I drove meekly to Mallory, where later Ronnie Peterson's shunt in a March 712 made my antics look pedestrian.

I learned a lot that first year, especially during my short-lived career as chauffeur to one of Dad's patients. Ray had undergone a serious eye operation and needed somebody to drive him around East and West Yorkshire so he could carry on being a sales representative for AJ Gelfer, a big beast of the tie industry at the time. My googling has confirmed that, although this Glasgow firm's products still enjoy a good reputation in the milieu of the tie and garment world, it ceased to trade in the Nineties. But it was big enough in the Seventies to fill our red Volvo 144 with boxes of sample ties, invariably in the exuberantly wide bladed style that had become the norm in the era of Jason King and The Persuaders. I learned a lot from Ray, and whilst the Volvo lacked the Vitesse's sparkle, it was predictable and benign, even if its two-foot long gearlever and ludicrously weighted accelerator made it feel like a throwback to another era. I learned how to hustle through city traffic, how to pre-empt an overtaking opportunity, and how to parallel park everywhere from East Coast Hornsea to the dark satanic mill clichés of Holmfirth and Huddersfield.

Dad's Vitesse was struggling after three years of the constant stop-start, three-point turning use on his visits to patients, although the absent-without-leave synchro and rapidly wearing G800s were down to my more recreational use. Although the Triumph Dolomite had already been launched, Dad decided that another Vitesse was more fit for his purposes and I wasn't complaining – the Mk II Vitesse had another 10bhp, almost house trained rear suspension and overdrive on third and fourth. It also had those tragic stylistic nips and tucks that the British motor industry insisted on applying almost annually to its products, succeeding only in making ageing designs look as if they were increasingly desperate to reclaim their lost youth. The Vitesse's tidied up grille was bearable, but what you noticed first were the Rostyle wheels; the real things might have looked terrific on the Mk II Cortina 1600E (a car with lines that could almost have graced an Alfa), weirdly attractive on the P5B Rover 3.5, but they looked almost farcically unsuited for the Triumph's 1959 Michelotti lines – which always had been more 'sui generis' than generic. And the plot unravelled completely on closer inspection, as the Rostyles were actually ill-fitting plastic wheel trims roughly tacked on to the same old, plain old steel wheels that the Herald family had been using for a decade. But ersatz wheels apart, the Vitesse was a hoot; not only was it quick enough to stay with the Mach One Mustang I raced along the Leeds Ring Road, but its previous inclination to premature oversteer was now in rehab. With the right combination of power and steering lock a slide was still provocable, but by invitation only – rarely was it the uninvited gatecrasher. Most of the time …

The end came unexpectedly and violently. Dad had asked me to deliver the car to Wakefield for a service, and I was to ensure the car was at the garage by 8.30am. It was a misty winter morning, bitterly cold, and as I drove to Castleford the grit laid by the local Council peppered the underside of the car reassuringly – there was not a hint of ice. As I left Castleford towards Wakefield the fact that the steering occasionally felt much lighter failed to register, but I was irritated at the slow progress being made by the car in front, which seemed to be taking exaggerated care on the wide, straight, and very smooth tarmac. I changed briskly down to third and accelerated hard into my well rehearsed overtaking routine but, almost instantly, I realised I was no longer in any meaningful control. I sawed at the wheel in the haphazard fashion you used to see people do in bad British films, but I succeeded only in over-correcting the previous over-correction of the enormous oversteering lunge that the unseen black ice had triggered. I hadn't noticed how the grit had stopped pinging the car's newly Ziebarted underneath as we left Castleford for Normanton, which was then, and possibly still is, the candidate for the most dour looking village in Yorkshire. The Vitesse spun viciously down the road, somehow avoiding the oncoming traffic, then banged across the high kerb and hit a lamppost squarely in the centre of the passenger door. The accident still had energy to burn though, and the car buckled and bent around the lamppost itself, which ended up a foot to my left, deeply embedded mid-seat in a confusion of twisted metal and vinyl. I was unhurt apart from a badly bruised shoulder and severe injuries to the ego. And Dad? He told me not to worry as he had managed to write-off his Aunt's Rolls-Royce in some tram lines during his medical student days in the Thirties. He meant well but there was still the feeling that not only couldn't I ever be a doctor, I couldn't even crash with quite the same distinction as he had.

5
ESCAPE FROM KRAKATOA

*So astounding are the facts in this connection, that it would seem as though
the Creator, himself, had electrically designed this planet just for the purpose
of enabling us to achieve wonders, which, before my discovery, could not have
been conceived by the wildest imagination*

Nikola Tesla, *The Transmission of Electrical Energy
Without Wires as a Means of Furthering Peace*

There's a wholly unremarkable Ford Focus on my drive. It has a 1-litre, turbocharged, three-cylinder engine and it's capable of an equally unremarkable 120mph (195km/h). It will hit 60mph (100km/h) in a mediocre 11 seconds from standstill and, on a recent 400-mile (650km), non-stop drive from Melvich on the North Coast of Scotland, it sipped petrol at 40+ to the gallon, despite cruising at a speed that would have sullied my driving licence if I had been intercepted by the Orwellian glare of a safety camera. There's a much wilder car in the garage in the form of a 400bhp per tonne Caterham Seven and, later on, I will noodle on (and possibly on and on) about the joy of Colin Chapman's best prime number. But let me talk now about why I am only impressed by cars like my white goods little Ford if I first think about how cars were back in the days when *Atom Heart Mother*, *Nursery Cryme*, and *Old Grey Whistle Test* soundtracked my life, and the three TV channels force-fed us pap like *Blake's 7* and *On the Buses*.

The 2015 Focus has broadly the same performance as a late Sixties Rolls-Royce Silver Shadow except that its engine – a sixth the size of the Shadow's – consumes quarter the amount of fuel. The Focus would out-accelerate a Mercedes 230SL, and an MGB or TVR Grantura would have been left trailing in its wake, and, even in the early Nineties, a six-speed gearbox would have been almost unknown outside commercial vehicles and supercars. 20 years before then, even a five-speed box was only found in exotica like Lamborghinis, Ferraris, and Aston Martins, with more blue-collar sports cars like the Corvette or Cobra getting by with at least one fewer ratio than even a 2017, cheap as chips, Suzuki or Hyundai can boast. All round disc brakes were not unknown in the Seventies but even then you would see fifth-hand Fords or Hillmans sporting stickers alerting you to the car in front's awesome braking ability – 'Beware. Disc Brakes fitted.' Until the Eighties, turbocharging was confined to the nutjob BMW 2002 Turbo, the glacially cool Saab 99, the more feral 911s, and the 'unsafe at any speed' Chevrolet Corvair; fuel-injection was a defining feature principally of Mercedes with SE badges – stoff einspritzung; and those of us unable to afford a Jensen FF could only avoid locked brakes by applying the more organic remedy of cadence braking. Given the Focus's gratuitously wide low-profile 235 section tyres, it would probably outcorner most Sixties sports cars too except, I suspect, the ones made in Cheshunt and Hethel, the sports cars with a green and yellow badge on their noses. Even the space saver spare in my last car, an inoffensive soft roader, was 20mm wider than an E-Type's 185 section tyres. Until the Nineties, traction control was via the medium of an educated right foot, stability control could be affected only by deft and busy hands, and launch control was enabled by an abruptly withdrawn left foot combined simultaneously with a sharply depressed right one.

But context is all, and although judging a car from the past by modern standards may be instructive, the judgement should never undermine the reputation of the car in period, because otherwise a Nissan Juke would eclipse a Lancia Aurelia, a 3 series BMW turbo diesel would outshine a Cord 812SC, and even a Dacia Stepway would outscore a Morris Bullnose or a Ford Model T, and that would simply never do. I guess I must have driven upwards of 2- or 300 different cars, I have owned over 30, and if I really cannot say anything interesting about the Renault Clio I hired at Rome airport last year, I can tell you about the cars that have shone the brightest for me, or which were so irredeemably dreadful that they are quite unforgettable and yes, I am talking about you, Suzuki SC 100.

I bought my first car when I started work in 1975 and it was a microcosm of everything good, and much that was bad, about the late-Sixties British car industry. It was a 1969 Riley Kestrel 1300, and it therefore represented the last moribund gasps and twitches of the once revered marque which had produced the sporty Brooklands and Gamecock prewar, and the elegant RME Pathfinder postwar, the six-cylinder engines of which had been the basis of the ERA R4 Grand Prix racers of the Thirties. A firm with form then, but under the dead hands of BMC and its successor BMH, it had fallen on hard times, begging for buyers' attention with the hint of sportiness provided by a house-trained Cooper-S engine complemented, if somewhat incongruously, by the 'Tudorbethan' wooden dash. The Riley was fishing in the same pool as its near identical stablemates in BMH, distinguished only by the subtlest variations in the DNA sequencing of the Issigonis-designed ADO16. Or, worse still for their international sale prospects, only an Englishman could really understand the exact societal subtext of each marque. ADO16 had been a clean-cut ground-breaker of a car on its 1962 debut; Alec Issigonis had designed the Mini's big sister, employing the transverse A Series engine and Hydrolastic suspension in packaging that was equally masterful but far more practical for family buyers. But instead of honing the car's potential, BMC deployed its full complement of badge engineers to produce first the Austin version (austere and ill-equipped), then the all but indistinguishable Morris, supplemented by the Wolseley (plusher, determinedly unsporting, and with only the sexy little radiator grille light to name-check the marque's heritage), my Riley, MG (clumsy grille and the spurious glamour of a rev counter) and, unforgettably, the Vanden Plas (yet more wood, real leather and the inescapable reek of suburban aspiration).

My Riley's body language was further nuanced by the addition of a tiny Astrali steering wheel, a six foot long whip aerial that described a perfect arc from front wing to rear rain gutter, a Hesketh Racing Teddy Bear decal and the almost mandatory aerodynamic windscreen wiper trims – a couple of quid from the Motorists Discount Centre and ensuring, in a Le Mans sports prototype sort of way, that visibility was maintained even at the sort of speeds a Riley 1300 could only achieve if driven off a very high cliff. Mechanically the Riley was both willing and robust and, although the rev counter seemed to be developing early onset dementia, I could live with that as the thrashing noises emanating from the engine room gave ample warning of when I was straying into the no man's land of 5500rpm and beyond.

The Riley took me to Cadwell and Mallory, Silverstone and Santa Pod with an enthusiasm that matched my own; it bounced down desolate fen roads as I pike fished the Lincolnshire drains, and it took me into the forest tracks of Dalby and Cropton to watch the Seven Dales and RAC rallies. But after only months of ownership the plot unravelled as I was driving between my new home in Lincoln and my parents' home in Yorkshire. There's a stretch of road between Lincoln and Gainsborough with a long, unsettling sequence of humps and dips; they are severe enough to confuse and distress any shock absorbers no longer in the first flush of youth, but the Riley's reaction was unprecedented. The car rocked up and down, as it always did on that road, but the spooky new reaction was for the floor to set up its own counter-rhythm, an unscripted syncopation that could only mean bad news. It did, as peeling back the driver's carpet enabled me to see daylight along a split floorpan. Further work (the due diligence I hadn't been diligent enough to do before I bought the Riley) revealed the newspaper and filler packed sills of the car, which had been transformed from Kestrel raptor to pig in a poke before the year was out.

Enter Krakatoa, in the form of a 1969 MG Midget. Inflation being the underpaid articled clerk's new best friend in the mid-Seventies, a backdated pay deal enabled me to euthanase the Riley and buy a pukka sports car. MAL 705E was finished in sloppily applied yellow ochre paint, had an enormous Peco exhaust, a leaking hood, 4.5 J steel wheels shod with cheap crossplies, and a long list of previous owners. Midgets were aptly named, but the tight and low driving position – augmented by the snappiest gear change this side of a Caterham 6 speed – and its quick, near telepathic steering made it outrageous fun even at pedestrian speeds. There was far less grip than even the Vitesse I'd killed, and it became entirely normal to exit any corner in town or country with half a turn of opposite lock. But there was a problem: I had bought yet another bloody pig in a bloody poke. The chassis might have been game for a laugh, but the 1275cc A Series (just like the Riley's) never brought too much to the party, as its claimed 70-odd bhp felt about half that. My engineering prowess has never been great but even I was able to diagnose that the MG had piston ring problems because, apart from the deteriorating performance, any attempt at meaningful acceleration produced a cloud of blue smoke of volcanic proportions, which not only engulfed the car behind me, but traffic on the other side of the road, pedestrians, and most street furniture. I might never forget the almost shocking intimacy of driving the two-seater sports car whose manufacturer's marketing tactic at the time was the deployment of very hot girls in very short dresses with the strapline: 'Your Mother Wouldn't Like It,' but the MG flattered only to deceive. The day of the old school, front engine, rear-wheel drive sports car was almost over for those of us who couldn't run to a Lotus, and everybody knew that an RS1600 Escort or Cooper S would annihilate even the Midget's big brothers: the everyman MGB and the tragedy called the MGC.

I very nearly bought a Lotus and it is to my eternal regret that I couldn't find enough cash at short enough notice to buy the Elan S4 Sprint Coupé I was offered in early 1979. The price? Read this and weep – a mere £1100. Its owner had worked for Team Lotus in 1977 on Mario Andretti's ground effect pioneering Lotus 78, the car about which its driver had said "Man, it's just painted to the road." The Elan had been painstakingly restored to better than new condition and the test drive confirmed everything I had ever read about Elans, and I had read a lot. The trademark snickety-snick gear change felt like an old friend before I had even reached top gear, the cockpit had room and comfort to spare, the engine might have fluffed a little at low revs but fizzed and barked round to the redline. The ride made most cars feel like trucks, and the steering was on the sublime side of heavenly. And if you tell me that there has ever been a small sports car more fit for purpose, better packaged, better performing, or better looking than the Lotus Elan I may have to ask you to step outside. The Elan's predecessor, the Elite, may have an even bigger fan club, but if the earlier car's fragility and more mouth than trousers 1220cc Climax engine do it no favours, the unassailable fact is that the Elan is just achingly sexy, in the same way as Ferrari Dinos or Bugatti Type 35s manage to be. Online polls invariably place the E-Type Jaguar on the top step of vehicular beauty contest podiums, but that perhaps tells us only that the voting public won't allow their attention to be drawn away from the Jaguar's ludicrously priapic nose for even the seconds it takes to notice the comically narrow track and incongruously upright windscreen. It's great in plan view and pretty good in profile but just bloody awful when it comes to down the road graphics. And if the Jaguar is blatantly about erectile functionality then the Elan's subtlety and build is entirely feminine: the Audrey Hepburn to the E-Type's Clark Gable.

When the Elan deal fell through I did think about buying another MG, maybe a B GT, a car whose near ubiquity has prevented its perfectly proportioned styling from ever getting the recognition it merited. If it had been built in tiny numbers in Sixties Milano or Modena it would now be a Pebble Beach invitee instead of a cheap retirement treat for summer weekend runs to the pub. But driving an MG instead of an Elan would have felt like settling for Diana Dors when you'd fallen for Diana Rigg. You might have had fun, she'd even make your friends love her too, but you'd never, ever escape the fact that she was just the wrong Diana.

Obviously, I then bought a Citroën 2CV 6 – in fact it was the only possible candidate for my new car. I had replaced Krakatoa with the only Ford Escort GT ever made that understeered, for which I had found a buyer. But I was so disappointed that I couldn't buy the Lotus that I used the sale proceeds of the Escort to buy a Citroen 2CV6 . If the Elan and I were fated never to be an item then at least I was confident that the Deux Chevaux's legendary eccentricity might beguile me. It didn't disappoint; and although I had reservations before committing, they were dispelled after borrowing my friend Steve Hardy's green 2CV for the day. Steve was evangelical about the Citroën's abilities and thought nothing of driving his to Provence every summer, returning a month later laden with Châteauneuf-du-Pape and charcuterie. Steve wasn't your typical Seventies 'Lincoln Yellowbelly,' as some citizens of the cathedral city, located miles from anywhere, would have regarded a day out in Nottingham as dangerously edgy. Curious at what I'd discover, I drove east from Lincoln, across to Horncastle on the edge of the Wolds, then north to Tathwell's lovely church before heading back to Lincoln, through that never-never land of one-horse hamlets that nestle at the end of deserted roads between Nowhere Much and Nowhere At All. Driving a 2CV is more involving than any other car I have driven except a Caterham; Mazda may make much of Jinnba Ittai philosophy with the MX5 – 'horse and rider as one' – but you feel an intimacy with the little Citroën that is every bit as direct, and the equine connection is irresistible, no? Its steering may be surprisingly heavy for a car running on 125 section Michelin X's, but the connection between front wheels and hands is shockingly direct to anybody used only to the soothing cosseting of electric power steering. Grip was extraordinary and, despite the levels of roll being more commonly experienced on maritime transport than terrestrial, my bright orange bolide rarely showed signs of understeering distress. The controls were out of step with every other car you could buy – apart from another Citroën – but I quickly understood that it was the stifling conformity of mainstream manufacturers that made Citroën's vision all the more refreshing. Why not a dash located gear change, especially one you needed to employ so frequently? Of course first gear should be a straight pull back from reverse because, if you are manoeuvring in a tight space, how much more logical is it to locate the two gears opposite each other? Second and third were the most commonly used gears and so they were also opposite each other, with the cruising-only top a right twist and push away. Need to carry bulky stuff? In five minutes you can take the seats out, remove the bootlid, and roll back the roof. Putting all your oeufs in just the one basket and need to drive over a bumpy field? Easy, with suspension that legend tells us was engineered for precisely this purpose. I drove my 2CV flat out, everywhere and always, and if heel and toe down changes needed more of a sustained kick to the accelerator than the blip normal cars needed, then so what? Well timed overtakes of 65mph (105km/h) coaches felt like slipstream battles on the Monza banking, the revs in the little flat-twin spiking as I picked up the draft 30 yards back, and surfed it as late as I dared before committing to the outside lane and steeled myself for the backwash of air as I drew level with a Wallace Arnold Leyland's front wheels. And thick snow would go unnoticed as I threaded my way through the flotsam of wheel-spinning Cortinas, and the jetsam of abandoned Marinas and Triumph 2000s.

I replaced the 2CV with a daft Suzuki SC 100, a bad joke of a car labelled 'Whizzkid' by its advertising copywriters. My first new car, I had been taken in by *Motor*'s uncharacteristic excitement at the combination of economy and performance that their suspiciously fit road test car had demonstrated. My 'Kid' was sorted for neither ease nor meaningful whizz, struggling as it did with a gutless engine and all the directional stability of tumbleweed in a tornado. It did, however, boast an early and analogue version of traction control: the engine would cut out if any hard cornering was even vaguely suggested. But Japanese cars had already started to be become hugely sought after in the UK and, after driving the now forgotten and unloved Datsun 120Y in the mid-Seventies, it was obvious why Japan would soon dominate not only the UK market, but everywhere else too.

The 120Y was an object of sneering contempt for everyone who knew the difference between a Mexico and an RS 1600, and every trousers-alight journalist with a press fleet payola BMW 2002 and a free lunch beano to attend. But to anybody who had been the butt of yet another under-equipped, cynically engineered, and badly built horror story from Leyland or 20th century schizoid firm Rootes/Chrysler/Talbot, the 'born to be mild' little Datsun was close to revelatory. My Dad's last British car, the Triumph Dolomite that had replaced the death-by-lamppost Vitesse, had consumed no fewer than five gearboxes in its first ten months of life, its snappy new overhead cam engine might have been praised in the magazines, but Dad's example would run on for up to half a minute after you had turned the ignition off, locked up, and walked away. The bloody thing would sit there, banging and jerking as if it had automotive Tourette's. Worse still, its nearside front suspension had collapsed at 80mph (130km/h) as, early morning Silverstone bound, I was turning into the downhill right hander over one of the highest viaducts on the A1, at Wentbridge. My knuckles may have been white and my passengers in shock, but we stopped short of the Armco – just. And I regarded the Dolomite's attempted suicide as the same cry for help as the one made by a friend's late and unlamented Marina TC, which had decided to end its short, and entirely miserable, life by understeering into yet another unfortunate lamppost.

Sorry, yes, the 120Y. It was as important as it was ground-breaking because it was one of the shockingly few cars that was exactly fit for most people's purpose. It started from cold, first time, every time. It ticked over without hunting, hesitation or histrionics. Its heater worked perfectly; it toasted your toes and demisted the screen. You could even see out of the back window as, instead of the tragically cheap and nasty plastic stick-on heated screen you'd had to buy from Halfords, there was one integrated in the glass which, just like an E-Type's, was even tinted. The gear change was as amazingly light as the clutch, and the synchromesh was unbeatable. And even the radio wasn't the aftermarket device you had to buy for everything else, it wasn't only standard, it was even built into the dash. Uninspiring and conservative it may have been, but unlike virtually every UK-built car, the unassuming little 120Y was robust, totally reliable, and generous in its equipment. Dull prophets aren't given to fiery oratory or spectacular deaths, but the unhonoured little Datsun told us our future with an uncanny foresight, even if only the acutest ears had heard its shy little voice.

But if Datsuns are about heads, then Alfa Romeos are only about hearts. You only have to look at an Alfa Romeo's badge to be halfway to the bedroom; on the left hand is the red cross of Milano and, on the right, there's a snake devouring a human – the symbol of the ruling family of the city, the Viscontis. It may be a cliché, but everybody who loves cars just has to acknowledge that driving, or, better still, owning, an Alfa is a notch on the bedpost which is compulsory, even if the consummation can end in disappointment, recrimination, and regret. A Ford might be the Monday sitcom, a Mercedes the Wednesday documentary, but an Alfa could only ever be a Saturday night opera. The plot might be risibly unconvincing but with arias so lovely and a libretto so knowing you could not help but suspend your disbelief and surrender to the moment. And you don't even need to drive one to love one; just look at and listen to a Thirties' Tipo B, a twin-cam GTA or GTZ, or (sigh) a 33 Stradale. And could *The Graduate*'s Benjamin Braddock really have snatched a Katherine Ross victory from the jaws of defeat if he'd driven a Toronado instead of a Duetto? Or fast forward 40 years, and if you tell me that an 8C Competizione isn't of the most aching loveliness I just won't be taking your calls any more, it's just so over between us, okay?

I will confess to being almost moist with anticipation at the prospect of my first drive of a V8 Ferrari, a Porsche 911, and a single-seater racing car, but the long day's drive I took in my first Alfa from a Manchester garage to my Lincoln home – via any road that looked as if it might be as long as it was winding, regardless of its direction – was just as unforgettable. The Sud Ti might have had a flat-four and not the trademark straight-four twin-cam power of a Giulia or a GTV, but, after enduring the cynically lazy efforts of mainstream Ford and Leyland and the wheezing impotence of VW Beetles, my Alfasud astonished as much as it invigorated. It may have had the typically simian driving position of most Italian cars of the era, but if my straight arms and bent legs made me feel I was driving something with a prancing horse on the side, precisely why was this the shortcoming that the road tests had highlighted? Its composure was astonishing; not only was the ride just on the comfy side of firm, but its resistance to mid-corner bumps and frost heave was otherworldly compared to anything I had driven before. The Sud boasted five – count 'em! – closely stacked gears, all for driving, none for cruising, selected by a beefy gearlever sprouting from a gaiter that might have come from a Maserati. It had all-round discs that sloughed off speed with eye-watering efficiency, steering that was entirely uncorrupted by torque steer or kickback (but which still telegraphed every nuance of the road), the hitherto unknown luxury of a driver's footrest, and – how I loved this smallest of things – the red light that stayed on until the engine was warm enough to play as hard as its driver wanted. Like it? I bloody adored it, and even now I cannot drive by a dry-stone wall without remembering the echo of the Sud's rasp; the trademark sizzle and pop that wasn't heard again until Subaru added its own bellowing refrain to the flat-four score.

My Sud, perhaps uniquely, didn't rot, and its only theatrics were a disinclination to keep its driver's door closed on left hand bends on exceptionally cold mornings, and even that amused me more than worried me. It's the Alfa DNA, it is why they are the best of good companions. The Mark I Golf GTi that replaced the Sud came close to being a parody of German thoroughness, even if its 21st century beatification seems to be gilding a lily which was far from unflawed in period. The Sud had more grip, an infinitely better ride, much better seats, steering that sang instead of mumbled, more room, and an exhaust note that sounded like an aria compared to the GTi's industrial drone. But it was the stopping and going that most clearly defined their differences; the Sud always felt as though its natural pace was 10mph faster than the speed at which you were travelling but its irrepressible brio was writing cheques its little flat-four couldn't honour. Its brakes could make you believe you were a hard charging Gilles Villeneuve though, slicing down the inside to scalp a last lap victim, so late and so effectively could you apply them. The Golf really didn't want to slow down much at all; its brakes were barely fit for purpose to the extent that I had simply run out of road more than once, and had slid muddily into field entrances and mercifully empty farmyards. Worse still, I had the very public humiliation of being forced to slither down the wrong side of the road to avoid the unexpected queue after a blind corner – and yes, of course I was driving like a 30-something with a fast car and a slow brain. The Golf never encouraged me to drive at any speed, high or low, it wasn't an Alfa-esque co-conspirator, but an entirely passive and totally obedient servant except where brakes were concerned. Want to start an overtake at 70 in fourth and finish it at 105? But of course. Rarely drop below 95 on an afternoon-long drive across deserted fen roads between Lincoln and the Norfolk coast? Kein problem, mein Herr. And, most unforgettably, want to explore the wilderness beyond the Great Glen in a maximum attack drive on the A87 under the gaze of The Five Sisters of Kintail followed by a low gear amble along the single tracks to Glenelg and beyond? Aber natürlich.

Most motoring journalists will tell you that the most common answer to the inevitable question – "what car would you recommend?" – is a Golf and I can't disagree. The two Mk2 GTis I drove for 100,000 miles were as fit for purpose as any cars I have owned, but their very virtue made them seem just too sensible once the small hot hatch revolution gained momentum in the mid-Eighties. And I tried most of the new breed of rocket shoppers – such as the Renault 5 Turbo that gripped like a limpet and accelerated like a 911 (or at least it did once the yawning chasm of turbo lag had been crossed). The 205GTi was the best looking of them all and, if I didn't warm to how heavily its steering loaded up in hard cornering, its trademark lift-off oversteer was joyous when induced deliberately, if downright scary when it gatecrashed your party. Perversely, I opted for the most flawed hot hatch of them all, and whilst it may now be an imprisonable offence for any journalist not to use the word 'icon' when describing the 205, it's also the law that the Fiat Uno Turbo should be dismissed with a sneer. So obviously I bought one, had a riot for a year, and then bought another one. It was almost all about the engine because the chassis was seriously flawed; it ran narrow 175 section tyres that struggled to deliver horsepower to tarmac in the dry, and just shrugged and gave up in the wet, when wheelspin was common in the first four gears. It had ludicrously uprated springs compared to the inoffensive standard Uno, and its ride was consequently so hard that the seatbelts were the only thing stopping you hitting the roof on poorly surfaced roads. Its clutch cable was directed over a succession of pulleys via so long and circuitous a route that it would snap every few months and, even with a freshly installed new cable, the clutch had what LJK Setright termed a "sharply projectile" action – I suspect it was easier to avoid a stall on an F1 car than it was on the little Fiat. The electrics were often consumed by demons, with my first Uno doubling the readings on most gauges when the thermostatic fan kicked in, and though this was reassuring on the fuel gauge, it was terrifying on its oil and water temperature counterparts.

But every sin, every shortcoming, and caveat was forgiven (if never entirely forgotten) when I floored the accelerator because the Uno Turbo was just insanely quick. Or so it felt, the road test figures never quite conveyed the apparently bottomless well of available acceleration. For a turbo car it even made a gorgeous noise too, a hard-edged howl that's pitch tracked exactly the amount of boost it was being given – a figure you could check on the manically flickering gauge in your eye-line. With my good friend Richard Daly, I drove my first Turbo to Imola for the San Marino Grand Prix: a 2000 mile (3200km), six-day road trip that featured a soul-stirring blast down a deserted Route Napoléon on a sun-dappled May evening, Verdi on the stereo and an endless succession of sweeping curves through which to spear. Later, we dropped down from the high pastures of the Alpes Maritimes to Grasse and then, as dusk fell, we purred along the Promenade des Anglais in Nice, city lights twinkling on a serene Mediterranean. And we felt like bloody heroes.

There have been lots of cars since the little Fiat but, once I was able to feed my lifelong addiction to the Lotus/Caterham Seven, I realised that, Lotus Elise and Exige apart, nothing short of an unaffordable Porsche or a pie-in-the-sky Ferrari could ever give me the kicks I now could get with every single mile in a Seven. Seven driving is a parallel universe to everything else, it's the one where Colin Chapman's 'added lightness' gives an interconnectivity with the road that is inconceivable to the driver of an M3 or an AMG, and it's one that I will explore properly in the chapters that follow. But first, just let me bookmark the two cars that both felt like the future, and that most epitomise how innovation can inspire even more than it can excite, and how, and how you shouldn't set too much store on what people say they want as, in Henry Ford's words: "If I had asked people what they wanted, they would have said 'faster horses.'" Reader, I give you the NSU Ro 80 and the Tesla Model S.

In popular legend, the NSU is now firmly resident in the dustbin marked 'seemed like a good idea at the time,' a car whose notional USP, its Wankel engine, went from the future of internal combustion to the same evolutionary cul-de-sac that made the dinosaur and dodo extinct. And like many an automotive legend, its apparently glib basis is eclipsed by a more robust truth, because the Ro 80 was the car that, more than any other, became the template for the supremacy of German manufacturers in the 21st Century. When I drove a friend's Ro 80 in the Seventies I was in awe at the near electric motor levels of smoothness, the utter unflappability of a rotary engine compared to the asthmatic wheeziness of the straight-four which, then as now, was the default choice of power for the European family car. Mazda stuck with rotary power for decades after NSU abandoned it, and, with the loophole-exploiting, four-rotor-shrieking Mazda 787B it even won Le Mans; as I write, Mazda still remains the only Japanese firm to have done so after Toyota's last-minute tragedy of 2016. Even Mercedes had a one night stand with Felix Wankel in 1969, the result of which was the C111, but the Wankel's thirst, unreliability, and emissions stopped the relationship from blossoming into marriage. So it isn't the engine that rules us from the Ro 80's grave, but it is virtually everything else. From its "intuitively aerodynamic" shape, as Stephen Bayley put it, to its semi-automatic gearbox, this car saw the future, and moulded it in its image. Look at the low bonnet, the deep windscreen, the powerfully muscled hips, the high tail, even the detailing of the lights and wheels, and you can see exactly how it influenced the 'Vorsprung durch Technik' of the Audi 100, and every one that has followed. Or look at the Chris Bangle designed 5 Series BMW of 2003 and tell me he didn't have a picture of an Ro 80 on his studio wall.

And finally, The Future. I rode in a friend's Tesla last year and I am still reeling. The acceleration made my R400 Caterham feel almost pedestrian, as the only time I have felt such a sustained, and almost bruising, push was in something with a Boeing badge on the front. And whilst the smoothness was eerie – progress punctuated only by a distant hum and a murmur from the suspension – what made the biggest impact of all was the dawning realisation that to think of a Tesla as just as a car with an electric engine is entirely to miss the point. The thing is more like the smartest of smart phones, but it's also one that can drive you to work, take your family on holiday, and keep you safe whilst doing so. Its functionality is dazzling, life enhancing, and unprecedented. It's an indictment of the industry's innate conservatism that it took a tech royal like Elon Musk to disrupt the orthodoxy that has stifled innovation and ignored the gigantic changes in attitude and behaviour of the last decade, the same lazy orthodoxy that thought giving its cars a sat-nav and a USB port was enough. Yet a Tesla is as much good companion as mere transport, the car that, whilst second guessing what you want, knows just what you need and, best of all, it can make you smile every time you turn the volume up to 11 and make your passengers gasp when you select Insane Mode and enter a brave new world of acceleration.

In 50 years' time, powering a car by employing a steel box to set fire to a liquor refined from long dead marine life won't feel any more ludicrous than fuelling it with Unicorn sighs then igniting them with dragon's breath. Tesla has shown us that, if we can be brave enough to learn from Fukushima and Chernobyl, if we can ignore the sideshow distraction of windmills on our hills and Archimedes' Screws in our rivers, and split some more atoms instead, we can keep on keeping on indefinitely. But enough of polemics already, you've bought a car book, so let me talk about the determinedly analogue Seven – the number that is the answer to more questions than you could ever imagine ...

6
SEVEN, THE MAGIC NUMBER

You ain't a beauty but hey you're all right …

Bruce Springsteen, *Thunder Road*

I saw my first Lotus Seven at a Tadcaster brewery car park in 1968; it was sideways as it pirouetted around the line of red cones delineating the route of the autotest I had seen previewed in *Autocar*. The driver was called Arnold Pratt and he was wearing shirt and tie and the sort of crash helmet you'd have worn to ride your born-to-be-mild Ariel Leader bike to the bookies. His fashion sense may have been on the dull side of staid, but his commitment was almost insane – the little maroon car was adopting angles of yaw that his Mini and MG driving competitors could never dream of emulating. Mr Pratt (Arnold would be too familiar for a man in a Viyella shirt and a red tie) didn't just compete in autotests either, as later in the year, I saw his S2 Seven in the High Eggborough Autocross and at Harewood Hillclimb, still being driven with the same brio. I had seen the Lotus Super Seven in my *Observer's Book of Cars* but, in the forward-looking, white heat of technology-focussed Sixties Britain, I had loftily dismissed the car as being some cranky irrelevance from ancient history whose spidery looks were just an embarrassment after the jaw-dropping cool of the mid-engined Lotus Europa. Or the Elan, come to that, the car that had special relevance to me that day, as I had just blagged my first ride in one. I had taken the bus to Tadcaster, walked to the famous John Smith's brewery, but had found no sign of any motorsport going on. I had started to walk disconsolately back to the bus stop when a surf blue Elan S3 Coupé stopped outside the brewery entrance, its driver's body language telling me that he was almost certainly looking for the same thing as I was. A passer-by told us to try t'brewery up t'road on t'way to Boston Spa, and with a sense of entitlement I hadn't known I possessed, I walked briskly round to t'passenger side of the Elan and lowered myself into that exquisitely cosy cockpit. It was only a mile to the Bass Charrington brewery, but I felt like royalty because this was me, 15, shy with girls, but only sitting in a bloody Lotus Elan, wasn't I?

Sevens started to further permeate my consciousness that year. I never did pretend to have a clue what *The Prisoner* was about (I struggled to keep up with *The Avengers* and stuck with it only because I was besotted with Mrs Peel) but I did remember the weird little sports car, KAR 120C, in which Patrick McGoohan had zoomed down an empty runway in the title sequence to the frantic tom-tom beat that soundtracked almost every TV action sequence at the time. I saw the odd Seven racing at Rufforth and, with the launch of the Ford Crossflow powered S3 later that year, I read more about them, especially on how this featherweight car with the retro looks could out-accelerate every Jaguar and Aston Martin and out-corner everything that wasn't another Lotus. It didn't take long for me to learn how the alchemy of light weight and clever design could humiliate cars whose huge power advantage was so brutally negated by weighing two or three times the Seven's mere half ton (500kg). As Colin Chapman had put it, "More power makes you quicker down the straights, but less weight makes you quicker everywhere." In 1968 Lotus' triumphs and tragedies were daily news, from Jim Clark's death at Hockenheim in a Lotus 48 F2 car and Mike Spence's death at Indianapolis in the Lotus 56, to the almost theatrical triumph of Graham Hill, who won the world championship in the Lotus 49, and left us thinking just what would Jim Clark have achieved in that car? Or in the 72 that superseded it, the wedge-shaped racer that won nearly everything but killed Jochen Rindt in the process. Is there a parallel universe where Rindt is a footnote, a Cooper driving nearly-man, and where Clark is the elder statesman with six world championships, the last in the Lotus 79 wing car?

In my 20s and 30s, I might have had lurid fantasies about the predictable objects of desire – Debbie Harry, Kate Bush, and Michelle Pfeiffer; the inevitable 911 Carrera RS, Khamsin, and Berlinetta Boxer – but whilst I already knew that, outside my dreams, Michelle and I wouldn't be driving to dinner in my Maserati any time soon, I knew that if ever I had the money to buy one and the garage to stable it, I would own a Seven. I did get the money and the garage eventually, and after over 100,000 miles (160,000km) of Seven driving I still can't stop smiling, because Seven is truly a magic number which just never stops giving.

In a quantum physics, wormholes, and Philip K Dick sort of way, I had actually experienced the Seven's successor before I drove the original because, in 1977, I had owned a Clan Crusader. That was 20 years before I drove its predecessor, itself an evolution of the 1957 original. Confused? Okay, well try to think of it in musical terms; if an original Seven was the Beatles' *Revolver* and the Clan was *Let It Be*, then an S3 Caterham Seven was a digitally remastered *Revolver*, with three bonus tracks and a signed photograph of George Martin. And *Revolver* was always the best Beatles album anyway, with *Let It Be* more of a Phil Spector penned suicide note than a celebration. More Clan explanation needed for any reader with less unresolved obsessive–compulsive issues than the author? Very well, but remember, I'll be asking questions later …

Paul Haussauer had been a Lotus designer, working on the Elan S3 and S4, and had proposed a successor to the Seven to Colin Chapman. It incorporated the original's lightness but in a modern closed coupé, more fit for the purposes of the Seventies sports car buyer, whose appetite for the hair shirt parsimony of the 1957 original had long since waned. But Chapman felt there was some life in the old dog yet, and had commissioned the mongrel Series S4 Seven to cater for buyers with a Lotus appetite but an MG budget. The beach buggy-esque, hippy vibe of the S4 might have amused the motoring press on its launch but the car dated as quickly as paisley and patchouli and, within three years, Lotus had given up on the S4, sold the S3 rights to Caterham, and decided that if it could beat the grandees like Ferrari and Porsche on track, it could beat them on the road as well. But, when its first effort was the underpowered and under-developed tragedy called the Elite 503, it was clear that even Colin Chapman could make the same mistakes as even the biggest manufacturer – just think Ford Edsel (but try not to think about the symbolism of that bloody radiator grille), Triumph Stag (great noise, lousy engine), and the AMC Gremlin (no, sorry, there just aren't the words).

So, back in 1970, Haussauer set up a cottage industry skunkworks in Norfolk, and pressed on with his vision, helped by his moonlighting mates from Lotus. The result was a fibreglass coupé with a rear-mounted Imp Sport engine – only 875cc but enough to push along its 1350lb (620kg) briskly enough to humiliate anything with an octagonal MG badge on the bonnet. Clan Crusaders ended up being built in Washington, County Durham, for reasons more connected with tax breaks and government grants than the sort of motorsport heritage that makes Norfolk and Northamptonshire the closest England has to Modena. *Autocar, Cars and Car Conversions,* and *Autosport* loved the Clan, and even the iconoclastic, immensely tall, and hugely erudite LJK Setright effervesced with an uncharacteristic enthusiasm that, to the relief of at least some of his readership, was expressed entirely in English, with not a Greek epithet nor Latin maxim in sight. It turned out that not only did the little Clan go far quicker than its modestly sized engine (Coventry Climax roots, but still only 55bhp) might have suggested, but it cornered like an Elan whilst sipping less petrol than a Mini. Better still, it repeatedly won its class in production sports car races, finished a fighting second on the Manx Rally and went on to win the Tour of Mull against a phalanx of Escort RSs and Datsun 240Zs ...

Nigel MacKrill is the man responsible for having wiped out the Marina TC mentioned earlier in this book, and not only did he persuade his father to replace the maimed Morris with a thuggish 'droop-snoot' Firenza, he also found my Clan and rescued it from West Country oblivion. My car, OPT 440 J, was the fourth built, and Nigel found it in a state of advanced decay in Bristol. Unaccountably, the original twin-Stromberg Imp Sport engine had been replaced by a standard Imp engine which didn't muster much over 40bhp and even its near 60mpg didn't compensate for its lack of punch. Nigel, with help from friends Alan and Ken, rebuilt the car, and, after I had persuaded my employer to give me a loan to buy a 998cc Hartwell Rally Imp engine, the Clan was transformed. Quick enough to embarrass a 3-Litre Capri on the straights, it would shame anything short of an Elan or a Marcos on the bends, facilitated by almost telepathic steering and huge grip. Impeccably mannered too, unless you were stupid enough to lift off or, worse still, actually brake mid-bend when, just like an early 911, the weight transfer would unsettle the heavier rear end, resulting in huge oversteer. And, of course, I was stupid enough; I already had form in stupidity. Whilst demonstrating the Clan's grip on the huge roundabout underneath the M1 in Leeds, I had forgotten that there was a 'give way' sign half way round, giving priority to M1 bound traffic over the local stuff. I nearly ran out of lock as the car went from gentle understeer to a huge tank slapper of an oversteer wobble, but somehow I kept the car on the road (to the relief of my ominously silent passenger). Actually, he was the very man, Steve Fox, who later bought the Clan from me when I had one of my periodic outbreaks of common sense.

The Clan would have made a lovely little Lotus, and had far more in common with the Elise – which rescued the firm in 1996 – than the succession of increasingly desperate attempts at upmarket Lotuses (never 'Loti,' thank you) that punctuated the firm's history after the demise of the Elan and Europa in the early Seventies. Their quick-to-date, flat-surfaced styling meant that the Elite and Eclat honoured only Lotus' trademark 'E' nomenclature, whilst ignoring the feminine delicacy epitomised by the Elan. And not even the shock of the new Giugario styled Esprit (and Peter Stevens' more housetrained evolution, the S4) was never quite enough to prevent buyers' apprehension about Porsche-sized pricing giving them two cylinders short of proper bragging rights. And if the V8 Esprit swan song had doubled the cylinder count, its flatplane crank rasp meant that it could still never even hope to threaten the hegemony of the 911's flat-six howl.

Sevens, now Caterham branded, were omnipresent in British Club racing throughout the Eighties and Nineties; the infamous 'Black Brick' raced by Rob Cox had punctuated its succession of race wins with implausibly fast lap records, and even the more modest Sevens raced by drivers such as John Lyon and Mark Goddard were beating cars designed 30 years later. In the USA a Seven's diminutive size had attracted snorts of derision from the good ol' boys who raced against it in the Nelson Ledges 24 Hours Race, but the snorting stopped when it won outright, having completed an estimated 7000 overtakes. Caterham's celebrated 'Too Fast to Race' slogan reflected the fact that some championship organisers were growing so tired of a Fifties sports car beating the modern stuff they wanted to see winning their races, that rules were introduced to stop Sevens even competing. I just had to have a Seven, and thanks to a legacy from my mother, bless her, I went shopping for a Seven in 1997.

I tried a Westfield first, but it was a decision of the head and not of the heart. It was quick, roomy, and felt like it could be just the best of good companions, but its genes were too far removed from the Anthony Colin Bruce Chapman DNA I wanted to experience. Only a pukka Seven would really do and, on a Seven owning colleague's advice, I introduced myself to Derek Moore of The Classic Carriage Company who were based in the stables just behind Shaw's Hairpin at Mallory Park race circuit. Derek was the most helpful man I have ever met in four decades of car purchasing and, even now, Caterham themselves would struggle to emulate his commitment to looking after his customers. I made many visits to Mallory, toyed with a crossflow Sprint, sighed that I couldn't afford the 'who spilled my pint' thug of a 2-litre Vauxhall, agonised over an S2 Cosworth, but when I saw K5 FUN I knew instantly that this time it was the real, 'coup de foudre' deal. So starry-eyed and speechless had I become that I could only sigh 'yes' to a smiling Derek, who had saved this trump card until now. K5 was a 1993 1.4 Rover K Series powered Supersport, which meant 130bhp at a screaming 7400rpm, an alleged 100lb/ft torque at 5000rpm and, in my early version at least, a Ford Sierra MT 75 five-speed gearbox. My car had been a press car, originally registered K4 FUN, and featured leather just about everywhere (seats, dashboard, you name it), had flared wings and chrome headlights, had so-called 'Prisoner wheels' (that man Patrick McGoohan again) and featured paintwork in Porsche Cherry Pearl Metallic – a deep, lustrous red that might have looked dull on overcast days but turned the Seven into a catwalk queen on sunny ones.

I hadn't driven a Seven, ever, before I drove my own Seven from Mallory to North Yorkshire. That I would love it was a given, as hadn't every journalist from Roger Bell to Steve Cropley assured me I would do so? That I would feel a sense of almost unbearable euphoria was only to be expected: I had waited nearly 30 years since I had seen Arnold Pratt's S2 performing in the brewery car park. That I would feel enormously self-conscious hadn't occurred to me at all, even though I should have remembered the sort of reaction the Clan had triggered in the remoter parts of Lincolnshire on summer evening runs with an OS map and no particular place to go. As far as I know, the locals are still talking about the dart profiled blue sports car that buzzed through Claxby Pluckacre and Aby with Greenfield one Wednesday night, just as the dominoes were finishing. Mind you, down in Whipchicken Fen they still haven't recovered from the time that an Austin Metropolitan nearly took a wrong turning in, oh, '59, was it boy? But if the Clan made ripples, the Seven made waves, and in my early days of 'Sevening' I found the constant scrutiny almost spooky. It was my very own Strand experience.

Meaning what, exactly? Back in the early Sixties a new brand of cigarette called Strand was launched with a huge advertising campaign whose strapline was 'You're never alone with a Strand.' This was meant to convey that a few drags on the eponymous gasper would transform even the most tongue-tied social outcast into an urbane charmer, whose company would be valued by the 'beau monde.' But, far from making Strand cigarettes an affordable passport to social elevation, the advertising sent out the subliminal message that I would be condemned to inhabit the world envisaged in Sartre's "Hell is other people" quote, with paranoia the result. I may not have had quite the full Strand deal but being looked at by every driver of every vehicle, every bus queue, and every bunch of kids at every school crossing exposed me to a scrutiny I wasn't fully prepared for. But after 20 years of Sevening I have developed an immunity, and I have also learned to anticipate how each social group will react.

Young kids and older women first: every child from three to ten, and nearly every woman over 60 will widen their eyes, point, shout and laugh when they see a Seven. The most common greeting comprises the words that could have been uttered back in the Thirties:

"Nice car, mister!" Older men always ask the same, damn fool question: "Is it a Morgan?" And they obviously get the same answer. And younger men between 12 and 22 are conflicted between being regarded as uncool for staring, and missing the opportunity of telling me they know what a Seven is. Middle-aged men either ignore you altogether (this trait being especially noticeable in, yes, Morgan drivers), ask you if you built it yourself, enquire if it's based on a Sierra like the one their mate (actually somebody they've never exchanged more than the time of day with) has built, tell you that it would be better with a Rover V8 (despite my telling them there's no room and that the weight would destroy the handling) or, especially at motorsport venues, sidle over shyly and say they're thinking of getting their own Seven and what do I think? Yet there is one social group, tragically, which affects never, ever to notice the middle-aged bloke in his daft sports car, and that is every woman between 17 and 60, except the packs of feral, 'three sheets to the wind,' high-heel-tottering, 20-somethings on a hen party raid. They might wobble mid-selfie, shriek something risqué, but they sure as hell brighten my day even more than I brighten theirs.

But being the centre of attention wasn't the most startling aspect of driving a Seven, what really shocked me was how utterly unlike a Seven felt to anything else I had ever driven, Clan included. It was the little stuff to begin with, the fact that, even though I was wearing my thinnest soled and narrowest shoes, I couldn't help hitting two pedals at once, which was fine for heel and toe down changes but unsettling for everything else. I was hypnotised by the view down that surprisingly long louvred bonnet, especially the sight of the reverse of one chromed headlight reflecting its twin against a background of rushing green verges. I knew the steering would be sublime, so quick, so nuggety with feedback and feel, and I had guessed rightly that the gear change would be on the short side of sharp but what I hadn't expected was the most graphic lesson in physics I had ever experienced. Granted, that didn't take too much, as my 15-year-old self had quickly lost all interest in heat transfer and the electromagnetic spectrum, and had affected an arty disdain for learning the exact use of sines and cosines, but within five miles of leaving Mallory I had learned more about mass and inertia than any 40-something lawyer had any reasonable cause to expect. It's that Colin Chapman added lightness thing again, but if you have never driven a car weighing quarter the weight of a Range Rover, half the weight of a Fiesta ST, or a third the weight of oligarch favourite, the daft Bugatti Veyron, it is an utter revelation to drive a car that seems to be subject to entirely different laws of physics. Add a passenger, though, even a light one and you feel the braking distance increase and the acceleration decrease far more than you ever might have imagined. You might expect an electric response to the accelerator, and you get one, but you struggle to acclimatise to the fact that when a Seven isn't speeding up it's slowing down. Lift off the power after accelerating and there's no inertia to maintain your progress, you just bleed away all speed with astonishing rapidity, thanks to a lightweight body with all the aerodynamic qualities of a house-brick. Any slippery and massy modern car will take a mile to stop from 80mph in neutral but a Seven will be stationary within a few 100 yards. Seven brakes are tiny little discs, and even 'big brake' upgrades are toytown stuff compared to the giant ceramic jobs that any self-respecting supercar now boasts but, with only minimal planning, you can drive a Seven at absurdly high average speeds on the twistiest of roads without even brushing the middle pedal. But if you do brake, you invariably stop far before you intend to. These characteristics, allied with the ability to change direction in an eye-blink, mean that, even in busy motorway driving, a Seven stretches both the time to react and the space in which to do so and that makes for the curiously relaxed, stress free travel you would never expect to find in a raucous little sports car.

There were some honeymoon parallels in my first months of Seven ownership, and that of itself should tell you just how intimate a bond a Seven and its driver can create. There is the initial 'shock of the new' enthusiasm, which you have to exploit as frequently as possible to confirm that you're not actually dreaming, that you really can enjoy yourself so much and so regularly but after the first few months you start to question whether you are confusing frequency with quality and whether the pleasure is an end in itself or the means to something less ephemeral, something substantial enough to create a relationship you couldn't have imagined when you made that first move. And so it proved with the Seven; I learned quickly that short, 40-minute blats were unfulfilling, that journeys were always better seasoned by a destination and, whether visiting a friend or taking in a race meeting, the longer the journey and the earlier the departure the more I would savour the experience.

I learned lots of other things too, and principal amongst them was that my Seven might have looked fast in the road test figures but that most of the time it rarely felt more than brisk. The engine was a gem, though, making a deep bassy grumble below 3000rpm, giving way to a baritone growl up to 5000rpm, changing to a tenor shriek that climaxed at 7600rpm. In the right place and at the right time it was an addictive thrill to drive a car that sounded like Laurent Aiello's BTCC Nissan but, when all I wanted to do was to overtake the old couple's Nissan Micra bowling along at 55mph, I just hated having to make so much bloody noise that the Nissan would jink towards the kerb as the banshee howl from the Seven terrified both driver and passenger. The problem was an engine with no meaningful torque below 5000rpm but an unquenchable appetite for revs beyond, exacerbated by gearing that was comically unsuited to a light car with a far racier power plant than the mardy old Pinto which was the normal partner for an MT 75 gearbox.

I had kept every Seven road test for decades and I could recite the words of the performance car test of the 1.4K SS almost verbatim, as it positively fizzed with enthusiasm at 'the perfectly chosen ratios' of the five-speed box. The journalist who wrote the piece should remain nameless, but was called David Vivian, and his text was so hopelessly wide of the mark that I came to wonder if he'd done anything more than recycle the press release over slightly too long a free lunch.

The gear ratios were indeed perfectly chosen for the demands of a fully laden five-door 1800 Sierra pulling a caravan between Manchester and Scarborough but they were utterly, spectacularly and uselessly unsuited to the sort of questions a 1400 screamer of a Seven might ask. Because first gear ran out of puff at little more than 30, but second peaked at

70, third at 90+, and fourth well into three figures. Fifth? God knows; at 7600rpm you could have set the controls for the heart of the sun and arrived there before next Tuesday week, so stratospherically long legged was the gearing.

Caterham sorted the gearing with its in-house six-speed, whose top gear was equivalent to the five-speed's fourth. I didn't know, or care, what Mr Vivian's verdict was on this innovation but every test I did read positively bubbled about the transformative effect of a gearbox that was now absolutely fit for purpose. But at two grand for a new box, I acclimatised to the fact that if I couldn't out accelerate a decent Golf much over 60mph, I could outpace just about anything if the road was winding. Even superbikes? Easy; they might disappear to distant dots on the straights but as soon as braking or cornering was involved I would be tracking their every move from as close a distance as didn't seem too aggressive. The irritation about bikes is that, despite my making every effort to assist them when they wished to overtake me, only twice has a biker made even a token effort to help me overtake when I have caught them. The usual reaction is denial and obstruction, as if I had mounted some sort of existential threat to their wild child ego. I blame Marlon Brando's *The Wild One* and *Easy Rider*'s Peter Fonda and Dennis Hopper …

I'll tell you more about track days later, but a day at Cadwell Park made me really start to thirst for more power. I would zoom through the uphill left-hander at Coppice at a buttock-clenching 90mph (145km/h) in fourth, but on the climb up to Charlies the revs would fall away and third was needed just to maintain speed up the hill. The curse of the lower powered Seven is that, although it is easy to lap far quicker than anything short of a supercar, the lap time is achieved much more by late braking and fast cornering than it is by straight line speed. Two cars epitomised the difficulty – an MGB GT V8, which would burble away from me on every straight, but delay me on every corner and – the ignominy – a Volvo T5 Estate. If it had been driven by BTCC Volvo pilot Rickard Rydell, I could have lived with the humiliation but, as the driver was a mild-mannered vet from Batley, I was mortified. I couldn't get by him except by a rule-breaking dive up the inside into The Mountain which startled the vet as much as it made me feel like Gilles Villeneuve.

Something Had To Be Done. My Seven's original Michelin MXV tyres might have been the rubber more suited to a heavyweight Mercedes 300E but I found them impossible to heat up, wear out, or grip as hard as their sexy tread pattern had suggested they would. I had replaced them with aggressive, near slick Yokohama AO32s, and found new levels of adhesion that, allied to much more progressive breakaway, made me much faster on the road and track but, even then, I was hampered by far less power than I felt the car deserved. The disease, which Seven owners term 'upgrade-itis,' might be highly contagious and ruinously expensive to cure, but once the patient is back to full health, the sense of euphoria is joyous, at least until the next outbreak. In 2004, after already having bought a decent roll over bar, FIA spec race harnesses, and adjustable shock absorbers, I took the braver step of buying a 1.8-litre, 160bhp Rover VVC engine from a Cheshire firm who had acquired a number of low mileage, ex-Rover test cars. My engine came from MG's too-late-for-the-party Elise, the MGF, and it utterly transformed my Seven. With lightened flywheel and competition brake master cylinder, the car went from mild to wild.

The Sierra box was no longer a hindrance with so much torque; overtaking became near subliminal, nobody kicked sand in my face on trackdays any more, and I was looking forward to a long and happy future with K5 FUN when Caterham pricked my complacent balloon by introducing the Duratec-engined R400. The Rover K series was light, keen to rev and sounded even better than a Lotus twin-cam, but it had not one but two Achilles heels. It could develop an unhealthy taste for head gaskets, and in its higher tuned versions, such as Caterham's ballistic R500, it demanded regular 'refreshes' – a euphemism for expensive rebuilds, which were the price paid for 230bhp at a rabid 8800rpm. The Duratec's 2-litres developed 210bhp, but it was no high maintenance drama queen, apparently being near unburstable and, better still for road driving, had almost diesel levels of torque. *Evo*'s Chris Harris raved about it and, coming from a man who, like erstwhile *Autocar* colleague Steve Sutcliffe, was a racer as much as a writer, I took notice.

Far too much notice in fact, as to scratch an itch, just out of curiosity, I booked a test drive at Caterham Midlands, who were then based a mile or so from where The Classic Carriage Company had been located; useful, as 20-odd years of attending Mallory Park race meetings meant I knew the roads well enough to exploit the R400's potential. Or so I thought – because the reality was that the six-speed test car was as insanely quick as it was absurdly entertaining. On first exposure, the gearbox felt as though it had been fitted with a long first, but five nearly identical second gears, so little did the revs drop between changes, and the gear change action echoed the rifle bolt cliché so beloved of road testers with limited vocabularies. There were a hell of a lot of gear changes, too, as the R400 seemed intent on reaching three figure speeds on the shortest of straights. Sadly, I also realised how baggy and tired K5 FUN's chassis had become, as the R400 rode, steered, and gripped with a tenacity that both thrilled and terrified me.

And of course I bought one; I had the money, a well-paid job with the baby boomer's privilege of a final salary pension, but mostly because, in my world, and maybe yours too, 'want' can so easily become 'need.' Ordering a new Seven involves ticking far more boxes than you might imagine buying such a stripped-down lightweight should require. Paint (really), windscreen (ditto), hood, heater, FIA spec roll bar, leather seats, decent harnesses, and oh-so-race car-sexy Stack instruments added more expense than I had contemplated when I first checked the borderline affordable list price. Colour became an absorbing challenge, as, although I wanted to have some sort of homage to the car's motorsport heritage, Lotus' trademark green and yellow was the most common of all Seven liveries. Black and gold JPS or red, gold and white Gold Leaf fag packet livery looked wonderful on a Lotus 49 or a 72, but faintly absurd on a car designed in 1957, and it was only whilst flicking through my 1967 *Automobile Year* that the problem was solved. The Grand Prix season review featured a photograph of Mike Spence's BRM P83 mid-air at Nürburgring, and its dark green-blue body and orange nose band looked utterly sensational. Problem solved, and later I even remembered that the garage Mike Spence ran also sold Elan BRMs in the same livery ...

R400 JPA arrived in October 2007, and if Caterham's pre-delivery inspection and customer care hadn't then been quite so cynically inadequate I would have been overjoyed instead of merely excited. The first problem was easily overcome, but surely delivering a 30 grand sports car should not have to necessitate your customer having urgently to find a petrol station to supplement the pitiful four litres left in the tank? I wasn't impressed by being given a handbook for a car with a different engine, and the damned thing looked flimsier than the one that came with my fridge freezer. Worst of all, I discovered that my car was so fast that the Stack's speedo registered 524mph, and this in only second gear on Northallerton High Street ... And Caterham fixed it so well that, after my first 300-mile round trip back to Leicestershire, at an indicated 65mph I was overtaking the shoals of 5 Series BMWs on the M1 North as though they were parked because the speedometer was now under-reading by nearly 30%. But, after a near meltdown on my part and a final tweak on theirs, R400 JPA and I were ready to go adventuring ...

7
TRACKS 'N' HILLS 'N' HOLE SHOTS

Get your motor runnin'
Head out on the highway
Lookin' for adventure
And whatever comes our way

Steppenwolf, *Born to be Wild*

It had been raining since breakfast time, and now hailstones were peppering our old stone cottage on the North York Moors. I had hoped the thunderstorm would be heading for the North Sea but, if it was, its big brother was trying to catch it up before it reached Whitby. Since being caught in a desolate Highland glen by an especially vicious storm a few years earlier, my enjoyment of the spectacle had been replaced by stomach churning fear, which I sometimes label as brontophobia in a doomed attempt to make myself sound more victim than coward. Obviously this convinces nobody, including myself, but this time there was another reason for the nerves: my instructions were to present myself to the staff at Croft race circuit in two hours' time, to be briefed on my track debut in my first Caterham Seven, the 1.4 K Series Supersport. Nerves had been jangling the night before, but with the added spice of meteorological unpleasantness I was dry-mouthed and twitchy; I already knew that K5 FUN didn't relish the wet, but the prospect of combining smooth tarmac and a sheen of hail with a skill level more plodder than Prost was making me pray for salvation by rain check. There was to be no escape; the cheery woman at the circuit office assured me the afternoon session was going ahead and laughed as she told me some of her regulars preferred the wet because it was so much more fun. Jesus, the absolutely last thing I wanted to hear was that I was about to be subjected to humiliation by Yorkshire 'Regenmeisters.'

I had actually done one track session before, two if you include an illicit lap of Silverstone Grand Prix circuit in my Riley 1300 after the Daily Express International Trophy in 1975. The victor, Niki Lauda, was already on his way home, the last support race had finished, and nobody had seemed too fussed as I eased the Riley on to the tarmac at Becketts but, that said, my time was not going to trouble James Hunt's 134mph fastest lap. The thing is that, unless you were called Noel Edmonds and could afford to hire Thruxton to show your Ford GT40 off to your mates, track days were virtually unknown until Club 89 broke new ground (and you can hazard a guess when) by allowing road cars to be driven on track. But I wasn't tempted: I doubted if the cars I was driving in the early Nineties, my crappy little Citroën AX GT especially, would have made it home after a good seeing-to on track. But in 1993 I had found a cheap day at the Jim Russell racing school at Donington, and I enjoyed the best of times in a Group N Vauxhall Astra GTE and a Formula Vauxhall single-seater, under the tutelage of former F3 driver Scott Stringfellow and another driver who had better remain nameless. Scott was charm personified, and his colleague might have been good enough for a BTCC drive, but his customer care was seriously compromised by his communication skills – "Are you bloody deaf? Why aren't you doing what I've told you? You deaf or something? If you've got a hearing defect then tell me about it" – and all I'd done was to screw up my line, just a little, into the Old Hairpin. But, brusque tutor apart, I had been given a taste of the track, and I'd driven as fast as I'd dared through the Craner Curves; ten days later, as I watched Ayrton Senna's McLaren do 170mph at the same spot during the European Grand Prix qualifier, I was speechless. A pity I didn't stay for the race. Oh yeah, that race …

Five years later I felt like the new kid starting at big school as I drove through the Croft paddock, parked up, and tried to look more confident than I felt as I walked towards the briefing room. There were lots of cars, from Westfields to 911s, a thuggish looking E Class AMG Mercedes, and the bizarre, but somehow comforting, sight of a red Ford Escort Estate with a load bay full of spare wheels. Miss Congeniality in the circuit office was going to be disappointed as the sun had burned through the clouds, the fast-drying track surface now wreathed in spirals of vapour. But now I wouldn't even be able to blame the wet for my risibly slow pace, and I could already visualise the line of WAGs and hangers-on holding their sides in helpless mirth as I droned by the pit wall, 20 seconds a lap slower than the Escort Estate. My nerves had already transformed the Escort driver into a serious player, a wolf-in-sheep's-clothing mensch with a penchant for humiliating the pansy in the Metallic Cherry Pearl Caterham. Because, of course, I had fallen victim to track day virgin syndrome, which afflicts nearly everyone who isn't blessed with the effortless confidence that great racing drivers ooze from every pore. Read Tommy Byrne or Johnny Herbert's autobiographies, and it's shockingly clear that they just knew they could not only do this stuff, working out lines and braking points almost instantly, but do it so well that self-doubt was never in their lexicon. Just like a Senna or a Schumacher, if they weren't quickest it was nothing to do with them, but down to poor set up, a tired engine, or any of the myriad excuses that racing drivers have employed since the dawn of competitive motorsport. But me? I knew that even my low-powered Seven should humble most cars, most of the time, and at any track that didn't feature Mulsanne or Mistral sized straights. And I also knew that I would be overcautious, beset by self-consciousness, and counting the hours until I could go home and return to being as dull a plodder as a public sector lawyer is invariably assumed to be. In Paul Simon's words – "Maybe I think too much."

You can guess what's coming; I stopped fretting before I had even left the pit lane and, within two laps, I was fizzing with exhilaration and laughing with relief. It was an utter revelation that not only could I apparently drive fast enough to catch rather more than I was caught, but that a Caterham could feel just so unbelievably alive and responsive. I thought I had pushed hard on empty country roads, but nothing prepared me for the extraordinary grip I found as I turned into Clervaux bend before following the long right hander of Hawthorn. And if I had rarely been especially hard on the brakes before – I had always found speeding up the fun part, with slowing down just the necessary evil before the buzz of a bend well taken – now I was finding the 'who blinks first' dilemma of how late I dare hit the brakes a game I really didn't want to stop playing; especially when I realised how much more natural it felt to heel and toe down through the gears when my right foot was pushing on the brakes with an assertiveness I had never needed on the B1257. The best parts of Croft, though, are the ones that only drivers and marshals get to see properly, as the speeds are too high to allow the public to get close – the deliriously fast run between the third gear Tower Bend, and the double-apex Sunny via the hold-your-breath-fast Jim Clark Esses and Barcroft. Only small movements of the little Momo wheel were needed to thread the needle between the left, right, and right sequence, but I started to realise just how different the car felt if I turned a few feet earlier or later, and how eloquent the Seven's feedback was when I did the right thing at the right time.

And I soon learned that doing the wrong thing at the wrong time could have drastic consequences, as I spotted wheel tracks leading through the infield barley crop and saw the inverted Peugeot 306 GTi 6. Another beginner, he had found out, in the hardest of ways, that sharply lifting off the power in the most 'wanna play?' hot hatch of the Nineties wasn't the smartest move to make after carrying too much speed into Jim Clark's eponymous bends. As the session ended and I drove back to the paddock, I reflected on the sheer amount I had learned, especially about myself. I bathed in the exultation of not having been as amateurish as I had feared; and, if I thought I had driven quickly on the road before, I had never driven so fast, and never with such total immersion that some of the exhilaration could only be savoured after the event. I learned, as never before, just how a Seven's flyweight mass endowed it with an almost surreal advantage over the conventional fast car; I was amazed, and hugely smug, that I didn't even think about braking until long seconds after the brake lights had appeared on the flame spitting Evo and the Carlos Fandango special edition Impreza. And instead of looking and feeling hot and bothered after 20 minutes of having been driven so hard, the Seven just reassumed its Clark Kent level of self-effacement as it muttered uncomplainingly back into the pit lane, as if to say "What the hell did you expect? I was born to do this stuff." Unlike the poor AMG Mercedes, now plumed by shimmering heat haze from every orifice, and reeking of cooked brakes and hot oil. The poor brute soon retired hurt, and was last seen exiting on an RAC recovery truck.

I really had not expected that driving on track could create an almost zen level of calm in me; the concentration might have been just as sustained and intense as I had imagined, but completely absent was nearly everything that fogged my thinking on a public road. No need to worry about speed limits, random dogs, deer, and cyclists, unexpected blind bends, oncoming traffic, and high kerbs. There was no need even to angst about what a tragic spectacle a middle-aged man in a noisy sports car can make, and no time at all to worry about the presentation I was doing tomorrow on the latest daft government initiative. I might have been spending too much money already on Aston's pastimes but now all I wanted to do was more of this, but faster and better.

Track days aren't timed, and doing so (except by data logging) is forbidden, but there are ways of doing it surreptitiously, especially with a friend as a co-conspirator. Stopwatches don't lie, and what I learned over the many trackdays I did at Croft both encouraged and depressed me. With a combination of an uprated car and better technique I was delighted eventually to have shaved 15 seconds a lap from my debut times, and I was childishly pleased to discover that I was lapping quicker than the sideways 500bhp Mustang I had seen win a historic touring car race. However, I was still embarrassed to be lapping a couple of seconds slower in my upgraded VVC car than a Caterham Graduate racer could achieve with less grippy rubber and a 40bhp deficit. But overtaking a Porsche 911 GT3 one lap and – yikes – a GT2 the next did restore some self-confidence, and even that feat was eclipsed by the guilty pleasure of making a colleague revisit his breakfast after fewer than three laps. Tim had been expecting a light-hearted passenger jolly and, after the sight of R500s and 911s blitzing past the pit wall in a Doppler blare of noise had made him uncharacteristically subdued, exposure to the level of cornering force the Seven could muster made him wave his arms in 'game over' defeat; full face helmet was removed with only seconds to spare. Tim's wife took his place and didn't bat an eyelid, even when I increased the pace from mild to maximum attack.

Just when I was developing a mild 'been there, done that' swagger at my local circuit, the confidence I had built up was swiftly eroded by my first track day at Cadwell Park: the circuit that not only offers the best spectating experience in the UK, but which can transport you to heaven or hell when you drive it. Le Mans winner Roy Salvadori may famously have said "Give me Goodwood on a summer's day and you can keep the rest" but, as Goodwood has now become as much a part of The Season as Henley and Wimbledon, it cannot eclipse Cadwell's classless allure, at least not in the view of this chippy Yorkshireman. And since when did former airfield Goodwood have the gradient that makes a good circuit a great one? Cadwell is located in the high chalk pastures of the Lincolnshire Wolds, and it caresses the folds and rises of the terrain like a lover. Its width may mean it is better known for bikes than cars, but if it was good enough for Formula 3 – at least until Senna's Ralt RT3 made its bid for the stratosphere in 1983 – it was good enough for both K5 FUN and R400 JPA. Cadwell can look far slower on the TV than it is to drive, as the camera just loves to linger over the relatively slow speed drama of The Mountain, but from Barn to Mansfield Cadwell is extremely quick, and nowhere better illustrates its speed than Coppice, the ultrafast uphill bend leading to Charlies blind double apices. It took some acclimatisation, but when I first steeled myself to lift off only for an eye-blink before turning in at close to 100mph, then speared round the corner, pushed down in the seat by the extraordinary grip that the gradient offers, I was near ecstatic. And Cadwell's every prospect pleases; solve the problem of Charlies and then savour the brief respite as you watch the buzzards wheel high above the Park Straight before the big stop into Park itself. Then it is time to hang on tight during the crazily long Chris Curve until the Gooseneck demands inch-perfect precision before the freefall downhill into the 'don't mess with me' challenge of Mansfield. Cadwell always demanded far more from me than I could give, and would leave me dry throated and shaky after ten laps, but I loved it as nowhere else. But unless you have experienced Cadwell in the wet, you would never have guessed that the place has such a bipolar personality. When the rains come the good day sunshine host is replaced by the knuckle dragging lout who just can't wait to find an excuse to spoil your day.

Cadwell is often described as being a mini Nürburgring, and whilst the comparison is a bit daft – the 'Ring is six times longer and Cadwell doesn't look much like the set for a Wagner opera – both circuits become extremely difficult to drive in the wet. The Lincolnshire Wolds may receive a third of the annual rainfall the Lake District receives but, when it does rain at Cadwell, the natural bowl layout of the circuit means that it is quickly affected by rivulets of water streaming across the track, which then create pools of standing water. One of the greatest wet weather drives I have seen was JJ Lehto winning a Formula Ford 2000 race at Cadwell in near monsoon conditions; watching him jink and slide his Pacific Racing Reynard 87 SF through the rushing stream of brown water at the foot of the Mountain so impressed me that I was sure he would be a Grand Prix winner. He wasn't, but at least he won Le Mans and wasn't the underachieving disappointment that some of my other tips for the top have been (yes, I'm talking about you, Dave Walker and Jan Magnussen). Recalling how so many of Lehto's fellow racers, quick drivers nearly all of them, had struggled even to stay on track, even at lap times ten or 15 seconds slower, with my almost non-existent ability I wasn't exactly looking forward to my first wet Cadwell.

My wife Joanne rarely accompanies me to motorsport events, she's more than smart enough to recognise an obsession when she sees one, and her enthusiasm for passengering in the Seven had always been kept well in check but, just this once, she had agreed to come with me to Cadwell. Obviously and inevitably it was pouring, and the driver briefing in the circuit café (windows steamed up, heating full on) was strict, stern and serious; on the pain of being sent home there would be no, repeat no, heroics. The track was borderline dangerous, there was standing water at Coppice and the trees bordering Hall Bends, the Hairpin, and Barn would keep the track wet long after everywhere else had dried out. I had noticed sniggering from the pair of likely lads to my left, heard their mumbled words of dissent – "we've paid our fucking money," and I resolved to keep as far away from them on track as possible, whilst employing my trademark 'steady away' pace. Joanne was a trouper, she hadn't said a word as I half spun out of Mansfield, locked up into the Hairpin, and flared the revs with wheelspin out of Barn; but, even above the VVC's growl, I could hear her gasp as we crossed the start-finish line and saw the debris arcing skywards in the mist and spray hanging over Coppice. I slowed down and tried not to gasp too as I saw the smoking wreckage lying across the full width of the track, and then noticed the crash helmet lying upside down on the kerbing. The helmet belonged to one of the likely lads, mercifully, it was unoccupied, having been torn off its wearer by the violence of the impact, which reduced the Ginetta to its component parts in seconds, and on only the first hot lap. Joanne hasn't nagged me too much since about coming to another track day ...

Post-millennial track days were very different to the amateur hour high jinks I had so enjoyed at both proper circuits, like Croft, Donington, and Cadwell, and cheap as chips days at kart tracks and airfields. I gradually found myself in the minority of drivers who actually drove their track cars to the circuit instead of towing them there in the five grand Raceshuttle trailer. I risked becoming the odd man out by not having sets of both slicks and wet tyres, let alone a natty race suit, set off by a Senna replica helmet and FIA compliant pixie boots and gloves. I was starting to feel like the country bumpkin who had gatecrashed the society ball, and I couldn't help thinking that some drivers' testosterone swagger might have been better directed into proper competition instead of the ersatz racing into which trackdays were appearing to degenerate. It wasn't just the driver demographic either, as some race teams were also using track days as cheap test days and, whilst it's fun to watch a proper driver in a proper car attack a bend with a commitment that confirms I shouldn't think about giving up the day job, having to spend quite so much time looking in the mirrors to spot the slick shod racer about to lap me – again – did nothing for my enjoyment. This was never more in evidence than the spring day when I took my 1.4K powered Seven to RAF Binbrook, which lies just a few miles north of Cadwell. Home to Lightning interceptors in the Cold War but now disused, many of the former airbase's runways were being dug up for recycling and the remainder had been laid out for an impromptu track day. Every bad lad in nearby Scunthorpe with a hopped-up Nova shod with a set of third-hand slicks had turned up, which was only to have been expected, but I was taken aback by the sight of the big rig race transporter with the Carlin Motorsport signage. Carlin had brought along two Porsche Supercup 911 race cars, one of which was driven by an Italian racing driver, who looked as only an Italian racing driver can – designer shades, three-day stubble and a leggy supermodel of a girlfriend with cheekbones the likes of which are very rarely seen on even the best night out in Grimsby. The other 911 was driven by one of those hard as nails Kiwis, sparing in conversation but the best of wing men, the guys like Denny Hulme, Howden Ganley, and Graham McRae who have peppered UK motorsport since Bruce McLaren first arrived in 1959.

The Carlin Porsches were so insanely quick that I found myself being overtaken by them every three or four laps, and at my puny 100mph (160km/h) down the long straights I felt as though I was parked as the Porsches slammed by at 150mph+ (240km/h), leaving that trademark flat-six howl in their wakes. The reason they were there? The Supercup race, which supported the Monaco Grand Prix, was taking place the next weekend, and Trevor Carlin had chosen Binbrook as the best circuit to replicate Monaco's trademark tight turns. It is not quite the first comparison I would have made; granted, a couple of tricky second gear corners had been created with road cones but the run off was endless, the straights were both wide and long, the surface was abrasive enough to arrest a Lightning, and the elevation changes were near non-existent. Worse still, the Mediterranean's trademark shimmering blue wasn't going to be threatened by the Humber's matte brown oozing, nor was the La Rascasse bar going to be eclipsed by nearby Grimsby's Yardbirds Rock Club (Google review: 'Great place.' Don't judge a book by it's [sic] cover, the staff are firm but fare!! [sic]) nor was the town often the mooring of choice for the sort of yacht that is owned by a Briatore or an Abramovich.

If I have learned one thing from driving my Sevens on racing circuits, it is an even greater respect for the professional racing driver. Club racing is such a broad church that it can cater for the rising star as well as the middle-aged plodder, and if some cars are impressively fast, others can be on the pedestrian side of stately, but quite how even a slicks and wings Formula Renault driver (let alone his bigger budget Formula 3 counterpart) can manage the level of concentration, possess the speed of reaction, and the razor judgement to keep up such a dazzling pace leaves me reeling. A morning of driving my 220bhp R400 at duffer level pace leaves me aching and thirsty, incoherent, and half drunk on adrenalin to the extent that I simply cannot imagine the physical and mental resources any half decent racer can apply to his driving. I once spun 720 degrees out of Croft's chicane, having failed to show my own regenmeister credentials; I still remember not having a clue which way I was pointing, let alone exactly what had happened and why, and how I then just sat in the car for half a minute to recover my composure. And what would Gilles Villeneuve have done? His spatial awareness would have ensured he knew exactly the pace and direction of his rotation, he would have kept the engine running, and would already have selected the gear he'd use to fishtail back on to the track, having lost five seconds at most. And if I think back to the first turbo era Formula 1, powered by engines with huge lag but the power delivery of a roadside IED, please tell me how a Senna or a Mansell, let alone a midfield De Cesaris or a Cheever, was able to cope with 1000bhp, stick shifts, and steel brakes for two hours – around bloody Monaco? It's beyond me, it's probably beyond you too, in fact it's beyond anybody either of us has ever met and that alone is why Grand Prix racing became such an absorbing passion.

I couldn't resist a day at Harewood Hillclimb school; I have already written about my marshalling days there in the early Seventies, and I have remained a regular visitor since. The course had been extended significantly in the mid-Nineties, meaning that the old starting area, where I had marshalled for years, was now about a third of the the way along the 1600-yard (1450m) course. I had driven, and been driven, up the old course on countless occasions, and whilst some of my ascents had been brisk, in cars such as a Series 4 Lotus Seven and a growly 3-litre Ford Capri, discretion was needed to avoid a bollocking from the Clerk of the Course. K5 FUN was in its 160bhp manifestation on my Harewood day, and I soon realised that the school nomenclature was well chosen. The day was entirely different to the relative free-for-all of most trackdays, as the emphasis was very much on educating pupils on how to do this hillclimb stuff both properly and well. Harewood has a beautifully converted stone barn as a classroom, complete with video screens, white boards, and venue maps; the tutors are invariably hillclimb alumni and often include former champions, a treat that is like getting some free advice from Sebastian Vettel at a Snetterton track day.

Nelson Piquet once said that "driving in Monte Carlo is like riding a bike in your house," so ill-matched was car to circuit, and his words rang true at Harewood, as a hillclimb course it feels just ludicrously narrow compared to a race circuit or airfield track. Whilst it's easy enough to take a racing line at Donington, angling from one side of the circuit to the other just like a proper racer would, it's much harder to do so on a well surfaced farm track. There's rarely more than a couple of feet (0.6m) of tarmac either side of even the svelte hips of a Seven and, until my instructor demonstrated just how much I could exploit such a narrow ribbon of road by taking an apex far later than seemed geometrically possible, I struggled up the hill incoherently. My progress was marked by furious bursts of power, locked up braking, and the scrappiest of cornering technique – which looked even clumsier on the video debrief than it had felt on board. Hillclimbing may lack the speed and adrenalin rush of a circuit trackday, and I did secretly miss the wannabe racing driver buzz of following, catching, and overtaking the car in front (especially if it was the sort of modded-to-hell-and-back Nissan or Subaru about which 14-year-olds of all ages get so moist), but the scalpelled precision that a speed hillclimb demanded was hugely enjoyable, as was the fact that, unlike on a trackday, I could ignore the mirrors completely and concentrate body and mind for the 70-odd second ascent. And the more I concentrated, the longer the course felt, and the more I was able to analyse each move I had made on what felt like a puzzle you could spend years trying to solve, none more than the eternal mystery of the final bend at Harewood – the blind entry Quarry. How does anybody programme their brain both to avoid braking embarrassing yards too early, or to brake so late as to risk the public humiliation of spearing off the track within touching distance of the finish line? And when you are driving your Gould single-seater with a 600bhp V8 behind your shoulders, which has just peaked at 145mph (235km/h) on the top straight, how does your brain even have the time to function at all?

If Harewood epitomises an affluent and posh Yorkshire, where it can seem almost compulsory to arrive in a new Boxster or a shiny Jaguar F Type (it's a Jag sort of place is Harewood, lying between moneyed Leeds and fur-coat-but-no-knickers Harrogate), the York Raceway caters for a far wider demographic, as drag racing has an appeal that covers both the bluest and whitest of collars. It doesn't matter whether you arrive in a Caterham Seven, a Nissan GTR, a knackered Mondeo, or an artfully rusted Rat Rod – you will be made just as welcome. The Raceway is located pretty close to the middle of nowhere, and if the access track could slow down an M1 Abrams battle tank, the agricultural reek makes you regret you're in an open car, the laissez faire, access all area vibe of the Raceway's paddock makes me regret leaving it so long after my last visit. I will write more about drag racing's unique appeal in a later chapter, but let me talk now about what it's like to be a participant in a drag meeting. Uniquely in motorsport, anybody can turn up in just about anything with two, three, or four wheels, and run their machine down the same quarter-mile strip as the big boys with their heavy metal machines in Pro ET and

American Superstock. Can you imagine running a track day during the lunch break at a BTCC meeting? No, me neither ...

'Run What Yer Brung' – RWYB for short – is the 30-something quid opportunity to find out just how quickly your car will accelerate, or more accurately, just how many fractions of a second you can so easily lose by screwing up your start or botching a gear change, and all in public too, with a commentator whose dry-as-a-bone wit offers no hiding place. Nearly every circuit trackday involves no scrutineering other than a noise meter check but in drag racing, even if yer runnin' what yer brung, there is a five-minute bonnet off and wheel kicking check – but no noise test. I strongly suspect that drag racing's outlaw persona would mean that any noise test it did require would only be to ensure that the number of decibels your car could generate was loud enough to cause hearing damage to onlookers, and the triggering of car alarms in the farthest reaches of the eroded WW2 concrete that is, laughably, called the car park. When it comes to doing the running thing, you are usually paired with somebody else running what he brung, and hence I've run against everything from Imprezas (from which there is clearly no escape at any track event I attend), turbo nutjob hot hatches of every hue and valency (and sometimes further enlivened by the wizardry of NOS – a nitrous oxide system), and drag racing's signature tune – the bellow and crackle of a big-block V8.

There's a tendency for motor racing people to sneer at drag racing's apparent simplicity, it's all-over-in-seconds brevity, and its corner free lack of challenge but I think the real reason many affect their disdain is a class thing, as if young people with a high tattoo count shouldn't be allowed to devalue such a middle class pursuit as motorsport. Me? I love the strip, even if I am the possibly the only reader of *The Times* who is driving today, even though I am two or three times older than the Nova and Civic drivers whose foxy girlfriends I can't help but notice, and even though I am usually the only runner with a drop top sports car – apart from the TVR Griffiths and Chimaeras whose owners seem to love this stuff even more than I do.

I learned that the secret of making a good time is all about the start – apart from those bits that are about changing gear as fast as hand and feet can move and (how can I dare to admit this?), not being so stupid as to lift off the accelerator, not at the place that most regard as being appropriate – the finish line – but 20 yards before, devaluing my standing quarter-mile to a standing 420 yards. My times were hardly noteworthy anyway; in the mid-14s with VVC power and the low 13s with the Duratec powered R400, and I blame this on being a fat bastard with reactions slowed by the ravages of both time and wine. But what a kick it is to show off to the crowd, with some gratuitous tyre warming and the proverbial 'dab of oppo,' as 220bhp squirrels us sideways on a damp track; what a thrill to hear a Mustang's V8 over my left shoulder as it strains to catch up after my hole shot (ie the perfectly timed and executed getaway), and what humiliation to be beaten so soundly by cars that really shouldn't see which way I went. It was flattering to be asked by the blinged up Asian guy in his lowrider Civic Type R whether my VVC had been "... well messed-with" (he was surprised it wasn't but glazed over during my Colin Chapman monologue), and it was as extraordinary as it was humbling for my near 450bhp per tonne Seven to have been left gasping in the black smoked wake of a bloody Škoda Fabia. A diesel Fabia, whose proud owner told me just how much he had spent on his sky-high boosted, torque drenched Czech hatch, the street sleeper stealth car that would shatter the ego of any Focus ST or Boxster driver who hadn't even noticed the little hatchback with the baritone rumble and the big, black drainpipe of an exhaust.

Trackdays sharpen your understanding of how quick a good driver in a pukka racing car can be, hillclimbs leave your mind reeling at how anybody can attack Shelsley Walsh or Barbon with over 1000bhp per tonne and putty-soft slicks, and running what yer brung leaves you beyond coherent speech when you try to imagine what deploying the 10,000bhp of a Top Fuel dragster to reach 250mph (400km/h) in under five seconds must feel like. And yet, whilst all trackwork has, at its heart, the inverse equation of the shorter the time the better the result, it can be just as gratifying to prolong the moment, and whilst Tantric sex has a place in some lives (mainly Sting's, I reckon) then stringing out a solo Seven tour over a five-day 1500-mile (2400km) marathon leaves me with just a smug a smile as a post-coital Sting's smirk. As you now are going to read in the next chapter ...

8
REFUGE OF THE ROADS

We are all in flight from the real reality
John Fowles, *The French Lieutenant's Woman*

These are the clouds of Michelangelo
Muscular with gods and sungold
Shine on your witness in the refuge of the roads
Joni Mitchell, *Refuge of the Roads*

4.30am can be the best of times or the worst of times. The worst of times used to come when I had angsted all weekend, fretting about Monday's all-day negotiation session, but the best times come when I wake on a May morning and remember that in 12 hours' time, I shall have driven 400 miles (650km). Because today the Caterham and I are off adventuring again, and to the best of destinations: the one that lies somewhere north of the Great Glen. So what if the alarm was set for an hour later? At the dawn of this long drive day I'm happy to be awakened by the first blackbird, as I'm instantly suffused with the simple joy of just being alive and almost breathless with the anticipation of driving a fast car over the roads I adore. And so what if they are the same roads? It's always a different journey, whether punctuated by chance encounter or dramatised by sun and shadows chasing each other over Rannoch Moor and white horsed Loch Linnhe. I couldn't help hiding a smile when an acquaintance told me how much she loved the Highlands, how accommodating she had found the gift shops and cafés in Pitlochry, but actually no, she had never been further than Aviemore. I knew she didn't believe me when I told her that the best stuff doesn't really start until beyond Great Glen, where, suddenly, I will be quite alone in a small car in a huge landscape, all traffic having evaporated within a mile of leaving Invergarry. A crow's flight from the Great Glen to the north coast may only be a 100 miles (160km) or so, but, if you do it my way, there's 300 miles (480km) before you see that dark line of the North Atlantic. And, better yet, you see it first from the ribbon of road that jinks and twists through Strath Dionard: the desolate wilderness of rock and mountain that can be as eerie as it is majestic.

In 1984 I had driven my 1124cc Citroën Visa Super E, three up, to Altnaharra in Sutherland for a week's trout fishing, and although the little Citroën was more willing than capable, we had still travelled 520 miles (840km) from home, and the further north we went the more astonished we became at the extraordinary landscape. We tracked across an empty Strath

Oykel, the mist now shrouding the hill as we listened to Talking Heads' *Remain in Light*, and every nerve crackled as we heard *Listening Wind*'s spooky lyrics, as if for the first time – "Mojique smells the wind that comes from far away ... he feels the power of the past behind him ... the wind in my heart ... drive them away." The song was about a Native American, one man's freedom fighter and another's terrorist, but I only realise now why it might also have felt like the perfect soundtrack, so meet and right for the wilderness we drove through, as *Psycho Killer* David Byrne was born a Scot ... That night we drove up to the high ground above Loch Naver and we spoke in whispers; because never had we experienced such total silence, a peace characterised by so much more than the simple absence of sound. Something else had filled the aural vacancy and, if at first it was unsettling, we soon acclimatised to the feeling of being in an outdoor cathedral with mountains for walls, a northern sky for a ceiling, and silence for a choir.

There were many trips north to fish the wild lochs of Cape Wrath and Assynt, and even though the fishing was often more of a trial than a triumph, the brief twilight of a midsummer night and the exhilaration of drifting down a big loch in a small boat more than compensated. And so did the day-long drive from Yorkshire to the north coast, or vice versa; it had been fun in the Visa, and it was simply joyous in a 205GTI, never more so than on the Sunday morning when we left the Cape Wrath Hotel at 8.30am but didn't see another vehicle until an hour later. And that wasn't so unusual, as driving in the far north is not like driving anywhere else in Britain. Not only can traffic be non-existent, but you can travel for ten or 20 miles (16-32km) without seeing more than a solitary croft, hanging on to the side of a weirdly shaped mountain with an unpronounceable Gaelic name. In England, an A road is wide, busy, and often multi-laned, but my first reaction on seeing the northbound A838 at Rhiconich was disbelief, as not only was the road in three-ply – grassy middle strip flanked by coarse tarmac – but it was also little more than the width of a Ford Transit. At home, such a road would be classified only (and ironically) by being unclassified, the sort of road only the locals know, the road that had last been resurfaced when an Escort RS2000 was at the apex of my wish list. Yet single track roads necessitate a courtesy to, and an interaction with, other drivers, which are so at odds with the hair trigger aggression that a rat trap A14 or M25 can so easily induce. And when I read the magazine road tests that deconstruct every nuance of a car's handling up to and beyond the limit, I struggle to identify where, even in North Yorkshire, I can attack a road with enough vigour to attempt to do the same without risking prosecution or my taking a lead role in a horror story with a wide tractor, a narrow road and a blind bend as co-stars. But in the North West Highlands there are places where it is safe to push the envelope a little more than is possible on the much lauded, if overrated, Buttertubs Pass or the B660, the Cambridgeshire road that one magazine often uses as the key determinant of chassis ability, presumably faute de mieux. Give me the road from Loch Eriboll to Lairg instead; I may incline more to Dawkins than Deuteronomy but the stark majesty of those 70 miles can make even this heathen a believer.

So why did it take me so long to take my Caterham there? I guess it was the fact that not only did I have doubts about my own capacity to endure the intensity of a Seven drive over such a distance, but also a scepticism that such a stripped-down machine, as insubstantial as it was basic, so lacking in the conventional comforts that even the humblest hatchback can boast, could tackle a 1500-mile (2400km) tour without mechanical malady. It didn't help that my love of cars and driving wasn't complemented by any practical skill beyond the absolute basics, as I am not part of the ownership demographic that not only builds its car from component form, but also just loves to take bits apart for the fun of upgrading them. But as I read about the adventures of other Seven owners as they made solo drives across the Alps, Apennines, or Picos de Europa, and even from sea to shining sea in the USA, I couldn't help feeling timid and parochial, with Northumberland and Silverstone the limits of my ambition. And so, at 5am on a Sunday morning in May 2005, I set off from home with the far north my only destination and the open road my only route.

I needed the trip badly; my father had died in April, after a hideous six months that had seen him degenerate into somebody who I no longer even knew, and working had felt like wading through a swamp.

I needed the refuge of the roads, and I found it.

Endless low-pressure systems had been forecast, and rain was a frequent travelling companion, except when it really mattered. And it didn't matter too much as I drove K5 FUN, post 160bhp VVC upgrade, across the Pennines from Scotch Corner. It may be a long way from Scotland, but there is still a feeling of trip turning into journey as you turn west onto the A66 and start the long ascent up to Bowes Moor. When you escape from the motorway formerly known as The Great North Road, now the soulless A1, all camera surveillance and dot matrix signage, it's as though your journey turns from digital to analogue, from virtual reality to organic experience. As I passed the Morritt Arms at Greta Bridge I couldn't help but think of the Bentley Speed Sixes and Lagondas that would have been garaged there in the Thirties, as their owners made the first overnight stop from London, en route for the Highland hotel where they would spend a summer stalking stags and fishing for salmon. As the miles to Penrith slid by, I spotted those familiar reminders of the past – the decaying facades of long-closed garages and former coaching inns in the villages bisected by the road, then the wartime pillbox sitting right up at the top of the Eden watershed and the long-abandoned railway lines. The UK might lack a Route 66, but its English near-namesake still has infinitely more character than just about every road built since the Sixties. How I loathe their geometric conformity, those oh so carefully radiused turns and their risk-assessed sightlines designed to ensure that not even a Le Mans car in full flight could appear unexpectedly.

The Lotus Seven Club magazine is called *Low Flying*, and it is the perfect title, as nothing better describes the feeling of sitting behind that tiny windscreen, arms and legs at Jim Clark reach, and hearing that indomitable growl from the exhaust as the wind buffets your ears, each little bump and ripple feeling like the little patches of turbulence you'd encounter in a low flying Sopwith Camel. As pilot you're always scanning the instruments to check levels and temperatures, you're compulsively checking the cloudscape up ahead for rain, and you're ever vigilant in the search for the Fokkers who can spoil your day. And I've encountered more than a few of those on the A66 before now, believe it.

Range anxiety isn't confined to Nissan Leaf pilots, as few Sevens are happy to go further than 150 miles (240km) before inducing obsessive-compulsive petrol station location in their drivers. Having refilled near Lockerbie – like Dunblane and Hungerford a place now forever defined by just one event – I drove west to Hightae to meet my distant relative, Jimmy Somervail, a man who had absolutely nothing to do with Eighties popsters, Bronski Beat. It's the British Racing Drivers Club badge on the tired Polo's grille that gives the first hint of what the owner of the pebble-dashed bungalow in the inconsequential village used to be, because Jimmy was one of the Border Reivers, the 1950s Scottish race team that was famous for launching Jim Clark's career. Jimmy Somervail was a racing driver entirely devoid of ego, modest to a fault in telling me about his days of racing against Stirling Moss, Duncan Hamilton, and Mike Hawthorn. Oh, and Juan Manuel Fangio too. Jimmy's cars were the sort of old racing cars that could be picked up for peanuts in the Fifties; he bought Remus, the ex-Prince Bira ERA R4B, for £700, and his Cooper Bristol Formula 2 car hadn't cost him much more. On the wall is a picture of Jimmy at Silverstone and his D Type is leading Stirling Moss' Aston Martin DBR1. "Your finest hour Jimmy?" I venture. "Och no, I was being lapped, Stirling was just so damned fast" he twinkled before adding "But I was careful – and that's why I am here talking to you today." It's easy to dismiss the Fifties as an era of grey austerity and conformity, with society holding its breath before the technicolor explosion of the Sixties, but when I think of that yellow D Type howling around Silverstone on a summer day I understand that, for some anyway, the lights had already come back on during the previous decade. As I finish my coffee, Jimmy tells me about the week he once spent entertaining F1 journalist, and Colin Chapman confidante, Jabby Crombac in the Sixties; Crombac was staying in Britain between races on successive weekends and, at Chapman's suggestion, he had come up to Scotland, where Jimmy had done his bit for the auld alliance by educating Crombac in the ways of mountains, lochs, and whisky.

Jimmy waved goodbye until I was out of sight, and I settled again into the simple joy of a fast car on an empty road. It had rained earlier, and as the sun burned off the moisture, I could smell wet earth, wood smoke and, drifting up from the roadside woodland, the pungent reek of wild garlic. It's a smell I love as it's the essence of spring, and with the hot sun on my back I headed north on forgotten B roads, tracking the busy A74 a few miles to my East. There was no traffic other than the odd crew-cabbed pick up and, my mind now in neutral, I realised how I had already forgotten to remember to gnaw over the problems I had left at home. It looked like K5 FUN had come fitted with the optional exorcism and counselling pack too.

Glasgow ... and somehow, I ended up driving through the centre and was therefore the target of more attention than I had wanted, and if the waves and smiles from pedestrians were lovely, the traffic light grand prix antics of Novas and Civics were less so. But there was a perfect vignette in Clydebank, where mum and son wait at an empty bus stop; mum is in a hijab, but lad is in trainers and leisurewear. He's maybe eight or nine and he looks at the Seven as if it's a spaceship; we make eye contact and he smiles shyly. I wave back and mum's eyes sparkle as I set off with more exuberance than was really needed – even us intros can get a little extro at times like this. Within half an hour the serious part of the journey proper had started as I jinked and dived along the A82 to Crianlarich, Loch Lomond sparkling in the sun, the occasional Mondeo and Dutch motor home disposed of with a third gear sprint. There's a real serenity about long journeys in the Highlands and it was so easy for me to relax into a state of near euphoria as I tracked north, watching the weather patterns ahead, cloud massing over the high peaks, my eyes catching the peripheral glints of blue and silver from the steams tumbling off the hill. Beyond the Bridge of Orchy there's a dead red deer straddling the verge, hooded crows already on the case, and a mile or two later I notice the West Highland Line hanging on to the side of the mountain as it turns towards Rannoch Moor.

Bikes became an issue, and you probably know the moves in this game; the bellowing Ducatis and howling Suzukis overtake in a flare of revs on the shortest of straights, and when ridden in convoy you learn to expect just how fine the last rider will cut it, such is the ignominy of running last and the risk of being left behind. And yet, as soon as the road gets twisty again, you regain the quarter-mile you've just lost, and you fume and mutter as you track through the corners 20mph slower than you really want to. But Harley Davidsons never, ever present a problem: their owners might exploit that Hells Angel wannabe menace, but their pace is usually glacial, both on and off their bikes. And the aggressive bluster of a Harley's Vee Twin exhaust, absurdly incongruous for something usually so pedestrian, sounds so exuberant on the long uphill ascents that I can't help but laugh.

Halfway across Rannoch, after those straights that are long enough to stretch out of sight into the blue hazed distance, there's a hard left, and then the sharp cornered, steep ascent of Black Mount. It's almost a given that drivers and riders of anything fast and noisy will play to the crowd here, as there's always a bevy of parked tourists at the top of the hill. Mums and grans may show some pursed lip disapproval, but I can see the dads and lads grin and wave as I charge up the hill in a blare of blipped downchanges and racer-quick up changes. I must have got it half right as even the pushbikers are waving and smiling now – maybe they recognise another refugee of the roads?

Glencoe is a few miles later and, is it just me, or does it disappoint, in just the same way as the Eiffel Tower or Trafalgar Square can? The trouble is, some images are so hardwired into our brains that exposure to the real thing can only disappoint. When you first see Stonehenge you can't help thinking that not only does it look just like a picture of Stonehenge but it's sort of, well, smaller than it should be. Glencoe doesn't lack scale but, just like visiting a grave, you expect to feel more than you do and then you beat yourself up for being an insensitive clod. I'm half bloody Scot – aren't I supposed to feel all fey and sombre? And I can't, simply because it feels expected of me.

Fort William – what's it good for? Another splash and dash of unleaded but absolutely nothing else; it may lie on the edge of the Great Glen, it may be overlooked by Britain's biggest mountain, and it may attract tourists, shoppers, and yachters from all over the Highlands but somehow, despite the new coffee shops, the bookshop, and the whisky shop, it still cannot help looking like an East German town at the height of the Cold War. All was forgotten within minutes, as it didn't even take me five miles (8km) to get into the rhythm of the road that tracks the Great Glen from Fort William to Inverness. The irony is that the A82 may be a good road, but it's never a great one and yet somehow it became one that evening. It was my Brigadoon moment, because no matter how many times I have driven it since, it has never revealed its magic again. But on this day, it was joyous; there might already have been 300 miles (480km) of road behind me, but now I didn't ever want to stop driving. What little traffic remained was dispatched with a third gear lunge that might peak at a 90mph (145km/h) gallop, but I'd soon back off to a 65mph canter, feeling almost blissfully happy, absorbed totally by the alchemy of road and Seven. 12 years might have passed, but all I need to do is to close my eyes and once again I see that blur of green to my right, the low sun highlighting the mountains across the glen, and once again I look down that blissful long straight above Loch Lochy. Lots of gear-changing before the tighter bends, the blips and barks of the down changes echoing from rock and stone, and the sound of birdsong as I crawled through the villages – why spoil somebody else's evening with my self-indulgence?

I parked above Loch Garry and a tired Golf stopped too, its owner ambling over to pay a compliment on my choice of vintage car. For once, I was just too tired to start my "Actually, it may look old, but …" riff as who needs a pedant on a Sunday night with a view like this one? On the road again, and I peeled off the A87 on to the single-track road that leads from nowhere very much to nowhere at all. I had booked a room at the Tomdoun Hotel, and, if I had to describe the perfect place to stay the night on a highland adventure, I couldn't have improved on the Tomdoun. If it had been in Hoxton, the Trip Advisor reviews would have extolled its boho chic, but at this stage of its life, Tomdoun was on the downward slide into the shabbiness that saw it close within five years. And, of course, I absolutely loved it; the view from its elevation above Glen Garry was sublime and the silence was a balm after ten hours of Low Flying. I ate oysters from Loch Leven, fresh haddock from Scrabster, and I fell into easy conversation with my fellow guests who had also found the hotel on the road to nowhere. IT homeworkers, a corporate finance couple from New York, two twitchers from Tyneside, and the local forester with whom I talked about the meaning of life, as is compulsory after a good cigar and a large Laphroaig. I walked into the dusk, or gloaming if you really insist, felt midges in my hair, and saw the red deer disappearing silently into the pine forest.

Awoken by swallow talk at six, I stumbled over the slumbering Labrador and his whippet friend as I made my way to the bathroom with the creaky plumbing and the peat stained water; there was none of that namby-pamby en suite stuff at the Tomdoun. It was what the Irish called a soft day, with insistent drizzle from the clouds that had rolled in overnight, but the sun burnt through as I started the descent from Loch Cluanie to Invershiel and, as I speared through those long bends that can make the A87 feel like Q3 at Spa, I could see the Five Sisters of Kintail rearing out of the sea loch ahead of me and I felt immortal. The Seven felt invincible, temperatures perfect, oil pressure just so, suspension firm but supple, and the gear shift feeling as though it was operating in warm honey. Life could still be good.

I didn't stop at Eilean Donan, as the world really doesn't need yet another picture of the most photographed castle in Scotland; instead I carried on up to the Kyle of Lochalsh, a town that is only rarely compared with Cannes, but which has a view over the Sound of Sleat to Skye that can lift the heaviest heart. A rambling chat with the guy who fills the Seven, self-service becomes rarer the further north you travel, and then the A890 to Strathcarron. The long ascent looks tough for the top-down MGB trailing the matt beige Peugeot 405 but, once overtaken, both cars diminish to specks within seconds as the Caterham storms up the hill with an urgency that thrills me, as if it's as keen as I am to see what lies beyond the next summit.

The drive to Ullapool was euphoric, fast, and serious across the great emptiness that lies between Loch Carron and Achnasheen, and even quicker, more urgent still, along the A835 to Ullapool. I had run in convoy with a Cooper S on our own mini-adventure, and we'd waved at the orange Murcielago heading south, with attendant TVRs looking like bait fish in the wake of a mako shark. I flashed the lights to say goodbye to the Cooper as he turned off for Ullapool and I headed for the best drive in the world. Don't just take my word for it; Phil Llewellin was one of *Car*'s elite journalists in the Eighties, had been everywhere and had driven everything. And his favourite road? Ullapool to Durness, via Assynt, Kylesku and Strath Dionard. And I am not going to be the one who disagrees.

It's the absences that most define the north-west corner of Scotland. There are no towns, very few villages, no roundabouts, no safety cameras, no yellow lines, hardly any trees and, apart from the BT vans that seem to breed in the Highlands, there's hardly any traffic. The absences mean that what is left assumes much greater importance and so Laxford Bridge and Ledmore Junction might have been signposted from 20 miles (32km) away, but when you arrive there's only a bridge over the River Laxford and only a junction where the A835 and the A838 meet. Nothing else, no café, no petrol, no house, nothing. There's only rock, heather, peat, water, and cubic miles of clean air rolling in from the Atlantic. Further south the mountains may be bigger, often of the 3000 feet (915m) or more that gives them Munro status, but in Wester Ross and Sutherland everything changes as so many of the mountains just rear out of the ground and stand alone. Some of them, such as the porcupine spine of Stac Pollaidh and the fish tail peak of Suilven, look so bizarre that you feel as though you have either wandered on to the film-set for a Tolkien fantasy, or you've been conscripted for a bit part in a Roger Dean album cover design. And there's even an echo of the environment in my Caterham; the car is stripped down to essentials, a machine that is so eloquently defined by its absences. It's an analogue anomaly in a digital whirlwind; my last Skoda (fit for purpose, frill free) was weighed down by acronyms – it had AWD, EBD, HiD, ABS, PAS,

HDC, TCS, CC, and A/C, and if I didn't like changing gear so much then DSG would have given me a full house. Sevens aren't like that, having only two acronyms. The default mode is FFS which is the abbreviation for the words you exclaim when you introduce 200bhp to a twisty road. The other mode is WTF, which engages progressively in proportion to the amount of standing water.

Into Sutherland and the hills were flagged by surrender-white cloud as I entered Scourie, the straggling village that is the last place to buy a coffee before the final stage to the north coast. And just as I was starting to fret about what might be waiting for me back at work there was an unexpected distraction – a middle-aged woman was taking pictures of the Seven, and was utterly absorbed in doing so. "Och, it's my new digital camera. I just had to try it out on your lovely wee car," and spoken in the singsong accent of Sutherland, which owes more to Scandinavia than Glasgow. "You'll have a cup of tea" – as much instruction as invitation. As we drank tea and ate homemade cake in the kitchen we were joined by a lamb, which had wandered through from the living room. "That's Charlie, he's living with us for the moment." And I felt as though I was playing a walk-on part in a Twin Peaks sequel ...

There's a loch called Loch a' Bhadaidh Daraich a couple of miles north of Scourie and you may have seen its picture in the press coverage of the Bentley Continental's launch in 2003. There had been the usual gushing praise, the recycled press release technical stuff, and an avalanche of clichés had been deployed to describe just how much better the reader's life would be if enriched by ownership of the reassuringly expensive Bentley. Just the car for these parts I had thought, a 6-litre W12 powered behemoth with a dipsomaniac's thirst. But the loch with the Gaelic name has darker memories for me as, in August 2000, Jon Stevens, one of my closest friends, had died when his Audi S4 left the road above the loch, speared across the Armco barrier and sunk into the deep, dark water. The passenger escaped but poor Jon didn't. He was somebody who rarely left room for error, whether his own or anybody else's, and that August night he had ran out of luck. It's as simple, as banal, as pointless, and as tragic as that and I have loathed Audis ever since. I stopped, stared across the loch, I thought of the times we had shared over three decades, and I left with my usual muttered "Oh bloody hell, Jon."

The drizzle stopped as I left Rhiconich and the sun started within a mile. My mood changed from introspection to exultation as I passed Arkle and Foinaven (the mountains after which the horses were named) and started the final descent from Strath Dionard to Durness. The Seven popped and banged on the over-run as I freewheeled downhill, gully scarred mountains to the east and the azure sea to the north. I had done it; no, we had done it, this daft little relic of a Fifties sports-racer and me, on our dreamtime adventure.

That night I stayed in my old haunt, the Cape Wrath Hotel, with its third world creature comforts, appalling food, great wine list, extraordinary guests, warm welcome, and a panorama from the dining room like a preview of heaven. That night I sat on the veranda with a Lagavulin and the best cigar I could find, and I wrote down what I could hear. There was wind from the sea, cold and edgy; oystercatchers piping over the Kyle; corncrake scratching out its trademark call and there were cuckoos – the Highlands are full of them in Spring. Nothing else; no people, no cars, no planes, no trains, no radios, no TVs, and no phones. Simply and exquisitely nothing. I loved it, and I slept at peace.

12 years later, and there have probably been 20 Scottish tours, and that isn't counting the day long drives from home to the Borders or Dumfries and Galloway. I don't need an excuse to drive the Seven but I do like to create a reason, a destination at which to arrive. It might be another trip to the Jim Clark Rooms at Duns, possibly the most low-key shrine to a world class sportsman there has ever been (and all the better for it), or it could be the drive north, then west, to David Coulthard's outstanding little museum at Twynholm. But the day trip favourite must be the early morning drive up Dere Street – the Roman road to Edinburgh which follows the A68 as often as not – to the Scottish border at Carter Bar. It's invariably cold and windswept, but its elevation means that the views are often breathtaking, and after a bacon roll from the lay-by café I turn west to enjoy the deserted switchbacks that skirt Kielder Forest. And, once the Solway Firth is in sight, I head for home on the North Pennines, often finding a reason to point the Seven's nose up the long climb from Alston to Middleton in Teesdale. It's often cold and hostile on the B6277, and even on a midsummer day it can feel as though I am driving in my own little February. It's the sort of place the holidaying caravanner will tell me, with a gravitas that suggests access to hitherto unknown meteorological data, that "it's a micro climate, it's got its own weather here." And only my politeness stops me asking whose weather you'd normally expect to encounter when you're 1600 feet up in Teesdale – Downham Market's? Or Basingstoke's perhaps?

But the memorable trips have always been the four or five day excursions to as far north as I can go. Much has changed since 2005, the Tomdoun and Cape Wrath Hotels are no more (one derelict, the other a superb makeover to a private home) but the hotels that have survived are a vast improvement on the austere hellholes that catered for the disappearing customer base of tweedy, braying Englishmen who had made the Highlands their playground for a century. I won't miss either the hotels or their customers, in fact Scotland feels positively enhanced by their absence, as it's become younger, funkier, confident in both its identity and direction. It makes a difference, and in a good way, to a driving holiday because I've found that conversation is now only rarely quick-sanded by the English preoccupations of class and wealth, and on the road there's just far more tolerance and good humour. None of the pursed lip, they shall not pass, light flashing disapproval that can punctuate even the most pedestrian of overtakes at home, instead there's often a wave and a smile at somebody enjoying themselves.

In recent years the R400 has traversed the notorious Bealach Na Ba in cloud and sun, dodged the late Spring snow showers over the Lecht, made the statutory lap of the 'Scotsburgring' (the road from Ballachulish that leads to Kinlochleven), been dwarfed by the red sandstone mountains of Torridon, and tracked the wild west coast from Gairloch to Ullapool. But two memories endure more than any other. The first was inspired by the near delirious 20-mile (32km) drive I'd made from Loch Assynt up to my hotel at Badcall

Bay; I had driven non-stop for eight hours, my arms ached from endless hairpins and gear changes, my ears rang from the assault of wind and exhaust blare, and the hailstorms had drifted in from the sea as I passed Ardvreck Castle, looking as sinister as ever on the banks of Assynt. The weirdly ramped mountain called Quinag drifted in and out of vision as the hail assaulted the windscreen, bounced off the wings and bonnet and ricocheted around the cockpit. And of course I didn't bloody stop, not even to erect the hood as ... I don't know, somehow I just wanted to overdose on being alive, and on using every sense and synapse to savour the synergy of weather, mountains, road and car that made me near delirious.

The second memory? Driving the magical route from Durness to Tongue on a hot-sunned, blue-skied day in early June. Traffic had been surprisingly busy the previous day, when I'd driven up from Strathcarron, and whilst the convoys first of Elises and then of Dutch Morgans had come close to being irritations on the single track, the howling Ferrari 250 SWB I'd seen was inspirational, even if my wave had been unacknowledged. Miserable bastard. But today was traffic-free as I tracked that magical road leading around Loch Eriboll. I'd seen the US Navy moored up here on a gunnery exercise in the Nineties but today not even a dolphin or seal, let alone the rumoured killer whales, was to be seen. It didn't matter, it was enough to thread the R400 from apex to apex and to hear the down changes echoing off the hard rock. Peat smoke on the wind, and I slowed to a third gear amble as I passed Danish ceramicist, Lotte Glob's, surreal rock garden, which lies between road and sea loch. She's an extraordinary woman, part performance artist and part potter, and she looks for all the world like a sunburned Patti Smith. She fires her work from local rocks, exhibits some pieces, sells others and even takes some pieces up into the high corries, where those weirdly humanoid sculptures are left for all eternity. It would make no sense at all in Haslemere, but it does make huge sense here, right on the edge of a continent. I passed Alan Clark MP's former estate, just the 18,000 acres (7300ha) for the man who admitted to being "economical with the actualité," but whose love of this wilderness, not to mention his XK120 Jaguar, his 2CV and Porsche 356 still endeared him to me as a kindred spirit. I stopped on the high ground to savour the view over the tiny Ard Neackie peninsula before heading east; I soaked up the sun and watched two ravens checking me out from the escarpment above me. I mused about whether even Sicily's Targa Florio could have looked quite as extraordinary as this, and then I wondered just what would a Ferrari 250P or 312P have sounded like as it blipped and howled its way up from Strath Beag, at the head of the loch. And would Phil Hill's Chaparral 2F have even fitted a road as narrow as this one? A car stopped, a new 5-series BMW with a Pringle clad driver and an ageing relative in the passenger seat. Pringle guy only wanted to check that I was okay, that I wasn't broken down or in distress, as this is what you do in a place as wild and lonely as this one. I smiled, thanked him, and said I was just drinking in that stunning view. He smiled back, appraised the Seven with a knowing eye, winked and said, "Bloody marvellous car that Seven, bet there's nothing better on roads like this."

And of course he was right. So forgive me if this chapter is more about the road than the car, more focussed on the journey than the destination but, for me, the vividness of the experience could only have been conjured through the prism of a Seven. Because, on this trip, and on so many others, the tiny little car designed half a century ago has been just the best of good companions. We sought, and found, our refuge of the roads.

Note – you might want to check out the postscript 'The Scottish Playlist,' where not only is there some serious stuff on the NC500 initiative, but also some suggestions on the mood music to enhance your tour of the Far North – think of it as an analogue Spotify, but don't bother reading it if you drive a car as noisy as a Seven.

9
LA MUCCA CHI RIDE

So, if I dream I have you, I have you
For all our joys are but fantastical

John Donne, Elegies

If Lotuses appeal to head as much as heart, then Ferrari can only be about heart. I fell for Lotus because of its iconoclasm, its delight in arriving at alternative solutions that were smarter, lighter, and better than the Brit fit-for-purpose conformity of the traditional British sports car marques. Whether Aston Martin or Jaguar, AC or Allard, the recipe for success was so often depressingly similar, with a big displacement, heavy but powerful six or eight-cylinder engine dropped into a chassis whose adequacy was rarely enhanced by much spark of originality, and whose attempts at aerodynamic fluency were rarely more than perfunctory. So what about that paragon of slipperiness, the D-Type? It's a shock to remember that its drag coefficient was just under 0.5. And a Lotus 15? A tad over 0.3 ...

I might also have fallen for Lotus because it elevated the status of smartarse to corporate mission statement, but my affair with Ferrari's prancing horse is entirely down to misty-eyed romanticism about the firm that, for decades, has behaved like a diva in an opera whose libretto cast most of its opposition as brigands and cheats. But things have changed at Maranello, hence the title of this piece, which I'll talk about later, but only after a short discourse on French cheese. Stick with me, it will make sense, but you'll have to wait a little longer to see why ...

I last made what can only be called the pilgrimage to Maranello in late 2007 and I wrote the notes that became this chapter a couple of days later in a hotel room in Siena overlooking one of the dark, narrow streets leading to the Piazza del Campo. It seemed the right time and the right place to reflect on just what part that bloody prancing horse had played in my life. Because it's impossible to be equivocal about Ferrari, even internet forum users don't post 'just my humble opinion' about Ferrari. So there'll be no craven nailing of any colours to the fence in this chapter, especially when the colours are black and yellow surmounted by the Italian flag.

Saints or sinners, the prancing horse has always crystallised opinion, even if our views have changed over the years. In my case they started to change during the Schumacher/Todt/Brawn hegemony, and then continued to do so as each successive road-going Ferrari seemed to be ever more targeted at the Premier League footballer and rich-brat-from-Saudi market. That's the price you have to pay for the transformation from legend to brand, or even to bloody icon, which is comfortably the most overused word of the millennium. And it just doesn't seem right that the preferred habitat of so many Ferraris isn't the open road or the European grand tour, but the tight little circuit of Kensington, the Targa Harrods perhaps? But I'd still give a kidney, and possibly even one of my own, for an F458 or F488, and I'd probably sacrifice a member of my family for a V12 classic such as a 365 GTC – which I'd take in blu chiaro of course. Rosso Corse may be fine on the racier cars, but the big GTs, just like every road-going Maserati, only ever really look right in blue, grey, or silver. On track, Ferraris still captivate like no other machinery; in recent years at Silverstone I have been in near ecstasy as I listened to the howl of a 512M ,and close to tears at the titanic noise that the ex-Phil Hill 246 F1 car made. And the day I stop feeling like that is the day I've lost my soul.

I was in the sixth form when I saw my first Ferrari, a tired old 330 GT, gathering dust in a Wakefield car park and flanked by an Austin 1800 and an HA Viva. It should have been the rose between two thorns, and a 330 GTC would have been, but the 330 GT was the squinty faced runt of the litter, that looked as though it had been knocked up by Pininfarina on the back of a fag packet during his espresso break. The passage of time, and its attendant nostalgia can bestow some glamour on old sports cars, but, even 50 years later, the 330 GT looks a dog in the classified ads, despite the 100-point restoration, the meaty provenance and the Concours d'Elegance plaudits.

My first Ferrari looked nothing like as stylish as the metallic blue Aston Martin DB6 I had seen the day before, snarling its way down Carlton Street in Castleford and turning nearly every head in the process, but the Ferrari had an indefinable allure that the sober Aston lacked, because it engaged me exactly the same way as the blues had when I first heard John Lee Hooker. No explanation was needed, no deconstruction nor nerdy analysis required, but instead there was an instant, total comprehension, and it felt as though that the blues had been something I had always just known, almost a part of my DNA. And so it was with the 330 GT; its lines might have been flawed, but they spoke of shimmering roads in Tuscany snaking through hilltop villages and scrolling around tight apexed bends. And all this would have been sound-tracked by a gratuitous howl from those four so-sexy exhausts. Long months would pass before I saw another Ferrari, but the drought was truly over when I saw a 275 GTB parked on a Leeds side street, and if ever a car could leer then this one did. I mentioned the gratuitous evil of an F4 Phantom in chapter one, and the 275 GTB echoed the "you lookin' at me?" swagger of the F4, as it was a car you really wouldn't want your teenage daughter to ever meet. Imperious in dull silver, Argento, it felt like the beat that my heart had skipped. But curiously I didn't feel envy, not the aching covetousness I felt when I saw an Elan or a Marcos Coupé, but instead I felt something almost spiritual, as though merely being in its presence was enough. That winter I read a road test of a 275 GTB/4 in *Car and Driver* and the copy was on the incoherent side of lyrical, riffing gloriously on the fact that, apparently, the bodywork was asymmetrical. An accident of construction rather than design I suspected and, just possibly, Lambrusco may have had something to do with it. If it was good enough for the race team mechanics, and it used to be even in the Lauda days, then surely an artisan deserved a drink on a Friday afternoon under a hot Modenese sun? Anyway, the GTB kicked out its 300bhp, revved to a stratospheric 8000rpm, pulled 160mph (255km/h) in fifth, and its shape –from snarly nose and shark gilled flanks, to its abrupt Kamm tail – made me fall in love. Jesus, I even knew where the '275' came from, it was the capacity of each of those tiny cylinders, and if I'd known where the silver one lived I would have stalked it, staked out in the shadows with my adolescent fantasies. Now you mention it, no, I didn't have a girlfriend at the time.

I had left school, just, when I saw my first Grand Prix Ferrari; a screaming, yowling 312B2, a red smear of noise and speed snaking around Becketts at Silverstone. It was driven by the Swiss buccaneer christened Gianclaudio Giuseppe Regazzoni, but who was universally called Clay, even by Silverstone's then rather stuffy commentary team. The race programme (for the British Woolmark Grand Prix 1971) puzzled me though, because if Gold Leaf Team Lotus and Yardley BRM were familiar enough (just check out the fag packet and aerosol liveries) who the hell was SEFAC Ferrari? Proudly, but quite inaccurately, I announced to my friends that the acronym obviously stood for Scuderia Enzo Ferrari Auto Corse and how come they hadn't worked that out for themselves? It was a decade before the rather more mundane truth emerged; SEFAC actually stood for Societa Esercizio Fabbriche Automobili e Corse and if its meaning is unglamorous, roll the syllables over your tongue and it still sounds a lot sexier than Team Surtees or Elf Team Tyrrell. And okay, Ferrari means Smith and Maranello is the town that feels like a Towcester or a Thame relocated a long way south to a hot plague plain tiled with ceramic factories but, just like John Lee Hooker, Ferrari's *Boogie* was *Chillen* that long-ago day at Silverstone. Starting from pole they lost but gloriously, tragically, as they so often did back then. Because, of course, Ferrari was flawed, massively and heroically, and that's why I could not but love them. There was none of the added lightness of a Lotus 72, no perfectly fit-for-purpose Tyrrell 003, nor the sci-fi cool of Ronnie Peterson's *Flash Gordon* inspired March 711 but the Scuderia's style and passione were enough to sate my hunger. Red flanks, white roll bar fairing, yellow shields on the flanks, and the signature wailing, feral scream of a flat-twelve, so much more urgent than a DFV's chainsaw buzz, the 312B2 felt like all that I needed and everything I loved.

But Ferrari lied when it suited their Machiavellian purposes, as, quite shamelessly, they would claim that a metalworkers' strike would prevent them from racing in the next Grand Prix but, translated from the Modenese, all this really meant was "we've fallen out with our driver. Again." Or "the car's even crappier than Ingegnere Forghieri told us it would be. And Il Commendatore isn't happy." It was a tragi-comedy that ran for decades before the team finally understood that V or flat-twelve muscle or V6 turbo power would never quite compensate for a mediocre chassis designed only to transport the precious motore around the circuit. They stayed in denial, with only occasional spikes of form in the Seventies (thanks to Lauda's searing commitment) and the Eighties (thanks to Gilles Villeneuve's heroics), until the Michael Schumacher panzer blitzkrieged the rest. Again and again, until it felt like some parody of a buy one, get one free deal, which devalued the triumphs almost as much as it humiliated the opposition. The stylish losers had been elbowed aside by the unsmiling victors who had forgotten all that Corinthian stuff about being gracious in victory. And we all had thought McLaren were the grey ones, until, in 2007, we saw Ron Dennis holding back tears, if only just, as he was screwed first by Alonso's treachery and then by Oswald Mosley's DNA – allegedly. We learned a lot about pride, dignity, and integrity in that year, and we learned something about ourselves too, as, back then, many of us felt moved by Lewis Hamilton, as if he were truly the chosen one. It was a season that felt like a Shakespearean tragedy, and after Ron Dennis was ousted from his own team in 2016 I realised that the 2007 season was Act 1 Scene 1. A tragedy constitutes the fall of a great man because of a fatal flaw in his character – so was it pride, inflexibility, or both?

But back to those years of Ickx, Merzario, Giunti, and the rest; that time before Grand Prix racing became F1; the time when I felt as though I belonged to a secret sect; the one where only my best friend could really understand how I grieved over the deaths of Rindt and Revson, Pryce and Pace. And grieving was something I had to learn quickly because in the early Seventies I had to do it so often. But I also adored the exclusivity of motorsport, and if that was just the same elitism as the Brooklands mantra of 'The right crowd and no crowding,' your problem with that is what, exactly? But the blanket TV coverage of the 21st Century has made everyone an expert on F1 (despite most of its audience never having even been near a race circuit, ever) and so I feel like the guy who first heard Richard Hell in 1973 and who in '77 was wondering just how contemptuously he could tell the latecomers that he was there first, surfing this one before it even became a New Wave. Just wish that guy had been me …

In Maranello, I stand on my balcony in the Planet Hotel and I watch and I wait for Ferraris to leave the factory gates, a short 30 metres away. It's drizzling and dull and, Christ, I'm in my 50s and shouldn't I have grown up by now, moved on to more adult stuff than watching sports cars that I could never even dream of owning? But then I hear it, long seconds before I see it, a ripsaw rasp echoing off the grey line of parked Ypsilons and Puntos; it's a 430 Scuderia, and it looks like a falcon scything through a flock of sparrows. Deep down I know that, actually, the celebrated noise is no huge deal, and that it's only impressive because of its volume, which is shockingly loud in a climate of EU compliance and drive-by humility. Some journalists may love it as they play their wannabe Jeremy Clarkson tunes in the tunnels on the Autostrada but me, I prefer a little more melody from my prancing horses. Listen to a 250 GTO, a 512 M, or a 312 T and feel the hairs on your arm stand up in response to that glorious whooping bellow. It's the passione thing again, the listener's visceral reaction to that otherworldly howl.

I stepped inside for a Prosecco (when in Maranello and all that) and what the fuck is that? I catch a glimpse, just, of the sharp-edged rear wing of an F40 that was accelerating impossibly, gloriously hard down the Via Abetone, sounding like a revolution until the driver lifted off in an anarchy of backfires and bangs as the unburnt Agip fuel erupted in the exhausts. 20 years on and The Old Man's swansong can still shadow its younger siblings. And how understated, how cool to call it simply and emphatically the F40, but how crass it seemed to call the latest bedroom wall fantasy an Enzo. (I wrote this in 2007, remember, and even Enzo now sounds preferable to the definitive article idiocy of the Ferrari LaFerrari. What the hell will they call the next one? Maybe they should take inspiration from their customer base, so may I offer the Ferrari Eurotrash GTO as a suggested new model?).

We dined at the Cavallino restaurant that night, and as usual it was full of eye-flashing locals celebrating something, possibly just the fact that it was a wet Monday night in Maranello, because it seems to me that if you're born Italian you are duty-bound to celebrate life as if you just had the one to live. So why is it only the Italians who seem to remember this, why do so many of the rest of us live the cliché and squander life like the rehearsal it isn't? The Italians congregate outside the restaurant for a quick-dragged Marlboro, all chat, and laughter, and gestured asides to their mates; but back inside, as the Americans' steaks arrive, they order four more to go, because it must be hard to make it through the night on just the one Bistecca Fiorentina. The waiter's shock is alleviated by a tip the size of Texas and it becomes obvious why, with red meat raptors like these guys, the USA rules the world. I note the loudest one's windcheater, bright yellow and logo'd 'Preston Henn,' and that isn't a name you're often likely to encounter in Easingwold or Masham. A distant bell rang; was Preston Henn perhaps a big buck corporate sponsor or even a racer's name? The American posse spoke at a volume that would have raised eyebrows in the sort of restaurants we normally frequent and God only knows what they would have made of the middle aged British couple on the next table, effetely picking their way through their polenta con tartufi neri. Hell, Preston's guys probably reckoned we were some sort of 'pantywaist goddamn democrats' … Joanne's subsequent googling revealed that, apart from being no stranger to brushes with the law, my fellow diner was in fact a GTP warrior, had won the Daytona 24 Hours, had finished second at Le Mans in 80-something, owned a 275 GTB Competizione, and now, just for fun, to pass the time, competed in the Ferrari FXX series. Thus dispelling my belief that one-make series for Italian supercars were the sole province of middle-aged wankers trying to impress their implausibly young girlfriends.

Before we left for Siena in our 1.2 Fiat Panda, on not-quite-qualifying compound 155/80s, we visited the Ferrari Galleria, but there was only one thing in the endless shelves of memorabilia that I truly wanted to own. It wasn't the Ferrari teddy bear and nor was it the monogrammed man-bag; not the Fiorano baseball cap nor even the Cavallino Rampante mouse-mat, but I did so want the 3.5-litre V12 from the Mansell and Prost era. It would have complemented my existing Ferrari collection just beautifully; you need to know that I already own not only a '59 Testa Rossa, but also a 250 GTO, 288 GTO and an F40 – all tipo

Bburago 1/12 scale, natch. Reality check needed though, the Panda's boot was tiny and the excess baggage charge would have been near life threatening. But what a something-to-declare for the customs guys a Ferrari V12 would have been, what a change from having to search the moister cavities of people to whom they had not even been properly introduced.

As we left for Tuscany we drove by the legendary factory gates and saw the gawpers and the gapers, their cameras and phones cocked and autofocussed, ready to pixelate the 612 shoving its really-not-very-beautiful-at-all snout into the traffic. Me, I'm pretending not to be a mere tourist, but a traveller, too knowledgeable to have joined the mob, the slackjawed Top Gear Tifosi who wouldn't know a Dino from a Daytona, the very same gene pool who rated the Testa Rossa (Tipo Miami Vice, not the 50's 250 TR) the most attractive Ferrari, ever. Jesus. Maybe that's why this lot didn't appear even to notice the 250 Lusso in steely light blue, sliding by on a creamy wave of V12 harmonics and looking like a Sophia Loren in a room full of Britneys.

And now I am in Siena, after a terminal understeer blast over the Passo della Raticosa, and I sit and I watch the sunset fade slowly on the perfect city. I'm happy, and how could I not be in Tuscany's jewel, but I know that I don't need to return to Maranello for a long time. In what feels like almost a tragedy, I am not entirely sure I want to ever own a Ferrari, even if the lottery obliges. And yes, I have driven one, years ago now, a friend's 328 GTB and it was ... well, it was just fine. Sorry to damn with faint praise, but it felt like meeting Jeremy Paxman and discovering that, actually, he was just like that Jeremy Paxman off the telly; the Ferrari had read the script and acted just as it should have done. Here was the trademark sticky click-clack gated gear shift, there was the metallic thrash from the engine room, sounding gratuitously loud. I loved the little prancing horse on the Momo wheel and the only steering that has felt better is on my Seven. But was it really that good, or did sense of occasion dilute my critical faculties?

Back in 2007 I didn't want the charmless and monosyllabic Kimi Raïkkonen to win the championship because the last Ferrari driver I really adored (and why should you be surprised after this cri de coeur?) was Jean Alesi. Only one lucky Grand Prix victory to his name, perhaps, but a heroic driver whom I will always remember for his display of brio at a cold and wet British Grand Prix practice. The rest of the drivers might have been cowering in the warmth of the pit garages, ignoring the public who had paid their wages, but not Jean Alesi. He had a crowd to please, a grandstand to galvanise, and he simply threw his Ferrari around Silverstone in a bouncing-off-the-rev-limiter blur of opposite lock and wheelspin. You couldn't see the man behind the helmet, but no-one doubted that the little guy from Avignon was seizing the moment, and who with a soul wouldn't have done the same? What Alesi did epitomised the spirit of Ferrari to me; style over substance, hope against expectation, and glory and theatre over bedrock pragmatism. This is what Ferrari first meant to me but now? Now is the time I need to talk about cheese ...

The title of this chapter means 'the laughing cow' in Italian, and you can read why I think it might usefully supersede the prancing horse shortly. But first I need to provide more insight into the laughing cow motif, and the starting point is your local supermarket. Skip this if cheese nomenclature isn't your thing, but if I've aroused your curiosity with my dairy diversion then here's what you do. Proceed to the processed cheese aisle next time you're in Tesco's where, like as not, just next to the Dairylea cheese triangles you will find their slightly racier French counterparts, La Vache Qui Rit, whose branding has a quite extraordinary provenance that dates from World War One. The name was created by the French and was the bovine livery applied to French Army food supply trucks. In a jibe aimed at the Germans, as you'd sort of expect in 1917, the words 'La Vache Qui Rit' were actually a corruption of the German Walküre, the statuesque and magnificent women from Wagner's *Ring Cycle* to whom many cinema goers were introduced by the use of *Ride of the Valkyries* in Francis Ford Coppola's *Apocalypse Now*, as in "I love the smell of napalm in the morning." Still with me? The illustration of a Valkyrie as a fat cow instead of a Junoesque mädchen was an effective piece of propaganda that, postwar, hadn't been forgotten by the French cheesemaker Leon Bel, who chose to apply it to his industrially processed cheese, and in doing so he perpetuated the anti-German jibe, even if its origin is now forgotten by many. If not by me, because when Joanne mentioned it, as part of her ongoing project to elevate me from uncultured clod status, it struck me that there was perhaps a perfect metaphor for Ferrari here as well. And this is why.

Ferrari produced its first car in 1947 (and how weird does it feel to remember that that was only two years before TVR did the same?) and, until Enzo Ferrari's death in 1988, its only real priority was racing, and racing alone. The road cars were just to offset the cost of the racers. Victory could, and did, come at any price for man and machine, and not for nothing was Ferrari's 1963 autobiography entitled *My Terrible Joys,* or *Le Mie Gioie Terribile* in its original Italian. Ferrari's sports prototypes might have wilted under the Ford sledgehammer at Le Mans 1966, but its frequent and dramatic lapses in form were so often compensated by renewed success, which would last a season or two before the prancing horse stumbled and fell yet again. Henry Ford might have "whupped Enzo's ass" at Le Mans with his GT 40 onslaught, but within five or six years Ferrari was yet again annihilating all-comers with the sublime 312P, which was as close as a sports racing car has ever come to being a two-seater Grand Prix car. But at the same time, after success in Formula 1 with Ickx, Andretti, and Regazzoni between 1970 and 1972, the '73 Ferrari F1 car was an utter dog, and had the further ignominy of having a chassis built not in Maranello or Modena, but in soulless Northampton instead. But, almost inevitably after such a nadir, it fought back under Niki Lauda's inspiration, when logic started to feature as much as emotion and the 312 T became the archetypal mid-Seventies Formula 1 car.

Road cars might have been just a necessary evil until the Eighties, but the present-day value and charisma of cars from earlier decades is almost in inverse proportion to the interest the firm's founder took in them. The 250 GTO was an expedient to win races, fashioned into shape more than it was styled, and for many years it was just another old and near irrelevant racing car. I remember parking next to Nick Mason's car, helpfully number-plated '250 GTO,' in the public car park at Silverstone in 1981. It attracted the same level of attention as an Aston Martin of similar vintage – there was polite recognition but not the adulation it would receive now – and apparently its owner had paid £35,000 for it in 1977. Not as cheap as you might think: that amount would have bought a fleet of five Scimitar GTEs or (shudder) ten Capri 1600XLs, but the GTO is now worth £30 million, maybe even more in a hot bidding war. How ironic it now seems that, as often as not, last season's Ferrari race cars used to be cut up and abandoned; most notoriously in the case of the legendary 'sharknose' 156 with which Phil Hill had won the world championship in 1961. There's a lovely picture in Rainer Schlegelmilch's *Sports Car Racing 1962-1973* of a 250 GTO in the mid-Sixties. New, it would have cost less than $20,000 but, in the state it was pictured at Nürburgring, I don't doubt it was worth much less. To say the car was well patinated would be too kind, as the thing looked knackered, dirty, dented, and battered; and it displayed an outsized prancing horse on its flanks that looked as though it had been painted by a nine-year-old. But, 50 years later, the only sky that old war horse is likely to see is above the pampered lawns at Pebble Beach or Villa Del Este, where its white-overalled minders will have pushed it out from secure overnight accommodation so it could be judged for originality and provenance, as if the thing had been assembled by master jewellers instead of Modenese artisans with a deadline to meet. Its owner will, likely as not, be a dotcom billionaire who wouldn't even have heard of a 250 GTO until he could think about buying one, and the main purpose of the purchase would have been to humiliate his rival masters of the virtual universe as they bid against him at the Gooding & Co auction. Reporters from the classic car press would get an attack of the clichés at the GTO's appearance, and wouldn't miss any opportunity to insert the words "holy grail" into their copy, and the retired racing driver judges might even try to pretend that this judging lark was the deadly serious business that classic car collectors seem to think that it should be. But what I really want to know is this. Just what would the GTO think? What if cars could talk? If that GTO has a soul – and anything that makes such a heavenly noise must surely deserve one – then doesn't it pine for its glory days when it howled down the long straights at Reims-Gueux under a Champagne sun?

It didn't take Ferrari too long after Enzo's death to start to plunder its heritage in earnest; the firm, which had once existed only to race, morphed into a big time merchandise outfit with a sideline in road cars, often as shouty and crass as some of its clients, and a subsidiary that might be a starring act in the Grand Prix circus, but whose objective may as well be to shift yet more merchandise. And Ferrari World in Abu Dhabi and Barcelona? The four million Google hits for Ferrari memorabilia? Its logo may once have been the Prancing Horse bequeathed by a WW1 fighter ace's family to Enzo Ferrari, but now? Now it might as well be a big, fat laughing cow, the cash cow being milked for every penny it can give, La Mucca Chi Ride.

But so what, do you really have to judge an artist by evaluating the entire career arc, why shouldn't you judge him only by his best work, or her best work? The title of this book is taken from a Joni Mitchell song on her 1976 masterpiece, *Hejira*, the album that crowned an extraordinary period of creativity, starting with *Ladies of the Canyon* in 1970 and, arguably, ending with *Don Juan's Reckless Daughter* in 1977. The early stuff was good, if never great and the many albums that followed were fine, but barely even good, at least when compared with her peak. Does that devalue her legacy? Of course it doesn't, and so it is with Ferrari, because in my world the last truly great Grand Prix car was the 641 in 1990, the last gorgeous sports racer the 512 M of 1971 (and I'll take the Sunoco Penske car please), and the last road car I truly coveted was the compact little F355 that replaced the dog's dinner F348 in 1994. By most objective standards the later cars, on both road or track, have been immeasurably superior and have often crushed all opposition, but it seems to me that they only did so after their creator had traded a lot of the soul that had defined the marque. Decades ago Ferraris were frequently flawed, erratic, shabbily made, and so often were left trailing in the wake of innovators like Cooper and Lotus on track, and Lamborghini and Porsche on the road; so how come so many of the older cars still have a magic that makes this baby boomer weak at the knees? You too? Maybe we should start a club?

Let's do it, and at our first meeting let's also reflect on the fact that it's part of growing older to fantasise about events that took place in our lifetimes, but which we were only ever able to experience vicariously. You need to know that I've got form here, as I'm the man who, when asked if he'd like a free ticket to see The Who, replied that he wasn't that bothered, as Emerson, Lake & Palmer were obviously the future of rock 'n' roll as we knew it. The ticket was to see the band at my university union; they were playing (and you're right with me) Live at Leeds. Anyway, back to cars, and the Geneva and Turin Shows of 1966 and 1967 were more than a big bus ride away, but I'd probably have walked there if I had known then what I know now. Not only was the Alfa Romeo Spider launched, and the achingly lovely Ferrari Dino 206S, but also the most beautiful sports car of them all. I may be in thrall to the Prancing Horse (you've noticed, right?), but for sheer, heart-stopping beauty, not even supermodels like the 250 GTO and the 330 P4 can eclipse the Lamborghini Miura. Just one look, that's all it takes – just drink in those Twiggy-eyelashed headlights, those taut-muscled haunches, and the Venetian blind rear window. Ferrucio Lamborghini's most raging bull was without either precedent or rival. The debutante 350 GTV might have been the best Grand Touring car Ferrari never made, but its sobriety and reserve fooled us all into thinking that Lamborghini's vision might have been much more acute than it was flamboyant. But we were wrong, and if ever a car was disruptive, as tech nerds might say now, the Miura was the one, even if nearly every successor, Countach excepted, has looked like a pumped up parody of its predecessor.

I realise now (and you probably did pages ago) that it isn't just Ferrari, but Italian sports cars, and Italy itself, which have the power to bewitch me. The big ticket V12s from Maranello and Sant'Agata are glorious, but even the more sober Maseratis and the Detroit muscled thugs from Bizzarini, De Tomaso, and Iso can make it feel as though somebody just turned the lights on. And that feeling went much further down the food chain in the Sixties, right down to the bargain basement Fiat 124 Spider and its even cheaper kid brother, the

850 Spider. The latter wouldn't have seen which way an MG Midget went, but the little 850 was the one to whom you'd introduce your parents. And the Alfa Duetto with its boat-tail charm? "Here's to you Mrs Robinson …"

I am going to end this chapter with something of which they rarely speak on my street – in fact any street apart from the ones outside places like Trinity or Magdalen College, Oxford – and that's nominative determinism, with a side order of the near unspellable onomatopoeia. I knew what the latter was, just, but the former sounded way beyond my educational paygrade, until somebody mentioned it on the radio (yes, Radio 4) and then, as I'm inclined to do far too often, I pondered on its possible relevance to my compulsive automotive disorder. Nominative determinism is the phenomenon that predisposes people to do work that corresponds with their name. So a Mr Fromage is the boss of Danone, which is big in dairy, Wordsworth was predestined to be a poet, and Reverend Vickers was never going to be a greengrocer. This phenomenon has a related manifestation which applies only to Italian cars – and if I'm half joking, I'm half serious too. Most car manufacturers' names are prosaic and describe nothing other than their creators; there's no subtext or nuance, no hint of ambiguity. Ford, Austin, Aston Martin, Honda, Toyota, and Renault are names that are just as likely to belong to grocers, sushi chefs or helpdesk gophers as to a car manufacturer, agreed? But Ferrari, Maserati or Lamborghini, just try saying them out loud, remembering to roll your tongue over the rrr's and lingering a little longer over the vowels. And what are you hearing? You've got it – you're hearing a fast driver skipping down three or four gears, revs matched just so on each change as a sports car, with a gratuitous excess of valves and cylinders, squirms into another hairpin in the Apennines above Modena. But what about Alfa Romeo, you say? Come on, it's the sound of the choir of angels that serenades your every journey in an Alfa. So what about Fiat then? Wake up, because everybody knows that Fiat is precisely the sound a blowing fuse makes in a Panda or an Uno …

10
THE GLITTERING PRIZES

No, there is no terrible way to win. There is only winning.
Jean Pierre Sarti, *Grand Prix* (1966)

1971 was a good year for me, as there were some pretty major rites of passage to notch on my belt. Not only did I pass my driving test, I left the loathed Queen Elizabeth Grammar School, immediately burned my old school tie with its idiotic Latin maxim, 'Turpe nescire,' grew my hair, and (may the church bells ring out) left home to start the first year of my law degree at the University of Leeds. Spring blossomed like never before: in March I saw my first Formula 2 race and, only weeks later, I was at my first Formula 1 race at Oulton Park, four years after reading my first Grand Prix report in *Autocar* (Monaco, since you ask, won by Denny Hulme's Repco Brabham in the very last Grand Prix before the Cosworth DFV changed the world as we used to know it). Club race meetings had now become part of the fabric of life, and I rarely missed a meeting at Croft or Rufforth. I loved it all, but I had now acclimatised to the usual recipe of battling Imps and Minis, a Formula Ford duel, a Clubmans' race, and the statutory guest appearance by local hero Tony Dean, as often as not in his Can-Am winning Porsche 908. I still struggle to understand precisely what satisfaction AG Dean got out of beating a Formula Libre field of Mallock U2s and a pensioned off F3 car in his 375bhp Porsche sports racer, but the massacre was always a treat to witness.

In 1970 I had also been exposed to the brave new world of big time, big buck, big bang single-seaters when I had marshalled the Good Friday Formula 5000 race at Oulton Park. Actually, hardly any racing per se went on, as in that stage of the Formula's evolution, the cars were a ragbag selection ranging from budget 'bitsa' specials to serious machinery like the McLaren M10B, and the diversity of the cars was reflected in the motley crew of drivers, who ranged from the 'coming men' like Mike Walker and Peter Gethin, to club racing old stagers like John Myerscough and Fred Saunders. From the marshals' post at Knickerbrook I don't think I saw a single overtaking move apart from backmarkers being lapped. That happened rather a lot, as fifth on the grid Ulf Norinder might have been five seconds slower than pole, but the big Swede still had 20 seconds in hand over the back of the grid. F5000 certainly had its glory days, especially in '73, but the '71 Oulton race was chiefly memorable for the waves of V8 bellowing that the ill-handling field left in its wake as it accelerated up Clay Hill, having lurched and twitched around Knickerbrook.

Mallory Park felt like a different world, and as soon as we arrived I was aware of an intensity that was entirely new to me. The circuit may be located in an unremarkable corner of rural Leicestershire, and comprise little more than a bloody great roundabout with a hairpin tacked onto its north east corner, but on that dull, grey March day, Mallory had transcended its country bumpkin status to become the centre of the motor racing universe. This was serious, and even as we walked down from the Devil's Elbow there was a hint of electricity in the air, as if the whole place had been charged with a sense of crackling urgency. Instead of the usual laconic announcements over the PA, instructing marshals to get into position in 45 minutes, today there was a crisply declaimed instruction for Mr Niki Lauda to report to the clerk of the course, and for the Frank Williams racing team to ensure their truck was moved – immediately. And the air was filled with that mesmerising rap of 1600cc Formula 2 engines being warmed up as team members pushed the Marches, Brabhams, and Chevrons into the pit lane below us. I'd been to Mallory before, and I suggested we moved up to Shaw's Hairpin as I knew we would have the closest view of the cars as they aimed straight for us out of the Esses. We heard the rapid fire up changes as the cars left the pit lane, and 30 seconds later they were jinking and squirming into the braking area in front of us. It was mesmerising, even in the early laps of the warm up. Formula 5000 cars might have made the ground shake but watching them tackle a tight corner was like watching elephants trying to roller skate – long on spectacle, but short on speed. The F2 cars were not only astonishingly agile, but were driven by the sort of premier league drivers I had only read about in *Autosport*. I must have osmosed the signature look of different drivers from the blurry black and white pictures in the race reports, as I recognised Jo Siffert in his trademark Swiss Cross helmet driving his ugly little Chevron B18; Henri Pescarolo too, his plain green helmet bobbing up and down in his March 712M. But nearly every eye was drawn to the yellow March that was so ferociously quick out of the Esses, braked impossibly late into Shaws, and was more exuberantly sideways through the hairpin itself than anyone else. One glance at the cocked to one side, blue and yellow helmet was all that was needed to instantly understand why Ronnie Peterson was a future Grand Prix star, as he seemed to be operating on an entirely different level to anyone else. And if a handful of other drivers shared his ability, none could match his commitment on that grey March day.

I was nervous about what to expect from my first Formula 1 race, as I found it difficult to imagine how it could possibly eclipse the sensory overload the big field of jousting F2 cars had created on Mallory's tight little 1.3 miles (2km). At least, now I could legally drive Dad's Triumph Vitesse, my friend Paddy and I were going to arrive at Oulton in time for the marshals' briefing. On our F5000 adventure the previous year we'd had no alternative than to hitchhike from Huddersfield, pre-M62 – despite our 4am start, we had only arrived in the lunch break, having walked through much of Cheshire until we were rescued by *Daily Express* reporter, Trevor Reynolds, in his Sunbeam Alpine. They were just perfectly matched: Trevor with his Fleet Street insouciance, and the Alpine, a triumph of louche style over lightweight substance.

Paddy and I were instructed to report to the Deer Leap marshals' post and, even in risk assessed 2017, the Deer Leap spectating area is almost within touching distance of cars accelerating out of Lodge. The prescribed standard for marshals' personal protective equipment was rather more relaxed in 1971, and I had prepared for whatever slings and arrows Formula 1 might fire in my direction by wearing the inflammable combination of my oiled cotton Barbour, and my borderline trendy desert boots. Such perfect wear for firefighting duties that I would have become an organic Roman Candle if I ever got near to a burning F1 car … or possibly even a carelessly discarded Rothmans King Size, come to that.

Some things happen so quickly that you somehow don't have time properly to enjoy them as they actually take place, but only in recollection, after your brain has processed the blizzard of stimuli and tried to make sense of them. My first sight of a Grand Prix car was such an experience, and who could have been a more suitable candidate than Jackie Stewart for creating those images that have never left me? I'd heard the perfectly matched downchanges of the first car into Lodge in the untimed warm up, but I couldn't see what it was, nor who was driving it until the exit of Lodge, which preceded the climb up to Deer Leap. Stewart's Tyrrell 001 was bigger, brawnier and much, much louder than any Formula 2 car, but it had an agility that matched anything I'd ever seen. I heard the rasping DFV accelerating the blue Tyrrell towards me and then, flighty on cold tyres, the car snapped sideways but was checked with perfectly applied opposite lock in less than the blink of my eye. The image has never left me, and I replay it often because it encapsulates the essence of all that I love about motor racing. I understood why drivers with the talent of Jackie Stewart weren't just far more skilled than the club racers I had grown used to, but were operating at a level that was simply beyond my comprehension. The man with the tartan striped white helmet was at the peak of his success, having won the championship in 1969, and if he had struggled with the mediocre March 701 in 1970, he went on to dominate the 1971 season in Derek Gardner's home-brewed Tyrrell. He didn't win at Oulton, though, as Pedro Rodriguez was having his last day in the sun when, for once, his BRM P160 matched his talent. Every lap, every single glorious lap, I heard that distinctive metallic howl as the BRM braked into Lodge, and I watched as it was provoked into a big, tyre-smearing slide on the exit, not a cold tyre hiccup like Stewart's, but simple, exuberant high jinks from the man whose passion was to kill him within three months. The race wasn't close, but it was enchanting, and notable for being the only time I saw the Pratt & Whitney-engined Lotus 56B, driven by Reine Wisell. This was the car whose throttle lag was so notoriously bad that power had to be reapplied before a corner even started to ensure that the car accelerated out of the corner itself. It sounded like an idling helicopter, and its disappearance from racing, later that year, went largely unmourned.

Post-race, we saw Pedro Rodriguez in the paddock, just as he was about to leave in his Bentley S1 Continental and, whilst his destination was obviously unknown to us, we just knew it was going to be a lot more glamorous than the "dark satanic mills" of West Riding to which we were returning. Anglophile Pedro wore tweeds, his trademark deerstalker surmounting Orbison-black hair and, whilst he should have looked absurd, we knew he was the coolest man in the paddock. He had charisma to give away, because he was the übermensch who tamed Porsche 917s, even, or perhaps especially, in the wet. There should have been an opera about the man.

I bet you are not too surprised to hear that I still have the Oulton programme. Of course I do, even if it's depressing to see that its format is still replicated in nearly every motorsport programme in 2017. It's badly written, unimaginatively designed, and is as good at giving readers information they don't need, as it is poor on telling readers what they do need to know. Did we really have to be told that finishing third in class in Mod Sports would net the lucky driver £6? But the period advertisements are a hoot – "Enjoy the luxury of COLOUR television on a brand new 3-programme TV! ONLY £1.29 weekly" and "LADIES: your husband or boyfriend is very interested in racing. How about you? Would you like a new car, a holiday in the sun or a new dress? Train to be a beauty consultant ..."

The British Grand Prix took place three months later and a combination of our ignorance of Silverstone's layout and my lack of sleep for the previous 30 hours meant that, not only did we end up on the Becketts banking with a view mainly comprised of the backs of other people's heads, but I dozed off altogether before half-distance. The race followed a familiar script: the Ferraris were fast but fragile and the Tyrrell was the former but not the latter, and I came away feeling slightly short changed. But on the way home I did have just a hint of what the Mulsanne straight must feel like in a slow car; I had seen a fast-moving, squat, yellow shape a long way behind us on the M1, but before I could alert my two passengers the Vitesse was rocked by the passage of a Ford GT40 travelling at the highest speed I have ever seen on a public road. It wasn't less than 150mph (240km/h), and if it was closer to 180 (290km/h) I wouldn't have been surprised, and the Ford disappeared as scarily quickly as it had appeared, leaving behind only the screaming yowl from the exhausts.

I made my first visit to Brands Hatch the following July and not only did I adore the circuit, I also started to learn how to watch Formula 1 cars properly. A group of us had planned to drive down early on the Saturday morning, race day back then, but after reading the *Autosport* preview on Thursday, I felt I just had to see more than the race itself. I took the midnight bus from Wakefield and, arriving two hours before my Wrotham bus left Victoria, I strolled around the London streets to soak up the dawn of the new day. I found myself on Ebury Street at one point and, remembering that this was the location of *Car*'s editorial office, I wandered down the road on the borderline delirious belief that I might encounter LJK Setright who, obviously, would have been enjoying his first Sobranie Black Russian of the day, leaning languidly on a Bristol 409 whilst reciting something from Aeschylus. Sadly, but not unexpectedly, Long John Kickstart turned out not to be at the office, and I decided he was probably enjoying an early morning thrash in a Miura instead.

Brands was a joy and a revelation; instead of Silverstone's dreary combination of vast acreage but zero change in elevation, here was the perfect amphitheatre whose intimate layout meant I felt as much participant as mere spectator. I wandered around the paddock where I eavesdropped on a conversation between John Surtees and Graham Hill, almost fell over the latter's Brabham BT37 and started to understand that I'd been cast in a walk-on part in the greatest show on earth. Being alone had its advantages too, as I simply went where I wanted, when I wanted, without the need for the polite negotiation that the company of even a single friend demands. Every prospect pleased at Brands and, after watching the hold-your-breath drama of Paddock Hill Bend, I walked back up to the high ground above Clearways for final practice (no qualifying back then, let alone Q1, 2 or 3). Tired from so little sleep (again), I listened to the cars as I lay, eyes closed, on the grass banking. Back then nearly every car had a Cosworth DFV and therefore sounded identical, but the two Ferraris, with their howling flat-twelves, were instantly recognisable. Eyes still shut, I followed their progress as they screamed on to the start finish straight, disappearing as they went up to Druids but reappearing at what was then still called Bottom Bend, then remaining in earshot as they accelerated up the long straight to Pilgrims Drop. There'd be almost half a minute to wait before the cars burst out of Stirlings and then speared down to my corner and, from my reclining repose, I could hear every tiny nuance of difference in technique from the two Ferrari drivers. The first driver's heel and toe downchanges were just so perfectly executed, revs matching each lap, every lap, and, as the driver turned in to Clearways itself, there was no hesitation, just absolute commitment, engine note first deepening as full power was deployed, and then doing that soulful Ferrari thing of traversing the entire musical scale, with a feral scream as the signature topnote. But the second driver lacked both technique and commitment; the revs sometimes ill-matched on the two downchanges and then a hesitant, on–off deployment of power in the corner itself. Lap after lap I listened and learned, and when I opened my eyes again I already knew what I would see. Arturo Merzario was subbing for Clay Regazzoni in the second 312 B2, and Brands was his first Grand Prix. Merzario was then most famous for his Marlboro man, cowboy hatted extroversion and, whilst he was a good enough sports car driver, he was clearly a long way short of team-mate Jackie Ickx's level of talent. Watching them confirmed what my ears already had told me, as here was little Art, bobbing white helmet so absurdly low in the cockpit, slanting this way and that over the bumps and dips and yet here was Ickx at his imperious best. Dark blue helmet with Kent cigarettes logo, every move relaxed, as if there were always time to spare. It was the same feeling you get when you hear Sinatra's phrasing or Clapton's soloing. Just how do they do that, how can they sound so utterly in control whilst operating at such rarefied levels? I still smile as I recall that cold and wet spring day at Brands in '74, when Ickx, in his borderline antique Lotus 72, simply drove around the outside of Niki Lauda's Ferrari into

Paddock, finding the refuge of grip in a way that I wasn't to see again until, in 2016, Max Verstappen made the rest of the Brazilian Grand Prix field look like amateurs when the going got tricky, and the tricky got going.

The '72 race itself was wonderful, with Fittipaldi, Stewart, and Ickx slugging it out in the early stages with Fittipaldi's black and gold Lotus 72 eventually triumphant. The red machines? Ickx retired with oil pressure problems, and Merzario claimed the single point for sixth. But never mind the race, Ickx's Clearways masterclass remains the memory that burns the brightest for me.

I missed only a couple of British Grand Prix in the next 20-odd years and I came to love Brands almost as a second home until, in 1986, Silverstone shamefully wrenched the rights away and bagged the Grand Prix rights all for itself; I was thus condemned to spending long, cold days on that windswept plateau in the badlands of the Northants and Bucks border. I learned to love even Silverstone, but it was never the 'coup de foudre' of Brands Hatch. They were just so different, with Silverstone perpetuating its trademark haughtiness, all blazered formality and clipped vowel commentary, whilst Brands was the ducking and diving 'Sarf London' player, never missing a trick, eyes on the main chance, Jag on the drive, and the trophy wife in the Tudorbethan detached. If Silverstone was a pillar of the establishment – a Harold Macmillan or Malcolm Muggeridge perhaps, then Brands was a David Frost: garrulous, cocky, and charming; or perhaps a diamond geezer Arthur Daley, charming your pants off whilst trying to sell you a warehouse full of dodgy gear. I suspected that the prize money for the winner of a Grand Prix at Silverstone would be payable, in guineas, by a cheque drawn on Coutts Bank whilst the Brands' winner would receive a fat wad of used tenners held together by a rubber band. Silverstone might have bagged the Red Arrows most years, but Brands was far more ambitious when it came to aerial entertainment, one year an RAF Harrier pirouetted so low over South Bank that most of the trade stands were blown over by its massive down thrust. They topped that – and how the hell did they ever pull this off? – when the New York bound Concorde gave two scarily low passes. Did they even tell the passengers first?

In the Seventies, Formula 1 was in danger of becoming a spec formula for chassis built by blokes in sheds and powered by a two grand down and a change of address DFV. Whether minnow size Connew, Lyncar, or Williams or the big fish like Lotus and McLaren, every car on the grid – BRM, Matra, and Ferrari apart (Tecno too in '73, if dogs count), was a variation on a familiar theme. Evolution was steady, almost entirely aerodynamic and, with the exception of the Peter Wright/Colin Chapman 'something for nothing' disruption with the Lotus 78 and 79 ground effect 'wing cars,' and, I suppose, the evolutionary dead end that was the Brabham fan car and the six-wheel Tyrrell, Formula 1 was slumbering on cruise control until turbocharging changed everything. But, like all good revolutions, it was far more of a process than an event, as the Renault RS01, which I saw wheeze and fart its way around Silverstone in 1977, was almost a pastiche of what I expected a Grand Prix car to look and sound like. That day all eyes were on James Hunt instead, if not quite as much as they had been the year before, when Brands Hatch went into midsummer meltdown with a crowd that had transformed itself into a mob …

Summer 1976 was notoriously hot and as a result most of the country had gone quite mad by July. The Third Cod War had ended (face was lost but lives weren't), the red top papers boosted their circulations with crazy stories of "well endowed" streakers and ice cream shortage shockers, labourers on the Humber Bridge went on strike after an attack by a plague of killer ladybirds and, weirdest of all, the country fell under the spell of a posh lad from Surrey with a patrician drawl and a dress sense on the grungy side of casual. James Hunt, in a spookily similar way to Damon Hill 20 years later, had risen almost without trace to Formula 1, having enjoyed only sporadic success in lower formulae. Both drivers found their mojo when the numbers got serious, showing that they could handle nearly 500bhp in Hunt's case (and rather more than that in Hill's) far better than they handled underpowered and over-grippy F3 cars. It was obvious what latent talent James Hunt had been hiding as soon as I saw him hustling the Harvey Postlethwaite modified March 731 in 1973, at a pace that no March had managed since the *Flash Gordon* inspired 711 two years earlier.

All racing drivers have a recognisable body language. Just think of Jim Clark's straight-armed artistry, Stirling Moss' languid recline, or James Hunt's signature pose of bristling, head-down aggression and an almost brutal exploitation of everything the car and driver could give. In '74 I had seen him drive the gorgeous Hesketh 308 to win the Daily Express Trophy at Silverstone and, with a McLaren drive giving the man they called Master James the equipment he needed to target a championship, Brands Hatch 1976 felt like high noon. Niki Lauda and Hunt may have been friends off track but, fomented by hysterical press coverage, the inter-team rivalry between Ferrari and McLaren was already toxic by July, and Brands was the perfect place for a shootout under a scorching sun. Even at 7am the place was feverish; we had queued at the nearest gate to where we had parked but, on seeing other gates opening whilst ours remained closed, the crowd in front of us simply smashed the fence down and barged in. Not even during 'Mansell mania' has Silverstone come even close to the anarchy of Brands Hatch 1976. Notoriously, Hunt was denied a restart after the first lap shunt, because Rule 78.01(b)(ii) said so (or so some FIA bloke claimed) but given the choice between a riot and a race the Clerk of the Course decided to choose the latter. Like Woodstock, the Third Test Match in 1981, and Foinavon's 1967 Grand National victory, the 1976 Grand Prix was elevated into legend as soon as it ended, even though the reality was founded on jingoism-fuelled anarchy. It really was the 'us and them' Grand Prix and, snobby elitist that I am, I felt as though my sport had been tainted, if not actually hijacked, by populism (it can happen anywhere, anytime, as 2016 reminded us). The fact is, I have never really cared over much about who wins a Grand Prix as long as the race itself is memorable; there is no such thing, – pace Maldonado, Brambilla, or Baghetti – as an undeserving Grand Prix victor, let alone an undeserving World Champion (yes you, Rosbergs major and minor). I would have made a bloody awful tifoso if I'd been born in Lucca instead of Leeds, because I wouldn't have left Monza on lap 25 just because the red machines from Maranello had broken. But Brands '76 was far more significant than I ever realised at the time, as it marked the beginning of the transition from simple motorsport enthusiasm to its simpleton cousin, fandom. More on this in the next chapter because now is the time to talk turbo.

The 1979 French Grand Prix may have been won by Jean Pierre Jabouille in the Renault EF1 turbo V6, but the victory itself remains no more than a footnote. The Dijon race assumed legendary status because of the extraordinarily intense battle for second place between Villeneuve's Ferrari and Arnoux's Renault, settled eventually in Villeneuve's favour by two tenths. But the real significance of the victory was that, after the last tango the DFV teams had danced in the two seasons since the Renault had first wheezed around Silverstone, the hegemony of the normally-aspirated engine was now under real threat. Since the advent of the 3-litre 'return to power' Formula 1 in 1966 a normally-aspirated V8, flat or V12 had seemed the only possible answer, even though the rules had admitted the possibility of a half-size, forced induction engine. But, despite the fact that turbocharging had already been employed in road cars as diverse as the Chevy Corvair, the BMW 2002, and the Porsche 930 (as well as lots of trucks), it had surprisingly little popularity in racing circles, except for Indycars, where the notorious lag from the popular, if ancient, Offenhauser presented little difficulty on high speed ovals. The Eurocentric view was that super- and turbo-charging belonged to the era of blown Bentleys and Bugattis, Maseratis and Alfa Romeos, and thus would stay forever marooned in prewar nostalgia. Grand Prix racing's engineering geniuses such as Colin Chapman and Gordon Murray were always much more focussed on what Mark Donohue had termed "the unfair advantage," and that invariably had manifested itself by creating more grip than finding more power. In 1968 Lotus had first fitted a wing to Graham Hill's 49B at Monaco, and wings quickly became universal (if often treacherous) in the following seasons. Slicks finally superseded treaded tyres in '71, and the alchemy of ground effect transformed grip levels from late 1977. The generation of ever increasing grip, now aerodynamic as well as mechanical, enabled the default DFV to last far longer than ever could have been imagined on its 1967 debut at Zandvoort in the Lotus 49. But the status quo started to quiver in the Summer of '79, and within four years the DFV was relegated to the status of also-ran until it was finally euthanised in '85.

History refresh done, what was it actually like to witness turbocharged Formula 1 cars from trackside? It was as exciting as it was unexpected, it was faster than we could believe and it was more spectacular than anything we had ever seen, could ever imagine seeing or, as it turned out, would ever see again. Spookily, the pace of change mirrored the power characteristics of a turbocharged engine as the faster things changed, the faster they'd change next, the pace exponentially accelerating until, inevitably, something just had to give. I am just glad I was there to see the big bangs of '84 to '87 before the declining whimper of '88 and the Year Zero reset of '89. The peak was reached in '86 and the three days I spent at the Grand Prix at Brands Hatch in July were the most thrilling I have ever spent at a race circuit.

In winter 1983 I had chatted to an Audi PR at the RAC Rally; her boyfriend worked for Williams and had told her about the extraordinary power being developed by the Honda

V6 Turbo in testing. Not normal boyfriend/girlfriend pillow chat it's true, but where had she been all my life? The young goddess mentioned the suspiciously precise figure of 824bhp and, shamefully, and possibly even chauvinistically, I assumed she had misheard because wasn't even the Renault only offering 20%, at most, over the best DFVs' 500bhp? But, by '86, 800bhp was kiddy stuff compared to the off the scale potency of the four-cylinder Brabham BMW and the 1000bhp+ of the Honda. Brands Hatch in '86 looked an even shorter circuit than it had been on my last visit, as the monstrously powerful turbo cars were devouring straights as if they were snacks, with corners now just the impediments to speed, rather than the key that they had been for so long. Such an abundance of horsepower might have created the freedom to drag around big acreages of downforce inducing wing, but just one look at a Benetton B186 or a Brabham BT55 in action told you what the real plotline was – insane acceleration and speeds never seen before at Grand Prix circuits. At the '83 European Grand Prix, Brands supremo John Webb had installed a speed trap just before the braking area into Paddock Hill Bend and we watched Mansell and De Angelis' Lotus 95Ts trading v-maxes in the 170mph (275km/h) territory, with Mansell almost inevitably posting the fastest time of 177mph (285km/h). So what was he doing in '86, in the Williams Honda, with another 400bhp to play with – 190mph (305km/h)? More?

Watching these monsters was a totally immersive experience, and a perfect example of the massive difference between being physically present trackside and watching the coverage on TV. With friends Richard Daly and Steve Fox, I watched from every point of the track during untimed practice and qualifying, but nowhere gave as visceral a hit as the climb up to Druids. We stood at the last point where the cars were still accelerating before they had to brake for Druids, and I'd be standing there now if the cars were still on track. Really. Because it was a show you could never tire of, the most dramatic thing we had ever seen. First there was the sound of rolling thunder along the pit straight, car still out of sight, and then it would appear quicker than you could blink, running fast and wide through Paddock, and passing you at a speed that made your heart beat faster, your eyes widen, and your jaw drop. At home you just might have made a cup of tea if the TV director had zoomed in on a back of the grid Osella or Minardi but, as I felt every car slam by in a sensory overload of speed and noise, seeing the drivers' total commitment and being awestruck by their sheer cojones made me realise that, in this most difficult and dangerous of games, even the lightest of makeweights are every bit as heroic as the front row prima donnas. We came to learn how, so unlike the DFV days, each car had its own signature noise and smell; the Honda and Renault V6s by far the rowdiest with their deep chested bellow, TAG McLarens had their cultured drone, the BMW powered cars a blur of industrial white noise and black smoke, but the Ferrari V6s, amazingly, were almost self-effacing. And yet what the Italian cars lacked in decibels they made up for with a reeking cloud of exhaust gas, smelling toxic, sickly sweet, and making our eyes prickle. It is now received wisdom that some teams, especially Brabham, had developed expensive and exotic tastes when it came to fuelling their racers but it was the Italians whose cars smelled most like an ICI plant with a health and safety problem.

And yes, I know, I've concentrated more on runners than riders so far, and I'm not stopping now, as I want to talk about the next iterations of the Grand Prix car, but don't worry, Mansell fans, the moustachioed maestro will turn up later, as will some other drivers who could transform a race into a drama. Anyway ... it isn't just my rose-tinted vision that makes me think that Formula 1 reached its apotheosis between '84 and '87, it is the unarguable fact that never have we seen more powerful cars. Never have we seen cars that had horsepower by the shedload, but were untamed by subsequent innovations such as the algorithmic intervention of traction control, almost infinitely adjustable engines and chassis, aerodynamic alchemy, carbon brakes, sequential (let alone paddle) shifts, and power steering. But there are still big lessons to be learned from that glorious era, not least the eternal truth that a healthy excess of power over grip is a key building block in making a Formula 1 race more of a gladiatorial duel than the back office obsession with strategy and tactics, undercuts and overcuts, that dominate modern Formula 1.

The decline has taken decades, though, and it didn't start to emerge into plain sight until the advent of the 2.4-litre V8 Formula 1, when I saw just how far we had fallen. The normally-aspirated engines of '89 may have lacked the turbos' sheer wallop in the early years, but power had crept up to nearly 1000bhp before the V10 was superseded by its noisy kid brother in 2006. The shouty little V8s may have been technical jewels, but they were more mouth than trouser, only developing useable power at stratospheric revs and, uniquely in my experience, being utterly identical in sound to the extent that I was quite unable to differentiate one car from another. But it wasn't like that in '89 ...

The turbocharged engines had had their wings clipped more severely each season after '86, resulting in the swansong '88 season being a Honda whitewash for McLaren in every race except one, Monza of course, just after Enzo Ferrari's death. Divine intervention, obviously, arranged by the Pope and prayed for not only by every Italian citizen, but also everybody blessed with an Italian heart in a northern European body. Yeah, me too of course, I even wore my black tie to work on 14 August 1988, not that anybody noticed – philistines. But even that win didn't assuage a season that may have given Ayrton Senna his first world championship, but still too often felt like watching the Mobil Economy Run. We knew that the next season wouldn't be DFV redux, but the glorious reality exceeded all my off-season hopes. *Autosport* Formula 1 editor Nigel Roebuck had written about seeing and hearing the Honda V10 powered McLarens for the first time as they tested at Silverstone, and he couldn't contain his excitement at this new breed of impossibly sleek racers singing the sweetest of songs from – wow! – only a bloody V10. We may almost acclimatise to the configuration now, as we can hear its distinctive howl from Lamborghinis and the more exotic Audis, but, back in '89, Honda may as well have announced that they were introducing a W9 running on fuel distilled from angels' tears.

I first saw the brave new world of normally-aspirated Formula 1 at Silverstone in 1989, and, after the droning of housetrained turbo engines in '88, the spectacle was arresting and overwhelming. No fewer than 39 cars were entered, which meant hectic pre-qualifying early doors followed by a full house of 30 cars in qualifying and a 26-car grid. It wasn't just the numbers though, but the diversity of solutions to the same set of problems; there were seven different engines, they had eight, ten, or twelve cylinders and there were more than 20 different chassis. Grand Prix racing wasn't exactly strapped for cash back then, but by 2006 budgets had grown even fatter, yet where was the diversity? Not only was a 90-degree V8 mandated, maximums for bore and stroke dimensions were laid down, no more than four valves per cylinder were permitted, variable valve timing was outlawed, and neither was more than one sparkplug per cylinder. No wonder each and every one of the bloody things sounded identical ...

The opening minutes of untimed practice at Silverstone in July '89 were mesmerising as, although the sledgehammer thrust of a big boost turbo had disappeared for good, the cars were scalpel sharp through Club Corner and they sounded utterly wonderful. I grew to love the doomy howl of the V10s but the screaming V12 in the Ferraris was, predictably enough, the most vocal of them all, sounding like a soprano in a choir of tenors. And, as I had finally stopped grieving over the loss of Brands Hatch, I came to know Silverstone so intimately that I knew exactly where to watch. It's a palimpsest of a circuit, with whatever represents the current configuration being superimposed on previous iterations, and they, in turn, on earlier layouts right back to 1949, when the old perimeter circuit was first used. Club was probably the finest place to watch a Grand Prix driver at work in '89, having superseded Woodcote's majesty when the latter was emasculated in 1975 by the inclusion of a chicane, and watching drivers such as Mansell, Senna, and Prost from close quarters as their cars speared through Club's savagely fast right hander was mesmerising. Bridge Corner, which had over a decade in the sun, was later to become an even better place to witness the artistry of an Alonso or a Schumacher, but the best l can say about Silverstone's layout in 2017 is that its run-off areas are almost certainly visible from space and that there must be, what?, at least three places where a car on track is in the same postcode as the spectator?

The V10 era lasted a satisfyingly long time, and if it was sad that we had lost the V8s and V12s, the pace of aerodynamic change and increasingly powerful engines made every visit to a Grand Prix a new journey of discovery. It wasn't just new drivers, but ever higher speeds and ever louder engines, as I discovered when the shriek from Diniz's Ligier Mugen pierced my left eardrum (as I recounted in an earlier chapter). Ear protection? Never without it now, mate, not since joining the Locking The Stable Door After The Horse Has Bolted Society ...

Hybrid engines, KERS, ERS and DRS? Azerbaijan, Shanghai, and Sochi? Jeez, I need some breathing space before talking about them, it won't happen until the next chapter because, just now, I'd rather talk about some of the Grand Prix drivers who have lit up my days since 1971. You know their careers already, and, even if you don't, Wikipedia is your friend, so I am going to concentrate on the memories that burn the brightest. Some you will already know about, others are just the vignettes which still resonate with your reporter, so objectivity be hanged. Let me start with Niki Lauda, the only man who has ever come close to being a hero to me, the man who BBC broadcaster Harry Carpenter described as the bravest he had ever met and who became the template for the modern Grand Prix driver. Just like James Hunt and Damon Hill, Lauda was a driver who raised eyebrows when he first appeared in Formula 1, as there hadn't been the inevitable elevation of a Senna or a Stewart, a Häkkinen or a Ricciardo, more of a murmured "what the hell is he doing here?" Lauda's trials in the awful March 721 during his debut Grand Prix season did nothing to dispel my prejudice as he then seemed just another Euro chancer who had made some ripples in Formula 2, but never quite enough to engulf a Peterson or a Cevert. But at the '73 Grand Prix, on the restart after the Scheckter shunt, who the hell was this, leading the field in a BRM that was more of an homage to its predecessor than a threat to the Tyrrells and the McLarens? It wasn't just that Lauda was leading, but the fact he looked so comfortable, so imperious, as he did so. The lead was brief, but it was enough to highlight what the driver could become, and Lauda's move to Ferrari came as no surprise even if the speed of the turnaround he engineered in the then struggling team did. The 1975 312T was a thing of rare beauty, Lauda's driving was sublime and, had the Nürburgring crash not happened, he undoubtedly would have achieved a hat-trick of championships from '75 to '77 – and he was only a few mistakes away from winning in '74 too. But I always remember him most for his British and Dutch Grand Prix victories in '82 and '85, both for McLaren, when the young charger had been replaced by the canny old fox. In '82, Keke Rosberg might have defied the laws of physics in the wickedly quick ground effect Williams in practice, with Lauda only fifth on the grid, but there was something almost inevitable about the McLaren's progress through the field. All you had to do was watch and listen, there was the metronomic consistency of line, the cornering pace that was blisteringly fast but only a butterfly's kiss away from a timewasting slide or twitch. And Lauda's gear changing! It was just astonishingly fast, very nearly as quick as today's paddle shift changes, which even a child couldn't botch, with downchanges a masterclass in timing, revs matched on each and every change. Like all great drivers it was rarely a question of whether the driver could win, but whether the car could.

Three years later I was at Zandvoort for the last Dutch Grand Prix, and for Lauda's last win. The circuit could have been located in Skegness – if with much better chips – and, as I strolled towards Tarzan Bend on a damp Saturday morning, I was astonished to find myself virtually alone, with none of the frenzied crowding I'd have seen at home. But it's Holland, stupid, and if the Dutch are good at one thing it's being laid back, no? The rain came down from a leaden sky, and I sheltered under the scrubby trees high up on the sand dunes, my Barbour waterproof zipped tight and my foul weather fishing hat pulled down hard to combat the North Sea wind. I heard German voices, one of them announcing "Das ist ein heftiges Hut!" to raucous laughter. "Danke," I muttered in return, frantically hiding my paperback copy of Sophie's Choice, a book that possibly, and I'm guessing here, didn't trouble the bestseller lists in Germany ...

In practice Lauda skulked around in his McLaren TAG MP4 2B, smooth as ever but an insouciant tenth on the grid, almost two seconds behind Piquet's rocket fuelled Brabham BT 54 on pole and 1.2 seconds adrift of team-mate Alain Prost, then en route to his first championship. On race day there was some showboating from Renault, whose pace suggested that running on fumes was a more likely reason for Derek Warwick and Patrick Tambay's retirements than the claimed transmission problems; and after both Rosberg and Senna had retired from the lead, and Prost had recovered from a pit stop hiccup, the race was transformed into a fight between the Austrian King and the French Young Pretender. Lauda had done his usual under the radar ascent of the order without fuss or drama, but things changed when Prost caught him, and the race started to look more like a Formula Ford battle than a Grand Prix played with big boys' toys. Senna would have barged Lauda out of the way, or tried to, but Prost was ever the gentilhomme, even with a championship to win. It was a privilege to watch two of the sport's smartest and neatest drivers showing that, when there's a chance to win and a win to lose, they weren't frightened of getting their hands dirty. I am rarely partisan, but I could not have been happier to witness Niki Lauda, the smartest and bravest driver of them all, on his seaside swansong.

Same year, previous month, a dank day at Silverstone: cold enough for me to shiver, and misty enough to delay practice. Late afternoon, and a brief window, track still damp but time running out fast. The story has it that Keke Rosberg dragged hard on his Marlboro Red (he wasn't going to be a Lites man was he?), ground the fag out on the pit lane, said "Let's do it" to his pit crew, climbed aboard his absurdly potent Williams Honda, and … just bloody well did it. 'It' being pole, 'it' being an average of 161mph with a slowly deflating tyre. The Finns have a word for it – they would, wouldn't they? – 'Sisu,' and it means strength of will, determination, and cold-blooded courage. Rosberg had overdosed on the stuff. In 1973, I had seen Ronnie Peterson from the same viewpoint at Woodcote, but then without the chicane, and he made his Lotus 72 dance through a choreography of instantly corrected 150mph slides, and I thought nothing could ever eclipse that spectacle. But Keke did, riding his 1000bhp monster as if the prospect of his tomorrow was more a hope than a certainty. It was majestic, courageous, and imperious, but my inner voice did just wonder how much faster he would have gone if that silly little chicane hadn't been stuck there in '75. And if the chicane hadn't been there, and if the Williams had got away from him, would the wreckage have landed in Towcester or made it to Northampton?

Two years later. Stowe Grandstand is packed solid, head-scratching crowd driven nearly insane by thunderbugs. 28 laps to go, and Nigel Mansell is 29 seconds behind team-mate Piquet. Bugs are forgotten, everything is forgotten, all we are doing now is counting the gap down – just as many of us had counted down the seconds to John Watson's capture of Arnoux's ailing Renault in '81 – but aloud and in unison. I don't enjoy team games. I have never been to a football or cricket match, and I think Rugby is fancy dress homo-eroticism, but on that day maybe I did get a hint of the terraces, as 1000 people whooped and cheered, fist pumped and air punched. Even self-conscious me was lost in the moment, and I can't deny that it was the most stupendous fun. And, as Mansell sold the dummy pass to Piquet then jinked around him to take the lead with two laps left, engine turned up to 11 but fuel down to mere vapour, it was simply amazing, the sort of thing that you might have expected at Brands, but here, in BRDC blazer and cravat territory, it was unprecedented.

But now I have to be really careful: I have to repeat the mantra 'judge the art and not the artist' before I say too much more about Nigel Mansell, the man about whom Lotus' team boss Peter Warr once said: "he'll never win a Grand Prix as long as I have a hole in my arse." As a Grand Prix driver Mansell became almost peerless, despite being underwhelming enough in his early years to have provoked Warr's withering verdict. He found his mojo in the Williams in '85, was dubbed 'Il Leone' by most of Italy in his Ferrari days, and the mojo was still working pretty damned well when he left Formula 1 in a huff and went CART racing instead, introducing the word 'Nigel' to the American lexicon and reintroducing the phenomenon of European drivers whupping some asses across the pond, as they might say in Indiana (but are unlikely to in Buckinghamshire). Five years later, '92, and I am standing just before the point where Formula 1 cars used to brake for Stowe. Not any more they don't, as they are all taking the right hander at, what at first seems to be, suicidal pace. You acclimatise quickly though – you get to the stage where you notice that the Jordans are out of sorts, the Brabhams don't even deserve the name any more, and that the pace of Herbert and Häkkinen's bargain basement Lotuses is not too shabby. And, after 20 years, I thought that I really knew how to watch this stuff: I knew where to look, and who to clock on my branded stopwatch because I've served my time, passed my 'been there, done that' degree with honours. I'm not some parvenu fan but an old hand. But just then, apparently from nowhere, there's a blur of colour, a whooping V10 scream, and suddenly I know nothing at all about motor racing, bugger all about who's hot and who's not, because just now I don't even believe my eyes, and I'm a tongue-tied tyro. The reason? Mansell, en route to a full house jackpot of pole (by just the 2 seconds over team-mate Patrese), victory (by 39 seconds, just to really humiliate Patrese) and, obviously, fastest lap. The Williams FW14B might have been a hi-tech wonder car in '92 but here's the thing – apparently Mansell was 35mph quicker than his team-mate at Stowe. 35mph … this in a sport that books a wind tunnel for a week to gain a tenth here, and spends a 100,000 for 2mph more there.

Back to '87, and the victory lap – do you remember those outrageous crowd-pleasing indulgences that the FIA, in everyone's best interests, stamped on soon later? 'Art/artist' I remembered, but I gave up as I watched Mansell kiss the tarmac in front of us before giving his usual 'my struggle, alone I did it, against all odds, just had to go for it, they've all got it in for me, people power, Murray' speech to whoever would listen. Great driver, but I'd hate to be stuck in a lift with him. Being unfair, am I, sneering at a true Brit hero? Never would I sneer at Mansell's artistry, but just read Russell Bulgin's July '91 interview with our Nige in *Car* if you think I'm being a tad unfair. Here's a flavour, on why Mansell won't talk about his past: "Number one, I'm not giving interviews at the moment," says Nigel, a faint patina of frustration surfacing; this – journalist, list of sanctioned questions, C90 rolling – is apparently not an interview. "I've got the utopia of a driver's position this year, inasmuch as we are racing to do the job." And the interview that isn't an interview at all rambles on in this vein until concluding with Nigel's parting shot to the man who was one of the greatest ever motoring journalists – "Thank you – and fuck off ..." And to his team PR – "No more journalists, do I make myself clear?" Bulgin concludes by mentioning that, within a week, Mansell gives a long interview to *Autosport*. It's an interesting vignette, and I remain forever bemused why the man who, on his day, could look like the best driver in the world, could also have appeared so tragically insecure.

You need to know that I have form for spotting drivers in junior formulae and recognising their talent long before the insular world of Formula 1 world does. 'Cos I'm the man who saw JJ Lehto put on a wet weather masterclass at a Formula Ford 2000 race at Cadwell Park, and told anybody who would listen that the Finn with the unspellable forename was the future of motor racing as we knew it. But he wasn't, actually, he might have won Le Mans, but he never thrived in the rarefied atmosphere of Formula 1. Neither did some of my other tips for the top – Jan Magnussen (amazing in Formula 3 but developed learning difficulties when he got to Big School), Danny Sullivan (another Cadwell F3 masterclass; ho-hum in Formula 1, but the Kentucky Kid done good back in the USA), and Takuma Sato. Yes really. Because I have never seen anyone drive a Formula 3 car with the energy, bravery, commitment, and sheer blinding speed that I saw when Sato blitzed the field at Croft in 2000, leaving an outright lap record that stood for years. But some heroism in Jordan and BAR apart, and a near win on the last lap of the 2012 Indy 500 (10/10 for speed, 1/10 for racecraft), until May 2017 it looked like it wasn't going to happen for Takuma, the driver who seemed condemned to be forever tilting at windmills. But the little guy who I watched as he drove the wheels of his Formula 3 Dallara only won the bloody Indy 500 didn't he? And I could not have been more overjoyed for him. Success seemed guaranteed for Gunnar Nilsson though, whose total mastery of his March 753 in Formula 3 was a joy to witness, one of those sublime 'man and machine in perfect harmony' gigs. But he was fated to win only the single Grand Prix: the Belgian at Zolder in '77. If he hadn't fallen ill, if he hadn't lost his Lotus drive in '78, just what spells would he have cast with the all-conquering Lotus 79? I even met him once, too, when, uncharacteristically, he crashed hugely at Silverstone in the little March 753, clambered nonchalantly over the spectator fencing, shook his head, swore, grinned, swore some more, said "hello," and cadged a Marlboro Red.

But I was right about Ayrton Senna. It only took ten laps in a Van Diemen RF81 around Mallory Park on 22 March 1981 for Ayrton Senna da Silva, as he was then, to convince me and, I'd guess, everybody else who was there, that the latest in the line of Brazilian drivers – going back to Emerson Fittipaldi in 1969 – was the star who would shine the brightest of them all. And in a constellation that also includes Nelson Piquet (senior, as if I have to remind you), and Carlos Pace (the driver who Gordon Murray told me was the one he rated above all others), Senna's star still deserves to shine the brightest. And yes, I did do some parenthetic name dropping just now: I once interviewed Gordon Murray, one of the most articulate men I have ever encountered, and it's a privilege I need to share, okay? Anyway, Ayrton Senna. What can I say that hasn't already been said about the man who was worshipped in life, and has come close to post mortem beatification? A premature death endows a glister to any career: are we really sure we would we feel the same about Jimi Hendrix or Janis Joplin, Jim Morrison or James Dean if they were now just washed up has-beens reliving their too-familiar pasts on daytime TV? How can we be truly objective about just how good the British *The Lost Generation* triumvirate of Tony Brise, Tom Pryce, and Roger Williamson might have been in Formula 1? Is it heresy to say that only Brise had both the steel and the speed? That Pryce had the speed but possibly not the steel? And that all we know about poor Roger Williamson is that we just don't know enough to be sure? But I knew, most of us knew, that Senna was not just astonishingly fast, but somehow just 'other.' Jackie Stewart was the template for what evolved to become the modern Grand Prix driver, Niki Lauda refined and improved the model, and Alain Prost followed it. Then Senna disrupted it, extracting the best elements of what it took to win, but discarding the rest without question or remorse; all that Corinthian 'it's the taking part' stuff may have disappeared with Mike Hawthorn's bow tie, but the unqualified will to win regardless of cost, risk, reputation, or popularity became Senna's defining characteristic. And his legacy too, because what was Michael Schumacher other than Senna v2.1? Lewis Hamilton v2.2? and Sebastian Vettel v2.3?

Senna the man was fascinating in that there was an unsettling and unprecedented combination of spirituality and hauteur complemented by a patrician sense of entitlement which itself was leavened with both philanthropy and compassion. But I cannot help feeling that both the man and his legacy may as well be consigned to join Russia in the Winston Churchill quote about Russia – 'a riddle, wrapped in a mystery, inside an enigma.' You can read about Senna in a score of different books but you won't read a better one than Richard Williams' The Death of Ayrton Senna, in which a proper journalist does a proper job, unlike some of the cut 'n' paste horrors rushed out to exploit Senna's grieving fan base, so many of whom had never encountered a death in Formula 1 until poor Ratzenberger's demise at Imola the day before Senna. That was the day the conspiracy theories started (and in our post-truth world they are still running) and the day when Niki Lauda reflected the Spring '94 zeitgeist so perfectly in one short sentence – "Today God took his hand away from Formula 1."

I watched Senna win in Formula 3 in the '83 season, when he seemed invincible until Martin Brundle rattled him and, for the only time in his career, he wobbled, as if his whole magic was deserting him. I never saw the biggest wobble, as, for reasons which I now know couldn't have been good enough, I missed the Formula 3 meeting at Cadwell Park when Senna achieved escape velocity at the Mountain, crashing out of practice and not competing in the race. But when I did see Senna in '83, he won as of right and on the many occasions I saw him in Grands Prix – at Donington, Silverstone, Brands Hatch, Zandvoort and Imola (in '87, thank God) – he was peerless. He even adopted a unique style in the turbo years where he would constantly blip the throttle to maintain boost under braking and the early part of the corner – at first it sounded like a car problem until we understood it was just the sound of a genius at work. I have never seen a better driver and doubt I ever will.

That's the end of a long chapter – I had a lot to say. History didn't stop in '94 but I found myself becoming less drawn to attendance at Grands Prix for the reasons I will discuss in the next chapter. TV viewing doesn't count as properly experiencing any race and, whilst I have enjoyed many Formula 1 practice days and tyre tests, I have seen just a handful of Grands Prix from trackside since the early Nineties. Enough to rate the same drivers you would rate, and never to be short of an opinion on the season, but my previous sense of immersion in Formula 1, that feeling of belonging that I had always found so addictive, declined on a curve that mirrored Grand Prix racing's transformation from a business-like sport to a global brand. As Ry Cooder sang on *Bop till You Drop*, "the very thing that makes her rich will make you poor."

It isn't customary both to begin and end a chapter with a quotation, but I make an exception now, as it encapsulates why Grand Prix drivers have exerted such a hold over my head and my heart since that long-ago day at Oulton Park. These words were said by an unnamed lorry driver to Gilbert and George, the London artists whose collaboration has appalled, amused, enchanted and outraged for half a century:

My life is a fucking moment; your art is an eternity.

11
SUPPING WITH THE DEVIL

Yeah, you do seem to have a little shit creek action going ... but, you know, FYI,
you can buy a paddle

Saul Goodman from *Breaking Bad*, Vince Gilligan

Mr Gradgrind is the teacher in Charles Dickens' *Hard Times* who gained his notoriety by saying: "Now what I want is facts. Facts alone are what is wanted in life. Plant nothing else and root out everything else. Stick to facts, Sir!" and facts are going to play an important role in this chapter, which is about how I've seen Grand Prix racing evolve during my 50 years exposure to the sport and where it is now. Complementing the facts will be opinions, primarily my own, although I am more than happy to steal other people's opinions as long as they suit my arguments, as one does. There's going to be no limp-wristed "just my humble opinion" equivocation about the bear pit that comprises modern Formula 1. Separation of fact from opinion should be easy, and 20 years ago I am pretty sure it was, but the second decade of the 21st Century has seen so much weird stuff going on that the ice that I thought would easily bear my weight might just turn out to be a damned sight thinner than it looks. It's not just global warming that's the problem but the ... ahem ... fact that web forums and social media now peddle 'fake news' and 'alternative facts' as much as the real thing, that expressions of opinion are often challenged as if they were errors of fact, and that even the most unshakeable of truths can be met with sneering disbelief. Faith used to be the opposite of science but in our brave new world they're ying and yang bedfellows. Season this with a pinch of self-righteousness, add a sprinkling of 'virtue signalling,' throw in a sacred cow or two and (no cliché unspared here) the appearance of a palpably nude emperor, and you risk entering what surgeons call 'tiger country.'

It's a tough job to navigate between the rock of fact and the hard place of opinion in a world that is making it increasingly difficult to identify one from the other. So that's the terms and conditions nearly done, that boilerplate legal stuff, which every vendor knows nobody will read (my guilty secret is that I used to write that crap for a living), and now's the time for Talking Heads' second mention in this book; here are some wise words from David

Byrne, from *Cross Eyed and Painless* –
Facts are simple and facts are straight
Facts are lazy and facts are late
Facts all come with a point of view
Facts don't do what I want them to
... Facts continue to change their shape

Fact one (of many): the 1906 French Grand Prix was the first ever motor race with the title of Grand Prix. It was held every year until 2008, with breaks only for the two World Wars and in 1955 as a mark of respect (and out of political expedience), following the Le Mans disaster of that year, which killed over 80 and maimed more than twice as many. Postwar, France has been represented by ten teams in Formula 1, and maintains a presence in 2017 with its works Renault team. Renault-powered cars have won over 130 Grands Prix, and at least 75 French drivers have competed in Grands Prix. But despite French drivers, French cars, and French engines having a century-long history in the sport, and despite the unassailable fact that France effectively invented Grand Prix motor racing and also hosts the world's most famous race every year – Les Vingt Quatre Heures du Mans – until its reinstatement in 2018 France's home Grand Prix was absent for a decade.

In the 2009 season, Grands Prix were held in at 17 different circuits, in 16 different countries. At least six of those countries had no meaningful history or current involvement in motorsport although several, notably Abu Dhabi, Bahrain, and Malaysia, have invested heavily in the sport, including the acquisition of interests in Formula 1 teams. In 2015, only five circuits enjoyed an attendance of 100,000 spectators or more and amongst this group only China has not been involved in meaningful participation in motorsport. Silverstone enjoyed an attendance of over 140,000, exceeding the number of spectators present for the Bahrain race by a factor of almost five. In fact, 30 per cent more people attended the Brands Hatch round of the British Touring Car Championship than turned out to watch the race in Bahrain. Maybe the no-shows are from people aware of Human Rights Watch's characterisation of Bahrain's human rights regime as "dismal," especially its marginalisation of the Shia population. HRW has also reported that "torture is a regular part of the legal process" in the country. Adultery and sex outside marriage is illegal, but, perhaps surprisingly, gay sex is not criminalised in Bahrain, unlike in another Grand Prix host country, Abu Dhabi, where 'sodomy' (as they still term it), is punishable by up to 14 years in prison.

Azerbaijan held its first Grand Prix at Baku in 2016; the total number of tickets sold was 28,000. Its Grand Prix was given the honorific 'European Grand Prix,' to the surprise of the relatively few people who knew where the country actually is: on the Caspian Sea, immediately north of Iran and east of Turkey, Syria, and Iraq. This, by the way, is the country that might have very deep pockets but has also gained notoriety for locking up journalists and bloggers who dare to criticise the regime. Reporters Without Borders ranked Azerbaijan 162nd out of 180 countries for press freedom.

70 per cent of current Formula 1 teams are based in England, most within an hour of Silverstone, and over 50 British Formula 1 teams have competed in Grands Prix – more than any other nation. Although Britain has hosted a Grand Prix every year since 1948, in 2017 Silverstone elected not to continue doing so after 2019 because the cost is becoming unaffordable; having started at £12 million per race it is likely to rise to as much as £25 million. And unlike almost every country that stages a Grand Prix, payment in Britain is made only by the circuit owners (the British Racing Drivers Club) and the Grand Prix does not benefit directly from any state support, and quite rightly so, in my view.

Bernie Ecclestone progressed from being Jochen Rindt's manager via ownership of the Brabham Formula 1 team, to the de facto owner of Formula 1 until 2017. He is worth, according to the 2017 *Sunday Times* Rich List, a comfortably affluent £2.48 billion. He is not the only one to have made a fortune from Formula 1 – former McLaren boss Ron Dennis is worth £450 million and Lewis Hamilton, crowned world champion for the fourth time in 2017, is reputedly worth over £100 million.

The admission price to my first Grand Prix in 1971 was £2, equating to £28 in 2017. Grandstand prices were £1, so £14 now. Admission prices to the 2018 British Grand Prix start from £155 and the most expensive grandstand costs £450. It is no longer possible for hoi polloi, you and me included, to gain access to the Formula 1 paddock; although, judging by the frequent appearance of sports stars, actors, and celebrities, access is easily available to some, regardless of their interest in or knowledge of the sport. Their main duties appear to involve wandering around the grid, hoping to catch the eye of a TV reporter, giving them the opportunity to reveal to a worldwide audience the gaping chasms of their ignorance about the sport they invariably call 'Eff One.' After the race begins they watch its progress from the back of the team garage where, ever aware of the ubiquity of TV cameras, they will obligingly gurn, applaud, and grimace at events that befall their host team during the race. I am not sure if these Very Important People ever actually see the majesty of a Formula 1 car in full flight from trackside, y'know, that sight that appealed to supporters of the sport in the first place?

Paddock passes were available for purchase by the public for Grands Prix until at least the early Nineties and, at most Grands Prix, a very relaxed attitude was taken by circuits and the Formula 1 community to public access. Both pit and paddock were easily accessible on the Friday and Saturday evenings before the race – Thursday and Friday evenings before the early Eighties, as Saturday was race day in Britain, South Africa, and elsewhere until the mid-Eighties. In front of me is a photograph I took at Silverstone in 1987, which shows an overalled Ferrari mechanic working on the suspension of Gerhard Berger's F1/87 in the pit garage. It was taken from a range of about ten feet and, at the time, the opportunity to take such a photograph seemed unremarkable; access like this was accepted by the Formula 1 paddock, but was a privilege I never saw abused. I said earlier in this book that, for a time, the Grand Prix spectator felt part of the show and, whilst it may have been only a non-speaking, walk-on part in Act Two, or part of the chorus in Act One, I never sensed any hard demarcation between players and audience in my first 20 years of Grand Prix attendance. We were all in this adventure together, but I was reminded just how much we no longer were when, in 2004, I watched a shrieking crowd pursuing the limo taking Jenson Button and BAR team-mate Takuma Sato into Silverstone and thought to myself "if you are so keen on seeing these guys why didn't you watch some Formula 3 a few years earlier, when you could even talk to them?"

In 1971, in Great Britain alone, no fewer than six races took place for Formula 1 cars; the Race of Champions and Victory Race at Brands Hatch, the Spring Trophy and Gold Cup at Oulton Park, and the International Trophy and British Grand Prix at Silverstone. Some races were almost full-scale rehearsals for a Grand Prix, featuring cars from nearly every team, but not every race had a full grid. Oulton had barely a dozen in April and the entry for most races, Grands Prix apart, was supplemented by Formula 5000 cars of varying performance. Whilst the fastest could humble a Formula 1 car, as Peter Gethin famously proved at Brands in 1973, the slowest were anything up to 15 seconds a lap slower.

In 1966, in the 'Return to Power' era of Grand Prix racing, the capacity limit doubled to 3 litres with a nominal 1.5-litre limit for supercharged engines – "nominal" because supercharging was largely forgotten and/or ignored after World War 2. In the next two decades, engines of four-, eight-, twelve-, and sixteen-cylinders were used, joined by six-cylinder engines as Honda and Ferrari followed Renault in exploiting the huge power that could be liberated by turbocharging a small capacity engine. Engine configurations used in this era comprised straight, V, flat, and H, although most engines exploited the full capacity limit, some teams, especially in the early years of the Formula, raced with 2-litre Climax engines. Even 1600cc Formula 2 cars were admitted to some Grands Prix, and the 1967 German race included nine such entries using Ford and BMW engines. But since 2000, only one engine configuration has been permitted in each of the three sets of governing regulations; 3-litre V10s until 2006, then 2.4-litre V8s and, since 2014, 1.6-litre turbocharged V6 engines, supplemented by energy recovery systems. There are limits on the exact specification of current Formula 1 engines that are so prescriptive that, as one commentator in *Autosport* said in June 2017 – "What's the point of rules requiring everyone to build the same car and engine, but in their own race shops?" Given Honda's unexpectedly dismal performance with its own engine, I have to assume that they relied on Google Translate for their copy of the regulations; but the intention, and effect, of the regulations was clear, effectively the same engine is being made, but at huge expense, by Ferrari, Renault, Honda, and Mercedes. For the first years of the new formula, the German engine enjoyed an advantage sufficiently large to make their cars almost invincible in 2014, with only three races being won by a Renault-powered car, and Mercedes remained championship winners over the next three seasons. Five seconds covered the grid for the first race of the 1.6 hybrid era, less than half the gap between first to last in qualifying at Brazil for the first race after normally-aspirated engines were reintroduced in 1989.

Don't fret, the commentary bit is imminent, but let me conclude the introductory fact-fest by turning, again, to the sordid topic of coin. All the figures are inflation adjusted and, more than any other metric, offer an insight into how the sport of Grand Prix racing has changed. Forgive the homophonic indulgence, but back in the prehistorical Prince Bira era, his ERA season in 1939 cost about $300,000; in the four decades that followed, team spends increased to annual sums of up to $10m in the Seventies, thanks to sponsorship from sources as diverse as petrol, booze, fags, condoms, tools, dodgy finance houses, coffee, cheese, and at least one art gallery. Even Jesus got in on the act at one point, as you will see shortly ...

In the Seventies and preceding decades, team numbers were tiny, with a handful of mechanics at each race, and hardly a PR person in sight. It was only in the Eighties that the immense amount of cash realisable by TV deals was fully exploited. Budgets rose to almost $300m in the Nineties, led by Toyota, which reputedly spent up to $445m on their Formula 1 team before realising that, not only were they unlikely to ever win, but that they might be able to finesse more bangs out of every buck by racing sports prototypes at Le Mans. Wallets bursting with so much cash reputedly enabled BAR to fit carbon fibre seats to the toilets in its hospitality area, and enabled Mercedes, in 2017, to employ the 700 staff who are retained for the sole reason of contesting 20 races per annum. None of the races, incidentally, will last for more than two hours, an hour shorter than the duration of many Grands Prix in the Fifties, and almost two hours shorter than Prince Bira took to complete the Monaco Grand Prix in the Thirties. Ross Brawn has described how Mercedes would run cost benefit analyses on the potential innovations and refinements suggested by its engineers, and how the rule of thumb applied to evaluation was that if $100,000 expenditure would produce a tenth of a second per lap improvement, then it was deemed to be worth investigating. A similar sum is the current cost of a front wing, the things that frequently get wrecked in the argy-bargy of the first corner of the first lap of a Grand Prix. Wings are worth about three of the type of multi-functional steering wheels that became universally adopted in the late Nineties, and which superseded the single function Momo steering wheel that was fitted to so many Grand Prix cars in the Seventies and Eighties. A similar Momo adorned my Uno Turbos and Golf GTis, and was a snip at 40 quid.

So, what can we learn from the preceding paragraphs? Lesson one is that, assuming Formula 1 ever owned a moral compass, the sport lost it down the back of the sofa a few years after deciding that racing in apartheid South Africa was a Bad Thing, but then, despite the election of Nelson Mandela marking the end of apartheid in 1994, deciding not to reinstate the South African Grand Prix. South Africa apart, only Morocco has held a world championship Grand Prix on the continent, the last Casablanca race taking place in 1958. Anyway, at some time in the first decade of the 21st century Formula 1 took the sofa with the lost moral compass to the tip, only deciding not to fly tip it because the negotiations on which team should do the job, when, and under what branding, stalled after three weeks' worth of wrangling, hissy fits, and posturing in the conference suite of the Heathrow Hilton. Formula 1 might never have been a beacon of transparency and business ethics, but when its commercial rights holder, Bernie Ecclestone, started hanging out with the kleptocrats and oligarchs running dodgy regimes in dodgier countries the rot really set in. Despite Europe hosting all of the team bases and most of the sport's global audience, Grands Prix started to be held in any country whose leadership was willing to stump up the necessary sum – inevitably a huge amount – and which might usefully have been expressed as multiples of 30 pieces of silver. The fact that a country may have had the dreadful human rights record of Bahrain, the borderline totalitarianism of Azerbaijan, or the near total disinterest in motorsport of a Turkey or South Korea was apparently of no concern to either the sport's participants nor many of its fans. "Sport and politics don't mix," the teams say, "I'm just worried about tyre choices" said Sebastian Vettel in front of a backdrop of palls of smoke from fires lit by the protesters in Bahrain and to the sound of police sirens. And only true grit Mark Webber was enough of a grownup to say publicly that a Grand Prix should not have been held there.

But what about the fans? Some sports fans often have very strongly expressed views on matters only marginally connected to their sport of choice. Remember how, egged on by the tabloid press, football fans had a huge attack of self-righteousness when FIFA purported to stop Our Lads wearing team shirts that incorporated the Remembrance Day poppy? But were motorsport fans remotely troubled by the fact that protesters are routinely banged up in jail without trial in more than one Grand Prix venue? Or were they troubled by the sight of Bernie Ecclestone buddying up to Vladimir Putin at the Russian Grand Prix in Sochi in October 2014, just months after Russia had annexed Crimea by force and ousted the Ukraine government and armed forces from the territory? This, incidentally, was the same Putin whom Ecclestone had said should be in charge of Europe. The fans weren't bothered a bit, and if you hang around some Formula 1 web forums you can soon see why. It may just be the biggest legacy of Margaret Thatcher that we have ended up in the so-called gig economy of the second decade of the 21st century, where even those of us who were not born entrepreneurs are expected to behave as if we were, and to applaud, without reserve or cavil, anything that perpetuates the success of a brand. Because brands and branding have almost taken the place of religion in the eyes of an increasingly secular fan demographic, in contrast, ironically, to the rise in religious fervour and intolerance that characterises so many of Formula 1's new territories.

As I finalised the last edit of this chapter in late November 2018, the name 'Matthew Hedges' was heard in every news bulletin. He was the British academic who had been sentenced by a court in the United Arab Emirates to life imprisonment on the charge of spying for the UK government. Hedges had been in jail – sometimes in solitary confinement, often handcuffed and blindfolded – for six months, his 'trial' lasted less than five minutes, and he had no access to a lawyer. The sentence was imposed on 21 November, just two days – two days! – before first practice began for the Abu Dhabi Grand Prix. Was a single voice of concern or objection heard from anywhere in the Formula 1 community? Despite its habit of 'virtue-signalling' its support for any cause that might suit its own self-interest, the Formula 1 paddock's silence on Hedges' plight was deafening. Hedges was released on the day after the Grand Prix but I still question how I can love a sport that inhabits a bubble so opaque that the outside world can be neither seen nor heard. Or is it just plain and simple moral bankruptcy?

Hold that thought while we think about a Brazilian driver, Alex Ribeiro and two former British Grand Prix drivers, James Hunt and Mike Beuttler. Whilst you may know all about Hunt, Beuttler's name is now only a footnote in Seventies Grands Prix as he rarely troubled the sharp end of the grid and never finished higher than (a then no points scoring) seventh place. Ribeiro also enjoyed an undistinguished Grand Prix career in Hesketh, March, and Fittipaldi cars between 1975 and 1977, but is remembered chiefly for his unusual choice of sponsor. And now let's consider the off-track behaviour that made James Hunt so notorious, and I am not talking about the jeans and sneakers (as they were called then) that became Hunt's trademark déshabillé look, and that he wore especially at events where stuffed shirts were near mandatory. Let's focus instead on the autumn of 1976, and the few days immediately prior to Hunt's title winning drive at Fuji Speedway when – egged on by his mate Barry Sheene – Hunt, reputedly, had sex with a number of air hostesses. Quite a few, by all accounts.

Now let me return to Mike Beuttler, who raced between 1971 and 1973 in various March Formula 1 cars, and died in 1988, in San Francisco, from an AIDS-related illness. Beuttler never came out during his racing career – hardly surprising given the homophobia of the era, and the fact that Grand Prix racing was almost a parody of robust heterosexuality at the time, with even punters like me being simpered over by scantily clad lovelies (copyright *The Sun* 1973) giving away free packs of John Player Special cigarettes.

Alex Ribeiro was best remembered for his fervent Christianity, which he proclaimed on his race cars by carrying the logo 'Jesus Saves' in very large, joyous lettering. Apart from L Ron Hubbard's sponsorship of an Indy car, advertising Hubbard's 'Church of Scientology Dianetics Research Foundation,' I struggle to think of another example of religious endorsement of a race team. Alas there is insufficient space here to list all the drivers who either thought they were God and/or behaved as if they were.

Now let me remind you again about some of the territories where Grands Prix take place in the 21st Century, the time when most 'civilised' countries show little more than polite lip service to organised religion, employing it principally to add gravitas and ceremony to the more formal state occasions. And let's speculate on the fate that might have been in store for James Hunt in October 1976 if the Grand Prix season had been concluded in one of the states that lie 5000 miles to the west of Japan. A prison sentence, with 31 other air hostesses being taken into consideration, and hence a possible second of three consecutive world championships for Niki Lauda? What about Mike Beuttler? Prison again, and, depending upon the precise location, if the 'offence' had been committed in 2017, the poor guy would have risked being thrown off the top of a block of flats. Ribeiro? Even Jesus might not have saved him from a full house of apostasy, heresy, and blasphemy.

40 years ago, Grand Prix racing's heartlands, Europe, North and South America, Japan and Australia, were far less liberal states than they are now. Gay sex is not the unspoken horror it was then, and cohabitation between hetero- or homosexual couples raises no eyebrows –

with the possible exceptions of places such as Turkey Scratch, Arkansas and Mavis Enderby, Lincolnshire. So what the hell is our sport doing by running races in countries that are so at odds with the libertarian and secular meritocracy that, in my less cynical moments, I still believe Grand Prix racing to be? In our more tolerant times, why are Grands Prix taking place in countries so at odds with our own values and that apply medieval laws to 'offences' that we have not criminalised for decades (or even for centuries, in some cases) and that have often had no meaningful involvement in, nor enthusiasm for any type of motorsport?

At least some of the answers can be found in the fact that until 1978 when, sparked by James Hunt's world championship in 1976, the BBC started to broadcast the highlights of every Grand Prix, enjoying Formula 1 was nearly always a vicarious experience. You had to read about a race rather than watching it, except for the annual chance to watch the British Grand Prix at Silverstone, Brands Hatch or, in earlier times, Aintree. Until 1978, even as a fervent follower of the sport, I often had to wait until the Thursday following a Grand Prix to find out even who had won it by reading either *Motoring News* or *Autosport*. It seems extraordinary from my 2017 perspective that, before 1978, I can only recall watching three Grands Prix on TV – the 1967 Italian and the 1970 and 1972 Monaco races. Each was memorable. Monza for being the only race where I watched Jim Clark live and where, after his extraordinary recovery drive, the race was only decided by a last lap bare knuckle fight between fellow champions Surtees and Brabham. The 1970 Monaco race was all about Rindt's astonishing drive in the ageing Lotus 49 that, ultimately, lost Jack Brabham what had looked like an easy win. And the 1972 event was Jean Pierre Beltoise's day of days: the BRM was far from being the best car on the grid, and Beltoise far from the best driver, or so their previous form had suggested, but so assured was their win that it looked inevitable, just as Olivier Panis's Ligier win at Monaco was to do, 24 years later. Two Frenchmen scoring their only win, and at the same circuit, in the same conditions, and for teams whose glory days were a decade earlier, it's a lovely symmetry, no?

TV coverage is the single biggest factor in making Grand Prix racing what it now is, warts and all, as the sport's potential has been exploited to produce the blanket coverage that we now expect. But the principal reason behind the TV exposure was not to enable existing or new fans to watch the sport, but to leverage the sport's value by exploiting its appeal to create vast income streams for some, if not all, participants and an ever-flowing tsunami of dollars to the sport's commercial rights holders. This is familiar territory, of course, for anybody with a working knowledge of the sport, even though I suspect nobody will dare to write the full story until *The Times* has published the obituaries of Messrs Ecclestone and Mosley. Seriously hard work was involved in creating the current model of Grand Prix racing, nobody doubts that, but was it really a couple of billions worth, and did nobody think about the collateral damage to the sport's heritage and reputation?

There is a real irony in how the media tail began to wag the sporting dog, to the extent where nearly every facet of the sport's fiscal value now derives from the cash cow of TV coverage. But enough of the animal metaphors, motorsport has always enjoyed interest from those who can only watch, and this interest goes back in time via the 'right crowd and no crowding' ethos of Thirties Brooklands, via the Targa Florio, the Nürburgring, and the Indianapolis 500 to the hordes who watched that first French Grand Prix in 1906 and the Gordon Bennett races that preceded it. TV first began to cover motorsport because vast numbers of people were already watching races from trackside, and had been for decades, and those spectators were sufficiently enthused to devote both time and money to watching motor racing. Broadcasting technology advanced until, during a five or six-year period that began some time in the late Seventies, a paradigm shift took place. Until the shift occurred, Grand Prix racing, and in fact motorsport as a whole, had been a niche sport enjoyed only by a relatively small community of highly informed and passionate enthusiasts. I was one of them, and possibly you were too, but I am still struggling to accept that the price that I, and people like me, have paid for today's blanket coverage of Grand Prix racing has actually been worth it.

So what's the problem? Surely I am just an elitist dinosaur if I object to a wider audience enjoying my sport? Is it that I just don't like the fact that my hairdresser is just as likely to ask, or tell, me about 'The F1' as my, or her, next holiday and that my neighbours are as likely to share their thoughts on Lewis Hamilton's tattoos as on the general election? Or is it that I don't like website forums becoming ablaze with micro analysis of what their posters have just spent the last two hours watching on their big telly, aided by a director deciding what shots to show them and by a commentator telling them what they just have seen, and thus amounting to what is little more than the visual equivalent of a pre-masticated snack? It might be, at least in part, but the problem is a little more nuanced and a lot more serious, or it is if you really care about what motorsport actually means. I think it was *Motor Sport* magazine's Simon Taylor who described the problem the most succinctly, when he wrote that motor racing used to be a pyramid, with Formula 1 at its apex and, lying beneath it in increasingly wider strata, Formulae 2 and 3, junior single-seaters like Formula Ford, club racing and, right at the base of the pyramid, cheap as chips speed events. Indycars and International sports car racing were also near the top of the pile whilst, slightly off centre, was the sui generis stuff like drag racing and rallying. And the mystery of the pyramid was, actually, that there was no real mystery at all: the categories at the bottom were just as much a part of the sport's continuum as the ones higher up, you just needed more talent (usually) and a lot more money (always) to progress. For decades this model worked well as drivers knew what their career path might be, team owners knew what categories best suited their budget and skillset and spectators knew where they might see a future Grand Prix winner racing in the early part of his career.

But it isn't like that anymore. Because Formula 1 now enjoys an existence only marginally connected to other branches of motorsport, it has built a pyramid of its very own, and it's a very big one. At its apex, the atmosphere is so rarefied that it can only be enjoyed by plutocrats and the altitude is so elevated that, most of the time, the clouds of sponsor and media dollars completely obscure the lower levels. And, as for the other pyramids, those tumbledown edifices containing the remainder of what motorsport used to comprise, they are rarely in view at all and, even when they are, Formula 1's elite tend to avert their eyes, just as they do from the São Paulo favelas surrounding Interlagos, as they do from the migrant workers in Bahrain, and as they do from the sight of civilians like you and me through the tinted glass of the Paddock Club.

But if it was just the elitism, the tunnel vision, the obscene budgets and the narcissism of modern Formula 1 I could almost live with that, but the bigger problem lies with the absurdity of the regulations. They now result in racing cars that weigh far too much, a lardy 722 kilos (1600lbs), 50 per cent heavier than most Formula 1 cars of the last six decades, and this excess weight is entirely attributable to the insanely complex power units that might be technical marvels, but the inconvenient truth is that they still produce less power than the smaller capacity turbocharged engines of the Eighties did. It gets worse, as the engines (or power units as they are termed in 'Newspeak') are so complex that their design and construction can only be undertaken by the few multinationals brave enough to devote hundreds of millions of dollars to powering a handful cars on 20 weekends a year. Formula 1 became embedded with the grandee car manufacturers when Renault, BMW and the rest joined Ferrari and Ford in the early Eighties, as turbocharging brought new opportunities and technical challenges. We thought it was a Good Thing at the time, as wouldn't it mean the end of the DFV hegemony (with which we were becoming ever so slightly bored), and a return to the glory days best exemplified by the prewar Mercedes and Auto Unions about which old men then still enthused and whose enormous power outputs had still remained unrivalled over 40 years later? But we were wrong, the sport was now supping with the devil, egged on by the Mephistophelean media.

Things went wrong because, just as media exposure expanded and its influence increased, so did the power wielded by the car manufacturers. For far too long they have been the only organisations rich enough to make engines for Formula 1 cars and, in the case of works teams such as Ferrari, Mercedes, and Renault, have been almost the only concerns, Red Bull apart, able to pay for the staggeringly complicated research and development needed to make their racing cars competitive. And, unlike Ferrari, for whom racing has always been at their essence, other manufacturers need to exploit their investment and have done do so by using their leverage to make the regulations relevant to their corporate objectives. Since 2014 we have had ghastly sounding, massively complicated and ruinously expensive Formula 1 power units and all for one reason only – the firms that make them want to be seen by the public as being environmentally responsible by making hybrid powered racing cars. "It's because of the green lobby," commentators will say and I don't believe a word of it. I have never heard any spokesperson from any environmental body say words to the effect of "those bloody V10s and V8s really bugged me, you know? All that noise and only, like, 2 or 3mpg? Dude, it was just horrendous! But these V6 turbo hybrids, you gotta love 'em, right? Only 105 kilos of fuel for a 200-mile race; they're almost running on fresh air man!"

Although I think hybrid engines have no place in Formula 1, they absolutely do have a vital role in endurance racing but unfortunately, Le Mans apart, nobody actually watches it any more (the Formula 1 pyramid effect at work) so where's the business case for the investment, what will it do for a firm's brand equity? Sports car racing has always been the real home for the clever innovation that ultimately might produce benefits to road cars, despite Formula 1's self-delusion that its own technical advances bring such improvements, or, in some cases, that those advances were even created by Formula 1 in the first place. Turbocharging? I have already mentioned that Chevrolet, BMW, Porsche, and others were using turbos years before they appeared in Formula 1. Ground effect? Jim Hall was pioneering this dark art down Texas way on his Chaparral sports cars years before the wing car Lotus 78 disrupted the status quo in 1977. Carbon fibre? I was using a Hardy carbon fibre fly fishing rod years before the McLaren MP4/1 raced. I can think of only three things that Formula 1 has created which have been widely used on road cars – paddle shifts (pioneered by John Barnard's sublime Ferrari 640 in 1989), raised noses, and diffusers. But only paddle shifts have any practical relevance as, even though the humblest Vauxhall Corsa might sport a trompe d'oeil raised nose, it has no practical function, and remains a homage to the look pioneered by Harvey Postlethwaite on the Tyrrell 019 in 1990. Rear diffusers decorate almost everything from diesel SUVs to hot hatches but, in almost every case, they are no more than costume jewellery. Diffusers certainly worked on a 900bhp Lotus 98T, but on a Citroën Picasso? Not so much ...

Crazy costs (whose collateral damage is thin grids), dubious race locations, excessive media and manufacturer influence, silly power units, surely I can't have even more dislikes? Of course I have, and tyres are very close to the top of my list of shame. If Formula 1 wants to be seen to appease the green lobby, then why does it encourage the consumption of specially made tyres at the rate, typically, of 12 tyres per race, or one every seven minutes? To spice up the show, its defenders might argue, but my response is you have just got to be joking, right? Pit stops break up the rhythm of any short duration race and are executed primarily to achieve the oxymoron that is overtaking in the pit lane by an undercut or overcut, the terms used to describe staying on track shorter or longer. Timing of pit stops is principally decided by the team's software, tyre changes typically last less than three seconds and they are only remotely interesting when something goes wrong. It was exactly the same in the days when refuelling was permitted, when only the risk of a fire from a fuel spill enlivened the spectacle from the viewers' perspective. Cynical? Maybe, but search YouTube for 'Jos Verstappen pitlane fire,' and the top three clips have had over 2.5 million views. But, disasters apart, I can absolutely guarantee that in 2047 nobody will be reminiscing about Mercedes' pit stop strategy in the 2017 Canadian Grand Prix – "wow, the algorithms those guys used in Montreal ... just totally awesome." But if I am wrong and such a person does exist then tell me this – would you want to invite them round for dinner? I thought not.

And if pit stops don't help, too much aerodynamic grip is absolutely guaranteed to transform a race into a procession. Overtaking in a Grand Prix should never be easy – this isn't NASCAR – but it should be possible. So why isn't it possible at most circuits, most of the time, except by the use of the lazy, cop-out Drag Reduction Systems? DRS, let me remind you, enables one driver to overtake another, not by the traditional tactic of outbraking his opponent, but by simply driving past him at a higher speed down the straight, just as you and I do when we overtake the Honda Jazz that has been holding us up on the twisty bits.

Then there is excessive radio communication (can you imagine a James Hunt responding to a blokey "Mate, we need to push harder" with anything other than a languid "I'm not your mate, you tiresome little man; now do me a favour and fuck off."); the emphasis on team strategy instead of driver tactics; and finally – at last! – an increasingly surreal penalty system. This has been insidiously infecting Grands Prix for several years but, as I write, continues to plumb new depths of absurdity. Drivers and teams are penalised for having an engine that breaks, something that highly stressed engines have been doing in motor racing for over a century, paying the price for pushing boundaries. Penalising breakage is done to save costs, apparently, thus leaving enough cash for the 30-grand steering wheel and the 100-grand wing, so come on, you know it makes sense. And even more crazily, drivers are penalised for behaving like racing drivers by trying – sometimes over ambitiously, sometimes too robustly – to overtake the car in front. That's the car he has been stuck behind for 30 laps because the airflow turbulence it created has stopped his own car's aerodynamics from working properly. And what happens when the guy behind tries a move, as he is paid to do and for which we pay to watch? Cue faux outrage by the leading driver on his car to pit radio – "Look, look, what that nasty man behind just did! He nearly pushed me off! He – cue gasp of disbelief – he exceeded track limits! He tried to overtake me – and it's so unfair!" or words to similar effect. Do we really want a once noble sport being diluted to such a parody of its former self?

So, have I fallen out of love with Grand Prix racing, buggered off to find pastures anew where I can seek the company of other disillusioned old farts and watch something else instead, convincing myself that Moto GP or NASCAR is just so much better? Actually, no, I watch every Grand Prix, every qualifying session and, if I spit and froth sometimes, doze off after 20 laps of Sochi, or snort at the ersatz Hockenheim, I still think that Grand Prix racing is the most exciting, most immersive, most multi layered, and most nuanced sport of all. Undoubtedly, it is the pre-eminent branch of all four wheeled motorsport, and that isn't a tacit admission that I prefer Moto GP, but a reflection of the fact that my interest in, and knowledge of, bikes and bike racing is perfunctory at best. And yet Grand Prix racing can, and should, be improved because I don't think that a Formula 1 car should sound like a piece of white goods and amount to not much more than a giant iPhone with a car app. Nor do I think that Grands Prix should be won or lost by undercuts, overcuts, or by the application of penalties to team or driver except in the most extreme cases, such as cheating, race fixing, or ramming opponents.

The sport has never shown itself in a good light when it comes to introducing changes in the regulations: self-interest always fogs debate and far too many people in the sport seem incapable of taking any objective view of it. I give you Max Mosley, who, despite 40 years spent in and around motor racing, once asked veteran Formula 1 journalist, Nigel

Roebuck, whether it was true that the race-going public not only enjoyed the awful noise that racing cars make but, apparently, even felt that it was a vital part of the sport's appeal. Or those responsible for the new rules in 2017, who decided that faster was always better, even though the price paid for a couple of seconds a lap was to make non-DRS enabled overtaking even closer to impossible. I watched 2017's final Grand Prix yesterday, from – God save us – the Yas Marina, during which the first 12 cars circulated in grid order for much of the race. Is that what racing is meant to be about, driving line-astern for 80 minutes? If Formula 1 can't get it right for themselves then maybe I can help? And so here is my 'food for thought' effort, unpolluted by any interest other than to make Formula 1 great again – snappy slogan huh?

This is what Pete Lyons, the greatest Grand Prix journalist of all, thinks the best racing car should do: "Make us step back in fear when it fires up … trying to watch its acceleration [will] almost snatch your eyeballs out. It should pound the ground, bring you running to the fence and hurt your ears. [It should be] the car you'd be most scared to drive." The current iteration of Formula 1 cars certainly don't lack acceleration, but frighten and try to deafen us? You'd have to be a very sensitive snowflake to be at much risk of either. Aided by Pete's vision my basic recipe is simple – a Formula 1 car should have 40 per cent more power than a Grand Prix driver needs but only 50 per cent of the grip the driver wants, thus re-emphasising the role of the driver and giving the lie to the guff about this being essentially a team sport. It isn't, or at least it shouldn't be. And, whether watched live or on TV, noise is undeniably a major factor in enjoying the sport, and, whilst the best turbocharged engines can almost wake the dead, nothing compares to the pure song of a high-revving, big capacity, normally-aspirated engine, and if it has ten or twelve cylinders then so much the better. Not too high revving though, as my proposed 4-litre engine capacity should ensure the requisite 40 per cent excess of grunt and the modest rev limit of 12,000 will mean that, unlike in the 2.4-litre V8 era, conrods won't need to be forged from unobtanium nor valves made from extruded angels' hair. And that should mean engines that are affordable enough for off-the-shelf units to be made by race firms such as Cosworth as well as by whatever manufacturers remain, and ideally they should be as few as possible.

Aerodynamic grip has been the ruination of decent racing for decades, and must be reduced to a level where cars can run closely, can overtake each other without the need for DRS or reliance on pit stop strategy. Actually, and I suggest you might take a deep breath if you didn't watch racing before 1983, pit stops won't feature too much at all, except in the case of force majeure events such as punctures, engine malfunction, or rain. That's because, rather than relying on the rubber compounds that are now used, and which score a PR own goal every race by wearing out in minutes, tyres will be constructed durably enough to last a full Grand Prix. Isn't that a much better advertisement for a Pirelli, a Bridgestone, or a Michelin than the present orgy of conspicuous consumption and profligate waste? Bingo – we might just regain the holy grail of races being decided by driver tactics and not team strategy.

I also want a far more relaxed attitude to on-track behaviour to encourage robust overtaking and risk-taking, with most shunts being classifiable as racing incidents, the inevitable price paid for on track competition. There would be no penalties for blown engines or broken gearboxes as, call me old-fashioned, isn't having to retire from the race and having to pay for a new engine a disincentive enough? Or do people think that, back in the Eighties, Zakspeed used to blow up their engines on purpose as attention seeking behaviour, maybe even a cry for help? Blue flag hysteria, where lapped cars are meant to dematerialise for the leader's convenience? Bugger that, leading drivers can find their own way by, surely, and if they can't then maybe they should consider another career?

Venues? Easy – just race in more places where they like racing and fewer places where they don't. It's easy enough to work out, really it is, just count the crowd numbers and find out where the drivers come from. This will mean the imminent demise of such nonsenses as the not-so-Grand Prix in Baku and I hope, the opportunity to do something really fun like a Scandinavian Grand Prix, because isn't it about time that the sport acknowledged the contributions made by K and N Rosberg, Häkkinen, Räikkönen, Bottas, and Peterson, with honourable mentions to Salo and Wisell, Kinnunen and Bonnier, Nilsson and Johansson. A street race around Helsinki or Copenhagen would be a joy, but why not a midnight sun race above the Arctic Circle?

Grand Prix weekends will take a different format too, as Formula 2 will stop being the support band nobody has come to see, but will headline their own European championship, which will come to a circuit near you next season. And in the winter there'll be a revival of the Temporada and Tasman series in the warmth of a South American and Antipodean summer. The new Grand Prix support act will be an elevated Formula E, with a 30 car grid featuring, compulsorily, at least one driver from the top ten Formula 1 teams and with the single make cars being prepared, managed and maintained by staff seconded from the highest scoring four teams in the previous years' championship. Other support races will be at the organisers' discretion, meaning one race weekend might feature Australian Supercars, another Indy cars and another historic Can-Am cars. Why not, what was so great anyway, about the previous homogenised package of events – didn't they only serve to make one country's race look and feel like everywhere else's?

So I'm dumbing down am I, committing the cardinal sin of diluting the sacred brand? And don't I risk ensuring that somebody will squeal triumphantly, as if it were the end of an argument and not the beginning of one, those tired, clichéd words – "But, but you can't uninvent technology – so there!" True, you can't, but you really do not need to uninvent in order to prevent a technological advance being exploited. You just get a decent lawyer, with a Formula 1 engineer or two at his side, to write a rule preventing its use. This approach can work, and it is why Formula 1 cars no longer run on rocket fuel, nor do they have ABS, fully automatic gearboxes, skirts, ground effect fans, fully enclosed bodywork, six wheels, or gas turbine engines. The sport has always attracted the geniuses, the disrupters, and the left field thinkers, the men like Colin Chapman, Adrian Newey, Gordon Murray, John Barnard,

Ross Brawn, and Mauro Forghieri, but far too often those in charge of the sport have fallen under these men's spell and allowed the sport's raison d'etre to be devalued, its reputation tarnished, by being bullied into accepting that almost any price is worth paying to encourage technical smartarsery.

And it isn't, because, at the very essence of Formula 1 (and every other form of motor racing) lies not design flair, tyre choice, nor pit stop strategy – not even speed and noise – but a single, binary question. And it is this: when two drivers are side by side, entering the braking area to the corner ahead then all that matters, the only thing we both crave and love, is the simple mano a mano drama of who blinks first. That's it, the mother lode, the DNA, the source code of it all. And it's a tragedy that the vested interests and the tunnel vision of the sport have been ignoring that one immutable truth for far too long.

And breathe ...

12
SOUTHERN COMFORT

Going down to Rosedale, take my rider by my side.
You can still barrelhouse, baby, on the riverside

Eric Clapton, Crossroads

"Honey, its two-twenty miles to Charlotte, we got ourselves a full tank of gas, a half pack of cigars, it's not dark, and we're wearing sunglasses," I drawled.

"Hit it," said Joanne. With an inner 'yee-hah' I pointed the Mustang's snout onto Interstate 85 North and unleashed the 300 horses under my right foot. Goodbye Atlanta ...

End of *Blues Brothers* pastiche. But in October 2013 on this, my first visit to the USA, it was impossible to feel that we weren't driving through a film set, with a soundtrack of the last century's greatest music. When you see the sign for Chattanooga, Memphis, or Nashville, when you see those *Deliverance*-spooky Arkansas woods on the west bank of the Mississippi or you drive your pony car on the Blue Ridge Parkway through the Great Smoky Mountains you feel an inevitable sense of déjà vu. And how could it be otherwise when you are as steeped in Americana as I am? From John Lee Hooker and Ernest Hemingway via Kacey Musgraves and E Annie Proulx, from *The Last Picture Show* to the inevitable *Bullitt*, the Big Country has shaped me every bit as much as my European heritage. In so many ways it felt like I was coming home.

It was early fall (just get used to it, okay?), and we were headed for the Bank of America 500 at Charlotte, North Carolina – which is the ground zero of NASCAR, the stock car championship that was first distilled from the murky world of moonshine running on the dirt roads south of the Mason-Dixon line. I had never watched a NASCAR race on TV, and only rarely had I bothered to read the race reports, but somehow I had absorbed the iconography of the good ol' boy racers, with names like Yarborough, Earnhardt, Petty, and Busch already familiar to me, not to mention the late and great Dick Trickle, the guy who had a hole drilled in his helmet just so he could spark up a Marlboro under the yellows, and whose name is so extraordinary that every so often I have to Google it just to confirm I haven't imagined it. After decades of watching Old World roundy-round racing, I could hardly wait to experience

NASCAR racing and to discover for myself how it would compare to European racing on road courses. Clay Regazzoni might once have said about oval racing: "It's easy, it's a-left, a-left, a-left," but, if drivers like Juan Pablo Montoya were struggling, I suspected that this apparently simple thing might just be a bit more complicated than my Eurocentric mind had expected. And remember Dan Gurney's words about NASCAR, perhaps with Regazzoni's thoughts in his mind: "People used to say about oval racing that all you had to do was turn left. But you're up against the guys who are best in the world at turning left. A 100-yard sprint is pretty simple too, until you come up against the best 100-yard sprinters ..." Dan also memorably described racing a NASCAR sedan on a road course as "like trying to dock an aircraft carrier." If those words had been spoken by Zeke Labonte of Possum Pelt County, Alabama you might easily dismiss such wisdom, but coming from Daniel Sexton Gurney, Le Mans winner, Belgian Grand Prix victor (in his gorgeous Eagle-Weslake), NASCAR, Can-Am, and Champcar winner? You've heard about US journalist David E Davis' campaign in 1964 – "Dan Gurney For President"? You have? Then you wouldn't have argued with Dan, no sir.

Plenty of web forum users tell me that the chalk of Formula 1 is not a patch on NASCAR cheese, but most of those boys have only watched on TV, and I suspect half of them don't even leave their bedrooms too much. So here in the real world, just what was the hugely hyped NASCAR really like? The answer may surprise, because NASCAR is absolutely not better than anything we have in Europe, but it is very different, not least in the fact that, unlike most road racing, you don't pass the other guy by slowing down later than he does but by going faster than he does, if not in the same daft way as Formula 1's DRS enables. NASCAR is intensely, holler out loud exciting at times but, whisper it, can actually get a bit dull some of the rest of the time. The races are long, twice as long as a modern Grand Prix, and you need to concentrate hard to get the best out of what it has to offer, and that isn't easy when the cars are lapping every half a minute and covering 90 yards a second. But here's the thing that really counts – when the game is played in the nearest you can find to a Roman amphitheatre, when there are 44 huge cars on track, pushing out 38,000 horsepower and running six inches apart from each other, when they're filling the hot and humid air with heavy metal thunder and you're drinking a very cold Margarita on a North Carolina night then, frankly my dear, you don't give a damn ...

Day one at the speedway was the bizarrely entitled Bojangles Pole Night, which sounds splendidly louche in a Spearmint Rhino sort of way, but it turned out that the eponymous Bojangles is a chicken 'n' biscuits franchise. And biscuits, we had already established at the hotel, aren't of the homely McVitie's Digestive genre, but a doughy sort of scone, often submerged in gravy, not of the Bisto persuasion but comprising a lumpy soup nightmare. Avoid. Charlotte Speedway is huge, incorporating the 1.5-mile quad oval with its 24-degree banked turns, a huge infield and grandstand seating for thousands of fans of this most blue collar of All American sports, and two rather over-awed Brits. "It's Bo Time!" the commentator boomed every minute or two during practice and qualifying on the largely deserted Speedway track – one of our first surprises was how very low attendance is on

Thursday in contrast to the teeming thousands on Saturday night. It suited us, as we could sit where we wanted and move around to experience this entirely new motorsport from every possible angle. As far as pit and paddock access is concerned, Bernie Ecclestone would have scowled in his scary pensioner in a Warhol wig way as, unlike at Silverstone or Sepang, the paying public aren't just nuisance civilians, fit for fleecing but little else, but genuinely welcome guests who can go more or less where they want, when they want. There is no need even to walk very far either, as one of the many local volunteers would inevitably appear in a golf cart and say "How y'all doing? Now you just tell me, Sir, where you folks wanna go, y'hear." You'd give him a couple of dollars for the local charity he was supporting and then you'd be whistled along to just anywhere you wanted. Believe me, it was a revelation, if not quite so much as the sight of the fat bloke in the white Bojangles chicken suit who joined pole-sitter Jeff Gordon on the podium.

When the Sprint Cup cars first emerged, I could not stop grinning like a kid on Christmas morning because these brutes of cars have massive presence, and their whole body language just exudes menace and potency. Imagine a modern single-seater, with its sculpted carbon aero, high revving engine, and tech heavy paddle transmission, the whole deal weighing next to nothing, its algorithms transmitting endless data back to its mother ship and all this under the control of a nine stone teenager who isn't even shaving yet – and then imagine the precise opposite. Think 3400lb (1550kg) (three Lotus 49s or two Morgan Plus 8s!) of three box old school saloon. Okay, 'sedan.' Bolt in an 8-litre V8, clothe the whole thing in some facsimile body with underpinnings apparently made from girders left over from the Forth Bridge, then get a tough guy called Greg Biffle to drive the thing. Aerodynamics? Hell yeah, there's a spoiler bolted (and I mean bolted) to the trunk, and a clear plastic strip up one side of the rear window. I'm sure it does something important in the maelstrom of turbulence created as the car runs 200mph (320km/h) just inches from a steep wall, but I haven't a clue precisely what. But whatever, when a race car sounds this good I don't really care about detail, would you? Of course I had elected to sit in the front row of the grandstand, and as the first car exited Turn 4 I was more terrified than thrilled because, even with the car still a quarter-mile away, I heard the feral howl of a World War II fighter plane in a steep banked turn and as the Toyota or Chevy dopplered past at crazy speed there'd be a percussive whoomph which, as Jerry Lee Lewis almost put it, shook my nerves and rattled my brain. "Feels good … ," as Jerry Lee had leered so lubriciously. And Christ, I did feel good as the gush of warm night air hit me, and I knew that I wanted more of this, a lot more. This was analogue racing with no gear shifts, except when getting up to speed, no braking (the only reason cars have brakes at all is to reduce the risk of Greg or Brad running over their own pit-crew); it's racing stripped of everything except raw speed and a thunderous backing track.

European racing could learn a lot from NASCAR; it isn't quite the access all areas some might imagine but even compared to series like the BTCC the showmanship and fan friendliness is amazing. Because, I suspect, the American fanbase simply wouldn't put up with anything else. As we watched the Nationwide cars practice, we stood next to the pit lane, close enough to feel the waves of heat coming off the cars as technicians checked tyre wear and temperature. The hot air washes over me, there's the smell of hot engine and burnt rubber, and I feel more a part of this show than a mere spectator, just like I did in Seventies' Formula 1 at Brands Hatch. 'Nationwide'? It's not the High Street UK bank but NASCAR lite, sponsored by a US Life Insurance outfit. To my uneducated eyes the cars look the same, sound the same, but push out only 700 horsepower (only!) and lap about 10mph (16km/h) slower than a full fat NASCAR racer – so just a 185mph (300km/h) pole lap, then. Wander into the paddock and let me share a guilty secret; I just loved the team trucks – so much sexier than the DAFs and Ivecos that clutter the M1 at home, and which have all the style of a microwave oven. NASCAR trucks are immense Peterbilts and Kenworths, which look absurdly sexy with a huge vertical radiator, priapic bonnet, narrow screen, and exuberant exhaust stacks venting 15 feet above the tarmac. I can't help being reminded of the sinister truck that co-starred in Spielberg's *Duel* with Dennis Hopper. Driving through Georgia we had already noticed that US trucks were often the fastest things on the Interstates and, lined up in the Charlotte paddock, they were nearly as big a draw as the race cars.

Another feature of the infield was the hardcore race fan, none more so than the apparently legendary Sofa Man. He is a fixture in NASCAR, or so my new best friend Ernie the Californian trucker told me, and, on top of Sofa Man's RV parked inside Turn 1 was a large wooden platform upon which was an array of distressed armchairs and sofas, all the better to recline into as the race progresses. School buses were popular too: you know, those yellow jobs familiar from every US movie? Groups of fans buy the buses, scroll some dubious artwork on the side, load them with beer and barbecue and then work hard on enjoying a lost weekend with their buddies. It'll never catch on at Snetterton, it'd get you a lifetime ban from Goodwood, but I reckon you'd be just fine with your bus at Santa Pod, where any English reserve went missing for good back in '72 …

Qualifying for the Sprint Cup racers was the highlight for me. The cars run singly, like Formula 1 did once, and they run two timed solo laps before the next guy thunders out of the pit lane. Laps were over in 25 seconds at an average of up to 194mph (315km/h) but, watching carefully, I could see differences in technique and learn how to tell the really fast and furious guys from the merely fast ones. Despite the sheer speed, I sensed immediately that to be good at this game a driver needs millimetric judgement and the ability to treat the car with a surgeon's delicacy. Some drivers did both of their allotted two laps and others relied on a single banzai lap when the commentator would announce "One and done." In an English accent, whether Watford or Workington, these words would sound plain daft, but in a lazy Carolina drawl? As cool as you like, boy. As the driver crossed the finish line he'd kill the ignition and the car would put on a son et lumiere display of yellow flame and a deafening Ker-phut before silently freewheeling at 180mph (290km/h) into Turn 1. This wasn't some parping little four pot Ford in British Touring Cars, no sir, this was blue collar belligerence at its all-American best. Remember Rockingham? Not North Carolina but Northamptonshire, where, in a triumph of hope over experience somebody built a banked oval, down the road a piece from damp and cold Corby. I missed the Champ Car visits in 2001/2 but I did get around to watching an ASCAR 'Days of Thunder' race there once. It had a pathetically sparse grid, no crowd beyond the few regulars who had turned up to wave their giant foam hands and little green flags, to our toe curling embarrassment. Under the cold, grey Midlands sky there was neither spectacle nor atmosphere and the whole deal was consigned to the bin marked 'two nations divided by a common language.' It felt like your nephew's pub band rehearsal instead of a Foo Fighters gig or like forcing down a Wimpy, if you can still buy them, when only a Big Mac would do.

Food, yes, on day two it was time to check out the on-site catering a little more diligently; a bucket sized Margarita sharpened our appetites as we browsed, although not quite enough to even consider buying one local speciality. Read this carefully – two Krispy Kreme Donuts separated by cheese-topped bacon and the whole lot then deep fried. This truly was TV's *Man v Food* made flesh – and naïve Brits like me had thought TV producers made most of this stuff up, but apparently not. You're still peckish? Then try this bad boy grilled cheese sandwich, weighing in at a hefty seven pounds and incorporating four pounds of cheese, two pounds of pulled pork and, just to top off the feast, a modest pound of bacon. Shuddering, we settled for chicken fillet sandwiches, the healthy option endorsed by a 2D, life-size, cardboard cut-out (wasn't it?) of Danica Patrick. It works for her, she's tiny and gorgeous, if a tad skinny compared to the Carolina norm, but we were the only customers. Real NASCAR fans survive on an exclusive diet of buckets of beer and dumpster size helpings of BBQ pork products, believe it. Replete with our liberal elite, Yankee chicken we watched the first race, which was for the Southern Outlaw series. No, me neither, so here's the picture. Try to imagine Frankenstein cars , part Buick sedan and part Ariel Atom and you're getting there. The recipe was to insert a thumping great V8, then bolt wide slicks onto a *Mad Max* homage chassis and then you're good to go. The Outlaws raced on a 440 yard oval using the start/finish straightaway (yeah, I'm still doing it, don't stop me now) and the pit lane, joined by two constant radius curves. Yes, it's a big roundabout ('gyratory' over here) and the cars were quite a spectacle, in a lumbering sort of way, even though my traitorous mind kept whispering "An R500 Seven would leave this lot for dead" as the Outlaws' repertoire was seriously lacking in the high G cornering department.

The morning of race day was relaxed, as you would expect when the race doesn't start till 8pm. Our Holiday Inn in Concord entered into the spirit by putting on a free barbecue and raffle, and we happily chatted to everybody we met including, in my schoolboy German, to the dour NASCAR fan who'd just flown in from Lausanne. But even Lukas was easier to understand than Mike from Connecticut whose body language was as friendly as every other race fan we met but whose accent was incomprehensible, as mine seemed to be to him. That two nations division thing again. Joanne won a seven foot tall cardboard cut-out of Brad Keselowski who, like many NASCAR drivers, has a name that's a struggle to say and a bugger to spell. Brad would have cost us 1000 dollars to fly home, so he was adopted by Kyle and Julie, and was last seen lying in state in the back of their SUV with New York plates, accompanied by the Coors beer cooler we'd won as well, but which we swapped for a NASCAR blanket. The Holiday Inn, Concord, was a whole lot more fun than the Chichester bed and breakfast we'd stayed in the last time we went to Goodwood. Falling into the American way of life worryingly easily, we didn't even bother to walk the 30 minutes to the speedway but caught the bus instead, sitting with a couple who had driven 17 hours nonstop from their home in northern Indiana, and a retired couple who'd driven from California – which, Mediterranean ferries and scary jihadi risk apart, would be equivalent to me driving to watch Jason Plato in a BTCC race in Cairo instead of Knockhill. Our arrival at the speedway was greeted by a highwire act performed by a Mark and Lijana Wallenda, who set off from opposite ends and crossed in the middle; we could barely watch. High wire angst isn't often an issue at Mallory Park.

The Star-Spangled Banner followed. In England many of us, me included, are a bit sneery and feel post-colonial guilt at overt displays of nationalism because, to postmodern smartarses like us, it can all seem quaint to the point of embarrassment. It's like buying those Battle of Britain prints from the small ads in the *Express*, it's all a bit too Brexit and Vera Lynn for me. But patriotism feels different in North Carolina and I wasn't discomfited when everybody stood and yes, I'll even admit to a lump in my throat, so humbling did it feel to be surrounded by good people with such deep and genuine love for the Land of the Free. But now that I'm a sneery hack writing about it back home in the Land of the Cynical, all I can hear is Noel Coward saying "Strange how potent cheap music is." But as you were, because back in Charlotte there was more emotion as the famous words "Gentlemen, start your engines" boomed out of the PA system, and they were spoken jointly by members of the US and UK military, which was a surprise. Did they know we were coming? The sound of 44 cars exploding into life fired up the crowd and, as the racers came by on their pace car laps, the atmosphere was a *Saturday Night Fever* for anyone with petrol in their veins. The opening laps were mesmerising, but within 30 minutes the race became ever more difficult to follow, even with the benefit of big screen, audible commentary, and scoreboard. In road racing you get a respite of a minute or so until the cars appear at your corner again but at NASCAR the racing is just relentless. I tracked the top six, and my neck ache lasted until Sunday night, but the rest were just a multi-coloured blur. And yet, the more I watched, the more I understood how much trust each driver had to place in the others as they ran inches apart at 200mph (320km/h). And, in contrast to road racing, where overtaking is often over in the blink of an eye as one driver outbrakes the other, here the overtaking could take over a minute. You'd see one car spear down low and dirty before running high into the next turn, and then just c..r..e..e..p by the other guy. It is connoisseur stuff for the seasoned race fan, but, because you hold your breath for the duration, you are near blackout by the time it's all over, and you need to be revived by yet more margarita. And it's all so nerve jangling because you know the wreckage from a misjudged overtake wouldn't hit the ground until the Georgia state line.

But it wasn't all thrill-a-minute stuff that night in Charlotte. In fact a lot of the race was actually uninterrupted by incident or overtaking, let alone the secretly hoped for fistfight feuding in the pit lane. Three hours of racing, remember, and the middle two hours were not the closest racing I have ever seen. There was the odd engine blow up and spin though, which would bring out the pace car and the crowd would stand up as one, all a-whooping and a-hollering as the yellows were replaced by the greens. Obviously, I neither whooped nor hollered, for I am a middle class Englishman and therefore crippled by self-consciousness. So no Yee-ha's from me y'hear? But the last 20 laps nearly made me break my hollering embargo as I was on my feet throughout when the racing finally exploded into the action we'd come 3000 miles (4800km) to see; right here, right now, the lead was changing constantly and I was buzzing. Fortuitously, there had been a final yellow flag period, attributed (to no-one's great surprise) to some debris on the far side of the track. Call me Mr Cynical Limey, but I believe that caution periods attributable to some hitherto unseen debris are not entirely unknown in races that need livening up. And it certainly worked at Charlotte as the yellows triggered the final round of pitstops – theatre in themselves – and then near anarchy broke out in the final dash to the flag. Any one of six drivers could have won but in the end it was our new cardboard friend, Brad the Unspellable, who finessed the victory and celebrated with tyre burning doughnuts (donuts, if you will). In Formula 1 you get fined for doing this, as behaving like a racing driver is now forbidden, but I suspect you'd be fined if you didn't do it here …

Would I do NASCAR again? Yessir, without a doubt, and, whilst it's like the BTCC in that it has a pantomime cast of heroes and villains, our domestic series would need a massive dose of testosterone before it could even begin to be compared to NASCAR. Sorry, but wheezy little turbo straight-fours don't really cut it, and drivers called Colin and Gordon lack verbal charisma compared to the Dales and the Clints of NASCAR. Who did I rate? I had only seen Juan Pablo Montoya and Danica Patrick race in other disciplines, but neither impressed me much in NASCAR; my tips for the top are Kasey Kahne and Kyle Larson, both of whom showed real speed and aggression on track. But as far as I am concerned they are all bloody heroes, as are the fans who welcomed two ignorant Brits with open arms, and could not have been more helpful or friendly – it was a revelation.

We left Charlotte the next morning and spent the next ten days and 2000 miles (3200km) heading – via the Smoky Mountains and rural Tennessee – to Memphis, the Mississippi Delta and beyond. Walking along Memphis' Beale Street was surreal: rock 'n' roll on every corner, and catfish and hush puppies to eat. Listening to live blues in Clarksdale, home to nearly every blues great you've ever heard of, was my secular equivalent to an audience with the Pope or a pilgrimage to Mecca, and driving down Highway 61 one day and repeating it the next day was wonderful – Highway 61 Revisited made flesh. The Mustang purred along the empty highway between the cotton fields and the Mississippi levee, as we cruised down to Rosedale on an empty highway; no cliché was unspared on this road trip. And the Mustang? The pony car was terrific, cost $30 to fill up, and turned out to be a wonderfully civilised tourer. I didn't open the hood (I'll stop this soon) although my ears quickly established that it wasn't the V8 that 'proper' car guys tell me is compulsory, before reminding me that only pantywaist fags drive a poverty spec V6. Sticks and stones, mate; my effete Mustang still made a creamy V6 snarl when the auto eventually worked out that a little more go was needed and, if I pushed the gas pedal even harder, the thing went as if there was a hellhound on my trail, a real risk when you drive past a certain crossroads on Highway 49; just listen to Robert Johnson to find out why. Everywhere we went it felt as if we were living in a retirement home for old Can-Am cars as my head was constantly turned by the rugga backbeat of a big-block Chevy, but instead of an M8F McLaren, or even a Corvette or Charger, there would be a big old pickup driven by some good ol' boys, lollygagging by at 40mph. I adored it all, especially the accents I heard, none of them more impenetrable than in rural Tennessee, deep in 'happily-married-to-your-cousin' territory. Just sayin,' y'hear? I stopped at a gas station a hell of a long way from anywhere else, and it looked like nothing much had happened here since Eisenhower had been in the White House and gas had been 30 cents a gallon. Just fire up your iPhone, check out Edward Hopper's 1940 painting Gas and you'll be right there. Struggling with the ancient pump, I was rescued by an old lady in work coat and slippers who made even Dolly Parton sound like Her Majesty the Queen – "Honey, y'all gotta persh erp the levver on this permp. Like this, see honey?" We even encountered the statutory swivel-eyed nutjob, and oddly enough this was also in Tennessee. He was articulate, olde-worlde polite, but he was scarily intense too, especially when he told us: "Sir, you and your good lady are living in the End Times. Praise the Lord." It was all the United Nations' fault apparently, Barack Obama was deeply implicated, as was 'The New World Order' and those "('scuse me ma'am') faggot bankers" on Wall Street. With astonishing prescience, the Old Testament had already spelled out this alternative truth. I guess I must have dozed off in Sunday School when we did that bit.

And so there was another vote for The Donald on 8 November, 2016 ...

13
SEASONAL VARIATION

Spring passes, and one remembers one's innocence.
Summer passes, and one remembers one's exuberance.
Autumn passes, one remembers one's reverence.
Winter passes, and one remembers one's perseverance.

Yoko Ono

What you've read so far in this book is a combination of reminiscence and opinion, with the bonus of some gratuitous sniping at targets who have only themselves to blame, but, with a deferential nod towards Mandy Rice Davies, I would say that wouldn't I? It's an age thing too: the older I get the more convinced I am that my opinions are sound, reasonable, and rarely, if ever, wrong. But this chapter is different as it comprises a series of individual reports of motorsport events I attended between early April 2017 and late March 2018. The reportage is not the familiar 'who won what' stuff, as this is only important on the day of the event itself, but if you really need to see the results, then nearly every organising club or event promoter posts them on their website anyway. "Nearly," as some clubs, such as the Vintage Sports Car Club, have websites that are only accessible to paid up members. Wonderful event it may have been, I didn't lose too much sleep worrying about who had won the VSCC's Lakeland Trial. What I most want to achieve in this chapter are two things. The first, and the more important, is to demonstrate the diversity of motorsport in Britain and to prove that the public perception of motorsport as comprising solely what you can watch on TV is mistaken. There is a huge amount of motorsport taking place across the country on every weekend between March and November, but because it attracts no mainstream TV coverage, virtually no press attention (sadly, not even from local newspapers), and precious little coverage on motorsport websites, the existence of such a wealth of activity is largely unknown except to its participants (and the sometimes pitifully few people who make the effort to turn up and watch). I have already talked about the effect of heavy TV coverage on Formula 1 in Chapter 11 ('Supping with the Devil'), but even in the context of club motorsport the ripples can still be felt from the Formula 1 ocean. Quite simply, the impact of TV on sport of any type is now so great that without TV coverage, I suspect that the sport can be regarded by some as being lacking or deficient in some way, and probably not worth making the effort to watch live. But when the sport is televised then, almost regardless of its actual quality, it is deemed to be worth watching from trackside as well as from sofa. In short, TV coverage doesn't just showcase a sport, but it validates and enhances it too and, in some cases, TV comes unhealthily close to actually creating the sport itself. In the case of rallycross, TV was the creator, of course.

The second thing? I want to paint as accurate a portrait as I can of what it was actually like to attend an event, what the best and worst bits were and why, and to find out what sort of people attended – were they old, or young; were they black, brown, or white; rich or poor? I wanted to talk to as many people as possible including racers, team bosses, commentators and journalists, and anybody else whose views I thought might be worth hearing. And whilst I am happy to give a flavour of the event, about which cars looked or sounded best, which race thrilled and which bored silly, or about which driver could hold the longest and most elegant slide, or about the history of a car or driver, I am absolutely not writing race reports in the traditional sense. So if granularity is your thing, and you really, really, need to know who won the Historic Formula Ford race at Cadwell, who set the fastest lap in the restart of Race 17 at the Silverstone Classic, or who was on pole for the BTCC race at Croft then you'll need to look elsewhere. Whilst I am far from the first to do this style of reportage, it's now far rarer than it used to be to read a report that describes the atmosphere, the touch and feel of an event, as well as the nuts and bolts of fastest laps, poles, and podiums. Even rereading stuff such as reports of Seventies race meetings in *Autosport* can now provoke more questions than it can provide answers. I am looking at the copy from 19 July, 1973 (kept only because it contains the report of Peter Revson's victory at the British Grand Prix, which I watched at Chapel), and in the back pages there is the usual series of race reports from club meetings at places like Croft, Cadwell, Lydden, and Llandow. They are far more detailed than their modern counterparts, and are printed in a tiny font to create the space to relay the fact that at Llandow "Chris Meek had non-started the Princess Ita Pantera which should have been on pole" and that at the foot of the Mountain at Cadwell the heavy rain had created a lake "3½ inch (9cm) deep" (I love the ½ inch (1.2cm) by the way), and that "the day had a morning after feel about it." But I am still left wondering what sort of people attended, did they all wear flares, smoke Rothmans? Were cheesecloth shirts much in evidence? And in what vehicles had they driven to the circuit? Any nostalgic TV drama such as *Heartbeat* or *Life on Mars* that tries to evoke the authentic Seventies feel will be suspiciously full of gleamingly restored Mexicos and Capris, Marinas and Minis, but the grim reality was that you'd see far more moribund 20-year-old cars back then than you would now, in an era of cheap PCP finance, when just about anybody can afford a new Golf or Audi A4. Back in the Seventies you might admire the new 3-litre Capri and Alfa Giulietta parked in the paddock, but look around the spectator car park some more, and you would soon find some ghastly little Berkeley two-stroke parked next to a distressed TR3 and a rusting Morris Oxford. And only if you were really lucky would you see the yellow Elan or the E-Type drophead that the nostalgia industry might have convinced you were near ubiquitous in 1973.

Something happened to the British psyche during the Nineties that resulted in the nation preferring to look back rather than looking forward. I don't know if pre-millennial angst was the cause, or maybe it was the rich seam of premature rock star deaths to mine, or the tsunami of emotion triggered by Princess Diana's death when English upper lips stopped being stiff and started to wobble, and in 2017 they are wobbling still. At some point between 1992 and 1999 the nation decided to forget all that optimistic, white-heat-of-technology stuff that had kept our eyes focussed on the future in the Sixties, and we became instead besotted by the past, or at least by our selective memories of it. In his novel *The Sense of an Ending* Julian Barnes wrote: "... all our past just gets transferred into well-honed anecdote" and who am I to disagree? In previous chapters I am sure I have been guilty of allowing my own memory to become the treacherous companion that fogs truth, and that's why, just this once, I want to tell you just how it was, rather than how I have chosen to remember it.

My plan was to achieve spontaneity by having no real plan at all; whilst some major events such as the Silverstone Classic were booked months in advance, I only decided to attend many others a week or so before, and sometimes much less than that. Exceptionally, I only committed to attend a couple of events late in the morning of the day they actually took place. My choice of interviewee was entirely random, and whilst I asked the same preliminary questions to almost everybody, others only occurred to me during our conversation. All interviews were taped (on the analogue Philips Dictaphone I stole from work the day I retired), all the extracts from conversations are quoted more or less verbatim and none were pre-vetted by the subject before publication. My biggest objective was to highlight the sensations of experiencing real events as they took place around me, interpreting what I saw, deciding for myself what were the highlights and lowlights, and doing all of this in the open air with the wind, sun, or rain on my face and using each of my senses to experience something actually, in real time and in real places. This was all real-world stuff, neither scripted nor planned, and resolutely analogue and organic.

You can only get an impression of what races were really like to attend from relatively few journalists, and even fewer who are still actively writing. *Autosport*'s Seventies' Grand Prix reporter Pete Lyons and its Eighties' touring car reporter Joe Saward are two obvious examples of writers who didn't just tell you who won, but what it was really like to be at Monza or Brno. *Motor Sport*'s legendary Denis Jenkinson was also guaranteed to provide the reader with a very personal take on a Grand Prix weekend and, whilst his account would often be over-opinionated, unfairly biased, and a triumph of subjectivity over rationality, even decades later his reports are still a joy to reread as you can almost smell the campfires at Watkins Glen and hear the tifosi baying for a Ferrari triumph from trackside at the Parabolica. Of contemporary motorsport journalists only a very few really stand out in their ability to convey the mood music of an event and not just its nuts and bolts, and they include Sam Posey and Simon Arron. American Posey is very much the Renaissance man, not only a successful race driver but also an architect, broadcaster, painter, writer and, yes really, a leading authority on model trains. This is what he says about Le Mans: "... when you have experienced a classic Le Mans evening, you will remember it always ... that marvellous northern European light, the light of Monet, the light of Gothic cathedrals, is one of the few things that is constant in a race that is perpetually reinventing itself." Simon Arron epitomises the enthusiast turned journalist, and, despite having reported on Grands Prix for *Motoring News* for many years, he still writes in *Motor Sport* about grass track racing and club bike racing with just the same affection and knowledge as he applied to describing the driver who answers (if you're lucky, it isn't guaranteed) to the name of Kimi Räikkönen. Arron's description of the charmless, but bafflingly popular Finn reads: "... lawnmower raspberry trifle Trojan T101 watercress Dijon mustard double dip recession pantomime horse Ford Corsair 2000E albatross Skimbleshanks The Railway Cat Mesopotamia binoculars cement mixer Van Der Graaf Generator butterscotch." I couldn't have put it better myself.

It's a high bar then, but this is how it was for me in the 12 months that began in April 2017 ...

HAREWOOD – 9 APRIL 2017

Harewood Hillclimb does not deserve to be damned with faint praise but this wasn't quite the season opener I had planned. I should have been at the Goodwood Members' Meeting a fortnight ago, and I had made the 250-mile trip down to Sussex but, by then, my back was misbehaving so much that I couldn't walk more than a few yards without yelping pathetically. And if I have learned one thing from previous trips to Goodwood it's that whilst most spectators think it's compulsory to watch between Woodcote and Madgwick, by far the best views are at the back of the circuit. But sadly, as even walking from the car park to the circuit entrance would have been agonising, I drove straight back home and then I grumbled for days. But hey-ho, Harewood is not only a damned sight cheaper than Goodwood, the catering is nearly as good and the views over lower Wharfedale make even the South Downs look underwhelming. But you'd maybe expect a Yorkshireman to say that.

You already know from Chapter 3 that I first went to Harewood Speed Hillclimb back in the late Sixties, and unlike many venues, Silverstone for one, it's an even better venue now than it was back then. The original course was extended in the early Nineties to make it the UK's longest mainland hillclimb, and if its 0.9 mile (1.5km) length is much shorter than the venues used by the European Hillclimb championship, it still offers a challenge for drivers of anything from old style Minis to high powered, slicks 'n' wings single-seaters. The British Automobile Racing Club owns the Harewood site and runs all the events that take place here, including today's 'Spring National Hillclimb.'

What used to be two long bus rides and a 30-minute walk from home is now a brisk Sunday morning drive down the route of the old A1 between Boroughbridge and Wetherby. Whilst I was annoyed that my back made driving my Caterham out of the question, the trip along the deserted old trunk road was still lovely, with blackthorn in bloom and lines of daffodils on what used to be the old central reservation. Traffic was nearly non-existent, and

I encountered just a few serious cyclists and a handful of rally-plated classics – a growly old 911, a Triumph 2000 and the inevitable MGBs and Minis – en route to their next time control.

Harewood costs a tenner to get in, the trackside parking is free, and so is the programme. It's well produced and, ignoring the "Alpha Romeo Berlina" clanger (properly an Alfa Romeo 1750 Berlina), it is error free and carries just the right amount of information for a first timer to understand what's going on. There's 148 cars in the hilltop paddock, a queue for bacon sandwiches, 30 minutes before practice runs start, and it was time to talk to some drivers.

I started with Jimmy Johnstone, who had brought his race-prepared 200bhp TR6 the 20-odd miles (32km) from his home near Boroughbridge. "I drove at Harewood at its first meeting in '62 in a Mark I Sprite. The quickest car I have driven here was my Brabham-Buick V8 in '69, when on the old course I did a 42 second run. That was then the quickest ever two-wheel drive time, as the record times back in those days were set by four-wheel drive cars like David Hepworth's (in his Hepworth FF Oldsmobile – Traco V8)." I asked Jimmy what he found so appealing about speed hill climbing. "People are wrong to compare it with circuit racing – it's totally different. I invited Mark Campbell, a friend who races the quickest TR5 in historics, to come and have a go here but he refused, saying he wouldn't be precise enough for the special demands of hillclimbing. I've known some racers who have come here, boasting they'd blow us all off and they've gone home after practice, despondent! There's no such thing as the perfect run, it's always the target though ..." I asked Jimmy about the hardest part of the course: "The Esses! The secret is not to keep trying all the way through them as if you try too hard you just lose time. Quarry (the blind final corner) used to be a problem for me but I cracked it when I half spun my little 1100cc Brabham on oil there and got a class record!" Today might have been Chinese Grand Prix day but this driver wasn't sad to miss it. "Ten years ago," he said "you couldn't drag me away but now it's a farce – DRS and suchlike is a nonsense. But here I'm actually doing something I enjoy; I may be 77 but I still love it."

I had assumed the born to be mild Nissan Leaf was just someone's random transport but as it had race numbers on its flanks I just had to investigate. Its driver was Jeff Allan from Birmingham, and he'd driven the car up last night. "I'm hillclimbing the Leaf to find out just what the best performance an all-electric car can achieve. I love Harewood – and it's great it's got downhill bits too – and I don't mind admitting that Chippy's (the very tight bend named after local hillclimb driver Chippy Stross) is a challenge – I had an off there in my TVR. I've been doing this since 2002; I started with a Cerbera and moved up to a T350. I bought a Tesla as a road car, so I thought I'd try a Leaf on the hills." I mention to Derek that it seems to be compulsory for every serious car guy to sneer at electric cars and I wondered if he'd got many funny looks in the paddock. "Not much at all, actually" he told me, "There is a lot of interest though. I do think electricity is the future, and hydrogen for heavy trucks." And this from a former TVR driver; we live in interesting times ...

Time for some heavy metal, and the brutal looking red Gould GR55B was being driven – for only the second time – by Nicola Menzies from Kincardine who mentions that her car has about 700bhp. Yikes. She loves the challenge of hillclimbing over circuit work – "and it's more exciting." She enjoys Harewood because "… it's longer than most courses, much more open, with longer straights but some tight stuff too." Nicola is another driver who rates both the Esses and Chippies as the hardest corners, and, like every other driver and spectator to whom I spoke, she loves the grassroots friendliness and openness of hillclimbing.

Now for a more traditional hillclimb mount, a Radical PR6 with a supercharged 1400cc engine producing 325bhp. (And if I think about this, it's still a shock to recall that's 60bhp more than the first 911 Turbo, and about the same as Denny Hulme's 1967 championship-winning Repco Brabham.) The Radical is being driven by John Prickett, from Howden in East Yorkshire, and he tells me that it's his second hillclimb car, the first being a Quest Terrapin single-seater. John enthuses about the friendliness of the hillclimb community, both amongst drivers and spectators, and he then looks at the sunlit paddock and, Chinese Grand Prix or not, he wonders why anybody would prefer to stay at home in front of the TV when they could be out in the fresh air at a place such as this.

There's only a couple of hundred cars in the public car park, and, not for the first time, I wonder just why grassroots motorsport is so woefully under-supported. BTCC and F1 may be standing room only, but everything else? Not so much. The previous night I had checked on the PistonHead's website for any late Harewood news, and the solitary post about the event had not attracted even one reply – unlike the multi-page thread about a breakfast meeting in Malton, which I recalled from my last visit mainly comprises scowling lads in Clios and ST Fiestas showing off their cars' accelerative prowess by leaving black lines on the industrial estate's access road. I might applaud the effort made by the Porsche dealer who organises the day, raising a hefty amount for charity but if … ahem … petrolheads happily attend bacon butty fests like this one, or the many car shows that now take place on a muddy field near you every summer, why do they avoid events when really fast cars and drivers are given a mile of uphill tarmac upon which to play? Or is actually showing enthusiasm like mine uncool, even a bit nerdish? Maybe I am what is technically termed a 'beard.'

In my world, hillclimbing offers a real insight into how a car handles, how much acceleration it can muster, and it's possible to monitor car and driver progress on live timing screens, just like on the timing app on your phone that you downloaded in a doomed attempt to prevent you dozing off during the Grand Prix. On Harewood's top straight there's also a speed trap, and nothing better illustrates the gulf between road cars and racers than the speeds reached on the short straight between Farmhouse and Quarry. YouTube warriors may get terribly excitable about the pace of a Civic Type R or a Nissan GT-R around the Nürburgring, but, if they left their bedrooms a little more and watched some real life in 3D instead, they might have to recalibrate their likes and prejudices a little. Because the GT-R would struggle to reach the mid-to-high 80s here, 10mph less than a fast Seven or Westfield (or, shockingly, even a well prepared 205GTi), 20mph slower than a bike engined single-seater, and anything up to 60mph slower than a Gould. And just watch how different cars and drivers tackle the long-left hand Farmhouse Bend; if you want understeer explained, then just watch the scrabbling front wheels of the old-style Cooper S. Oversteer? Then check out the triumph of tyre-smoking, big-power-over-small grip that is a TVR 350i – this musclebound example sporting an oversize 4.8-litre V8. Perfect balance, poetry in motion sort of thing? Try a well driven Force Suzuki or a GWR Raptor. Its slicks, downforce, and featherweight mass allow access to G-forces you'd only get to experience in your badass Nissan GT-R if you crashed it into a wall.

After lunch I drive down the bumpy track to the start line and, as usual, only a handful of spectators have left the hilltop car park to savour the experience, very close up, of cars starting their climb. And whilst an Elise or a Formula Ford Jamun is unlikely to quicken the pulse with its getaway, a big power Impreza or Mitsubishi Evo can become quite the drama queen, as launch control algorithms get all hot and bothered deciding just how to share out 500bhp between the four semi-slick tyres. Many lose time by just bogging down off boost over the first few feet, but one brutally stripped-down Subaru just squats and goes, all four wheels spinning in unison as it bullets down to Clarks corner. Today's a low-key meeting so the big single-seater count is lower than an RAC championship round, but it's nearly six months since I last saw a Gould do its stuff and even this single swallow guarantees the summer to come. The GR55 freewheels silently down to the starting line, slicks encased in plastic covers to repel grit and maintain heat, then the covers are stripped off, the slave battery is plugged in, and there's a brutal flare of burnout revs. On the line, green light, a moment passes, another, in your own time, revs spike and then? And then it's just ... gone, as it's somewhere else in a heartbeat. Today I don't walk down to the exit of Clarks or down to Chippies, but either bend enables you to stand just feet away from a 1200bhp per tonne single-seater (eat your heart out, 1900 kilo Bugatti Veyron fat boy). It's a brutal spectacle, and, if it lacks quite the sledgehammer punch of a Top Fuel dragster, it still feels as though the laws of physics have taken the day off.

I damaged my hearing doing start line marshalling in the Seventies, but today hillclimbs are calmer environments and, now I'm almost a grown up, I can admit that they are both safer and better. I talk to Eddie Kaps, the RACSMA official who monitors sound levels, and I just had to ask him if the Nissan Leaf had even registered on his kit. "Oh yes it did; the ambient level's at 55dB and the Nissan got as high as 60dB. Tyre noise, that's all." The noisiest? "Hmm, some of the single-seaters are 100dB+ and if one of the turbo cars banged and popped within range possibly rather more." God knows what an unsilenced DFV registered – but if engines had been a little more housetrained back in '72 I wouldn't now need to access the subtitles quite as much on TV ...

Verdict

1. Summary – A perfect example of low cost, accessible, inclusive, and absorbing motorsport. A great diversity in competing cars; they span half a century, range from 900cc to nearly 5 litres, feature flat-fours; straight-fours; V, flat, and straight-sixes; and V8s; they include turbocharged, supercharged, and naturally aspirated engines; sequential, H pattern, and

automatic transmissions; and both two and four-wheel drives. And the Leaf of course. The crowd? Predominantly white, middle aged and middle class, but with lots of lads and dads and quite a few mums and daughters. Litter is just about non-existent, and if you have ever been to a race circuit the day after a BTCC meeting you will know exactly why this is worth mentioning.

2. Nature notes – and why not? You need to know that I'm a paid-up tree-hugger who doesn't believe that it's actually compulsory for every motorsport enthusiast to be a climate change denying right-winger with a Jeremy Clarkson habit and a Pringle sweater. Willow warblers and chiff-chaff in the hillside woodland, no swallows yet, but a couple of martins and Harewood's signature red kites checking out the paddock every hour, on the hour.

3. Catering – Deep joy, Harewood is one of the few motorsport venues that understands that it's no longer 1981 and that some people don't actually survive exclusively on a dog-burger and fizzy pop diet. The Harewood catering team (a group of ladies who look as though they might have first met at the local bridge club) produce home cooked lasagne, roast beef, fresh salads, good coffee, and bloody good cakes. I only wish they serviced Croft as well.

4. What could be improved? – The access to the lower part of the course is unpublicised and sometimes its existence seems unknown, even to the car park staff. The first half of the course offers very close up views over a range of corners but far too few people take advantage of this opportunity. Installation of more audible PA and timing screens at the bottom of the hill would make it an even better viewing experience. And, as not everybody might want to drive down the bumpy access track, why not introduce a minibus shuttle service? For a couple of pounds, spectators could get a better idea of the challenges of the course itself and any older or disabled visitors would be spared the steep climb back to the paddock. An honesty box payment with profits to, say, the Yorkshire Air Ambulance – and I won't even claim my usual consultancy fee …

5. Website – Harewood has a dedicated website and it's a model of good practice. Results are archived, there's decent history and gallery sections and, best of all, the full entry list of each event is posted up to a week before the event takes place.

CROFT – 30 APRIL 2017

Today I really should have been at Donington for its Historic Festival. It has disappointed in recent years because its bizarre timetabling meant it felt like a weekend race meeting stretched over three days, but this year common sense had broken out. It would now be possible to watch a full day's racing as, unlike in previous years, I wouldn't have had to endure interminable practice for old Jaguars and the like before – at closer to 6pm than 5 – I'd get to enjoy the sight and sound of a grid full of Chevron B8s, GT40s and Lola T70s. But a poor weather forecast and my ongoing back problems meant it would be Croft instead, just 30 minutes up the road from home. But I was still grumbling to myself that the two or three miles (3-4km) I would normally walk at Donington would have been reduced to some walking stick enabled forays of 100 yards (91m); sometimes it's not only Tesla drivers who can suffer from range anxiety. If not quite to the extent that this Caterham driver does in the North West Highlands ...

It's nearly half a century since I first went to Croft as a sixth form slacker and I have missed few meetings since the circuit's renaissance in '96, after a 15-year hiatus when rallycross had been the only show in town. Whilst journalists from pint-sized Home Counties can get cringingly 'Ee Bah Gum' about the fact that Croft is in Yorkshire, that is only just true as the circuit's real character, most of its crowd and many of its regular competitors come from Teesside, Durham, Newcastle, or Darlington. Croft lies only a couple of miles south of the Durham border, but it is nearly as far from Sheffield as Bristol is from London and, as the North Sea is only 20 miles away, when there's a gusty breeze from the east, Croft can be "colder than a well digger's ass," in Tom Waits' words.

Today's meeting was firmly located on the left-hand side of the keyboard, with only the Northern Saloons and Sports car series round hitting the high notes with a full grid but that alone would make it worth sitting through the sparse grids of Clubmans, Clios, and 2CVs. The latter's 18 car grid would normally have exceeded the critical mass of cars needed to make a race watchable, but today it was only half of what was needed for the 2-hour Endurance race, its title presumably meant to apply to everybody present other than the drivers. But that's okay, motorsport at this level is more about those who do rather than those never-weres who just sit and watch, your correspondent included.

TS Eliot was right when he termed April "the cruellest month" as there had been frequent night frosts and edgy northerly winds, and I wasn't too surprised to notice that the beech trees were still not in leaf as I drove round to the season ticket holders' parking area next to the chicane. My mood was good though, as, for the first time in almost a year, I hadn't wasted time explaining to the security staff, yet again, that actually (no, listen please), yes, I really was entitled to park in the place that the circuit website had assured me was mine to use. Given Croft's fall from grace with many National championships, trackside parking remains the only reason to spend the £145 on a season pass, just £10 less than a season pass for both Cadwell and Snetterton. Most drivers who haven't raced at Croft before seem to adore the circuit, or at least tell the commentary team that they do, but so many teams and drivers stay away, apparently believing that Croft is somewhere near the Orkneys rather than a few minutes from the A1, a couple of hours north of Donington. But the circuit, which used to call itself Croft Autodrome, has had its glory days – from Surtees, McLaren, and Hulme in big banger sports racers in the Sixties, to the wonderful years of Formula 3 and GT meetings in the late Nineties and the early part of the Noughties. Back then, seeing a McLaren F1 GTR in John Nielsen's hands, or Sergio Perez, Sato, or Button in a Dallara F3 car was always special, and made even more so when it was almost in my own back yard. Crikey, I even saw Danica Patrick race here in '99, during that era of weird looking Formula Ford cars that looked wider than the Formula 1 cars of the time. I saw a very young Kimi Räikkönen win at Croft in a winter Formula Renault series race, and a couple of years later Lewis Hamilton did the same thing, taking his first victory outside karts. Bet he hasn't been back since though, but I do wonder what lap time his Mercedes WO8 EQ Power + would do here – low-to-mid-50 seconds? Snappy title for a Formula 1 car by the way. But at least the noise of the hybrid V6 wouldn't upset the neighbours, unlike the noise the rorty little Dallaras made, which ended up being loud enough to be heard in the High Court. But the 60-strong field of Lotus, Brabham, and Tecno Formula 3 cars back in 1970 didn't seem to upset anybody in those more tolerant times, even though those screaming little 1-litre racers were audible at my sister's pub six miles away. Formula 3 has never reached quite those heights again, not since that wandering band of racer brothers gypsied their way around Europe on a shoestring, racing at Chimay or Karlskoga one week, and Cadwell or La Châtre the next. 'Sic transit gloria mundi' – I believe they speak of little else in Dalton-on-Tees – 'all worldly things must pass.'

There must be, gosh, almost as many spectators as there were for the last Grand Prix in Baku, so getting on for three figures, and the familiar faces of the regulars wave to me as I park up. Over the last decade we've spent hours chewing the fat between races about who looked quick in qualifying, whether that guy with the Cayman will do better or worse than he did last year in his CSR Seven with the paddle shift, and if anybody knew why the last circuit manager left so abruptly, or so we had heard. It's worryingly close to *Last of the Summer Wine* territory, but the slightly unsettling thing is that only a couple of us actually know each other by name. It was like that at school too, where Christian name usage was an informality too far, or maybe it connoted an intimacy that was too girly? There's a doctorate's worth of sociological research here and tell me this, do we have tongue-tied counterparts at the Stadium of Light, Lords, or Goodison Park, happier to share a game than a name?

Today's programme cost £3 and echoes the same format that was already looking tired in the early Seventies. There's a circuit map, a bit of text about the championships competing today, the event timetable, some tedious guff about which points win prizes, and an entry list. Little about class lap records, nothing about forthcoming events, and, brief description of flag signals apart, very little to make a newcomer feel either well informed or welcome. It must feel like a private members' club to the car mad kid who is experiencing his first hit of live motorsport. Two typos only, "Westfiled" and "Caymen," and even a pedant like me will let the copywriter off with a caution for that, unlike the mandatory custodial sentence that should apply to "Marshall" and "Donnington."

The meeting's format entry is another echo of the Seventies, but this time in a better way, as today is a rare example of cars and karts on the same bill, and, as somebody who once scared himself silly in a 250 Kart in the wet, I was looking forward to watching just how fast those buzzing little Jade Hondas and Anderson KTMs would go. The answer was about a second a lap quicker than Colin Turkington's BTCC BMW 1 Series, but on a budget that wouldn't have kept the touring car crew in rear view mirrors. Karts might lack the heft of a touring car but their speed through Hawthorn's long radius and the chicane that follows is almost frightening, with drivers' hands constantly at work to check the twitches of oversteer that punctuate the many bumps on the right hander. Then it's the who-blinks-first showdown into the chicane itself before the karts disappear down towards Tower, where more overtaking takes place than anywhere else on the circuit. I've watched many races down there, but not for over a decade as, bless them, the RACSMA decided that it was too dangerous to do so. It left me wondering about the story of the tree falling down in the forest and if there is nobody there to hear it does it still make a sound? There's an echo of this, possibly a silent one, when you're watching at the Chicane, Clervaux, or Hawthorn, and you're sure the outbraking move is shaping up for Tower but you don't know until the next lap and what if the guy who was overtaken gets his place back out of sight at Barcroft? Did it happen at all?

The commentator, David Smales, sounds like a familiar voice from local radio, but that's not a criticism, it just reflects his familiarity with his own patch and if his style is more conversational than rapid fire that just reflects the fact that a 20 minute race for a dozen identical Clios will rarely trouble anybody's adrenalin gland over much. There's the scurry down to the first bend on lap one, some elbows out aggression through the next couple of corners and then, just like far too many Grands Prix, it descends into a second apart high-speed convoy for the rest of the race. It lasts for 20 minutes but felt rather longer. Clubman cars next and whilst the race is no closer, when cars are this absurdly fast, the speed alone compensates for the lack of wheel to wheel stuff. Clubman racing has nearly always been like this, even in the days when my old race programmes tell me I was watching Harvey Postlethwaite and Patrick Head taking their baby steps towards Formula 1. The cars lap in the low 1 minute 22 seconds and only a pukka single-seater will corner quicker; I remember watching a Clubman's car rocket through Cadwell's crazily fast Coppice last season at an approach speed of over 130mph, not too shabby for a car powered by the pushrod engine that first saw life in Mark I Cortinas. First time winner, James Clarke, punches in lap after lap of searingly quick times, correcting slides before I even register them and winning at a canter. He is 17 today, a year younger than I was when I failed, time and again, to master even the reputedly idiot proof gearchange of that bloody Triumph Herald.

David Smales doesn't need to feign excitement for the Northern Saloons and Sports car races, not when there's a 30 car grid of such gloriously diverse cars. What a contrast to the grey porridge conformity of most spec formulae this series is; there are cars from 1-litre to four, turbocharged and normally-aspirated, there's bike-engined screamer Westfields, an ASBO-loud Metro Turbo, a 205T16 tribute act, Andrew Morrison's World Touring Car specification Seat Leon, more BMW M3s than you can shake a stick at, and a host of singleton entries including a French refugee in the form of a Mégane V6 Trophy. It might look like a Manga comic rendition of a touring car racer but its sequential box down shifts into Clervaux are soul stirring, almost musical. Mr Commentator Smales is kept busy talking this race but, there being no nit too small for me to pick, why does the name of every single car smaller than a BMW 3 Series have to be prefaced by the word 'little'?

Unusually, the NSSC race wasn't very closely fought, but Mike Cutt's red mist recovery drive in his M3 from a stalled start was spectacular until he was overtaken by his own rear wheel and had to Reliant Robin his way to safety behind the Armco. And what a rare pleasure to be able both to watch and to listen to the differences between front, rear and mid-engined cars exhibiting such a range of sounds and cornering style. Why has the racing world decided that racers and public alike prefer the stifling conformity of identikit cars in single make series?

I stayed for only the first few minutes of the 2CV Enduro, but long enough to be reminded that whilst some may sneer at 600cc two-pot racers on rubber band tyres, not only does a phalanx of 2CVs create a spooky echo of the sound of the Halifaxes and Lancasters that once were based here, but the lap times were comparable with some of the track day tyros I have seen who, just like me back in '97, had a fast car but a slower brain. I'd pay to watch a race prepared 2CV hunt down a Boxster, or harry an RS Focus, or an Audi S3, wouldn't you?

Verdict

1. Summary – Club racing is often poorly publicised, under reported, and poorly attended in spite of the fact that it offers accessible motor racing to drivers and spectators alike. Little effort is made on local TV, radio, or newspapers to preview or to report on Croft club race meetings, even though every Hebden Hedgehogs cricket match will be reported, over and over again. Poor PR by BARC, media aversion to motorsport, or the belief by local media that motorsport begins and ends with either Formula 1 and/or the sexy local lass doing well in Autograss. It's a combination of those factors I suspect, but the near glee with which the local press reported Croft's court cases, about noise related nuisance and planning consent issues, suggests there's even more prejudice than there is apathy. Some might say that it's strange that those locals who professed to be traumatised by the distant noise of silenced race cars were apparently unaffected by the proximity of the East Coast Main Line, the busy A167, and the flight path to the Durham Tees Valley Airport (snappy title eh?). But for those who do turn up to Croft, there's the freedom to watch close racing from a range of different viewpoints and to inspect cars and talk to drivers in both the pit garages and paddock. Croft Clubbies are a Good Day Out, and I remain bemused why BTCC racing at Croft might attract 20,000 people but we never see them again until the series' next visit. Are they all slumped in front of their 50-inch TVs watching Plato and Turkington exchange insults and paint at the next round of the BTCC panto? Are they kidding themselves they're watching motor racing when all they're actually doing is watching telly in their front room?

2. Nature notes – Arrive early enough and you'll see roe deer roaming over the far side of circuit. But today it's the swallows that beguile, jinking low next to Croft's many small copses to catch hawthorn flies. An early cabbage white butterfly is busy on the dandelions, and warblers and skylarks soundtrack the day, interrupted by show-off rooks and jackdaws. There's a view of the Pennines to the west and the North York Moors to the south east from the freshly mown grass banks and there's little litter, unlike after a BTCC round when the place looks like a

bloody landfill site. Yes, I do plead guilty of sniping at touring cars and I accept that I am a serial offender with 100 similar offences to be taken into consideration. Still, BTCC and criminality haven't been exactly strangers to each other at some times in the past. Damn, that's 101 ...

3. Catering – The good news is that at least we can give thanks to the circuit for getting rid of the last lot, whose noisome speciality was pommes frites a la Pollokshields. Overpriced, tepid, overcooked, cynically dreadful chips accompanied by burgers with absurdly upbeat names and tasting of damp trainer, and not even one of your own. But it could still be 1975, just like most other race circuits I assume, it is with caterers serving up the same greasy fare of the burgers and bacon, donuts and chicken nuggets we ate when Harold Wilson was in Number Ten and drink driving was compulsory. Is it what we want, or do we get what we're given, put up and shut up? The hot chocolate I'd bought at a winter rallycross meeting for – £3 was it? – came in a small Styrofoam cup, wasn't even warm, let alone hot, and comprised an emetic, unidentifiable dark coloured liquid tasting so toxic I spat out the first mouthful. The coffee they gave me instead was just about recognisable as such, but you'd never see its like on the High Street at Starbucks, or even at a motorway services. In 2017 most of us grab a sandwich from Marks and Sparks, Pret a Manger, or Greggs; we get a latte from Costa, or buy a cappuccino from Starbucks or Caffé Nero. Is it really too much to expect something comparable at the race circuit where we spend a long day?

4. What could be improved? – Unlike Harewood, which BARC manage beautifully, on a bad day Croft can feel like meeting the country bumpkin cousin with learning difficulties. Its regular staff are invariably friendly and helpful, but there seems to be a high turnover of security staff, leading to what I will euphemistically call "misunderstandings" on parking, access, and just about everything else.

The PA system, which has often struggled to be heard above the wind, was instead turned up to 11 today, and was probably more audible a mile (1.6km) away than the cars were. I rang the circuit office to ask if they might turn it down, but the recorded message told me it was closed until Monday; it wasn't the end of the world but not for the first time did I wonder how much MotorSport Vision might improve the customer experience if they took the place over. Croft look after the grounds well but, unlike Oulton or Cadwell, the no man's land between spectator enclosure and Armco here is littered with Styrofoam cups, the remains of touring car front splitters, associated debris and, accumulated detritus.

The loss of Tower Bend viewing apart, Croft offers a range of spectating experiences, either from high grassy banking or down 'n' dirty at trackside. The entrance to Clervaux is a wonderful spot to witness just how fast some cars can corner but why does the circuit allow transporters to be parked almost touching the catch fencing, thus denying easy spectating access? It's a part of the paddock, that is understood, but the last circuit manager agreed that it would easily be fixed by painting a white line a few feet back from the fencing. I'm still waiting, and I'll even paint the bloody thing myself ...

Communication? There's a hard core of season ticket regulars; we used to get a free polo shirt and baseball cap, and programmes were also included. Now it's a laminated ticket and the chance of a spat with the guy on the gate about parking. Tesco and Amazon bombard me with information and requests for customer feedback, but only the Silverstone Classic, Santa Pod, and Charlotte Speedway have done the same in the motorsport world. How about emailing your customers now and again, how about inviting them for a pre-season coffee and bacon sandwich, how about fostering a sense of community?

5. Website – BARC has its own Croft website and – if it's not exactly startling – it's okay, as is the main BARC site. But, unlike Harewood, only rarely is the entry list or timetable uploaded on the circuit website. Want to know how to do it better? Just Google Santa Pod …

YORK RACEWAY – 1 MAY 2017

It's 23 years to the day since Ayrton Senna died at Imola (did Jo Siffert's death in '71 still feel so recent in '94?) and it's time to go to the site of yet another World War II airbase. Today it's the former RAF Melbourne, now the York Raceway, and it's located a few miles south east of its more famous neighbour, RAF Elvington. Both bases were home for Handley Page Halifax squadrons and, although Elvington entered the national consciousness when Top Gear's Richard Hammond was seriously injured in his 2006 jet car crash, its real claim to fame is that it's where the wonderful Yorkshire Air Museum is located. As I drove past I could see a Buccaneer parked out on the runway and, nearby, the Victor V Bomber which looks like an escapee from a *Tales To Astonish* pulp magazine. And in the far hangar I knew that 'Friday the 13th,' the Halifax bomber that was lovingly rebuilt by the museum's volunteers, would be silently brooding, ready again to reduce today's visitors to awestruck silence.

It was the Spring Nationals meeting at the strip, catering for everything from the guy with the old Volvo Estate in Run What Yer Brung to the 10,000bhp insanity of the Firestorm Funny Car. As I parked behind the weather-beaten grandstand I heard the signature tune of the sport that, just for one day, can transform a lonely corner of rural England to Orange County, California. What I heard was the deep lunged bellow of a Chevy big-block rat motor erupting into joyous life. I can't help smiling; there may be none of the glamour of Goodwood or Brands today, but with a venue so joyously anarchic, so free of the hi vis jobsworths employed at almost every other venue, who couldn't resist the outlaw chic of a day at the drag strip? The crowd isn't huge but the average age is 20 years younger than at any race meeting, there's lots more women and kids, you can hear East European accents as well as Yorkshire ones, and there are more than a few black and brown faces. Nobody ever seems to comment upon drag racing's cultural diversity, but they should, as this branch of motorsport reflects 21st Century Britain far more than the monochrome demographic of circuit racing.

There's a high tattoo count as well, but who cares? If tatts are good enough for Lewis Hamilton then that's just fine by me. And at least Lewis wouldn't get a bollocking at the Raceway from some pompous guy in a blazer, like he did when he took Roscoe and Coco, his Snapchat starring bulldogs, to a Formula 1 paddock. Dogs seem almost mandatory at the Raceway, with Staffordshire Bull Terriers a favourite and whilst Google tells me they are "energetic and playful," I suspect that might be just a little euphemistic. But I'd love to see somebody try to take Tyson the Staffy to the Goodwood Revival.

I want to talk to Graham Beckwith, who enlivens every meeting with a stream of consciousness commentary on runners, riders, and just about anything else that he thinks is worth sharing. He's funny, hugely well informed, knows everybody and bubbles with enthusiasm. The man on the mic is just bloody relentless as he's talking nearly non-stop from bacon sandwich time to tea time. I wanted to find out what motivated him to take on the task that most of us would screw up in the first minute and discover how he manages to infuse his commentary with a zest that few race circuit commentators can match. The man's got so much whizz, but he does his thing with so much ease – never pass up another laboured Pulp reference. Graham's from Flockton, near Barnsley, which is a good start as people from Barnsley aren't noted for being either self-effacing or burdened with the sort of self-consciousness that crippled your reporter as a young man (not now though, as you can tell from the oxymoron that passes for my dress sense). I hadn't made an appointment, I'd just spoken to the ladies (I use the word advisedly) who were signing on the Run What Yer Brung guys, and not only did they conscript Graham as soon as he arrived, they brought me coffee in, what looked suspiciously like, a china mug. In his dark brown voice Graham told me he'd first become involved with drag racing nearly 50 years ago: "I came to one of the world record attempts at Elvington, when Arnold Sundquist had brought his jet car over from Sweden. And I started commentating when, as a marshal for the Pennine Drag Racing Club I was working over at Aintree for a big drag event. There was a Scots guy, Billy, who was supposed to be the commentator. He wore dayglo green micro shorts, a huge orange sombrero and little else but his commentating style was to say "Will you just look at that?" a lot, because he knew nothing about what he was supposed to be commentating upon and there were dragsters, jet cars, a wheely truck, even a guy driving a bus on two wheels. He asked me to help him out, gave me a mic, I said hello to the 2000 people in the grandstands and that was it, I was away."

I ask Graham about how he can keep up the crowd's interest at an event where literally hundreds of runs are made down the strip, he said "It's sometimes hard for people to grasp the basics of drag racing; at its simplest it's just a straight lane race between two cars when the lights change but the sport has evolved to make it a fairer competition, so with a handicap system a slower car can arrive at the finish at the same time as a much faster one. There's a lot of maths involved ..." So how do you big that up for the first timer here, I asked, "I don't need to, the sport can big itself up. The faster cars are just phenomenal, awesomely powerful, spectacular to look at; image has always been a big thing with drag racing, so the sport can speak for itself even if you don't grasp all the technicalities. You can just enjoy it as a spectacle." I'm interested in just how Graham seems to know every single driver on the strip, not just the boilerplate stuff about their best elapsed time at the last meeting but the anecdotal details that can make listening to him sound more like a confidant than a commentator. "Well, so many drivers are personal friends anyway, and they come and tell me about the new heads they've put on their car, and I know the people who build the cars, even the people who paint them ... drag racing is like a big family." So, I ask, why should the public come and watch the sport? Graham chuckles before saying "It's easy to look like a lairy, big lad out in a supercar on the road but they really get brought down to earth here. When you see some of the cars here that look normal, but which can turn in phenomenal performances on the strip ... they'll blow supercars into the weeds! And top fuellers ... the statistic I most like is that the power needed just to turn the supercharger is twice the power of a Formula 1 car. It's a marginal sport but it's easy to sell any sport that makes that kind of power. And for boy racers, or tuners as I should call them now, this is the best place to test their work. And they are not old farts like us either!"

Graham becomes sombre as he remembers the fatal accident that occurred here in 2011, when Kasey Dixon-Granger's Cortina crashed at 130mph (210km/h). He reminds me that drag racing is still one of the safest motor sports in the world, and that, even in the rarefied world of 11,000bhp Funny Cars, "accidents are big ones, but the driver walks away. Safety is paramount for us." It's still remarkable to see how many of the cars competing today commemorate Kasey, and not in the mawkish or flamboyant way that is so often found in 'civilian' life but quietly and respectfully. They're tough people in this community, but their hearts are definitely in the right place.

Before leaving Graham to fire up his mic, he smilingly recalls his late friend Sammy Miller, the American driver whose rocket powered dragster's 3.62 second, 382mph (615km/h) quarter-mile at Santa Pod in 1979 remains unbeaten. "He was an honorary Yorkshireman too, loved his Yorkshire puddings did Sammy." This was my cue to talk to Roger Goring from Rotherham. He looks and sounds normal, but this guy's race car doesn't have an over-boosted four-pot turbo or even a Hemi V8, but a jet engine which came from a Northrop F5 Strike Fighter. Roger drives Firestorm, which looks like a Mustang would after you've drunk a 20oz (0.6ltr) bottle of Jack Daniels Old No.7. So why not a normal dragster Roger? Silence. "Umm ... good question ... okay ... conventional dragsters, especially top fuel or alcohol cars, come with their own problems and jet cars are a cheaper way of going very, very fast." It turns out that Roger started on two wheels, building and tuning bike engines, and he also crewed for another driver's jet car until he had a go himself and said to himself "Yep that's me, I want one of those." As you would, but only if you were more like Roger and less like me ...

The Mustang is a new car but in his last jet car he was doing over 15 meetings a year and I can testify that if you were within 200 metres of the thing, you'd feel a great rolling wave of heat wash over you, the air would reek of jet fuel and the noise was probably audible in the next county and I could not have loved it more. Roger runs over the full quarter-mile on some tracks but half that on the bumpier tracks like this one and he tells me that Firestorm has run its best quarter at 5.92 seconds and 247mph (400km/h). So how does that feel Roger? "Well, a good Ferrari will go 0-60 in, I don't know, three and a half seconds? I'm doing 200mph (320km/h) by then ... I don't actually black out but we're pulling 3.5G on acceleration and it feels absolutely unbelievable." Roger tells me, in a voice that he might use to talk about a quiet round of golf, that he crashed his last car at nearly 250mph (400km/h) and walked away without a scratch. We talk about aerodynamics, which are rather more relevant to jet dragsters than the daft diffuser on the back of my Focus. Roger doesn't get any wind tunnel time but he says "I have a friend who works in Formula 1 who has helped me a lot, he's got access to a lot of advice. I also work closely with Hanna Motorsports in the USA, who do have access to wind tunnels and run a similar car to mine. You need to find out about this stuff when you run a jet car ..." I leave Roger to his preparation work with crew chief, Helen, and whilst I don't tell him this, if I meet anybody this year with more of the Right Stuff than he has I will be amazed. Or more enthusiasm, as Roger sounds as excited as any other fan about 1500bhp bikes and 7 second street cars. What a contrast this man is to the studied indifference and perverse insularity that so many people choose to affect in motorsport's higher echelons.

I amble over to watch the rumbling majesty of American Super Stocks and Pro ET, cars that might have started their lives in sleepy Californian suburbs back in '69, but which have now been re-engineered as 800bhp monsters, which deafen onlookers and fog them with tyre smoke from the trademark burnouts that make circuit racers look very lacking in the trouser department. It's showboating, cloud pleasing theatre, and after the 400 cubic inch (6.5ltr) behemoths have smeared the strip with their rolling thunder, the sound hangs in the air for long seconds before silence returns. And I wonder again, as the sound drifts east over the Wolds, does it drift into some forgotten valley where, on still nights, the distant echoes of Merlin and Hercules V12s still resonate?

I watch more runs, smile at the screaming Punto turbo as it melts its front tyres in a pre-stage burn out, admire the urban camo look of the brace of Astras as they post times quicker than a 911, cringe as the Jaguar V12-engined dragster gets into a huge tank slapper on its debut run, and I cough from the thundercloud of diesel smoke pouring out of a Land Rover – yes really, but it's not the same sort of Defender you'd see on the road, not even the Bear Grylls Special Editions, sporting their asinine 'One Life Live It' logos and their virtue signalling stickers. You know the sort. Anyway ... this Land Rover's got an exhaust the size of a factory chimney, big fat tyres, a nose down stance and a 5.9-litre Cummins V8 Diesel. It posts the same time as the original AC Cobra managed, a high 13. And what a contrast the demure Golf R presents, its launch and DSG gear shifts made perfect by algorithm, not technique, and running a startling 12.89 quarter – but thank God the enormous white 'Honey I'm home' American estate car is even quicker, and who wouldn't prefer the bad boy backbeat of a pushrod V8 with enough Detroit muscle to make the front wheels paw the air? That'd get you sacked in Wolfsburg, assuming anybody at Volkswagen is old enough even to remember rear-wheel drive.

Graham's now talking ten to the dozen on the PA, one of the startline marshals looks like Mark Rylance, and the guy in charge down there may have a prosthetic leg but covers more ground in a day than many circuit marshals manage in a season. Have you seen the size of some of those guys? I can talk, the only thing that prevents me getting to be an even fatter bastard is the prospect of not fitting in my slimline Seven …

Time to leave and I can't help noticing the car parked next to me: a matte military green Škoda Fabia, badged 1.8 8v D (ironic, postmodern? Search me), with the driver's door secured by a padlock. And parked in landscape format opposite me, flanked by an Impreza and an Amarok in portrait, is a Chevy Apache 32 Pick-up. It's in the same pale turquoise as my Dinky El Camino was back in '61, and its quad headlights come from the era when double headlights, at least in styling terms, meant a whole lot more than just double the number. The Chevy is just so redolent of tumbleweed junctions somewhere out west, dust devils, ponytailed girls, and moonshine, and my cup overflows when a girl in rockabilly retro denims and headband poses for a selfie in front of the little Chevy. And so I wonder if, out here in the East Riding Panhandle, Western Swing's now officially a thing? Or should that be 'thang,' honey?

Verdict

1. Summary – It's £15 to get in and there's no programme, but it's a full day out and ten minutes' walk around the paddock will tell you everything you need to know. Still in doubt? Just ask, as there's no privacy boards nor security tape nonsense at the strip and I've yet to meet anybody who isn't happy to talk. Action is usually non-stop, with queues of RWYB cars filling in the time between the heavy hitters who are competing formally. Information is instant, from two large screens, on driver reaction time (I'm usually nearly a second, one guy here today is a fifth of that), elapsed time, and terminal speed. The best cars today run high 8s and low 140mph. There's every configuration of car – front, rear, and four-wheel drive – and engines with four, five, six, eight, and twelve cylinders. There's lots of bikes too, even a two-stroke scooter, and I especially loved the '55 Vincent for its smell and its oh so English looks. I can watch cars do burnouts ten feet (3m) away, and, on the south side of the strip, nearest the right-hand lane, I can walk to the eighth mile (0.2km) mark, while muscle cars are getting down to work on the heavy lifting. In summary, a hugely enjoyable day out, free of corporate bullshit and hierarchy, laid back, laissez-faire, and a day's holiday away from CCTV and dash cam obsessed, risk averse, selfie mad, and half-asleep modern Britain.
2. Nature Notes – With this much noise and smoke? You're having a laugh, right? Actually, I did see a rook in the distance, heading towards Pocklington and flying as fast as its wings could carry it …
3. Catering and general facilities – You're not going to get haute cuisine at the strip, but the chips are good and I can buy a latte or an espresso, which is more than I can at many race circuits. Most of the infrastructure is pensioned off Portakabins and sheds but this place is run by volunteers on a shoestring, and they make up for a little roughness around the edges with sheer 'can do' enthusiasm.
4. What could be improved? – The access track can be a nightmare, demanding great care to avoid the Olympic scale potholes and ruts. Which is only to be expected from a runway laid

nearly 80 years ago, but if I were driving a SoCal Lowrider I'd take it steady … That nitpick apart, I wouldn't change a damned thing.

5. Website – Informative, detailed and colourful. The Raceway is also the only venue that bothers to send me an events calendar.

CADWELL PARK – 7 MAY 2017

There is never a bad time to go to Cadwell Park but there isn't a better time than this early morning in May, International Dawn Chorus Day on Radio 4 and an empty road in front of me. There's still a cold wind blowing from the north east, but when even the A1 is garlanded by bluebells and cowslips, and every view over the Vale of York is punctuated by yellow rape fields and freshly minted green hedgerows – it's enough to exorcise the memory of those black dog moods that haunted my December. The British Racing and Sports Car Club was hosting the day's racing, which would feature Mazda MX5s, Porsches, and other single make series supplemented by ancient and modern Sports 2000s and Formula Jedi single-seaters. It's typical modern club racing fare, and though it lacks the wildly modified saloons and sports cars I saw in my early years at Cadwell, there's full grids and the promise of close racing from the single make series and eye-watering speed from the screaming Jedis. This marque started life as a low volume producer of hillclimb specials in the early Eighties but their race series occupies some of the vacant space in UK single-seater racing, now that Formula Renault has effectively ceased as a UK series and Formula 4 (né Formula Ford) has positioned itself as being beyond the budget for club racers. Which is ironic really, as one of Formula Ford's founding principles in 1967 was its affordability, with cars having a price cap of £1000, about £13k at 2017 prices. A Formula 4 Mygale, without engine, is about double that figure and a season's racing will cost well into six figures.

I can never drive through Cadwell's parkland entrance without remembering my first visit here in '75, shortly after starting work as a trainee solicitor (or articled clerk as they were then, so quaintly, called) in Lincoln. I was well used to windswept airfield circuits by then, with Oulton Park the sole country cousin, but Cadwell was not only impossibly pretty, but it also offered a cornucopia of different viewing points, all of them gratifyingly close to the track. Bizarrely, the first car I ever saw at Cadwell was a slick shod and very raucous Datsun Cherry, the inoffensive little hatchback that was ubiquitous in suburbia but not a common sight on track, not even in the strange never-never land of the mid-Seventies. But Cadwell itself hasn't changed much at all since the days of flared trousers, cheesecloth shirts, and rampant inflation; although MotorSport Vision's tenure has improved what marketing wonks call the 'customer experience' immeasurably. Cadwell had been sliding into decay for years under the previous ownership and whilst I miss the shabby chic of the old bridge across the Hall Bends, which led to the most dangerous spectator area I've ever enjoyed, MSV have done the same terrific job here as they have at Oulton and Snetterton, and I'm sure they'll transform Donington too (which they took over only a few weeks before I wrote these words). Jonathan Palmer is a frequent visitor to his circuit portfolio, but it does help to have a helicopter. I saw him in the café last June, busy talking to punters like me, joking with marshals and racers and, at more length, chatting to the catering staff. It's like watching a video presentation on good management practice, and the motorsport community should be thankful for his efforts in transforming basket cases into showcases. The fact that some people still find reason to snipe at MSV, on racing websites especially, is more indicative of tall poppy syndrome (our national ailment), than of actual circuit deficiency.

A big field of MX5s and I already know what might go wrong here – just possibly, just a wild guess. I'm right: within a couple of laps of hectic qualifying, cars entering The Mountain sideways and sliding on to the grass on the exit, and a car slams into the barriers at Charlies, that fiendishly tricky blind entry corner on to the Park Straight. But no real harm done – even if the dents won't polish out without a sledgehammer – and within ten minutes the Lotus Elan clones are demonstrating their Jinnba Ittai responsiveness again. It's still a source of wonder to me that some of the people who think that watching Top Gear makes them car enthusiasts spout the same old drivel about MX5s and hairdressers, as if ownership of a featherweight car with a fizzy twin-cam four was evidence of a shortage of testosterone. I remember interviewing Jonny Leroux, of BookaTrack fame, and his mantra of the 'one tonne rule': the more a car exceeds one tonne in weight, the less suited it is to delivering track day fun. Remember Professor Gordon Murray's words too: "never confuse power to weight with weight to power" which is why the peerless McLaren F1 weighed almost a Caterham's worth less than the McLaren P1 and almost half of the Bugatti Chiron's mass. MX5s are just fine by me then, and prove that budget one make racing can be worth watching if the cars are rear-wheel drive and driven with brio. Three abreast from Mansfield to Hall Bends, a grassy excursion for the guy who blinked first and here's yet another pack of wheel locking Mazdas already, and so it continued for every lap.

But Sports 2000 cars are pukka racers, mid-engined, slippery, and genuinely fast, the Duratec engined cars turning in lap times that would humble a Porsche GT3 and even the near 40-year-old Pinto cars – all 130bhp of them – would embarrass all but the most insanely heated uber-hatch. I talk to John Fletcher, who prepares a Tiga SC 79 for customer Mira Feyerabend to race in the historic class. John's from near Worcester and started his race preparation business in 2016, but I wasn't surprised to hear he was a racer himself before family responsibilities meant an end to his adventures in the Royale RP21, which he once raced in Formula Ford 1600. I ask him if Cadwell has any special set up challenges and was surprised to hear that the set up for the Tiga was broadly the same for all the circuits the series visits; John's aim is to make the car "easy to drive, not too extreme in its handling." He says that drivers do find Cadwell difficult – "not just the undulations but the blind corners too. Our last meeting was at Silverstone so you can imagine the contrast." John comments on the improvements in circuit standards since his own racing days: "I remember when the toilets were just breeze blocks, if you were lucky, and now we've got hot showers, a good restaurant, hardstanding parking – the lot!" I'm curious to know what fee John charges for a weekend meeting, and whilst he'd rather I kept the precise figure to myself, I bet it wouldn't be enough to pay for a day's skinny latte bill for a BTCC team.

Back to the Mountain grandstand and what promised to be a hectic Fiesta race was emasculated by the first ever deployment of Code 60 I had witnessed. A car had crashed at Charlies – again – on lap one and all but two laps of the remainder of the race were run at 60km/h (37mph). The dinky little purple flags denoting Code 60 were easy to miss, unlike the traditional waved yellows which still are supposed to mean 'great danger, slow down, be prepared to stop' but are invariably so widely ignored that the new rule has been introduced. Obviously it works, in the sense that the removal of the crashed car could take place in entirely safe conditions, but so would stopping and restarting the race or (whisper it) waved yellows. At least it would if anybody still took any notice of them. Lots of people have told me since that Code 60 works well, that I'm out of touch, that marshals' safety is paramount, yadda yadda but I don't believe that a process that was originally designed to 'neutralise' an endurance race lasting six hours or more is effective if it reduces a 20 minute race to a 16 minute crawl bookended by four minutes of racing. If I'd paid a few hundred quid to race I am not sure I would be overjoyed to spend most of the race checking my speed was 60km/h (37mph). I assume, post-Brexit, that the more rabid right-wingers will press for Code 36–60km/h in Imperial mph?

There's no dark side to the Jedis at Cadwell as they are the quickest cars to race here since Ayrton Senna's crash at the Mountain in '83 resulted in Formula 3 never returning, except in historic racing, where the pace is a little gentler than the white heat of the Senna/Brundle war. The outright lap record was held by Enrique Mansilla's Ralt RT 3 for more than ten years until a Jedi undercut the Formula 3 time by almost 1.5 seconds, meaning an average speed very close to three figures. Yikes. The race is run at a speed that is almost too fast to take in after the furious-but-not-so-fast Mazdas and Fords, and every single car is airborne at the Mountain. It's a common myth, by the way, that car and bikes take off at the Mountain's peak, actually they're already well airborne by then as there's a slight dip a metre or so before the top which triggers escape velocity. And if you're thinking that, with this degree of obsessive observation, I really should 'get out more' or 'get a life' you're almost certainly right ...

I catch up with Jedi master Lee Morgan, whose laurel leaf garlanded Mark VI has won the race at an average of 96mph (155km/h), and he looks significantly less hot and bothered than your overweight reporter does after some pedestrian track day lappery in a Seven at Cadwell – damn you Morgan, with your youth and your talent ... Lee's from Telford and tells me that his Jedi's 1000cc GSXR bike engine gives a 600bhp per tonne power to weight ratio and that the circuit is ideal for this formula – "It's one of the best tracks we come to all year; it's so tight and twisty but our cars are so small that the racing is really close here. Overtaking's a challenge so when you do make a pass it's a bit more special. The Gooseneck is by far the hardest part, if you're an inch off line you can end up on the grass and the best section is Coppice and Charlies, where we are carrying a lot of speed – I'm doing 121mph

(195km/h) over the start/finish line so I'm probably doing about 130mph (210km/h) into Coppice ..." Lee loves Cadwell (doesn't everybody?) and together with Oulton Park it's his favourite track: "Silverstone National's just point and squirt in a Jedi." Lee's won over 20 times in this Formula, having returned to it after an expensive foray into Formula 3. "Been there (in F3) after winning this championship," he says, "finished fifth out of 15, maybe 20 cars, but my budget meant I couldn't get to the front of the grid, so ..."

Verdict

1. Summary – Cadwell Park is Britain's best circuit to watch club racing as it offers peerless viewing from a huge range of vantage points in beautifully kept parkland. MSV's attention to detail is as well-known as its affinity for red and white kerbing and the circuit staff's welcome and general customer care is exemplary. There is no litter, of any type, anywhere; and you can park where you like, unsupervised by anybody. The construction of the new bridge spanning the track between the straight linking Mansfield and the Mountain and the start/finish straight has improved access, but I am possibly not alone in mourning the loss of the old arrangement, which involved walking across the circuit between races. Much more welcome was the removal of the advertising hoarding that had obscured the view from Mountain entry to the start/finish for nearly 30 years. It cost me £13 for admission and programme, reflecting my official old fart status. The programme was more colourful and much more informative than the Croft programme from a couple of weeks before. Cadwell employs two race commentators, who today included Croft regular David Smales, and they are much more effective than the sum of their parts, keeping up their conversation to good effect during the Code 60 longueurs. There's also the facility for spectators and racers alike to text in comments to the commentary box but, disappointingly, they didn't read out my text saying that Code 60 was "a fucking farce ..."

2. Nature notes – Lapwings and buzzards are visible above Park Straight and skylarks are ubiquitous. Serenaded by wood pigeons and rooks from circuit woodland, which is maintained as a conservation area with no public access. And I fear that I may have 'something in my eye' when I see the memorial cross that commemorates "Jess the Cadwell Cat; Passed Away 2013 Aged 13 Years."

3. Catering – There's a clean, warm café overlooking the circuit and located next to the paddock assembly area. There's ample seating, big screen telly, and no 'no-go' areas. The food is traditional circuit fare, but well prepared and reasonably priced. My £2.50 hot chocolate was just what I needed to stave off the effects of the north easterly wind and was a welcome improvement on the gunk I had been sold at Croft.

4. What could be improved? – I'm struggling here. The only thing that could improve Cadwell would be to attract some higher profile championships here – F3 or F4 would be something to savour. BTCC? No thanks, as they'd only find something to complain about, and some might say that allowing the BTCC barmy army to come to Cadwell would be like giving a pig a strawberry.

5. Website – There's an MSV site which includes portals for each circuit and links to series organisers. Not flashy, no extra bells and whistles but entirely fit for purpose.

YORK AUTOGRASS – 14 MAY 2017

I last went to Holyhead sometime in the Nineties and, whilst waiting for the ferry, I solved the mystery that had been giving me sleepless nights and Joanne the loss of the will to live – she doesn't quite share my enthusiasm about all matters automotive. The insomnia inducing enigma was to establish where all the Ford Cortinas had gone to die. The Sierra superseded the Cortina in '82 but the mystery of the ageing Cortinas was solved when I saw that Anglesey was full of Mark III, IV and V Cortinas, as often as not in fading beige or gold. The once ubiquitous Cortina was now the default choice for every taxi driving Geraint and Huw. I was reminded of the Cortina's graveyard when I dropped in to the York Autograss track on a breezy afternoon, and realised that Autograss was the last stop before oblivion for many Nissan Micras, the puppy fat K11 model which was made in the Nineties and which has become a rare sight on the road.

Shamefully, I'd dismissed Autograss as, at best, a marginal and low budget category until I saw a round of the National Championship in 2016 and was overwhelmed at just how spectacular it was. York's meeting was very low profile, but it still had the holy trinity of factors needed to make any motorsport event worth watching – speed, poor grip, and lots of overtaking.

Autograss is simple; there's up to eight cars lined up abreast and they race over four laps, sometimes more, around an unsurfaced oval track located, as you'd expect, in a field. The track, at least in dry weather, is hard packed but once off the inside line, the surface becomes ever looser. Think of the marbles that litter the margins of a Formula 1 track and then multiply the debris a hundredfold and you're getting there. Cars usually race in one gear only and, except in the quickest classes, the drivers rarely trouble the brake pedal except to avoid a collision. Autograss caters from everything from pensioned off, stripped down Micras and Corsas to highly modified cars with a lot more power, delivered from engines like the old favourite 16V Vauxhall Redtop to, in the case of one special at York, a pukka Lotus twin-cam. The fastest cars look like a Funny Car would if it was based on a Sixties Mini Pickup; they are rear-wheel drive, softly sprung, and pull wheelies at even the hint of an opportunity. If Formula 1 is designer sushi, then Autograss is pie 'n' chips with lots of sauce on a Saturday night. And it is all the better for it.

The Micra races aren't fast, but they are close and entertaining, with frequent overtaking, monumental slides and more than the odd exchange of paint when fighting for a place. But it's the high-power, rear-wheel drive cars that can reduce a first timer to dropped-jaw delight and temporary loss of speech. The sheer grunt the cars deploy is mesmerising, with big speed obtainable on even the toytown straights, but the real party piece is the astonishing amount of oversteering high jinks in the corners. And I am not talking about the cliché of the 'dab of oppo,' which even the most timid trackday tyro boasts about, but massive, near 90 degree, bouncing-off-the-lock-stops, navigating-through-the-side-window, simply massive slides. But if the driver made the mistake of applying insufficient power the result was terminal, juddering, and deeply humiliating understeer. And it didn't stop until the car came to a halt, perhaps 20 metres away from the line it had been taking before the plot was lost.

Verdict

1. Summary – Just like drag racing, Autograss appeals to a far wider demographic than traditional circuit racing. At York there were lots of women and kids, and that was just in the driving seats of the cars taking part. It's another cliché, but today was genuinely 'a day out for all the family,' dogs were welcome (chocolate Labrador the dog of the day), there was an open paddock, it was only eight quid to get in and there was plenty of trackside parking. It's nearly half a century since I used to marshal at High Eggborough Autocross, but at York it felt as though very little had changed since those laid-back days. It was informal, very friendly, the PA worked most of the time, nobody was supervising my parking, and there was plenty of bumping and grinding on track – what's not to like?
2. Catering – £2.50 got me an ice-cold coke (the Real Thing too) and a hot dog, which was bad for me in every possible way; I enjoyed it hugely, obviously. Last time I was down Goodwood way, the down payment on a glass of champagne was more than my dinner at York.
3. Nature notes – as the track is right next to the busy A59 this was never going to be a long report. I saw some racing pigeons, and there were definitely trees of some sort in the distance.
4. What could be improved? – For this price, nothing.
5. Website – "York Autograss – More Than Just Another Grassin' Site." It's obviously run by volunteers, but I have seen far less informative websites run by major national clubs. Good effort.

HAREWOOD VSCC – 3 JUNE 2017

Vintage Sports Car Club events take place in an alternative reality far removed from the slings and arrows of what passes for normal life in 2017. Nearly a year ago the majority of the UK electorate, or at least those who could be arsed to cast a vote in the referendum, had decided to press the self-destruct button and leave the EU. A few months later, the Rust Belt vote outweighed the tech vote and elected a reality TV star President, with the attention span of an ant and the statesmanship of a pit bull. And now we have a general election in less than a week's time, and God alone knows why. But I can report today that Harewood is not consumed by election fever, and why would it be when cars like the 90-year-old Frazer Nash Supersport have already seen 17 different prime ministers leave Number 10, Downing Street? VSCC meetings attract the most eclectic machinery and the most eccentric owners you will find in any branch of UK motorsport: there's a high incidence of pink trousers and distressed Barbours, there are drivers with extraordinary names such as Al Frayling Cork and Amber McHamish, and there are cars with 10-litre aero engines, supercharged straight-eights and 4-litre fours. There's even a Thai bride or two here today, with the inevitably middle-aged and overweight husband in rather too close attendance. These lopsided alliances must make sense to the participants, even though I feel like washing my hands if I ever think about the details.

As I wander into the paddock I see the unmistakeable shape of a Lotus Six, alloy panels gleaming in the Wharfedale sun and I talk to its driver, David Cranage from Stratford-upon-Avon. Having owned Sevens for 20 years and coveted them for 30 years before that, I obviously have an unerring eye for the marque, so unerring that the car I had so confidently identified as a Six turns out to be a Series 1 Seven. I blame the narrow front track for my mistake as David politely corrects me; like everybody in VSCC world, David is the epitome of politeness. He has owned the Seven for three years and tells me it was built in 1959 at Cheshunt, being one of about 200 Series 1 Sevens made by Lotus, and the car was sold initially to a dealer called Connaught Cars, "… but it can't be the Connaught Grand Prix team as they went bankrupt in 1957 … maybe somebody bought them?" David loves early Lotuses. "In fact," he says, "I just love cars from that postwar period up until 1960. When the engine's in the front they are much more interesting, but I did like some early rear engine cars like Coopers and Lotus 18s." The Seven was built as a race car "… so the gearing's a bit wrong for hill climbing" and it has "… a 1460cc FWB Coventry Climax engine with probably 115-120bhp and, as you know, with Chapman it was all about lightness." It turns out that David has never even seen Harewood before, but even before driving the hill he is hugely enthusiastic about "… the fabulous view; it's fantastic, amazing, probably the best hillclimb in Britain." And these words make this Yorkshireman really rather proud. Before being lured away by the angry, insistent whap, whap of a supercharged six being warmed up, I ask David why people should come to a VSCC meeting instead of watching BTCC or F1 on the TV and he smiles, "because it's real, because you can get close to the cars, talk to the drivers, there's no status getting in the way like there is in Formula 1 – it's very informal and more like motorsport used to be in the Sixties and early Seventies. When I first went to Silverstone I remember standing next to Jackie Stewart and Graham Hill – you could talk to people then." This is my cue to mention that I had interviewed Sir Jackie for the Lotus Seven Club's *Low Flying* magazine just ten days earlier and yes, of course I was name dropping, both then and now – wouldn't you? Sir Jackie's personal mobile number is staying on my iPhone for good, believe it.

Practice gets under way and what could be more quintessentially English than watching and listening to a Lea-Francis Hyper slipping and sliding its elegant way uphill on a blue-skied June morning? The dale has a myriad of greens, there's three red kites showing off to each other above me, and the paddock smells of bacon and of racing cars and so God must be in his heaven, and all must be right with the world – or so it seemed for the few hours I spent in this tiny bubble of sanity.

I find Nick Hildyard, who comes from Hull and is driving a 10-litre aero-engined Théophile Schneider. "The car's from 1913, and it was found in bits by my friend David Baker; the engine is a 1917 Hall-Scott aeroplane engine. It's four cylinders, overhead cam driven by gears, inclined valves, roller rockers, and hemispherical heads – all well ahead of their time. We've got about 160bhp and 480ft/lb of torque. No front brakes ..." The car was built in Besançon, France but its early history as a sports tourer is unknown, with the aero engine being installed in the early Nineties. David loves the diversity of VSCC events and he's quick to remind me that although many cars may be centenarians, the technology some of them feature is still remarkable: "this car, flat out will do 120mph (195km/h) ..." David has driven the course of the first Grand Prix, the 1908 French, and tells me he is still in awe of the fact that the winning Mercedes' average was 67mph (108km/h), and this was on the dirt roads of the era.

Outside VSCC circles it's a truth universally acknowledged that the most characterful cars, the most stylish, and the most covetable were those that populated the motoring landscape when you first got interested in cars, but at the time couldn't afford to buy anything more than car magazines. I therefore can recognise the Cox GTM, the Porsche 914, and even the ex-Mike Wilds Ensign LF 3 at 100 paces (if not a Lotus Seven, it seems) but I have to check the badging on an Alvis to double check it isn't a Lagonda, a Talbot, or even an Aston Martin. Prewar cars do make lovely music though, even if their precise identity often remains a matter of conjecture. The exhaust notes can vary from soft gurgling (which, curiously, sounds uncannily like a Renault 5 Turbo) to the urgent, abrupt bark of the little Sixes that were once so popular, but which died out postwar after the demise of the 1600cc Triumph Vitesse 6. Olfactory delights are guaranteed, and never more than when standing downwind of the phalanx of Cooper 500s, whose JAP and Norton engines exude that unmistakable tang of Castrol R, the castor-based oil (yes, Castrol) whose smell is not only addictive, but which is also guaranteed to induce lengthy bouts of reminiscence in those of us who are of a certain age.

It's time to find a Bugatti owner to talk to, as the most elegant of all prewar racers is a longstanding personal favourite; I adore the svelte perfection of le pur sang Type 35 as much as I loathe the grotesque excess of the modern-day parodies, the Veyron and the Chiron. These are the cars whose design mantra seems to have been 'if enough's as good as a feast, then a huge amount more must be better,' and whose preferred habitat is thus South Kensington rather than the Nordschleife. As I know virtually nothing about the Type 40 Bugatti I decide to talk to its owner, Bill Clarke. I get today's first brush with real world politics, but sadly not my last, when Bill explains just why he needs to be evasive about not only precisely where he lives – "about 30 miles (38km) north of Belfast" – but also about just what other cars he has in his collection – "there's a reason for that." He's a lovely man though, soft spoken and intense, and he tells me that he has owned the Bugatti for 17 years, "it's a genuine Type 40, built in 1927, imported from France with an English body, we think by Jarvis," he explains. "The previous owner had it for 40 years. This is a four-cylinder

1.5-litre car – very similar to the Type 37 sports cars." Bill's in his 70s, I'd guess, and he tells me that he's always loved Bugattis: "ever since I was 18, which was a long time ago ..." Before I leave Bill to lavish some more TLC on the Bugatti's internals as "... it's not running very well today" – he praises Harewood's top of the hill paddock location and the efficiency of the meeting's organisation, and he chuckles endearingly as he tells me that every single corner is a challenge in this 90-year-old car. He's a typical Bugatti owner, I think, having talked to a few over the years – passionate about the marque, and with the good grace to share his enthusiasm. I remember the 80-year-old who wandered over to admire my Seven at a VSCC Cadwell meeting, he then answered my question about whether he owned a classic by mentioning that yes, he had a Brescia Bugatti, which he drove down to the Dordogne most years, and that his son ran a Type 35; he said it not to impress, but because he knew I'd be interested and, of course, he was right.

Today feels like the garden party where you half expect to encounter Bill Boddy or John Bolster holding court over a G&T, but also where you fear you might be exposed as a parvenu for having a less than encyclopaedic knowledge of Brooklands or, as 'The Bod' invariably termed it – 'The Track.' It is a shame that today the usual VSCC commentator cannot be heard over the public address – what he'd probably term 'the Tannoy' – as although today's voice is perfectly competent, he lacks the sheer eccentricity that is an intrinsic part of the VSCC experience. At my last VSCC Cadwell, the commentary had been a joy, almost like those rambling chats Test Match commentators used to indulge in when rain or poor light had stopped play. There had been an almost forensic analysis of the precise ownership history, modifications, and race record of some tiny little Austin Seven special, delivered in the tone of a retired Latin teacher from a minor public school, and then the conversation took a surreal turn, a stream of consciousness riff to his rather more contemporary co-commentator, Marcus Pye, on the best way to cook a partridge. And even when racing was taking place (and don't forget that the on-track action can be ferocious in vintage events) a particularly opportunistic overtaking manoeuvre would be celebrated with a Mr Chips-like "Oh I say, Tuppy – Glossop on the Riley's really putting on a show today." And I loved the old-fashioned equestrian usage – 'on the Riley' – which was so common prewar but is now only to be heard on days like this. I'm at a British Touring Car round in a week's time and I don't think I will be able to find a bigger contrast to today.

It seems only fitting to drive home on the route of the old A1, as deserted of traffic as The Great North Road might have been when the Type 40 Bugatti was still being run in. After dinner, I recount my day to Joanne over a little too much Pinot Noir, and most things seem right in the world until my little bubble of vintage car-induced complacency is destroyed by news of another ISIS-inspired attack, this time in Borough Market and taking place only a couple of weeks after the Manchester suicide bombing that had killed more than 20. As the singer Ariana Grande had so eloquently put it: "I don't have words." And I don't have any more today either ...

CROFT – 10 JUNE BTCC 2017

It was the best of times because I won't forget the sight of a 32-car field of Touring Cars squirming and sliding on a wet and slimy track. But it was the worst of times because those same conditions contributed to a multi car accident that left many cars wrecked and three drivers – Aron Taylor-Smith, Luke Davenport, and Jeff Smith with serious injuries and, as I write, Smith and Davenport remain in the James Cook University Hospital. I'll describe later about why the accident was foreseeable, if far from inevitable except to those blessed with 20:20 hindsight, but let me start this piece by trying to exorcise my inner snob.

The thing is this – I have been guilty of sneering at the BTCC's current iteration on more than a few occasions over the last couple of decades, since the Supertouring formula superseded the Group A formula in the early Nineties. The 550bhp Sierra Cosworths were replaced by far more housetrained 2-litre normally-aspirated cars, which may have raced much more closely than the Sierras ever did, but whose spectacle was often very tame in comparison. In 2017, the BTCC is still, essentially, a spec formula (with many parts common to all cars regardless of manufacturer), but with turbocharged engines now permitted; although not the same fire-spitting, wheel-spinning type of the anarchic Sierra epoch. My problem with the series is not only the 'push to pass,' fender-bending overtaking that wows the huge TV audiences, but also the pantomime villain melodrama of driver rivalry, and the fact that BTCC attracts what I am guilty of thinking are – sorry – the wrong crowd. I might have allowed some of the 'right crowd and no crowding' Brooklands mentality to have influenced me, but it's more than that. It's the fact that the only time I have seen drunken high jinks at motorsport events is at BTCC meetings (nope, I don't do Le Mans laddish weekends), the fact that there's an element of tribalism in the support demographic and, most of all, the fact that I am left wondering where the hell all these people are the rest of the year? Why do they attend this event but no others. Is the BTCC on TV because so many people watch it live from trackside, or do so many people watch from trackside only because it's on TV; and TV coverage, therefore, doesn't just stimulate interest but legitimise it?

I hadn't seen Touring Cars for a few years, as the Croft event often clashed with events that appealed rather more to my motorsport purism but, as populism is one of the words that define 2017, it was time I stopped sneering and started watching. And even though a family commitment meant I only watched Saturday's qualifying, I had one of the most thrilling days I have enjoyed at the circuit for a long time. And that was the last thing I expected.

A hard rain was falling as I left home in Thirsk and, apart from unfounded rumours of the sun having been spotted for up to five seconds somewhere down near Tower Bend, it rained the rest of the day with varying degrees of intensity. I had arrived before 8.30am and, to my relief, the security team were allowing season ticket holders to park in our usual reserved spot next to the chicane – bloody luxury actually, as I could read *The Times*' take on Thursday's General Election from the comfort of the new Yeti during the boring bits, and then watch the more interesting cars buck and squirm through Hawthorns, the Chicane, and beyond from the banking in front of me. And, as I was to find later, it was the 'beyond' bit that made the day so unforgettable.

Christ, it's only 10am and there's already more people here for BTCC qualifying than there is at 2pm on a typical club racing Sunday. There's more wives, kids, and girlfriends than usual; and damn it, I'll have to allow, grudgingly, that both the numbers and diversity of the crowd are making the circuit – which so often feels like a country for grumpy old men – start to sparkle, even under these dripping wet skies. Time to talk, and after a brief chat to the regulars, all of us trying to disguise our inner grump, I chat to Dave Webster, from nearby Darlington. Dave's "a motor dealer and builder" but his side-line – "it's just my pastime really" – is catering, and he's here today to do his bit in feeding the 5000. Dave specialises in venues like Croft and he rolls his eyes at the rain as he tells me how much the weather can affect business – "it can ruin it." Dave never has problems with his customers, "they're all good," and I suspect that if trouble did come calling it wouldn't be Dave who would come off second best. I've often wondered what it must be like working next to a track but not being able to see it, and Dave rarely gets to see any action: "but I like the single-seaters best," he says. (Hooray, another purist.) I ask if Dave has noticed his customers' taste in food changing at all: "Oh … yeah, probably, but what I offer is very simple – we do burgers, bacon, and sausage and that's it – and it's still what most people seem to want." Last question, Dave, how much do you take on a good day? Big grin. "A lot of money," he says with a big, dirty chuckle. I thought he'd take the Fifth Amendment when I suggest five figures, but he pauses and confirms, "… on a really good day? Oh yes, and I knew you'd come down to money!" Before I wander off to the paddock we can't help chatting about the election, the outcome of which is "strong 'n' stable" Theresa May going from hero to zero overnight, and hanging out with some very odd folk, not the sort of people you'd normally find in her fragrant Maidenhead constituency. Yup, our Theresa's so banjaxed, so she is, that she's hanging out with 'Norn Iron's' nutjob DUP, where it's still just fine, maybe even be compulsory, to be a pro-life, creationist homophobe – in 2017. Dave and I agree that a wasted vote is the one that isn't cast, he says "I voted leave last year for the sake of my kids." And I thought it was the kids who were the Remainers but what the hell do I know any more?

I resist the temptation to watch the Ginetta Juniors practice as, whilst I'm sure the racing will be close, the spectacle of a procession of the little sports cars skipping from puddle to pond is easy to resist when there's a waterproof awning to shelter under and a guy in a Dunlop logoed shirt to talk to. He turns out to be a big fish too – Tony Duffy, Operations Manager of Dunlop Motorsport and, like nearly everybody else I meet today, he's happy to chat on the record. The obvious question is just how many tyres will his team be fitting. "On a typical weekend it's about 600; all the teams pay our agent before the race meeting." Tony tells me that Croft doesn't have any particular challenges: "It isn't hard on tyres really, unlike Thruxton where we have to produce a special tyre." I don't know how much time Tony spends at home, but I suspect he's not able to help out with the supermarket run as often as most of us. "Next week I'm at Le Mans," he says, "we've got 31 cars racing out of 60 in the race; we're doing more than Michelin this year, who've got the other 29. We do LMP2, the GT Pro, and GT Am, but we're not into LMP1." Tony tells me he's been involved in motorsport for about 15 years, which was actually less than I expected but – "I've worked for Dunlop all my life." I'm just a fan, but this is Tony's job and I wonder if he allows himself favourites – "I'm involved in motorcycle racing as well. I've got a team of people down in Catalunya this week – Moto GP – so we run Moto 2 and Moto 3 out of that paddock, and we're at the TT races this week as well – we won the Senior TT yesterday with Michael Dunlop, we're into everything." So who's going to win the Touring Cars this weekend Tony? He laughs "I've no idea," and laughs a lot more.

I reckon that if you turned up at any race circuit, anywhere in the world it wouldn't be too long before you heard an accent just like Tony Duffy's. It's a reassuring accent, making me think of Jaguars, Aston Martins, and Land Rovers, and it's probably the voice you'd most like to hear as you climb out of the wreckage. It's Warwickshire, of course, and Tony's accent reminds me a lot of the late hillclimb legend Roy Lane, and a good proportion of the guys I see working on historic Formula 1 cars at the Silverstone Classic. The UK car industry may have shrunk massively since the hegemony of British Leyland, but nearly everybody who's anybody in racing now seems to be located in that golden triangle between Birmingham, Oxford, and Northampton.

I watch the big beasts of the BTCC world tackle Clervaux in practice, and bloody hell there's a lot of them, 32 already, and none of them look like the makeweights who used to clutter up old time saloon car racing -- as we called it in the days of Escorts and Minis, Capris and Magnums. BTCC racers are ugly cars making an even uglier noise, but I can't deny the spectacle; it's sound-tracked by dyspeptic pops and bangs as the cars turn into the right hand corner at the end of the start/finish straight, with a good third of them slithering and bucking off track and on to the gravel. It may be predominantly a front-wheel drive field but there's no shortage of opposite lock theatre, and absolutely no sign of anyone taking it steady – the rule seems to be maximum attack and we'll repair the damage before qualifying. And I don't know what decibel limit these things are supposed to run at but I wish I'd picked up my earplugs from the Caterham before I left home ...

I mentioned ugly cars and I meant it; from trackside, only a handful of BTCC cars look less than a mess. It doesn't help that hardly any of the competing cars had an attractive shape before they were transformed into racers, with Passats, Toyotas, Chevrolets, and MG 6s looking about as sexy as your fridge and – help me on this one – does anybody actually drive an MG 6 or a Chevrolet Cruze, except at gunpoint? The only MG 6 I have ever seen was Jason Plato's company car in 2014, and I bet he parked it round the corner from his house. But the real problem, aesthetically, is the bloody awful liveries of nearly every car on the grid. The only cars that stand out are the Pirtek BMW 125 M Sports in arrestingly bright blue, red, and yellow strip; and the funky red and yellow Shredded Wheat Focuses. Good to see that the seam of irony has been well mined by these guys, with their three car team numbered '3,' '30,' and '300,' and prompting me to remind myself that, true to the values of the brand's

USP, I've never managed to eat more than two Shredded Wheat either. Has anybody? This brings me to the dog's dinner of the Subaru Levorg – an unfathomable name (except when reversed) applied to a ghastly looking car. Old style Subarus, even the bug-eyed Impreza, had a certain jolie laide appeal: looking like the girl you might not have noticed first at the party, but who was the one you really wanted to go home with, but the Levorg estate has looks only its mother could love. And the paint job? It's good to see that Stevie Wonder is still getting work, even in the unexpected role as graphic designer.

I decide to find Plato, primarily to justify making some smartarse link with a quotation from his philosopher namesake. Something like "I'm trying to think, don't confuse me with facts," or "wise men speak because they have something to say," would have been a good platform, but honorary Geordie, Jason, is hiding from his adoring public and so I talk instead to Michael Epps on the grounds that I've never heard of him, he looked pretty handy on track, and he's climbing out of his VW CC as I return from the great Plato hunt. Epps' team isn't in the posh end of the paddock and, whilst Plato gets his own garage, son of Hemel Hempstead Epps gets a team awning and a big brolly. But he's a good guy to talk to, with the sort of instant response and self-assurance that characterises so many racing drivers – they are not a breed given to either diffidence or self-doubt (both being my specialist subject at his age). Are you a Croft regular then Michael? "I'm a real expert – I've only raced here twice, that's it." He laughs. "The car's good and I like the track, it's quite technical, a lot of bumps, a lot of different lines you can use. The wet's good fun and we've performed really well so far, even with an old set of boots." I ask Michael what the high-speed Jim Clark Esses are like to drive today (choosing not to mention how they scared me silly on wet trackdays): "Yeah, sketchy but ... we're racing drivers aren't we, we're supposed to deal with that stuff. Just a few opposite lock moments, bit sideways, but it's front-wheel drive – just hit the throttle and hold on." I nod in assent, as if I'd do just the same myself. I'm intrigued to know what brings a young driver like Michael – he's 25 – to BTCC racing. "I did the VW Cup, and before that I did single-seaters – US F2000, Formula Renault, Formula Vee – so yes the VW feels a bit of a bus compared to some stuff. But this car really does reward a good driver – you have to drive these things a lot harder than people think – it does reward big cojones." I like this lad – he's a nice guy.

I try and fail again to locate my nemesis, Plato, and decide instead to talk to the ITV4 reporter who looks as though she has run out of people who are prepared to brave the incessant rain and talk to her. Very meta, an amateur hack like me interviewing a media pro like her but, whilst she's happy to chat about what I'm doing and why, she can't do an interview without getting consent from ITV4's head honcho. My irony gland starts to ache.

Whatever, the serious stuff happens in the afternoon and I know, to the inch, just where I'll be standing to watch the drama. There's a spot trackside about 75 yards (68.5m) beyond the chicane that, to somebody unfamiliar with Croft, looks an unremarkable section of straight, not even worth pausing there for a moment, because everybody knows it's the corners where the real heroics get played out. Usually, because if you watch motorsport properly you work out exactly where to watch, when, and how. And apart from the crew who have erected a bloody gazebo on the grass banking, very few others are in on this secret (note to self, bring my Stanley knife next time to remove these Poundshop marquees that ruin everybody's view, apart from the one enjoyed by their selfish occupants). The exit of the chicane is a very fast left-hand flick, and it leads on to the back straight and, eventually, to Tower (the best overtaking spot), and so a fast exit is the first step towards an outbraking move on the inside of Tower. In the dry, it's often flat out without an issue but today, with a track slicked by muddy water and punctuated by the divots cut by earlier miscreants, there was real drama each lap, every lap of Touring Car practice.

Two approaches were adopted. There was the Rob Austin approach of containing the slide with the sort of reactions and skill you might expect from somebody who has raced in Formula 3 and historic Formula 1, resulting in his Toyota Avensis slithering by with 30 degrees of opposite lock applied, foot hard down at three-figure speeds. More spectacular, if far slower, was the approach taken by at least half the field, which was to allow the car's outside wheels to kiss the grass and, as long as two wheels stayed on the tarmac, the drama was confined to a shimmy of the car's hips and a dirty cloud of mud and grass. But oh my, how quickly the drama could turn into crisis if the car left the tarmac completely. There were terrifyingly quick spins, back across the track and in front of oncoming cars and, for one of the Focuses, a clattering impact with the Armco. More dramatic still were the cars like the matte grey Cruze, whose driver exercised his inner Martin Schanche and strayed so far on to the infield that the tragic little Chevy was soon bouncing down the circuit's Rallycross track. It was thrilling, and whilst some drivers were really fighting the car and losing, others looked supremely confident, none more so than the drivers of the Subaru Levorgs I have just been so rude about. The two surviving Focuses also impressed, steaming out of the chicane with the proverbial dab of oppo already wound on, and arrowing past me in a blur of noise and colour.

Enjoy it? Too right I did; it was as exciting as it was unexpected, and my day reminded me that racing is racing, wherever it takes place and whoever is watching it. In the dry it might not have been as thrilling, but these guys take no prisoners and it would have been almost as hectic and much quicker. As it was, the cars were lapping in the low 1min 30s, which, bearing in mind that a 300bhp Caterham on slicks, in the dry, won't get much below 1min 27, is seriously impressive.

Things ended badly though, as seemed almost inevitable. BTCC qualifying was made more dramatic than usual as there was a risk of the rain getting even heavier during the 30-minute session, and this meant every driver was desperate to secure a good time as soon as they possibly could. Lots of cars were running closely together, and the conditions made it inevitable that mistakes would be made. It took an even shorter time to happen than I expected, with red flags waving within ten minutes. I didn't worry about the cause as sessions are red flagged far more often than they used to be but after 20 minutes I knew this wasn't a light shunt. And it wasn't; half a dozen cars had crashed between Barcroft and

Sunny after Davenport's Focus had sheared an oil line, the ensuing slick had removed what little grip there had been. Reactions to the crash were mainly sober and mature, with Alan Gow, the BTCC supremo saying that "The accident ... couldn't have been avoided ... it was the imperfect storm." Quite a contrast to one of the comments on an internet forum, from somebody who didn't allow his ignorance about which corner the accident had taken place on to prevent him from insisting that the circuit must be changed before the BTCC returned. Complacency is never a good thing in this sport, but having seen over 1000 individual races at Croft, with only one serious injury until today's accident, I think I can fall back on Mario Andretti's words after team-mate Ronnie Peterson's death at Monza in 1978: "Unhappily, motor racing is also this."

Verdict

1. Summary – Terrific entertainment from fast, noisy, spectacular, and well driven cars. The support races now don't include the luscious Porsche Carreras that used to feature. Alan Gow's strategy is clearly to prevent the support acts from overshadowing the headline turn. The Ginetta Juniors were unremarkable: the Ginetta GT4s were quick and made a lovely V6 snarl, but weren't a patch on series like the local Northern Saloons and Sports cars; the Clios were as exciting as you'd expect a field of identical hot hatches to be (ie not very); but at least the F4 single-seaters brought a bit of slicks and wings glamour to the party, even if they sound just like the cars the local yoof use to lap Thirsk Market Place.

2. Nature notes – The only sentient creatures stupid enough to brave the rain were BTCC spectators.

3. Catering – A bit more variety than usual but the Michelin Star will have to wait.

4. The programme was a glossy A5 job costing a fiver. It didn't match the production values of programmes during peak Supertouring in the late Nineties but then neither did the cars. The PA had been turned down from 11 and the commentary team of Messrs Hyde and Hartley was slick, professional, and entertaining. It was good to see more women working for the race teams: a decade ago the only women you'd see were half naked, and usually shivering, grid girls. People like Claire Williams, Leena Gade, Susie Wolff, and Monisha Kaltenborn are helping to change the sport whose sexism and misogyny had left it marooned in 1974 for far too long.

CADWELL PARK 17/18 JUNE HSCC 2017

Exactly 47 years ago, Richard Attwood was racing a Porsche 917 in the 24 hours of Le Mans. With his co-driver, Hans Herrmann, he won the race that formed the background of Steve McQueen's film, *Le Mans*. This was the film that, even more than *The Great Escape* and *Bullitt*, triggered McQueen's canonisation, and which was also responsible for the number of paunchy middle-aged blokes who wear Gulf-branded T-shirts. Attwood is as far removed from McQueen's Hollywood glamour as you could imagine, but I am still slightly star struck at talking to 'The Man Who …' Richard is racing a Porsche 928 today in the HSCC's '70s Road Sports Championship, primarily because 2017 is the 928's 40th birthday – and he's happy to talk.

"There's lots of corners!" is Cadwell first-timer Attwood's initial reaction to Cadwell. "The 928's a big old lump really, but straights have always been my strong point," he laughs. "The car doesn't like the kerbs – does anything? – and I'm just concentrating on learning the track and not looking for a time." Richard tells me the car will be looked after by various Porsche dealerships during the year, today being Leeds' turn, and he mentions that the 928 had gone well at Silverstone (where he finished third) "but it was wet, the car's big and heavy, and that's nice, but we're still a long way from the right setup. I don't think we'll feature here at Cadwell – I need nice long straights!" I ask Richard if he still thinks about driving his 917 at Le Mans and his answer is surprising: "Not very often, it's a long time ago but the horror stories I have of the '69 car will haunt me forever, it was such a wayward car, virtually off the ground at speed, and any quick corners we had to slow down a lot for. But it had massive speed down the straights if you could just hang on to it, you just needed the full width of the road." He reminds me of John Woolfe's fate – he was the English driver who had bought a 917 for the 1969 Le Mans "who shouldn't have been there, and he didn't survive the first lap. In '69 the car was extraordinarily difficult but by 1970 it was perfect." Before I leave Richard to talk about setup with his mechanics, he contrasts Le Mans then and now – "Le Mans, as an achievement, has always been a team effort, and it's much more for the manufacturers than the drivers. If you're in the winning car then you're lucky, and we had a lot of luck. Lots of people threw the race away; we weren't the fastest – we only had the 4.5-litre engine and most of the others had 5-litres. People think we were holding back, but that's not the truth, we were going as fast as we could with what we'd got, looking after the car, and we came through. We never expected to be in the lead, but after ten hours we were leading, which was ridiculous, we never should have been there. It was hugely wet, today there'd have been safety cars … actually I believe they'd have stopped the race, but in those days we had to cope with what we'd got, and we were managing the car, not the pits. These days it's a sprint race, the cars are bulletproof and I think the drivers race harder than in Formula 1, which is wrong. There's something seriously wrong with Formula 1 …"

Richard Attwood is 77, looks ten years younger, and answers every question in detail, quickly, and eloquently. Watching him from trackside, even in a short club race, you can see why he was such a formidable endurance racer. He has that economy of effort that delivers pace, that is only apparent from the stopwatch as it's so much quicker than it looks. He's a man in the Button and Prost school, or rather vice versa. And how can I not be impressed with somebody who also finished second in his BRM P126 at Monaco in 1968, as well as winning Le Mans, and whose road car, until recently, was a 400,000 mile Peugeot 405 Estate?

It's almost midsummer, and if Cadwell's woodland had looked even more glorious in early May, today's cloudless sky and 28°C heat more than compensate. I had set off from home at 5.30am and, because I was driving the Seven, my route was an analogue one, avoiding dual carriageways and snaking down through York, Howden, and Goole, then through John Wesley country in the Isle of Axholme until, after escaping Gainsborough, we had climbed up the gentle slopes of the Lincolnshire Wolds, that near empty landscape I have adored for 40 years. As ever, the Seven devoured the road, and overtaking the few cars I encountered was the briefest of formalities. But I was fairly sensible and I treated 30 and 40 limits as mandatory, 60 as advisory and 50 limits as a misprint of 60, as most of us do.

The HSCC was putting on a 22-race programme over the weekend, catering for an extraordinary range of machinery from late-Fifties Formula Junior single-seaters to the crowd-pleasing Mustangs and Cortinas, Imps and Minis in the Historic Touring Car Championship. Point of order HSCC, if these cars raced in period as saloon cars then what's with the retrospective rebranding with the touring car moniker? Nomenclature issues apart, the meeting's entry is a delight, with the feature race for 1-litre Formula 3 being a special joy, as the Hunt and Peterson era racers not only sounded divine (they weren't called 'screamers' for nothing) but they also had looks that epitomised the beauty that function bestows on form. Just look at a Brabham BT 28 if you're in doubt or better still look at Thierry Gallo's Tecno F3, the racing car that looks most like 1984 Madonna, sexy teenage attitude with a hint of puppy fat. Hmm, not quite sure what that comparison says about your reporter, so I will return to the safer, asexual ground of the huge entry of Formula Ford 1600s, which guaranteed that I would see more clean overtaking than in several seasons of Formula 1, and without a DRS in sight.

The contrast with the BTCC bandwagon I had watched the week before was an intriguing one. BTCC offers a package of races, four of which are for identical cars and one of which, the main event, is for cars with either front or rear-wheel drive but which all feature four-cylinder engines, as do all the BTCC support races except one. The main BTCC act is great stuff, as long as I give my inner purist the day off, but a racetrack's soundscape is important to me and this weekend I revelled in the taster menu of sounds which the HSCC offers. There was the three-cylinder, two-stroke fizz of a DKW, sounding like a castrato Ferrari, straight and flat-fours, straight and flat-sixes and V8s of up to five litres in cars such as the 928 and the trio of Mustangs. So that meant screams from the DKW, barks from the BMC A Series, potent growls from the 911, creamy howls from the Triumphs and 240Z, and burbles and bellows from the 928 and the MG V8s. Dare I confess at this point that I can do a really quite passable small-block Chevy impersonation? Running on 48 Weber IDA carburettors, natch.

There are two full days of qualifying and racing, and with such an extravagance of sights and sounds to experience, I opt to watch practice (let's park the 'Q' word, this is historic racing after all) from the Mountain, through the Hall Bends and up to the Hairpin, and to watch racing between Mansfield and the Mountain. The former gives me a close-up view of technique and speed and the latter enables me to see pure racing, none more so than at the hold-your-breath quick entry into Coppice, taken at almost 130mph (210km/h) by the insanely fast Mallock Mk 20/21 of Mark Charteris.

Through the Hall Bends nobody looks quicker, neater or more in control than Jon Milicevic in his Brabham BT 21B, but that was only to be expected. I first became aware of Jon's talent at exactly the same spot in 2010 when I was part of a small group of spectators who were captivated by the sight of Jon's Cooper T59 being driven at a speed that was so much faster than anybody else could manage that it came close to humiliation. Each lap we would see the little blue car arrow into the first apex, tail sliding, engine note hardening before it would be flicked perfectly into the second apex, driver's hands applying measured opposite lock with the ease of somebody whose talent is almost wasted in historic racing. Later the same day his 1100cc Cooper, without wings and running narrow treaded tyres, had left several slicks and wings Formula 2 cars in his wake, and it had absolutely no right to do this, just as it was never in the script that he would lap Silverstone quicker in the T59 than most Sixties Formula 1 cars can now manage. I interviewed Jon for *Low Flying* at his garage in Foster's Booth, just up the A5 from Towcester, and he was the antithesis of the stereotypical racing driver. Softly spoken, apparently devoid of ego, and with the sort of deep knowledge of and enthusiasm for the sport's history that drivers rarely possess. Jon tells me today that the little Brabham is far more physical to drive than the Cooper and that, post-race, his arms would feel as though they had enjoyed a good work out. He won both races with ease and again I wondered, how far could he have gone if he had opted for racing as a career?

As I wander down towards the Mountain grandstand, sheltering from the glaring sun under the tall beeches, there's a cameo that almost convinces me that there's a rip in the space/time continuum and it really is 1963 all over again. Because here's the Mallock U2 freewheeling down to the assembly area with its beaming driver enjoying a last-minute roll up ciggy before the race. You don't see that at the Monaco Grand Prix. And when I hear that the front engine U2 has to race in the rear engine (and therefore faster) class in Formula Junior because it was winning too often in the front engine class I wonder if Humpty Dumpty is now a big cheese in the HSCC – "When I choose a word it means just what I choose it to mean, neither more nor less."

The weekend's highlight is Formula Ford 1600, the formula that was introduced in 1967 and which is almost as strong now as it was then. Narrow tyres, light weight, modest power, and no aerodynamic grip are the ingredients that make this formula still the most capable of producing close racing and huge amounts of overtaking. What a contrast to the quick, but stultifyingly dull, Ford Ecoboost Formula 4 single-seaters I had seen the previous weekend which, even in wet conditions, had droned and farted their way around for 20 minutes, each car running a second or so behind the man in front and with overtaking happening only through mistake rather than opportunism. Formula 4 cars look awful and sound even worse, and if FF1600 is 1954 Elvis singing *That's All Right* then Formula 4 is the 1977 peanut butter sandwich fuelled *Way Down* decline. Anyway, there are over 50 cars entered, driven by young men in their teens and men old enough to be their grandfathers, and even though most just race for the sheer joy of doing so, they race bloody hard. There's seven or eight cars jinking and diving as one into Coppice, side by side at 115mph (185km/h), and from my vantage point on the apex, ten feet above the track and only 15 from it, I can see groups of cars scrapping into Mansfield, sliding wide out of it and regrouping for another lunge into the braking area for the Mountain. To my left is the steep ascent into the double apex of Charlies; on lap one of the second race, I watch as one car spins, Dick Dixon's Lotus 61 spins to avoid it and disappears from my sight towards the guardrail. I know Dick, as does almost everybody in the Formula Ford and Lotus Seven communities, and there's a sharp stab of worry that this time Dick has really hurt himself.

I needn't have worried: Dick's just fine, even if the car is a bit peaky after its Armco kiss, and he's working on re-securing the oil tank as I arrive on Sunday morning. I don't offer to help as my technical prowess is such that even ten minutes of my cack-handed clodhoppery would see the little Lotus out of action for the rest of the season, and so I talk to Boston-born Jane Dixon in the family motorhome instead. She and Dick are from Stanstead Abbotts, Hertfordshire, Jane is a former teacher and Dick is a retired firefighter. I know that sports cars and motorsport are a big part of their life together and I wanted to hear Jane's perspective. She tells me how Dick had wanted a Lotus Seven since he was a child, finally getting one when he was 18, "which he used every day to go to work, he had to shovel snow off the seats in winter." After sprinting and hillclimbing the car, something that Jane also did, Dick had bought the Lotus 61 "in boxes in the early Eighties and then he spent two years putting it back together." Jane tells me about her sprinting days in the Lotus Seven: "we had a women's series with at least 12 or 13 of us in the Seven Club's Speed Series. We were taken as seriously as the men and some of us, not me, were quicker than the men. I understood then what the appeal of the sport was, but I knew it wasn't for me so I bought a horse." Jane compares the atmosphere that prevailed in Dick's early racing days "when wives and girlfriends were discouraged from attending race meetings as they might be a distraction" with the present day "when women are really appreciated. The paddock is a very convivial atmosphere and I'm happy talking to anybody in it." Jane tells me that, as a teenager, she'd come to Cadwell on Sunday afternoons to watch the bike racing. "We'd have a family picnic on the grass bank above the track" she says, then adds that whilst race circuits have improved a lot since her childhood, the catering has a slightly retro theme – "we bring our own food and we don't want to survive on burgers and chips ..."

Verdict

1. If you wanted to show your maiden aunt the difference between oversteer and understeer then Cadwell is the perfect place at which to begin her education. The elevation of the spectator areas enables a spectacularly close view, and even Aunt Maud would have given a spontaneous squeal as young Benn Tilley's Lotus 22 snapped into oversteer at well over 100mph (160km/h) and 20 yards before the apex. And she'd have hooted and hollered as the Mini Cooper S slithered by, crabwise – the driver's foot buried to the floor, hands pushing the wheel as far left as it would go to counter the understeer, and the Mini's inside rear wheel

waving clear of the ground. And if you wanted to demonstrate that Lincolnshire isn't all flat fenland, that motorsport can enhance an already beautiful location, that historic racing offers a spectacle that rivals even the best of modern racing, and that MotorSport Vision really has done a brilliant job at preserving and improving Cadwell then you know exactly where you should be one weekend next summer.

2. You already know about wildlife and catering from my May visit, but I will mention the bargain price of a weekend ticket for 20-something quid, and the really, really crappy programme for three. I can get the entry and timetable already from the HSCC's excellent website, so why is the programme quite so useless? It's defined more by what it doesn't include than what it does; there are no lap records and nothing worth reading apart from some brief text about 1-litre Formula 3. There's the usual soul-destroying litany of race class structures: "Class D1 Formula Junior Cars built and raced between 01.01.61 and 31.12.63 with drum brakes on all four wheels (FIA category FJ/2D) fitted with engines of 1000cc or less." I know this stuff is important if you are racing or scrutineering, but does anybody else need this stuff? Mightn't they prefer to read about what it's really like to drive a Mustang around here? And when you have the excellent Marcus Pye and Ian Titchmarsh as commentators, you already know that no detail – including the chassis number of the Brabham raced here in '69 by somebody even I hadn't heard of – will go unearthed.

3. I stayed near Tealby at Bully Hill Top, a 15 minute drive from Cadwell, and over empty roads. Wold View Bed and Breakfast is the most peaceful location I think I have ever stayed in for a race meeting, or at least it is after the bikers have stopped arsing about and gone home. I can see the silhouette of Lincoln Cathedral 20 miles to the west, and there are rolling fields of barley to the south and east under a blue sky etched by swifts and swallows. Mid-June's late dusk and early dawn might reduce my sleep, but that feeling of midsummer euphoria makes me feel near-immortal, despite the mounting evidence to the contrary. There's sage-spicy Lincolnshire sausage for breakfast, and on the next table is Formula Ford and Junior driver Benn Tilley's grandfather – a former racer himself, who went to college with Roger Williamson (the sublimely gifted driver who died in a burning March at Zandvoort in 1973), and even in our short chat I can feel just how much the loss is still felt.

4. I am reminded of why a Caterham Seven is not fit for every purpose as I drive home in heavy traffic on the A1. It's 32°C, my left leg is being slow-roasted by the heat soak from the transmission tunnel, my right leg is being seared by heat from the exhaust, and my back is dripping with sweat. But I cope manfully as all I need to do is to remember those endless Friday morning senior management team meetings, endlessly droning on about key performance indicators and risk management. I remind myself that instead of talking management-speak bollocks, instead of playing bullshit bingo to an international standard, I'm now driving the 'too fast to race' sports car, I don't go to work on Mondays any more and that Cadwell and me, 40 years on, are still very much an item.

SANTA POD SUMMER NATIONALS – 24 JUNE 2017

What I don't understand is this – whenever Lord March invites some American drag racing legends to the Goodwood Festival of Speed, the combination of larger than life drivers and thunderously vocal cars receives a rapturous reception from the crowd and a glowing write up in the monthly magazines. *Motorsport*'s Simon Taylor once even gave his readership his trademark *Lunch With* long interview with John Force, one of the very bravest of the brave in the drag racing world, the patriarch of a dynasty of drivers and the man who won the Funny Car championship 16 times. But just the mention of drag racing in some of the places I frequent, both real and virtual, can trigger sneering from those who assert that motorsport begins and ends with circuit racing, and who think that even racing has been sliding into disrepute since Stirling Moss' Goodwood accident on 23 April 1962 brought his trademark 'let's fire up the Maser and find some crumpet' schtick to a premature close. There's an easy way to a counter this negativity, and it involves sitting next to me above the start line at Santa Pod as two Pro Modified monsters get ready to devour the strip in a seismic eruption of noise, smoke, and colour. Nothing prepares even the most seasoned circuit race fan for what a couple of thousand horsepower or so (each!) of 520 cubic inch V8s sound like as they power a machine with outrageous cartoon styling to reach a quarter-mile six seconds from standstill. And the Pro Mods will be doing 230mph (370km/h) or more during the final second. Oh, and by the way, these cars aren't even the really quick ones …

The Summer Nationals are held over the last weekend in June and, whilst the spectacle doesn't quite match the extraordinary sights and sounds of the Pod's (get used to it, okay?) Main Event and Euro Final, the smaller crowds and slightly more self-effacing machinery make this event an ideal taster before I return later in the year. It's a three hour drive from Thirsk, further than Silverstone, but a 5am start ensures I have time for a bacon and egg roll before inspecting the huge race paddock. 5am? No problem, as even after nearly half a century of motorsport I still get so excited at the prospect of my trip that I'll usually be awake an hour before I need to be, fizzing with anticipation of a long drive and a day to be spent doing just what the hell I want.

Even Santa Pod's name is unimprovable, as Britain's drag racing capital is located near the Bedfordshire village of Podington – the sort of quaint little place you'd expect to see Miss Marple driving her Morris Minor en route to the big house where she'd prove that the butler really did do it after all. Santa Ana in Southern California was where drag racing began in 1950 on the runway at the Orange County Airport, and it's a reasonable bet that some of the pilots there had also flown out of RAF Podington a few years earlier, when it was home to squadrons of USAAF B17 Flying Fortresses. Like so much of Eastern England, you can often feel closer to the USA than to London, the war having left its legacy of American DNA, evidenced not just by the Pod, but by the 'Fuck Off' crew cab pickups the locals love to drive, the line dancing *Macarena* and *Cotton Eyed Joe* tribes, and the rockabilly chic that might work in the Fens, but in Shoreditch or Sevenoaks, Hendon or Hoxton? Not so much. Even the commentary team sound a distant echo of the transatlantic twang adopted by pirate radio DJs I listened to on Radio 270 from June '66 until August '67, the now forgotten names such as Vince 'Rusty' Allen and Pete 'Boots' Bowman.

The paddock is already busy, and immediately I am reminded of just how diverse the drag racing demographic can be. There might be more Marlboro and vapes being smoked than at Prescott, and there's certainly more tattoos in evidence, but it is the sheer variety of people attracted to the sport that helps to make it so beguiling. Nobody looks twice at anybody else, even though there's goths and greasers, a hint of steampunk, toddlers, oldsters, and everything in between. There's long hair, buzz cuts, and dreadlocks; there's pink hair, blue hair, grey hair, and no hair at all; there's long shorts, short shorts, jeans, skirts, dresses, dungarees, and leathers; there's baseball caps and panamas; and it's not all just white people. What a contrast to my normal fare of club race meetings, where I feel I am surrounded by clones, and what a bloody nightmare that can be, living in a world populated entirely by fat middle aged white men grumbling that fings ain't wot they used to be and droning on about their old man ailments – "Oh I know, my back's just getting worse, and did you hear about poor old Hugh?"

I talk to the first driver I see; he's from Essex (in case you couldn't tell), he's Brian Pateman, he's driving a red '68 Pontiac Firebird in the Super Pro ET Class, and his car's toned 'n' pumped menace epitomises Detroit's Muscle Car glory days. "I've had the Firebird for 36 years, I used to drive it on the road when I was a young man and ..." He laughs. I think I've just triggered feel-good flashbacks of hot nights and even hotter Essex girls down Canvey Island way. So, the car then, Brian? "Yeah, I've converted it to race car spec, with race chassis and bigger engine, it's a 9-litre Chevy and about 850 horsepower and yeah, I've got nitrous oxide on it as well. I've done a 7.9 quarter and 169mph (270km/h)." Why drag racing, why not other types of motorsport? "I dunno, I've done a bit of karting and other stuff, but I love the power and the feel of drag racing. The challenge for me is beating the other guy; I've been National Champion in Super Gas and Super Comp so I've just stepped in now to Super Pro. I'm racing cars that are a lot quicker than me now so ... I might get a head start but I can't see them at the other end so it's a completely different game for me but yeah, it's going alright." Brian and the Pod go back a long way, he tells me: "I used to have a 3-litre Cortina and I'd bring it up here on test days, and I've progressed from there. Funny game ... it's a mental game. How much do I spend? Classified, that is ..." He laughs. I like Brian, I love the fact that he had a Cortina because it feels written in the stars that he should have owned Essex's finest export. And I like people like him too, as they're the sort of people who make this country tick, and most of them seem to be here today.

I walk towards the big wind turbines, which lie beyond the far end of the strip, and I smile at the juxtaposition of renewable energy and the drag racing credo of burning as much fossil fuel as quickly and as noisily as possible, for no purpose other than the existential sake of doing it. In fact, I smile a lot most of the day; drag racing has an inherent humour at its heart, the engineering and attention to detail on display wouldn't be out of place in a Formula 1 paddock, but the tongue in cheek wit and sense of absurdity – not to mention the sport's engagement with its public – would have merited a lifetime ban if a Formula 1 team had acted this way in the Age of Ecclestone. You would need to return to the Hesketh days for a comparison, but even their breath of fresh air was tainted by the reek of privilege and public school japery.

I walk by the team of Dutch racers, relaxing with roll-ups and "koffie" under the banner sign 'Orange Country Racers.' Brexit Britain, eh, where half of us can't speak a word of another language and yet here are these bloody Dutch – with their implausible height, their dope cafés, and their gorgeous women – and they're only making bloody puns in their second language, or maybe even their third? But I'm still smiling, and how couldn't I when the air is slowly filling with the sounds of V8s being woken from their slumbers, sounding like the dinosaurs in Jurassic Park would on the morning after the night before. There's coughs and barks and backfires, and the smell of unburned fuel mingles with tobacco and bacon to create the Pod's unique and addictive paddock perfume. I wander aimlessly, pausing now and again to admire the artwork on the race cars and to smile yet again at the language of the strip. At Silverstone you might see a T70, an RF84, or a G55, and, if you're really lucky, you might even see a B24 or a 312T, but here at the Pod there's Anger Management, Van with No Name, Dat Fing, and Miss De Meaner and, as often as not, there's exquisitely detailed paintwork to illustrate the name. Or there's 'rat look,' the subculture that involves running a car that looks like it's been left in a field since 1962, with the visible neglect sometimes complemented by randomly applied wire netting and gate latches. But the look of not-so-elegant decay might also be subverted by a good as new big-block Chevy and a trick transmission. Drag racing's iconography is infinitely more beguiling than the utilitarian prose attached to circuit racing kit. Omex, Emerald, Spax, SU, Hewland, and Scholar are, or have been, key brands in what drag racers dismiss as "roundy round" racing, but how can that Anglo Saxon reserve ever compete for verbal glamour with brands such as Moroso, Edelbrock, Hooker, Cragar, Holley, Yenko, and Milodon? You can almost feel that hot Californian sun on your back when you say those names aloud, even in Bedfordshire. Hell yeah, (see the effect all this stuff can have on me?). And I know that we English are supposed to be masters of understatement, but Cosworth even underplayed understatement with its Formula 1 DFV (Double Four Valve) and its Sixties Formula 3 MAE (Modified Anglia Engine – yes, really). Meanwhile, Chevrolet had the Rat Motor and the Mouse Motor …

Marc Henney is driving Ethanol Guzzler, a Super Pro ET dragster, and he's from Frankfurt. "It's a Chevy Big-Block 620 cubic inch and it's about 900bhp. I run 7.15s, about 177mph (285km/h). I come here two times every year. The European drag scene ..?" He gives an ironic laugh, "yeah … it's … yeah … it's okay. In Germany I race at Hockenheim and a little venue in the north. I like Santa Pod – nice track, friendly people." Marc tells me he grew up in the sport, "my father worked with the timing crew in Germany and so … I got the bug … I've been driving for 11 years now." Drag racing also has an active junior class and today there's 30 junior dragsters entered, and whilst their power plants have the humblest of origins, the cars reach up to 85mph (135km/h) in 8-seconds over the eighth of a mile, which is rocket hatch territory. I ask one of the junior team's bosses if I can talk to one of his drivers and he reappears from the caravan with all three of his girl racers. Morgan and Caitlin Wilson are from Scarborough, Charlotte Bradford's from Stafford, and they are all feisty, funny, and eager to talk. Morgan tells me: "I'm drag racing because my mum and dad met drag racing, and they used to race against each other at York, Avon Park, and sometimes here. I've been coming to the track since I was like four months old." Caitlin loves the sport – "It's fun, it's part of my life, it's like 'here we are' really, we've always been here." Charlotte loves "… the adrenalin and the people, everything about it." Is it just the speed or is it beating the other driver? "It's BOTH!" Big laugh from all three girls. I don't ask exact ages but they're all 16ish I'd guess, and Morgan tells me she's been racing for the last six years and definitely wants to keep on racing as she gets older. Charlotte's school friends – "don't believe me when I tell them about my racing," but Caitlin's close friends "… are all like, don't crash or die!" but so far, she hasn't even come close to the former. Morgan tells me about the Briggs and Stratton engines – "which are supposed to be lawnmower engines, but they've never seen a lawn in their life. They are purpose built in America – it's really big over there." I tell the girls that I used to drive a Briggs and Stratton powered lawnmower myself, and they seem remarkably impressed – either that or they're incredibly polite.

As I leave the girls chatting and laughing amongst themselves (and why didn't I meet girls like that when I was 16?), I am thanked effusively by another team member for wanting to hear what her girls had to say, reinforcing my growing belief that drag racing is more gender blind than any other type of motorsport. Charlotte, Caitlin, and Morgan are a credit to her, and I hope they go on to follow the footsteps of legends such as Shirley Muldowney or up and coming stars like Leah Pritchett and Brittany Force. The girls' utterly extraordinary reaction times, which are displayed when they race, leave me reeling – how do they do that? Later in the season, in the parallel universe of Formula 1, Sebastian Vettel expresses disbelief at Valtteri Bottas' reaction time as the lights went out in Austria – "0.2 seconds; unhuman." It isn't unusual at the Pod, Seb, you ought to get out more …

I really should be watching some cars in action from the grandstand by now, but I am distracted by a split-screen Corvette (has any American car ever looked as perfectly proportioned?) whose rear slicks are so immensely wide that they nearly touch each other in the middle. The 'Vette's being worked on, and – unlike in circuit racing where chassis fine tuning is a far more common sight than engine work that can't be done on a laptop – here there are four big men with big sockets doing serious stuff on the V8's half-exposed innards. Each cylinder is bigger than a Focus EcoBoost's whole engine.

Distracted again, because here's Another Small Fortune, a pukka dragster in Super Pro ET; the name's apposite because the crew chief tells me the crankshaft is broken, meaning driver Martyn Jones has time to talk to me. He looks and sounds a lot more phlegmatic than I would be if I'd just learned that my car was out of the meeting and would live up to its name by needing yet more of my cash thrown at it before it could race again. Martyn's an IT consultant from Hamble – "and what I should be driving is a blown – supercharged – Chrysler

Hemi V8; about 450 cubic inches and it makes 2600bhp – or it does when it's running …" Martyn explains how he runs in bracket racing, which involves the driver choosing a dial in time, which is his or her predicted time for the run, meaning that the emphasis is on driver skill at the expense of raw performance. Martyn's quickest permitted time is "six seconds flat, we can't go any faster and to do that I have to come off the throttle at 1000 foot (i.e. well before the end of a run). On the full-quarter? The quickest we have ever run is 5.79 seconds and 242mph (340km/h) …" Martyn has been racing since 1979, starting in "a small front-engined dragster with a supercharged 1071 cc Cooper S engine, but I rarely raced it as it was so unreliable. So many problems … I love the sport, it's spectacular, it's a challenge and if anybody thinks driving one of these things is easy I can show them how it certainly isn't simple. I've wanted to do drag racing since the early Seventies, when I saw the sport at Lee on Solent RNAS; I was 15. I do five meetings a year here and I couldn't run this anywhere else – no, not at York! Too bumpy …"

The siren call of cars and bikes running hard and fast down the strip lures me finally to the start line grandstand and I settle back to enjoy the show. There's probably 150 vehicles entered and a steady procession appears from behind the stand. Some of the milder street legal stuff may be undramatic as, however effective a road car an Audi S3 may be, even a perfectly executed hole shot (qui vive) from an S3 isn't going to trouble my adrenal gland but when its wild child cousins from VW Pro show up things get a whole lot more interesting. If you are of a certain age you will remember the asthmatic wheezing that was the VW Beetle's calling card, the sound of a four that was flat in more ways than one. That's the Ur Beetle of course, the kraft durch freude people's car with the dodgy parenthood, not the lukewarm Bauhaus pastiche that VW served up in 1998. Anyway … you will remember that Beetles never broke, but they never got anywhere fast either. But these ones do, even if they still have a flat-four, because they are boosted by turbochargers as big as a pedal bin and they're fuelled on stuff (stoff?) that makes your eyes stream. The Wizards of NOS decals remind you that laughing gas can induce mirth even if you don't breathe the stuff in – just watch a bellowing, barking Beetle squat down at the rear and wave its front wheels two feet in the air en route to a quarter-mile time a 911 Turbo couldn't hope to beat. But the sinister black Beetle with the So Cal body language is even quicker, and it is totally silent. Electrically powered, and the best burnout of any of its siblings. "The times they are a-changin' …"

I can, and do, soak up the spectacle for the rest of the day and if it was all good, I am still savouring two special memories. Watching and listening to Marc Harteveld's Pro Modified Plymouth Superbird, Voodoo Hemi, feels like having a front row seat for a preview of the apocalypse, my heart might be in rapture but my head is pleading duck and cover. Six seconds, smoke everywhere, 200mph (320km/h) and the crowd exhales in unison before whooping and hollering. I can't do this stuff, obviously, but I do essay a loud clap which seems to go unnoticed. The other memory? A Top Fuel bike that's what, because I have never, ever seen anything like this. It's a bike, but a very, very long one, and its engine has 1000bhp, about four times more than a Moto GP bike. This stampede goes through just the one wheel, remember, and the noise disturbs my chest even more than my ears and I seem to have lost most of my power of speech as at the end of the run all I can say is 'Jesus Christ ...' Depending on your preferred deity, you'd say something pretty similar if you had just witnessed a 200 yard wheelie and a 200mph (320km/h), 6-point something run. It is truly, madly and deeply astonishing.

Verdict

1. Summary – 20 quid entry fee (more than club racing, less than touring cars) and a pound for the programme. Unlike the tired old tat that masquerades as a programme in so much circuit racing this one is in what used to be called full colour. Yes, some race programmes still feature black and white photos, just as they did in 1969. The Pod programme is only 12 pages, but it still manages to tell newcomers what they need the know to understand what is going on, with a brilliantly concise description of each class.

Unexpectedly, on arriving, the security staff on the gate politely ask if they can inspect the boot of the Yeti. I had assumed its purpose was to intercept any bad lads trying to avoid the entry fee, a stunt I had last pulled at Mallory Park in 1973. It wasn't that though, as I was told the idea was to find and confiscate glass bottles (booze fine, puncture causing glass not so fine) and yes, terrorist bombs. It has finally come to this in 2017 Britain; I had seen bags being checked at Croft a fortnight earlier and today I also saw, for the first time, the Government advice posters on what to do in the event of a terrorist attack. Which essentially was to run like buggery and don't look back. Who'd have thought it ..?

2. Nature notes – This was never going to be a long report. But hold your horses – the Pod was visited by red kites at regular intervals throughout the day. And they seemed to like Nostalgia Superstock best of all. Good choice.

3. Catering – Yes, of course, there's burgers and there's fries and there's bacon and there's donuts. It seems to be the law that every motorsport venue sells them. But there was fish and chips and – wow – only a noodle bar. Which was good, no?

4. What could be improved? – Not much, if anything. The staff are friendly and efficient, the parking is a stone's throw from the strip, there's a circuit shop, covered areas where you can escape the sun and rain and an access all areas policy, except the startline grandstand. I happily paid a tenner to sit there but I can understand why some would pay ten times that not to do so.

5. Website – Top marks again. Instead of the staid and uninformative efforts I have seen elsewhere, it's funky, fun and tells me just what I want to know, even including an illustrated entry list.

Somehow drag racing at Santa Pod manages simultaneously to maintain an outlaw vibe, with its leather and bandana chic, but it also boasts the most diverse spectator and competitor demographic in any type of motorsport I have witnessed so far this year. It's an addictive combination of subcultures, and it's where badass biker meets Rammstein meets The Beach Boys, with a seasoning of Nordic steel, Dutch cool, and Essex geezer.

As I left the Pod I drove past a memorial to the US personnel who had been based at RAF Podington in World War Two. And I got to thinking; 40,000 US airmen were killed in the war and many of them were flying out of bases like Podington. And what could be a better memorial to those bank clerks from Vermont, shopkeepers from Maryland, and farm boys from Arkansas than the sound and fury of the strip with its V8 thunder and the Stars and Stripes snapping in the breeze above the same runway where, 70 years before, B17 Flying Fortresses had once lumbered into the air, bomb-heavy and bound for the Ruhr?

BARBON MANOR – 1 JULY

Even though Barbon is only 50-something miles from home it still takes at least two hours to drive there, as the road leading through Wensleydale is not best suited to making swift, or even modest, progress, not even when you are driving a Caterham Seven. The A684 is twisty and narrow, it has far more blind bends than open ones and in summer it is populated by holidaying drivers who like to watch the hills and dry-stone walls scroll by at a sedate pace. But the journey to Barbon is almost always worthwhile (almost? Read on ...) as the speed hillclimb at Barbon Manor takes place in one of the loveliest motorsport venues I have ever attended. The eponymous manor, a modest country estate house, hangs on the edge of Thorn Moor, on the western slope of the Pennines, and its steep access drive is the venue for today's British Hillclimb Championship round.

Barbon is far from being Britain's best hillclimb as its half-mile (0.8km) length contains just two left-hand bends, a short straight followed by a longer one, and ends in a right-hand hairpin at the summit. Even slower cars complete the climb in less than half a minute and the record time is almost exactly 20 seconds. Barbon is, therefore, a hill that is positively parochial compared to European venues such as Saint Ursanne – Les Rangiers with its near two-minute record time, and even Harewood is nearly twice the length. Barbon is a hill that favours big horsepower cars for the relatively long top straight and drivers with cojones sufficiently large to leave their braking later than late into the top hairpin. It's far less technical (the word racing drivers like to use for slow and tricky bends) than Harewood or Prescott but there are few places I would rather watch motorsport than at Barbon, sitting on the grass at the hilltop and watching the controlled violence of a single-seater reaching 130mph (210km/h) on a track ten feet wide, then braking impossibly hard into the final bend and deploying its 600bhp in a white knuckle ride to the finish line. And between runs, I can enjoy the perfect view of a perfect England, with grazing sheep in the pastures leading down to Barbon village and the parish church looking as only an English church can on a midsummer day. To the east and the north there's the infinity of peaks of the North Pennines and between runs you can hear only lapwings, curlews, and skylarks; on days like these it feels as though Santa Pod must surely be located on another planet.

Thanks to my 7.15am start, my drive up through Masham, Wensley, and Bainbridge was rarely interrupted by traffic, and even when I encountered any, it was the local farm lads pressing on in their Toyota HiLuxes that I caught, and not Hendrik en Janneke en route from the Rotterdam ferry at a heady 60km/h in their Westfalia RV. Above Hawes the road towards Ribblehead is a favourite route for loony tune bikers but this early in the morning there's just the one bike, which I smell half a mile before I see it, and it's a sedately ridden old BSA. We exchange thumbs up, one refugee of the road saluting the other, in this desolate somewhere lying miles from anywhere else. Then I take the tiny road leading down through Dentdale, limestone paved river bed running parallel to the road and an infinity of potholes somewhere far beneath me. Along here even 30mph (50km/h) can feel ambitious, 40mph (65km/h) insane and, as I drive along the cobbles of Dent's absurdly narrow main street, I return the smiles and waves from early morning fell walkers. Then it's the final steep climb and gentler descent through Barbon Dale, and I see the becks on Barbon Fell still flowing hard and strong after Wednesday's heavy rain. They were trying to tell me something, something that I only started to suspect when I saw the idling Porsche 911 and Focus RS in the village itself, their drivers talking to a local wearing (but of course) a Marlboro liveried body warmer. Cancelled, it's only bloody cancelled, the heavy rain that had enlivened the becks having also turned what is so aptly called the paddock into a mud bath. This news was on the website, which I hadn't checked since Tuesday, even though Barbon already has form on the cancellation front. Usually, it's the biblical rain for which the northwest is notorious but the last time I had driven home early was when a bump had appeared in the top straight, apparently almost overnight, and was only noticed when it surgically removed a low riding racer's sump at high speed.

I park on the outskirts of the village, next to Barbon Beck and decide what to do next. But it's a summer weekend, I don't even have to go to work anymore, there's a Caterham to enjoy and I am in some of England's most inspiring scenery and so what if a hillclimb is cancelled, it's assuredly a First World Problem, no? On traffic grounds I dismiss both a run through the Lakes and a Border Blat over to Duns and the Jim Clark rooms and I am just thinking about whether I will stay awake at the Croft club meeting when an old style Audi 80 Estate draws alongside. He's from Morecambe, is far from happy but cheers up when he tells me about his TVR – "My mate's Griff[ith] used to leave me behind but t'bugger doesn't do that no more. I've got a turbo on it now and I were pulling 160+ (260km/h) up [here he names a hill he assumes I know intimately but that I've never heard of] and before I could only do 145mph there. 500 lb ft of torque though … So what will that Caterham do then?" I tell him the Seven wouldn't do 145mph (235km/h) if it was dropped out of a plane, but I don't tell him that 145mph on a public road, let alone 160mph (260km/h), in 2017, is perhaps more than a little daft.

I drive up to Sedbergh, tracking the River Lune's meandering as it runs parallel to the A683 and then I take the A684 east along Garsdale which, staggeringly, is deserted until I cross the watershed and start the descent through Wensleydale. It was an intense drive, and the fact that I rarely strayed much over the speed limit says as much about the serpentine road as my laid-back mood. Which lasted until I saw the ambulance, blue lights ablaze and in a hurry, and then the queue of traffic with a police pickup blocking the road. 20 minutes passed in a pleasant reverie until we were waved forward, driving past the two riderless big bikes propped up on the dry-stone wall that were almost certainly testimony to fracture and bruising, and I hope nothing even worse.

90 minutes later I called in to Croft and it was obvious that the security staff had just taken delivery of even more cones and tape to deal with the influx of spectators, which today was threatening to get into three figures. Increasingly this year, and possibly not unconnected to the appointment of a new circuit manager, getting in to Croft has resembled trying to cross from East to West Berlin in the Cold War, with passes being scrupulously inspected by stony faced guards. I had known the people on the gate at Croft for years but this year they have joined the ranks of the disappeared. And it gets worse, as after I park up by the chicane two hi-vis clad security guys wander over and minutely inspect each of the dozen parked cars to ensure their papers are in order. And hold on, one car isn't displaying a pass! Cue much radio traffic, frowns and jobsworth body language, which is rapidly dispersed by the appearance of the burly marshal from the nearby post who owns the offending vehicle. Who would have thought it, a marshal using his own car to get to his position and then parking it where there's room for a couple of hundred more cars? Or there is room as long as you are not disabled, as the banking reserved for blue badge holder vehicles remains blocked off with a skip, as it has been for most of the year. Here's an idea – maybe the skip could be used, not as a road block, but to store the piles of rubbish (cans, bottles, fibreglass debris, Styrofoam cups, and a forlorn brolly) which are still here from the BTCC meeting nearly three weeks ago? I'm on a roll now and so maybe, just maybe, the security lads could be deployed to collect the litter instead of making visitors and marshals feel like trespassers?

I stay an hour or two and watch a couple of Caterham races – fast but not as furious as I had hoped and a Legends race – not as fast but far more furious. But then I lose interest completely, as a thin grid of junior stock hatch and an even thinner MX5 grid will not keep me awake. They might have done in April, when I have been known to spend a morning at a test day, so desperate can my habit become after a winter's forced abstinence. But in early July? Nah.

I had planned to stay at home on Sunday as Joanne might be incredibly tolerant of my motorsport addiction, but I still needed to build up some goodwill before I disappeared to Donington next weekend. But she is working on her latest talk on the WI and local history society circuit, it's about Ancient Greek Drama. You'll have maybe heard of this stuff even if you haven't seen it – Aeschylus, Euripides and Sophocles? Having attended a few such talks as Joanne's roadie I can report that the fearsome ladies of the WI are especially amused by the slides depicting the giant leather penises sported by the players back in the day in 500 BC (or am I supposed to say BCE now? Christ knows). Joanne's rehearsal means I can drive down to Harewood again to watch the round of the hillclimb championship – what should have been the second half of a weekend double header with Barbon.

I have written about Harewood already so you already know about the view, the food and the red kites, but I can report that the astonishingly accelerative Force Xtec was a special delight, that the visiting Channel Island sand racers were as bonkers as ever (think forward control, super-size Ariel Atom with a mid-mounted V8), and that the car I most wanted to take home was the yellow Porsche 911 RSR with its sexy hips surmounted by its duck tail spoiler. But I couldn't help thinking just what the Force would have looked and sounded like as it charged up Barbon, its braking provoking a cacophony of bangs and grumbles, and its acceleration being itself accelerated by the giant shove from the turbocharger. I hope to find out next season ...

DONINGTON PARK – 7/8 JULY 2017

We all know about Donington's prewar glory days, when the Silver Arrows jackbooted the homespun ERAs and Rileys into touch, and created a new generation of lifelong motorsport fans in the process. The vastly powerful Mercedes and Auto Unions even created their own iconography: They leap! They deafen! They blitzkrieg the opposition! Their drivers are übermenschen! But, when Tom Wheatcroft relaunched the circuit, his main focus was on the future, as the nostalgia industry hadn't really taken root in 1977. There might have been a museum on site, and even a life size replica of a Spitfire (Supermarine, not Triumph) overlooking the Craner Curves, but both the design of the new circuit and the programme of races looked forward, with only respectful nods to Von Brauchitsch and his Mercedes W125 and to Rosemeyer and his Auto Union Type C. Between 1977 and 1993 Donington hosted Formula 1, 2, and 3000 as well as Group C sports cars, and the venue was the very model of a modern race circuit. No more RAF specification latrines (such as the ones Silverstone still had), but spacious and clean Scandi-look bogs instead; no more dank and confined pit garages, but dry and spacious new build ones instead. In the Seventies, catch and debris fencing was the bane of any circuit that hosted anything more exotic than club racing, but Donington trod new ground by introducing run off areas with stout concrete walls to arrest errant racing cars. The result was a racing circuit in heavily treed parkland which offered close and unobstructed views of the track over almost its full length. And the racing was sublime; especially in Formula 2, the series that I adored for its close competition and jewel-like cars. Two memories still burn from that era, and the first was the excitement of standing in the pit garage as the two Ralt Honda RH6-84s were being warmed up in readiness for the circuit's last ever Formula 2 race in 1984. The V6's screaming howl was as demonic as it was addictive. Standing next to me was my friend David Bramhall, then a newcomer to live motor racing and quite unprepared for the assault on the senses of unsilenced racing engines. He soon got used to it, and apprehension's bitten-lip grimace was transformed into the beatific grin that a 24-valve racing V6 is guaranteed to induce. There in front of us, bending over the rear of the white Ralt and adjusting the wing, was its legendary designer, the 'T' in the BT designation of every Brabham racing car, Ron Tauranac. The second memory was from an earlier Formula 2 meeting when, within 20 seconds of the race starting, I had to duck and cover to avoid the flying debris, as what seemed like half a grid's worth of Ralts,

Marches and Maurers clattered into the wall at Redgate, coming to rest only feet away as shards of shattered wing and nosecone arced into the spectator area. Motor racing is dangerous, just like it says on the ticket.

And Donington had delivered so much more, such as the Gunnar Nilsson Trophy in 1979, featuring a high-speed display of Formula 1 cars, ancient and modern, including a Tyrrell for Jackie Stewart, a Mercedes for Juan Manuel Fangio and – crikey – only the Brabham BT46 Fan car. Add a race for the simply wonderful BMW M1 Pro cars contested by a galaxy of drivers, from Piquet and Hunt to Andretti and Jones, and my cup overflowed on that June day in 1979. As it did in 1989, when David and I felt the ground shake at the Old Hairpin from the seismic thunder of a full grid of Group C sports prototypes leaving the start a quarter-mile away. And even that wasn't peak Donington because, as "any fule kno," that was the European Grand Prix 1993, when Senna showed that his talent came from another world and when Rubens Barrichello also seemed to be another visitor from space, so searingly fast was he in the Jordan Hart 193. So why do we never forget the former, but struggle to remember the latter?

Donington, after a near death experience in 2009 triggered by an overambitious bid to become a grand prix circuit again, has now had reconstructive surgery and although some of the scars are permanent, at least the place now looks less like the victim of carpet bombing than it did five years ago.

This weekend I wasn't really here for the racing, as the Lotus Seven Club had chosen Donington as the venue to celebrate the Seven's 60th anniversary. Caterham was holding a weekend race meeting exclusively for Sevens too, and if the two events would have exceeded the sum of their parts had they been more closely integrated into one, there was still a buzz about Donington that had been absent from my last few visits. I think it is partly to do with the fact that if the Competition and Markets Authority approve, MotorSport Vision will be leasing the site, which can only be a good thing, and it's also because the circuit is now home to both BookaTrack, the Caterham dealer and track day operator, and a cluster of Formula E race teams. Weekday race circuits used to feel like the Marie Celeste, but now they are becoming the sort of place you'd find an excuse to drop into en route to or from a work meeting, or maybe that's just my guilty little secret? But the opportunity to enjoy a coffee in the fresh air while being serenaded by the sound of a growly race engine and quick-shifted gears is guaranteed to make my day a better one.

I had driven my Caterham cross-country from Melton Mowbray to Donington in loose company with 60 French, German, Swiss, and Italian Sevens who had already toured up through East Anglia from horrid old Dover. Whilst I loathe the 'yes, just look at us – look' vibe of convoy runs, often conducted as if the participants were bestowing favour on an adoring public rather than just pissing them off, I won't deny that there's something comforting about seeing the yellow Seven following me, a discreet quarter-mile behind, whilst 200 yards ahead the matte black CSR, and the green and yellow Roadsport tracks past forgotten villages like Wymeswold and Widmerpool (so that's the inspiration for the character in Anthony Powell's *A Dance to the Music of Time*?). Driving in the company of other Sevens can feel like taking the Patrick McGoohan role in an episode of *The Prisoner*, or maybe it is just starring in my own trite little soap opera, as has become customary in our age of selfie narcissism.

Donington itself was under siege by hordes of Sevens, ranging from the mild mannered little originals of the early Sixties: all skinny wheels and Weber carburettors, to the supercharged, V6 powered, carbon bodied monster packing an insane 520bhp. This is the car conceived by the late Richard Lee, an artist in carbon fibre composition and one of the pioneers in installing ever more potent engines in Sevens. Richard's eccentricity was legendary, and on our first meeting, on a Seven tour of Wester Ross and Sutherland, Richard had calmly walked around the dining room of our hotel and replaced each long life light bulb with a traditional old-style bulb as the new-fangled jobs apparently emitted damaging radiation. Or something. He was a sound believer in homeopathy, which sadly (though predictably), did little to help his terminal illness, and the song he chose for his funeral was Black Sabbath's Paranoid ... But he was a lovely man, and the car he created is a fitting legacy. It has a 24-valve Yamaha based V6, with Rotorex supercharger, Sadev sequential gearbox, and a similar power to weight ratio to Jackie Stewart's Tyrrell Formula 1 car. Cripes.

And there's plenty of Formula 1 cars to see in Donington's museum, even if one has to walk past a Kampfgruppe of World War Two militaria first. Donington owner Kevin Wheatcroft is wealthy enough fully to indulge his fascination with Nazi tanks, trucks, bikes, and guns, and he is eccentric enough (as if owning a Raiders of the Lost Ark style German half-track weren't quite enough) to own Hitler's bed and to have constructed replicas of the Auschwitz gates with their notorious "Arbeit macht Frei" slogans – or so *The Guardian* website told me in 2015. I am not sure what our German guests will make of this shrine to the Third Reich, and I don't wait to find out as I stride past the satisfyingly rusty remains of Nazi ambition and find some Formula 1 cars to admire. I have visited the museum many times before, but the opportunity to scrutinise the evolution of the racing car never palls. The elegant simplicity of a Sixties Formula 1 car, with its narrow treaded tyres, tiny cigar-shaped body unadorned by aerodynamic aids, is in such contrast to the latest cars on show from the 2.4-litre V8 era, which ran until 2014. Cars such as the garishly liveried Force India are not only enormous compared to their svelte little 1.5-litre and 3-litre predecessors, but their bodywork looks absurdly complex, with a forest of carbon winglets and vanes adorning the front wing. I wander on through the halls, past the Royal Bank of Scotland liveried Williams (the RBS saga ended so well didn't it?) and Adrian Newey's shrink wrap designed Red Bull and you eventually reach peak F1. I think that the cars from the early Nineties manage to retain some of the elegant functionality of their predecessors whilst previewing both the potency and complexity of 2017 Formula 1. Just look at Senna's 1991 McLaren MP4/6 and tell me I'm wrong.

There's one exhibit at Donington that always makes me want to weep and it is the touchingly simple tribute to Tom Wheatcroft's protégé, Roger Williamson. It is difficult to imagine some Grand Prix drivers ever having been young men, and I simply can't believe that tough guys like Denny Hulme and Clay Regazzoni could ever have been less than 35, but Williamson, just like Johnny Herbert, always looked more lad than man. Forever young then, but no ladder to the stars and dead at just 25. I saw Williamson race in Formula 2 and 3, and I saw his debut in Formula 1 two weeks before his death at Zandvoort, and my abiding memory isn't his speed, but his voice. I heard him being interviewed after another victory (and there were lots of those) and he stressed the importance, at Oulton Park's many corners, of "getting your loins roight." You can take the lad out of Leicestershire but – you know the rest, right?

Caterham Cars had organised a weekend's racing for Sevens, and they varied in specification from mild to wild and were driven by everyone from 'coming men' such as Vincent Beltoise to the 'never were's and 'never will be's. As I walk through the paddock, I sense that familiar combination of pre-race angst, all urgent activity, last minute adjustment and checks, and then the post-race downtime spent dozing in a folding chair, grazing factoids, Instagramming, smiling at a tweet on a smart phone, or maybe dreaming of the winter days when you dreamed of days just like this one. Then there's man hugs with your pals and fellow racers, the ready laughter deployed to establish your bloke credentials, but often a little too loudly and always a little prematurely.

I might have had Sevens for 20 years and 100,000 miles but when I'm driving mine I am far too preoccupied properly to appreciate the speed, and so watching cars like the hardcore 420R, which has a similar power to weight ratio to my own car, as they bulleted out of the Melbourne Hairpin was revelatory. God, but they were quick, disappearing up the hill towards Goddards in a rapid-fire succession of popped and banged up shifts on their sequential gearboxes. And even the relatively cheap and low power Academy Sevens provided proof, yet again, that the key to close racing and full grids is low cost, rear-wheel drive, less grip than grunt, and absolutely no aerodynamic downforce. It really is quite extraordinary to witness how the same car can be made to behave in quite so many different ways, as our little group of Yorkshire Seven owners witnessed, watching the progress of one driver especially (who politeness dictates shall be nameless) who demonstrated the Seven's full range of party tricks. We had first noticed the yellow Seven when, running an unthreatened last, its driver outbraked himself and explored the run off area. And on each subsequent lap he approached the corner as if it had appeared quite unexpectedly on a fast cross-country drive on unfamiliar roads. The next time round, our friend missed the apex by a good ten feet and lurched round in a tyre squealing masterclass of terminal understeer, but on the following lap he lunged at the apex with such aggression that the car spun broadside before he got anywhere near. The only time the yellow car went through the corner properly was when another Seven had spun, forcing an unexpected change of approach from our hero, who rocketed around the corner, line inch-perfect and looking as 'on it' as Lewis Hamilton in Q3. We cheered our man on the slowing down lap, still in a comfortable last place, and we weren't being ironic either, because we'd had as much fun as he had had, and our enjoyment was enhanced by being able to share our lofty appraisal of our victim's performance on each lap. As if we could do any better …

I write elsewhere in this book about the fact that the essence of motor racing is a binary question – will the guy behind get past the guy in front? Forget Formula 1's daft preoccupation with undercuts and DRS, what really matters – what only matters – and what really thrills is watching two cars, running inches apart, entering the braking area, and finding out who will blink first; who sells the dummy, feinting left but opting for right; who can turn in on the brakes best, close off the apex, and power away to look for the next fight to pick. And when there are a dozen 270R Sevens fighting over third and fourth places alone, elbows out and jostling, ducking and diving in a drama with a new script every single lap? Life can feel pretty damned good. I try to remember last time I watched from Melbourne – as it's a part of the circuit that isn't always used, and for years I have loved to watch the majesty of the downhill, hold-your-breath, don't flinch Craner Curves – and, shockingly, the last thing I can remember watching from this spot was the Deutsche Tourenwagen Masters – the legendary DTM – back in the Nineties. My antipathy to the BTCC might have softened a little since my Croft experience last month, but the sheer drama of the DTM cars made the BTCC, then as now, look like amateur dramatics in the village hall. The DTM cars were absurdly complex, the paddock had more trucks and hospitality units than a Seventies' Grand Prix paddock and, if the cars didn't overtake as much as Caterhams do, their stage presence, speed, and noise more than compensated. Their looks could make you swoon, because who couldn't love a Martini liveried Alfa Romeo with a V6 singing its tenor solo and conducted by the cooler than cool son of Siena, Alessandro Nannini? Not for the first time this long summer I find myself half in the present, watching whatever's in front of me, sometimes enthralled, other times indifferent, but half the time I'm in a reverie, smiling at past sights and sounds. Do the followers of the stuff I've never watched – the ball games, Wimbledon, the Tour de France – suffer from the same bipolarity, I wonder?

Verdict

1. Summary – The racing was peripheral to my reason for being at Donington but the circuit appears, at last, to be showing signs of recovery from its long malaise, rehabilitation now taking the place of intensive care. But it's still hard to reconcile the glory days of Formulae 1, 2, 3, 3000, and Group C with this homely location, the start/finish line sponsored by a pie firm (or was it central heating?), the pitted paddock, the abandoned hospitality suites and ageing infrastructure.

2. The viewing may be close and fun at Melbourne, but at everywhere else around the circuit the spectator is now located at least ten and sometimes up to 30 yards further away than he or she was when the circuit re-opened. Having seen the aftermath of Alan McNish's Formula 3000 accident, which killed a bystander here in 1990, and whose aftermath looked more like plane crash, I can grudgingly accept that our post-millennial obsession with risk assessments isn't always entirely daft …

3. It is now as long since Donington reopened for racing in 1977 as the reopening was from the prewar glory days of Mercs and Auto Unions. Your baby boomer reporter attributes this to not enough tempus but far too much fugit. Fugit's the word all right …

4. The museum is still worth visiting, despite the increased emphasis on militaria. The most frustrating aspect is the ill-thought-out design of the displays, which often juxtapose separate eras. And, if you are as much of a pedant as I can be, your suffering will know no respite when you encounter the signage. It is simply terrible – poorly written, often factually inaccurate, and littered with spelling and basic grammatical mistakes. I am far from perfect, but I suspect that whoever wrote some of Donington's signage still moves his lips when reading. It's that bad.

SHELSLEY WALSH – 22 JULY 2017

"How much?" are the first two words that North Yorkshire farmers teach their children. Intonation is important as the question has to be uttered in a tone that combines outrage, disbelief, and good humour. The question may be asked in many different situations, such as on the receipt of a quotation for a new milking machine or on being told by grandchild, Dwight, how much he needs to pay for the four 99 ice creams at the Osmotherley Show. And I was close to asking the question myself when I was told it would cost me £30 for a single ticket and a programme for Shelsley Walsh's Classic Nostalgia Festival. This was three times the ticket price for a RAC hillclimb championship round at Harewood, and after the guy on the gate confirmed that no, it wasn't a weekend ticket, "just for today, sir," I muttered to myself that this had better be worth it. And, actually, it was, if not quite in the way I had expected, as today turned out to be more about the people than the place. Not that the place wasn't worth a 5.30am start on a wet and wild July morning, as Worcestershire looked more wonderful the further west I drove. The wooded hillsides, smoked with mist and low cloud, reminded me of the Vosges and, just like Alsace, there was an unsettling awareness of being right on the edge with an imperative to tread warily on the borderlines between two countries. To the west I would see brief glimpses of the darker, taller hills delineating the Welsh Border and was it just me, or did I sense a bustle in the hedgerow? I can understand now why Robert Plant drew such inspiration from this mysterious and brooding countryside as, quite unlike Yorkshire's wide open and almost treeless 'take me as tha' finds me lad' Dales, here it was all wooded lanes leading who knew where and an intuited sense of dark whisperings in the black and white houses studding the hillsides.

Shelsley Walsh is the oldest operational motorsport venue in the world, with speed hillclimbs having taken place here since 1905, and today the venue was exploiting the burgeoning nostalgia market that monthly magazines such as *Octane* and *Classic & Sports Car* so love to feature. Shelsley's unique selling point this weekend was a celebration of the venue's close links with the Campbell family, Malcolm having competed here in the Twenties in Sunbeams and Talbots. It is also 50 years since Donald Campbell died at Coniston Water as he pushed Bluebird to 300mph, and his daughter Gina is here in person as the focus of the celebration. Record breaking, whether on land or water, has never captivated me quite as much as racing and competition, but nobody who was around in January 1967 will ever be able to erase the memory of that flickering black and white footage of Bluebird's nose rearing almost vertically before breaking up and disappearing beneath the surface in a starburst of debris. The Summer of Love that followed a few months later somehow feels far more recent, in full hallucinogenic colour, reeking of dope, and sounding sublime, but the Campbell crash now feels more like a folk memory bequeathed to us from our grandparents, as if record breaking for Queen and Country were forever marooned in the Empire days of the Twenties and Thirties. But if that thought renders poor Donald a man out of time it is not to underestimate his drive to match his father's achievements. There's a whole PhD to be researched on the reasons why so many racing drivers felt driven to emulate their father's profession. The litany of names includes the Brabham brothers, Jacques Villeneuve, Nico Rosberg, Max Verstappen, Michael Andretti, Hans Stuck, and Damon Hill. Hill didn't employ a ghost writer and his superbly crafted autobiography, Watching the Wheels, didn't shrink from describing what it felt like to be the introspective kid whose double world champion, Le Mans and Indy winning, after dinner speaking, risqué joke cracking, caddishly moustached charmer of a dad was the life and soul of everybody else's party. And oh, the sweetest irony of that dad never having been being crowned BBC Sports Personality of the Year, unlike lad Damon in '96.

I decide to speak to Gina Campbell if I can engineer an opportunity to do so, but first there's the second entirely new venue of the year to explore, the other was York Autograss, and the contrast could hardly be greater with this place. Shelsley feels like its own little alternative world where only good things ever happen and where only the nicest people go, and if it veers close to a suffocatingly middle class Utopia, the sheer beauty of the setting and the friendliness of everybody I meet stops me from reprising my chippy Northerner act. There are echoes of Goodwood, the paddock's covered garages especially, but here one (one? Get me, eh?) feels that the history isn't an alternative reality, because Shelsley really does feel as though little has changed since Raymond Mays attacked the hill in his ERA in the Fifties. There is even a commemorative plaque near the start line to Mays, and I wonder how many people here today are aware of Mays' 'colourful' private life and whether in today's more relaxed society he would have been able more overtly to express his sexual orientation.

Shelsley's layout is utterly beguiling, with a steeply angled start line overlooked by viewing points, and also by the perfectly named Vox Villa, from which the languid voiced commentator gives a stream of consciousness review of cars and drivers and their performance off the line. 20 minutes viewing is enough to demonstrate that front-wheel drive cars struggle to put their power down on this slope, that a Porsche 911 (in both traditional form as well as in the guise of the flat-six powered VW Beetle) has astonishing traction and that a World Rally Car Mitsubishi WRC 04, in the hands of Kristian Sohlberg, not only makes one hell of a noise but can also ascend the hill faster than anything else here today, including even the ex Derek Warwick Toleman TG280 Formula 2 car. The runs are competitive but so laid back is the atmosphere that caring about the actual times seems to border on vulgarity and so I decide to explore the paddock and talk to some drivers. As I stroll, I realise that I am possibly the only man in the paddock who isn't wearing plum or mustard-coloured cords, but distressed Wrangler jeans, virtually my sole trousering since my retirement in 2012. Anyway, jeans (or maybe Carroll Shelby dungarees?) are the only thing to wear when meeting an AC Cobra, no? The white Cobra had already caught my eye, as I love the shape of the early narrow-bodied Cobras as much as I loathe the steroid-pumped 427 parodies that so many replica firms turn out. Did you know that it's now the law that if you drive a Cobra 427 replica you must not only wear a bandanna and Ray-Bans, but you must also wear shit-kicking leather work boots as well? If a 427, even in original form, is a sledgehammer then the slim and delicate 289 is a switchblade. And this Cobra is even more understated, because its driver, Andrew Lovett, explains that it is actually a very rare 260 (denoting the US cubic inch capacity which translates to 4200cc). Andrew is from nearby Worcester, working at Listers Land Rover in Droitwich as retail manager, and says today "is the first time I've ever competed at Shelsley, although I've been coming here for years. The Cobra is my father's and it's a '62, so basically it really is an AC Ace with a V8 dumped in the front. This car ended up being used in the Shelby driving school and was used in *Viva Las Vegas*, so this is the actual car Elvis drove in the movie." Hell-fire is all I can think at this revelation, I'm no real Elvis fan but I have been to Graceland and, well, only bloody Elvis ... And whilst I don't raise the grubby question of price with such a polite young man I do wonder, with this rhinestone provenance, just what the auction reserve might be at Pebble Beach. I ask Andrew how often he gets asked if the Cobra is a real one; he rolls his eyes and laughs – "every single person outside the motorsport community asks that question. But sometimes I don't want them to know it's a real one, depends who I'm talking to. And yes, I prefer the original to the later big block cars." Andrew's take on motorsport is that it's a broad church and of course people should also go and see BTCC and Formula 1: "it's the pinnacle of the sport, it's where they're really pushing, the technology is great but this stuff, here at Shelsley ... this is where it all started."

Next I talk to John Newton from Deganwy, North Wales, and he is driving a gorgeously sexy TVR Vixen S2 with a 1700cc Ford Crossflow delivering 140bhp. It has the classic period modification of twin 45 Webers, the Italian carburettors that looked like works of art, sounded like angry goblins, and were found in everything from Lotuses to Lamborghinis in the Sixties and early Seventies. John had graduated to the stubby TVR from the even more petite Mark I Austin Healey Sprite – "which I still have and have had for 44 years. It's a 1380 cc, it's got a single Weber, straight cut gearbox and limited-slip diff." Not your standard Sprite then. John tells me that driving the TVR up the course "is alright, it's okay here but far more of a handful at Prescott where you've got to be quite aggressive, especially with the gear changing. Shelsley is short, yes, and the secret is keeping a car of this performance flat in third through Kennel and getting the Esses right. You need to have enough bottle to tackle the Esses as fast as you should, you normally brake too early and you need to be disciplined." Final question, John – do you ever think 'I wish this was an original Tuscan or a Griffith with a thumping great V8 up front?' He laughs. "Yes, an early one, oh God yes. But I'd never be able to afford one now, sadly, just the same as so many other cars I lusted after when I was young."

It's time to explore the Shelsley site some more and it's a big contrast to the Barbon environment of a lonely gazebo in a cow-patted field. It's like a little village down here; there are shops, a bar, a café, and even an open-air stage with live music and a dance floor. As a brontophobia victim (which sounds less wimpish than saying thunder and lightning scare me silly) at least I shall have somewhere to hide from the forecast thunderstorms. But the sun's shining now, and it's reflecting off the exquisitely proportioned Bugatti Type 37 that forms part of the Campbell display. The Bug's in French blue, naturellement, and I was just thinking that if I owned it I would spend whole days just worshipping those divine proportions when a vaguely familiar figure walked by, towards Sir Malcolm's Rolls-Royce Phantom 2. It's Gina Campbell, Donald's daughter.

"John, of course I've got time to talk to you, take as long as you need." I'm charmed immediately by this tiny, bird-like and endearingly animated woman. She tells me that she "... realised that my grandfather ran up the hill here, the organisers asked me to be their guest of honour this weekend and I jumped at the opportunity because to come and see these Campbell-connected cars is fantastic. And the whole event ... I'm just blown away by it. The camaraderie, the friendship and openness of everybody, the thrill of the hill – it's amazing." I asked Gina why she thought there had been such a resurgence of interest in the Campbell family's record breaking legacy, as 20 years ago it had been no more than a footnote in history but now a whole new generation of enthusiasts had wanted to find out more about the Campbell dynasty: "I think it's very much in the English psyche. We love our history, and things are circular and this year marks 50 years since my father died and so various places have put on events to commemorate his life and his achievements, not to mourn him but to celebrate him. Chris Evans said on the radio yesterday that it was also the anniversary of my grandfather doing a record run on Pendine Sands and so I was just meant to be here." I mention to Gina that having read Damon Hill's book recently I was reminded that being the child of a famous parent can be as much a curse as a blessing: "For me it's all good. I tell you – my father and grandfather's name is just ... oh, it opens so many doors for me. Look, if I wasn't Donald's daughter and Malcolm's granddaughter I wouldn't even be here so it's a privilege and an honour and it's very humbling to be part of that dynasty – it's a lot to live up to but I embrace it and I love it." Later, I see Gina being driven up the course in her dad's Jaguar XK 150 with the DC7 number plate and in her left hand she holds up Mr Whoppit, the teddy bear mascot rescued from Coniston immediately after the '67 crash. And quite unexpectedly, I find the sight so desperately moving that I feel close to tears. Embarrassing. And I wonder, was it simply empathy for another 60-something, as she remembered a lost father or was it (and this really would be worrying) a more teddy bear related emotion? That's a rocky psychological road I really do not want to drive down just now.

There's a man called Lord Lorne Jacobs who has built an homage to Malcolm Campbell's Bluebird record breaker of 1927. By the way, the 'Lord' bit is TK Maxx ennoblement as the title was an impulse purchase and the family seat is apparently a suburban semi in Northolt, or so I read in an *Octane* magazine feature. Jacobs' creation is far from an exact replica, but it is still a hugely impressive device, as I witness when it is driven up the hill by his ersatz 'lordship.' There's a 24-litre Napier Sea Lion aero engine up front, which its owner claims is developing 700bhp. If that's true, then Jacobs was being very careful with his right foot, but even so the spectacle is extraordinary, and it would be even more so at anywhere located outside Shelsley's timewarp bubble – where almost anything seems possible. Like every aero engined car I've ever seen, this one sounds as though its fire is permanently on the edge of either going out or exploding, so low revving is the engine but so thunderous are its power strokes. It's like hearing a Brobdingnagian Harley Davidson, which is another sentence I didn't expect to write, and the *Pseud's Corner* nomination can't be far away …

I wouldn't be at all surprised if most of the people at Shelsley weren't drifting into the same reverie as I did as the afternoon slid slowly by. Soothing tones from the commentary team were punctuated by the trademark whine of supercharged Austin Seven Specials, Buckleys (no, me neither) and MG TCs whilst distant strains of trad jazz, jive, and swing drifted up from the paddock, and I really wouldn't have been surprised if the time hadn't been "… ten to three? And is there honey still for tea?"

Verdict

1. Summary – An almost hallucinogenic escape from the reality of Trump, May, Brexit, and the rest of the horror stories and comedy acts of 2017. As a venue, Shelsley is bucolic perfection with a tangible feeling of history and heritage, which at times might come a little too close to smugness. As a speed hillclimb it's far more of a climb than it is a hill, as it's a short but very steep course that even slower cars ascend in the 30-40 second mark, and although the view is delightful, it can be restricted in places by the trackside privet hedge, which is both high and wide. Cue for some guerrilla gardening maybe? An hour or so with a Black and Decker hedge cutter would get the perpetrator in the stocks in these parts but it would do a lot for the trackside view. Uniquely, in my experience anyway, there are some 'no-go' areas reserved for corporate guests. On the evidence of today, very few of these important and doubtless high net worth people (or the filthy rich, as we used to say) could be arsed to turn up, leaving some valuable viewing areas tragically unused. What a shame it is that, even at a hillclimb venue, albeit a very posh one, we Johns and Mikes, Julies and Daves, have to be physically separated from the Ruperts and Hermiones, Tristrams and Allegras. Or maybe it's vice versa? But I enjoyed seeing a huge diversity of cars and the friendliness of both competitors and fellow visitors undermined the widely held Yorkshire conviction that people are far friendlier Up North. The absurd entry price was twice what I expected but the

74-page programme was well written and informative. Car parking was ample, if hilly (which I guess shouldn't have been too much of a surprise), and the event stewards were young, helpful, exquisitely polite, and the girls were distractingly good looking. I dare say the boys were, too, but I'm not one to judge.

2. Nature Notes – Who knows what nature of beasts were lurking in the woods? If the undergrowth was home for wild boar or wyverns I would not have been remotely surprised. But I was captivated by the pied wagtail that was happily foraging for treats on the track, flying up a few feet to avoid another racing car at the last second. Lots of pigeons in the woods, rooks and carrion crows were busy over the fields, and jackdaws were skulking around the Dutch barn next to the paddock. A man wearing a cravat, brass buttoned blazer and Panama hat who looked like a Nigel or perhaps a Henry jogged my arm and pointed out the two red kites spiralling on the thermals above us. Kind of him to share, and I resisted the temptation to suggest a trip to Specsavers as the kites were, in fact, nothing of the sort, but a pair of buzzards doing exactly what buzzards love to do on sunny afternoons.

3. Catering and general facilities – Harewood and Barbon have tents but Shelsley has a permanent café and bar. My sandwich was not even up to Tesco's value range, but the reassuringly expensive £7.50 fish and chips looked good and smelled even better. Lots of ice cream and drink outlets too, some trade stands and a classic car concours sponsored by *Classic & Sports Car* magazine.

4. What could be improved? – My minor cavils and carps above excepted. The day was almost perfect and exceeded my already high expectations. Add in a fly past by a Spitfire, which emptied the café in seconds, and my cup nearly overflowed.

5. Website – Up to date, nicely designed and informative.

SILVERSTONE CLASSIC – 28-30 JULY 2017

It's 7.30pm on a gloomy and wet July evening; it has been raining steadily for three hours, I've been up since before 6am, I have already spent eight hours watching historic racing cars, I've walked five or six miles over tarmac and cinder and the Thai meal I ate an hour go feels like it may have been a mistake. But I am standing in the rain at the entrance to Village corner, and I am captivated. And from the whoops and claps that spontaneously break out from the dozen or so people near me, I am not the only one who is thrilled to be watching a master class. It is the second day of the Silverstone Classic, billed as the biggest historic motor racing event in the world, and we are watching the race for pre-'66 Classic GT Cars, which means E –Type Jaguars, AC Cobras, a Bizzarrini GT and its kissing cousin the Iso Grifo, sundry Big Healeys and TVR Griffiths. And a Lotus Elan 26R, all 1558cc of it, in a race full of cars powered by engines up to four times bigger than the Elan's little twin-cam. But what does the second most famous Colin Chapman quotation say? "Adding power makes you faster on the straights. Subtracting weight makes you faster everywhere." I had already seen David Pittard's stealth grey Elan in dry practice, and its pace through Vale had been hold-your-breath fast – looking at least 15mph quicker than the V8 powered Cobras and TVRs: all bluster and swagger and whose pace came more from an adequacy of Detroit cubic inches than any finesse in the suspension department. But tonight that adequacy was a superfluity, an embarrassment of riches that couldn't be spent on Silverstone's rain-slick tarmac, and the Elan shone. It had qualified in the top ten, an achievement in itself on this circuit which lacks any slow corners, but now it was harrying the TVRs and Cobras every lap. Our little group watched the fight on the circuit's big screen and we saw the Elan lose ground down the Hangar Straight but then gain 30 yards more, as the Chapman alchemy struck gold and the Elan simply drove by the Cobra and started eating up the gap to the silver blue TVR Griffith that was running in third place. And then, big screen be damned, we were watching in 3D sensurround as the TVR twitched out of Farm, then squirmed, bucked, banged, popped, and flamed under braking for Village and despite all its machismo it was overtaken before the next corner by the lissom Elan, with the move looking as undramatic as it was inevitable. That's why we cheered, even your bashful reporter joining in, and that's why drivers love to race in historics – for the simple love of doing so, with not a championship in which to score, not a sponsor to schmooze but just a trophy for the cabinet to win and a damp kiss from the girl next door who was handing out the pots on the podium.

The Classic is a huge event, and attracts close to 1200 entries, ranging from oddities such as the Ogle SX1000 and the Dulon Dino to a horde of DFV engined Seventies Formula 1 cars. Added to which there are the endless car club displays on Silverstone's vast infield and, whilst I can easily walk past a line of Jaguar XKRs or Lamborghini Gallardos, there is the chance of seeing something really unexpected, none more so than the Ghia Willment Cobra I saw here a few years ago. I had read about this unique Cobra in a copy of *Car* so long ago that I had paid three shillings for the magazine, but there was the AC, looking like a VW Karmann Ghia would have if it had been force-fed steroids and then spent a year in the gym. Absurd, pumped up, testosterone drenched, a real knuckle-dragger dumbass of a car, but somehow it was even more memorable than the exquisite Gordon Keeble I had seen the same year. This year there are hectares of Porsches (everything from cheap as chips old 924s to a brace of big hipped hybrid 918s, and even the Le Mans winning 919), an acre or so of free range Morgans (starring a boss-eyed Aero 8), and a rood of Bristols, and doesn't the 401 look more modern each passing year, in just the same way as a Citroën DS does? As for the Seventies déesse, the Maserati powered SM, it may be finished in a very period metallic brown, but I suspect that it is still one of the very few cars that can make its driver look and feel as cool as Lord March.

I had arrived early on the first day of the three day meeting and I had wandered over to what is now called the National Paddock, the old pit complex that leads towards Copse. Possibly because I had driven the Seven a spirited 20 miles from my B&B only an hour earlier, I talked first to the driver of the lovely Lotus Six, John Cleland, who (like the David Coulthard who hillclimbs a Rover) shares a name with a more famous racer. John tells me that the Six has been restored to its original 1955 specification, with an 1100cc engine replacing the more powerful 1500cc version which had been fitted when singer Chris Rea had raced the same car in earlier Classics: "I can only do 100mph (160km/h) flat out, but if it rains ... then I can really make some progress." I walk behind the pit garages, see Lukas Halusa lowering himself into his father's 250 Ferrari Breadvan, and wonder why even the ugliest of all Sixties' Ferraris can still make me almost breathless with joy. Maybe it's the exquisite details, such as the silver-spoked steering wheel, the sexily wide wire wheels, and the quartet of extractor exhausts? How can it be that old Ferraris always succeed in looking like a Gina Lollobrigida, a Monica Vitti, or a Claudia Cardinale, whilst old Jaguars and Astons invariably look like John Mills or Anthony Quayle in *Ice Cold In Alex*?

I walk towards Copse and see former Grand Prix driver Howden Ganley in conversation with a Formula Junior owner; I wait, and my tentative "two minutes Howden?" is rewarded with "yes, no problem at all, fire away." And this may be a guy who never won a Grand Prix, but for me, and maybe you too, people like Howden Ganley are touched by enough magic to make talking to them unforgettable. Because at the time when I was invited to abandon O-Level Biology, and did so, breaking my GP father's heart in the process, Howden was helping Bruce McLaren build Can-Am cars, and when I was learning about the rule in Rylands v Fletcher in my law of tort lectures at the University of Leeds, Howden was driving a BRM around Monaco. "I'm here as patron of the Formula Junior Diamond Jubilee world tour; I've already been with them in New Zealand and Monaco, and it's California next month. I'm presenting the trophies and ... well, I just love all this stuff. One car to drive around here today?" He has a big smile and a wrinkled brow, "My goodness that's a question ... I might just go for the HWM Jaguar. Not something with a DFV, no, because I've done that and I love old sports cars. The HWM there might have been Tony Gaze's car which I saw race in New Zealand when I was 15 and I got Tony's autograph, I was a little shy kid." I ask Howden about his career in Formula 1, he says: "I drove a BRM P153 when I first came in, which I thought was wonderful, but I didn't know any better really, as I'd only driven an F1 car for Bruce [McLaren] very briefly in testing before. The P153 was great to race and the P160 was probably as good as anything in the field in late '71, but that changed when everybody else got more horsepower. The Williams was a good handling car on some circuits, so if I had to pick – actually, out of the whole lot the best car was the Matra I tested at Ricard, without BRM knowing. That car was brilliant, an absolutely wonderful car. I had a whole day there with them, it was an MS120C (or maybe D, was it?)." I mention the scream that made the Matra V12 so legendary and ask if, as a driver, Howden enjoyed, or even noticed, the sound it made or whether his sole criterion was power – "Oh, it's the latter, you keep pushing a car and think 'what's wrong with this thing?,' it hasn't got enough horsepower. And you get used to the noise, I drove the P153, 160, and 180, and I drove for Matra in sports cars as well. If you want noise, when I was a mechanic for McLaren for their first Grand Prix in Monaco in '66, that was a noisy car, it drowned out everything else. No horsepower but one hell of a noise!" We chat for a good 20 minutes more about Silverstone ("I redesigned some of the corners when I was on the (BRDC) board. But it's a great shame we lost Bridge Corner"), the state of Formula 1 ("I'm happy we're out of the contract. We absolutely had to get out and we'll see what happens. I can't say what else I might know ... But Formula 1 hasn't gone in quite the direction it could have and for sure it would have been better if it had.") I mention how sad it is that we have a Grand Prix in Azerbaijan but not at Kyalami in South Africa any more – "Yeah, I agree with you, I loved Kyalami and I loved the Osterreichring too, the 14 mile Nürburgring, they were just wonderful tracks and I'm so happy I got to race on them. Old Spa in sports cars was brilliant too and the young guys aren't getting that any more. But they can be consoled by the noughts on their bank balance ..." Ganley claims that "as former Formula 1 drivers me and Tim Schenken were unemployable so we set up Tiga (the racing car manufacturer) and actually made a wee bit of money. I really enjoyed it and couldn't wait to get up in the morning and design some new part." I mention I used to be a lawyer and could very easily wait to get up – cue huge laugh from Ganley. We talk some more, about Cadwell in Formula 3 ("I loved it but I still can't forgive that bastard Schenken for pushing me off there"), about self-publishing his autobiography (*The Road to Monaco*) and just as we part, I am introduced to his companion, hillclimber and Grand Prix driver Mike MacDowell's widow, and she is visibly touched to learn that I used to push-start Mike's Brabham Repco at Harewood 40-odd years ago.

I could have talked to Ganley all day, as I found him a very likeable man with a deep love of the sport but with only – only! – three days to enjoy this meeting I headed for the new Wing pit complex and tingled as first one and then a whole pack of DFVs were warmed up for the Historic Formula 1 qualifying session. I catch a brief word with Joaquin Folch, the Spanish driver of the Parmalat liveried Brabham BT49C – "Chassis number 10, in period Nelson [Piquet] and Hector Rebaque drove it. Silverstone? Oh ... in any car the circuit is very demanding, very fast corners which at first glance don't look so fast – it's very technical so the people with huge experience here have an advantage. Becketts is very, very good, full throttle, then the next one you change down, brake a little bit and ..." Further conversation was made impossible by an Arrows A4 starting up five feet away and I am reminded that unless you have stood next to a Grand Prix car as it erupts into life, you really have no idea of the sheer feral brutality of an unsilenced Cosworth DFV. It makes me want to laugh and cry at the same time, and I hope it always will do.

I watch the Formula 1 cars, and even though they are mainly driven by gentleman racers (aka very well off middle-aged men), even though their revs are restricted to 10,000rpm and even though these are designs from up to 45 years ago they still are an arresting sight, and stupendously fast compared to the D-Types, Cortinas, and Cobras that had preceded them. And not even in period, not even in the glory days of DFV garagistes like Connew and Lec, did we have 32 car grids. McLaren boss Zak Brown is driving a Williams and I wonder if he does so to exorcise the memory of the day job nightmare of running a racing car that breaks down during virtually every Grand Prix and whose Honda power unit struggles to pull the skin off the fluffiest rice pudding. And how I'd love to see his driver Alonso wring the neck of the FW 07 and how, even more so, I'd have loved to see Alonso drive the 1992 ex-Mansell

FW14B which was demonstrated the next day. From Farm Corner I could hear almost every single gearchange made on the full 3.6 mile (6km) circuit, and at full power the V10 Renault sounded like the essence of everything that has ever thrilled me in the sport.

In a pause between races I talk to Henry Hope-Frost, who is the roving commentator for the Classic (as well as Goodwood and much else besides) and I am intrigued to know just how hard it is to talk about a race meeting featuring over 1000 drivers – "Keeping up to date with the driver and car changes is a huge challenge, and as they print the programme weeks in advance it immediately becomes out of date. So working out who is in which car, trying to get a handle on start drivers is really hard, I'm running up and down looking into cockpits trying to recognise whose helmet is who. Covering in-race class battles can be tough too." I am intrigued about whether drivers are always happy to be interviewed before a race: "I've been doing this a long time and I've never had a problem with anybody. Historic racing is a sort of family affair, very friendly and even when some of the superstars come they can't believe how relaxed and friendly it is. No pressure, no debriefs or data to pore over, they're just here having a laugh and they're all amazed by the power and grip some of these old cars have." I ask Henry whether the buzz ever wears off of having a job like his – "If it moves and makes a noise, I love it – two, three, four or even six wheels. The Historic Formula 1 cars do something slightly unpleasant to me every time I see them, they're from my teenage years, but I love the big V8 sports cars too, T70s and so on. Silverstone? The drivers all love it, you can really stretch a powerful car's legs here, especially if it's got a lot of downforce. Some people say the circuit is sparse, or bland, but it is still the home of British motor racing, I feel it when I drive through the gates, it's our Wembley or Wimbledon, isn't it?"

A line of XJ220s, there must be 30 of them, and am I the only one who admires their owners' dedication but questions their taste in lavishing such care on what is, to me, the daftest looking supercar of them all? The Jaguar is ludicrously wide, but even its width is modest in comparison to its length, itself made to appear even more elongated by the huge overhangs front and rear. Add an interior that looks like a Vauxhall Carlton's and an engine that makes a bag of spanners sound tuneful and is it any wonder so many of the buyers refused to take delivery, having been short changed of both four wheel drive and a V12? But some love 'em, and in my world that's just fine, but if you want to know how this supercar gig should be done, just check out the Ferrari F40 parked near the pit garages. It's svelte, taut muscled and compact, and even motionless, Enzo's last hurrah from 1987 exudes menace. Fired up, turbo V8 spitting and barking, this analogue brute sounds venomous, just as every supercar should but now so rarely does. Ever heard a Veyron? White noise. Or even a 918? I've heard better MGBs. Aston Martins and AMGs? Algorithmically created exhibitionism for the rigours of South Kensington.

Next day I drove in early on the back roads from my B&B, 20 miles away in Priors Hardwick, this time in company with a Boxster S. Huge fun, if not quite as memorable as it had been in 2013, when I had driven in company with the Dutch doctors in their Maserati Khamsin and '66 Shelby Mustang GT 350. We'd drunk far too much together the night before, and I vaguely remembered arguing that the Miura was incomparably gorgeous before droning on to them about Philip Larkin's poetry – it was that sort of evening. I parked up in the Lotus Seven Club enclosure near Brooklands, walked the half-mile (0.8km) towards the National paddock and, after watching the hectic Formula Ford 1600 race (50+ cars, most of them involved in multicar dices), I admired the prewar sports cars as they assembled for their race. I am no expert on older cars, but I couldn't walk past the glorious Alfa Romeo without talking to owner/driver Roger Buxton – "I'm from Hammersmith in West London and my day job is a coal trader," cue much laughter as I reveal I once lived up t'road from t'pit. "This a 1930 Fourth Series 1750 GS Zagato (pronounced the Italian way), matching numbers and a complete provenance, even the original leatherwork. It's about 120bhp, a straight-six and it makes a very nice touring car. I've had it for about 14 years and I have done over 80,000 kilometres (50,000 miles). It's frightening to drive here," he roars with laughter, "particularly when you know you're preserving a piece of motoring heritage. The worst bit? Flat out down the Hangar Straight, and the best is flying around Copse. These are real cars and it takes a real art to drive them." Another charming man, the place seems full of them, and it feels as though we are all privy to a delightful secret we can only share with each other, if not with the outside world.

Sunday morning, and after watching a couple more races, including a delicious second helping of Formula Ford 1600, I wander through the old garages, admiring a Porsche 356 here and a Lotus Elite there, encountering Richard Meaden, the journalist who writes for *Evo* and, latterly, *Motorsport* magazine. Following on in the tradition of men like Paul Frere, Roger Bell, Marcus Pye, and erstwhile colleague Chris Harris, Meaden is an experienced and respected racing driver. "I'm not racing as much as the last few years, but I'm driving a Lotus Cortina and a Group A Rover in Supertouring. I actually enjoy swapping from one car to another, and what I most enjoy about historic racing is that all the cars are very distinct characters and all require something different in terms of the way you drive them … they're like people I suppose, you get to know their strengths and weaknesses. You adapt your driving to their personalities." Richard has been racing historics since 2012 and says: "Cortinas were the first thing I raced, and they're different to anything else and once it clicks … oh, they're just great fun and that's why you see all kinds of people racing them. They might have a Lola T70 or F1 car, but everybody loves racing Cortinas." And what about driving the Ford around a circuit designed to accommodate 800bhp Formula 1 cars? "It's actually really good fun, Stowe's great, Copse and Becketts are brilliant in anything. T70s are brilliant here, lots of power and they romp down the straights too. They're terrifying things when you fire them up – angry, very potent and you think 'I'm not sure I'm up to that' but when you drive them, they tend to do what they're told. It's huge fun but they're easier just to get in and drive, they are not the monsters they appear from the outside." ("They bloody well are to me" I suggest; Richard laughs). I want to get an insider's view as to how much of the *Evo* readership understands the appeal of historic racing: "I think they maybe don't appreciate how quick the cars are but I think more people are enjoying watching historics as most fast road cars are now so competent and quick, the driver's role is diminishing, the roads are now so busy that people want to connect with this stuff more, it promotes the joy of driving a 'proper car.'"

I am drifting through the last day in a state of near euphoria, pausing to watch one race from Becketts, another from Brooklands when reality bites. I am watching a race for prewar cars on a big screen when a car spins, rears up on to two wheels and ejects its driver – no seatbelts or roll bars in these old warriors. The director cuts to another image and I fear the worst, feeling the ache of anxiety and guilt gnawing away at me that my day's fun may be somebody else's death or injury. It isn't, thankfully, but three years ago Denis Welch's luck had run out when his 1960 Lotus crashed at Village, a reminder that what can be a routine shunt in modern carbon fibre single-seater can be catastrophic in a GRP and aluminium racer from the Sixties. It's too easy to forget, or simply to ignore, the dark shadows that can eclipse the sport on even the sunniest summer day.

Verdict

1. Summary – Comparing the Silverstone Classic to any other event I have attended this year is like comparing Glyndebourne to the local am-dram gig. The place is huge, and so is the entry and crowd. The access all areas policy which applies to the entire circuit, including many grandstands and the pit garages (right up to the pit lane itself, even in pit stop races), is a model of what motorsport events can and should offer. The crowd is at least 50% middle aged white men but the remaining 50% has a wider range of ages from toddlers to oldsters on mobility scooters, and the crowd also includes far more women than at most race meetings.

The commentary team is expert, likeable, and hugely knowledgeable; you feel in the company of old friends.

Under my car club deal it cost me £99 for a three-day infield pass (including a free ticket) and the slickly produced 200-page programme was a tenner. I think this value is unrivalled.

The Classic also offers a 'retail village' where you can buy anything from a Porsche 911 RS recreation to a chamois cloth and the Saturday evening offers live bands. They're usually tribute acts, sometimes to themselves, as in the case of Seventies rockers Suzi Quatro and Wishbone Ash, and the sounds on offer generally comprise the sort of music that people who don't really like music tend to enjoy. He said, condescendingly.

2. Nature notes – The infield used to be a working farm but now that Silverstone is a circuit within a circuit within a circuit there's far less habitat. Hares used to be a common sight on the Hangar Straight and this year I saw my first one for several years, as it raced down the track between Village and Farm. As at Shelsley Walsh, pied wagtails had a starring role here, supplemented by a large group, if not a murmuration, of starlings that were feasting on discarded pizza and chips. There's still woodland in places and the usual suspects were in evidence – sparrows, wood pigeons, and blackbirds.

3. Catering – Tex Mex, Japanese, Thai, Italian, US, Indian, and UK food. Craft beer and everything else you'd find in a hipster pub. The food may be more expensive than on the high street but most of it is a vast improvement on typical circuit food.

4. What could be improved? – I don't think I am the only one who regards celebrity races as oxymoronic and whose interest in watching a D-list celebrity drive badly is too tiny to register. The Classic needs to feature more single-seaters – Historic Formula 2 and F5000 would be ideal – and if it could attract more Can-Am cars than it managed in 2016 my cup would be in serious risk of overflowing.

5. Website – The Silverstone Classic website is excellent and is active all year round. I also use the HSCC website for results – so groaning with data is the site that if I have a pressing need to ascertain the lap time of car 32 in the Formula Junior race on its penultimate qualifying lap I can easily do so …

OULTON PARK GOLD CUP – 28 AUGUST 2017

Ever tried explaining the appeal of an activity you love to the friend who boasts of knowing nothing about it? I have, and it isn't easy to convey how heart-stoppingly exciting catching a big trout on dry fly can be, because to a non-angling friend it's just me, the 200 pound smartarse exercising his inner caveman by outwitting a four pound fish with a brain the size of a pea. Where's the appeal in that not so equal struggle, you demand? But now imagine you are a chess player, and you're demonstrating to your sceptical mate just how enervating and exhilarating it can be in those last few moves before you checkmate your opponent. You make the killer move, which your friend obviously doesn't recognise, at least he doesn't until the move is punctuated by a sledgehammer hitting the chessboard, showering the room with body parts of bishops and knights, shattering the chess board, and splintering the table into match wood. Get it now do you, pal?

If your friend doesn't get motor racing here's what he should have done on Monday 28 August 2017. Stand with me at Deer Leap during the Derek Bell Trophy as a Chevron B37 Formula 5000 single-seater thunderclaps past at 120mph (190km/h) just 20 feet away. You'd just heard the rumble of its pushrod V8 as the Chevron pulled 150mph+ (240km/h+) before braking for Lodge, then you saw the big red car with the tall airbox squirming through the downhill bend, but then, with no apparent passage of time, not even a second, the car is blowing the sky apart as it stampedes its way under the trees and past you towards Old Hall. You catch a subliminal glimpse of the sun glinting off the driver's visor and then your every sense is consumed by the urgent bellow of a Chevy small-block, which you feel as much as hear and only afterwards do you realise that your every emotion had deserted you except the fight or flight response your ancestors had felt when the mammoths got really mad. And now you can't stop smiling for a week. Job done.

This was actually my second trip of the year to Oulton, as I had been there in April for the British GT meeting, but my mobility had then been so crappy that my range was restricted to a few paces from the car. Even that was enough for me to realise that the series' health was rude, that the Mercedes AMG GT-3 is a stranger to understatement, that Lamborghini Huracáns look amazing and sound even better, and that racing a Bentley Continental GT3 feels like using a Tudor mansion for a Stormzy gig.

Today I'd left home at 5.30am, watched the huge orange sun in the mirror as it rose over Windy Hill and Saddleworth Moor, and I had arrived at Oulton Park before 8am. And the place looked simply glorious, with late summer mist rising from the avenues of trees and the smell of coffee and bacon drifting over from the infield campers. I parked next to the start/finish line amongst a platoon of orange clad marshals, a worrying proportion of whom seemed to be carrying even more extra poundage than I am. But at least there were plenty of women volunteers; in my marshalling days they weren't even permitted trackside and were condemned to paddock or admin duties. Today was the last day of the three day Gold Cup, the race that used to be a non-championship Formula 1 race before it had a 20 year identity crisis and vacillated between F3, F3000, GT, and touring cars before finally transitioning to an established historic race meeting. It's an identity that suits Oulton perfectly as its heritage is almost as rich as Silverstone's, but its parkland location is joyously bucolic compared to Silverstone's windswept acres of tarmac.

The Gold Cup sits between the Silverstone Classic's enormous, 1000+ entry extravagance and the relative parsimony of events such as Cadwell's Wold's Trophy and Croft's Nostalgia Meeting. There are over a dozen different races, some of which, principally the 50 strong Formula Ford 1600 field, are run on a heats and final basis. It's shocking enough to be reminded that the Rover SD1 s and Sierra Cosworths I had watched racing here in the Eighties are now historical relics, as are some of their drivers, as well as many of those watching them, but it's even worse to realise that the screaming BTCC Supertourers from the Nineties are as now as far back in the past as Sixties' Minis and Cortinas had been from the glory days of the '86 Bastos liveried Rover Vitesse.

The paddock is waking up slowly but some pit garages are already open and I take the opportunity to remind myself why I think that we reached peak single-seater a year or so after slicks and wings became de rigueur but five or six years before the dark forces of ground effect downforce changed the look and feel of racing cars forever. My eyes linger over those oh so soft curves of a Brabham BT 23 and a Tecno F2 before the past greets me abruptly in the form of a March 712, the very same car that I had seen James Hunt race here in 1972. It was the first time I had realised that the man they called Hunt the Shunt had real potential. Back then, his notoriety derived only from crashing frequently and from having thumped another driver, Dave Morgan, after they had collided during a Crystal Palace Formula 3 race. 45 years later (and how the hell did that happen, and how can Hunt have been dead for nearly a quarter-of-a-century already?) here's the car looking the same as it ever did in its blue and white Hesketh Finance livery. Somehow I doubt that its aristocratic sponsor ever financed a Marina or Cortina purchase for a Kevin or a Bob, but paid only for the more rarefied products of Dastle, Surtees, and March to be driven exclusively by James Simon Wallis Hunt. My eyes then linger on a March 782 and I smile wryly as I realise how quaint the March logo now looks; in '78 the stylised March logo in Data 70 font was so very now but in 2017 it looks as dated as if had been inscribed by a quill pen on vellum.

Cascades is a corner to relish, even though I am not as close to the track as I'd like, because the elevation of the spectator banking means I can see the driver at work and because the geometry of the corner reveals just how fast even a Sixties' saloon car can corner. Jonathan Lewis' 1965 Mini Cooper S evokes a collective gasp from the crowd each lap as it is pitched into the corner 20mph quicker than anything else, its tiny front wheels scrabbling in an extravagance of understeer before the Mini barks its way down towards Shell. And here's a rare bird, the very first Alfa Romeo 2600 Sprint I have seen in competition. It's a Bertone design by Giorgetto Giugiaro and it is a thing of rare beauty, if not quite as achingly desirable as its kissing cousin, the sublime Gordon Keeble GK1. Later, I talk to the Alfa's owner/driver Jon Miles, a big man in a big car. "I bought it because it's a little bit different and it gives me the opportunity to get into some of the more interesting events. It's my first venture into Alfas and I'm still thinking 'was it the right thing to do?' I also race a Mark I Escort and we do stuff like Le Jog and Rally of the Tests. The Monte Carlo rally we do every year and a bit of sprinting and hill climbing." Jon confirms my recollection that the 2600 has a triple Weber fuelled straight-six and says, "it was on the rolling road the other day at 193bhp but it's all at the top end. Round Oulton? Best bits are the straights and," (he belly laughs), "the corners are the worst. Druids is … umm … interesting and I'm new to the car and the tyres so I'm just getting used to going sideways really."

En route for another coffee I spot Katsu Kubota soaking up the sun; he's a Japanese racer I've seen in everything from the demure Lotus Cortina he's driving today to Historic Formula 1 cars and the rocket ship Group C Nissan R90 CK. I know it's a cliché, but it's also true that Japanese drivers are typically both fearless and fast and they also seem to thrive in the worst of conditions, possibly because Japan's North Pacific climate gives them ample opportunity to master wet weather lines. Katsu proves to be both polite and intense, and happy to tell me about his Oulton Park debut ("fantastic, first time here") and a lot more besides – "I'm racing the Cortina, yes, and also the Lotus 23B and Lotus 22. I drove those at Silverstone and also a Tyrrell F1. This year I've raced in Canada and I'm racing at Austin (Texas) and Mexico in a Lotus 78." So how long does it take you to get used to a different car, Katsu? "Exactly …" long laugh "… a car is a car, driving is driving; there's maybe later braking but it's okay. My favourite cars are carbon fibre, very stiff, lots of downforce … I've bought a Lotus 91 for next year and I'm driving a Lotus 72 at Monaco. And next year's Classic Le Mans, we've built another Nissan. I love racing in England, in Japan the most important thing in racing is safety but here … no! The most important thing is competition." We talk about Takuma Sato's Indy 500 win (about which I'm still grinning) – "I'm very happy for Japan and we have a lot of respect for him. Some people maybe don't understand the meaning of the Indy 500, but our Prime Minister Mr Abe awarded an honour to him – it's a great day for Japan."

I walk through the assembly of sports and classic cars on display and soak up Oulton's unique ambience. Silverstone can often feel aloof, Donington is currently long on shabby but short of chic, and Croft is hard as nails northeast, but Oulton has always succeeded in feeling like a country estate, with its avenues of mature trees, ornamental lake and a race track that feels as though it was created primarily to enhance the view. The crowd is very different to anywhere else too, with a high quota of old boys with a pension gold plated enough to run to a Boxster, cherished S2000 Honda or, inevitably, a sporty Jaguar. But God knows who owned the Burberry liveried XK8; in Cheshire it's got to be a Footballer's Wife right? And as the big cat must be at least a decade old, I'm thinking more Accrington Stanley than Man U?

As the sound of the ex John Surtees Lola T70 Spyder echoes around the circuit, lapping in tribute to the man whose recent obituaries devoted as much space to speculation on why he had remained unknighted as they did to his world championships, I find a posse of Eighties Historic Touring Cars in various states of déshabillé, which if anything makes them look even more potent. None of the namby-pamby laptop cosseting the younger Supertourers like Primeras and Accords receive from their carers, but tough love given to Rover SD1s and BMW 635s from big blokes with builder's bums instead. Steve Soper's far too dapper and slim to sport such an outrage and the man who has raced from Bathurst to Le Mans smiles when I tell him it's been a long time since I saw him racing a Fiat X1/9 in Modsports – "I'm driving the Bastos TWR Vitesse and yeah, I'm sort of getting flashbacks to an earlier life but the circuit seems a lot narrower than it did 25 years ago." I ask if more modern cars had appealed when Soper came back to racing after an injury: "... no, not really, I'm too old. I'm 65 now and I should be driving cars the same age as me, not any modern stuff." He's more downbeat than I expected, so I ask about the good times – what's the most memorable car you've driven, Steve? There's no hesitation, "BMW Le Mans Prototype, the V12 LM R. BMW commissioned Williams to build it; the car won Le Mans in '99 and that year I won three races with the same car after Le Mans. It's one of my favourites, it's still old but it does everything you want it to do and it brings back lovely memories. 700 horsepower, lots of grip, lots of downforce, and they still bring it out and let me do demonstrations in it. I did the Williams Jubilee at Silverstone in it. Other cars ... oh ... Sierra Cosworth, I drove a Texaco Eggenberger car at Goodwood this year and I thought the car would feel horrible and it felt fantastic with an awful lot of horsepower, fun to drive. That [the Bastos Rover] is a bit heavy to drive and clumsy round here, it'd be better somewhere like Donington or Silverstone – still fun, you just need to manhandle it a bit." Steve is mystified but enthused by the growth of historic racing: "it's taking off everywhere, I'm going to Zandvoort next weekend for a Masters race in a Lotus Cortina and there's a historic race somewhere nearly every week." Before leaving Steve to ponder the challenge of throwing the big Rover around Oulton again I ask what his take is on the current BTCC. "If you look at the TV and the crowds it's very difficult to criticise it but as a driver I am critical. I don't like success ballast, I don't like one of the grids being pulled out of a hat, and the cars are too heavy, too under-tyred, not nice to drive. But from a show point of view you can't really criticise it. I'm just pleased I was doing it when I was driving for BMW and Rover; to me the fastest car and driver should win and you shouldn't handicap people – it's rubbish."

I agree about BTCC in its current form in that it's difficult to knock its success, but it is harder still actually to like the product. I had enjoyed what I had seen at Croft back in June but that was mainly down to driver skill and dreadful conditions. I am reminded of just what a diversity of cars used to race in our premier saloon car – sorry, touring car – series as I inspect the ranks of old stagers, nearly all of which I had seen in period. Cars like the black VW Golf GTi Mk 1, the rowdy *Autocar*-sponsored V6 Capri, the big arched Mk II Escorts, and the white RS500 Sierra of Gianfranco Brancatelli. I catch a few minutes with the Italian whose career may have been blessed with success in sports and touring cars, but which also was cursed by having driven two of the worst cars ever to enter a Grand Prix, the Kauhsen and the Merzario. But, he says "I really enjoyed my single-seater life; so long ago now but you know, I was racing good drivers like Rosberg, Cheever but okay, maybe people remember me best from touring cars, yes?" Gianfranco looks like a 60-something Italian racing driver should do; he's whippet thin, sporting wild and mainly black helmet hair, he's demonstrative, friendly, and he's absolutely tiny. It's his first time here but says "I learn new circuits pretty fast. I walk them, then run them, and you learn the corners better than just driving." I had watched him race minutes before and I was shocked to see that despite his almost driving the wheels off the Sierra, this touring car legend could not keep up with the newer front-wheel drive Honda Accords driven by people who are far from being well known outside the historic racing bubble. I ask about this, mentioning that the Sierra must have well over 500bhp against the Honda's what, 300bhp on a good day with a following wind? "Ach, there's many reasons. Yes, there is turbo lag, the gearing is too long, I'm not getting out of fourth, not ever in fifth round here. But the big thing is the new cars have sequential boxes – is worth easy 150bhp, it saves so much time – and front-wheel drive … just so much better in slow corners."

Almost sated by such a feast of reminiscence it was time to watch some racing, even though competition is secondary in the world of historic motor racing to the opportunity to inspect such an extravagance of old racing cars at close quarters. There was the good – inevitably the close fought Formula Ford races, as often as not contested by the sort of young racing driver whose talent and ambition can't be demonstrated in the Formula's unaffordable successors; the relatively pedestrian – a thin grid of Formula Juniors; the spectacular – Mustangs, Cortinas, and Minis still re-enacting those battles from the Sixties on a stage largely unchanged from the days of Sir John Whitmore, John Rhodes, and Jim Clark and finally, the take-a-step-back adrenalin rush of the Historic Formula 2 Marches and Brabhams. And the Chevron B37. Which is where we came in.

It was just such a perfect day.

Verdict

1. Summary – A wonderful day, in perfect weather, with a big crowd who were unfailingly polite, knowledgeable and enthusiastic. Lots of family groups and kids, and plenty of places for them to play safely, thanks to MotorSport Vision's enlightened management. Predictably

enough, most of the crowd was white and middle class, but it was good to see some minority groups enjoying the day too. I loved the sight of the elderly Indian gent, wheelchair bound, surrounded by a big family group, smiling at the racing whilst puffing a steampunk style vape. Like Silverstone Classic, the HSCC allow free access to pit garages and the edge of the pit lane itself, which enables any racegoer to steep him or herself in the sight, sound, and smell of racing cars being worked on before exiting back on to the track itself.

£20 entry and a fiver for the programme, which was by some margin the best I have seen all season. 50-odd pages, printed on thick, parchment style retro paper, and featuring wonderful period advertisements. I loved the Elf petrol advert especially, from 1976 judging by the presence of the six wheeled Tyrrell P34. The strap line was "Now, for Britain, it's Elf!" and the main illustration was of a cleavage-revealing, bouffant-haired, and presumably French, woman holding a petrol pump nozzle in a vertical position whilst grinning inanely. The phallocentrism of Seventies' ads is really beyond parody ...

The expert Ian Titchmarsh and Marcus Pye were on commentary duties, and as erudite and entertaining as usual.

Litter? Not a scrap, anywhere, in contrast to the scruffy, neglected Oulton pre-MSV. Security? Soft touch and helpful.

2. Nature notes – If I could have got closer to the lake I might have had something more interesting to report than just the sounds of an English country estate in late summer. But that in itself was just fine; pigeons in the woods, a kestrel hovering beyond Old Hall, and invisible magpies cackling.

3. Catering – There was decent, if unimaginative and generic, race circuit fodder, reasonably priced. But amongst the car club displays and the now almost compulsory World War II re-enactors there was an artisan market selling craft beer, Cheshire Gin (no, me neither) and – deep joy – freshly made Indian food. Tapas too. Oulton Pork anybody?

4. What could be improved? – The timetabling could have been better, as the previous day had featured many cars I would love to have seen, but as there was only circuit action from noon it wasn't worth the 260-mile round trip. And yet, some of Monday, the final day, was taken up with lacklustre qualifying sessions.

5. Website – MSV told me the basics and HSCC everything else, including entry, timetable and, as usual, the lap time of every car on every lap.

TIME ATTACK – CROFT – 3 SEPTEMBER 2017

I know, you're thinking 'Not bloody Croft – again,' but just stick with me on this, okay? Because I am here today to see an event that, as its hyperbolic programme announces, has become "one of the most significant and engaging motorsport phenomena of our time ..." and which "has inspired an entire generation of enthusiasts from around the globe." It certainly inspired the drivers of the parptastic posse of Nissan Skylines and Mitsubishi Evos (other hysterical JDM brands are available) to double the 30-limit past my house early on this Sunday morning. JDM? Do keep up, because if the Time Attack sub culture is rich in one thing it is acronyms. Japanese Domestic Market, mate.

So, did Time Attack make me 'LOL,' realise 'YOLO' or was it just a 'PITA?' And what is Time Attack anyway? It is an evolution of the type of speed event (think sprints and hillclimbs) that has taken place for a century in the UK, not that you would ever learn that from its publicity. Its USP, and you do know what that stands for, is the fact that Time Attack also features some track day elements, with multiple cars running on track simultaneously but with overtaking taking place consensually. The objective is not to race but to set the quickest lap time during the session. The series can be contested by just about any production-based car, with a refreshingly relaxed rule framework allowing barn door size wings, massive diffusers and high boost engines delivering up to 700bhp, or even more, in the Pro Extreme Class (and where do you progress to next – maybe Big Budget Batshit Bonkers?). Most of the cars entered today actually occupy quite a narrow niche of the market, and if I was unkind I would characterise it as comprising the sort of cars you might see loitering in the darker corners of a multiplex car park on a Saturday night – Civics, Astras, Fiestas, Saxos, and the inevitable Imprezas and Evos. Today the menu is seasoned by a couple of Nobles, a Honda S2000, and a snarly Alfa Romeo 155 V6, making a grand total of fewer than 50 cars, or between one third and a quarter the size of a typical speed hillclimb entry.

The four-wheeled Time Attack entry was supplemented by the Lambrettas, Gileras, Aprilias, and Piaggios racing in the British Scooter Sports Organisation 20-minute races. Two wheels are outside both this book's scope and my real interest, but I can report that the scooters were ridden with brio, and looked faster than they actually were. It's a lazy comment, but I could not help thinking that parkas should have been compulsory race wear and that the race should have been sound-tracked by something from The Who. *Won't get fooled again* perhaps? Did I "smile and grin at the change all around"?

It is only 10am, two hours before anything happens on track, and yet there are many more people here already than for a typical club race meeting. And the reason is clear because, unlike a traditional race meeting, where spectators can sometimes be made to feel irrelevant, if not actually unwelcome, at Time Attack (not forgetting the Petrol and Pistons Car Show bit) the visitor is part of the show, or at least he is (and, WAGs apart, it is 'he') if he brings a pimped and primped rocket hatch that can be parked up next to a line of similar cars, bonnets propped up to enable the cognoscenti to admire the carbon fibre ducting, polished engine bay, and bad boy turbo. It is a culture alien to me but that only makes it all the more intriguing. There is an emphasis on JDM cars and iconography and, whilst the magpie approach the Japanese take to the English language was once seen as a rich vein of humour to Westerners (with a side offering of gratuitous racism), Japanese imagery and usage is now glacially cool, especially to young men. But smart Westerners, in an exemplar of meta branding, and thus big in what Google tells me is the metaverse, are now exploiting the appeal. You've noticed Superdry Japan leisurewear of course? Based in Tokyo maybe? Cheltenham actually …

The ambience is more tribal than I expected; on display, for example, is a whole bunch of modified cars signed Extortionate Obsession, there's the Modified Militia assembled in a corner of the paddock, and I'm inspecting a member of the Militia's Volkswagen Polo. It features the red webbing towing loop which seems compulsory kit in the Militia, but it must have only a cosmetic function as it appears to be attached to some plastic trim. I am struggling to decipher the precise message here as it may mean "my car needs this because I knackered the engine with that stuff I bought off eBay" but maybe the intended subtext is "I'm a bit of an operator, me, like. Yeah, mad for it, always in the gravel trap. Gotta push, yeah?" But it seems as counterfeit as wearing a parachute on the park and ride bus, or ski boots to the shops. And now I am really struggling with what this car is trying to tell me, as above the offside wheelarch is a photograph of Donald Trump, and who knows if this POTUS pic is ironic or adulatory? I then double take at the sticker on the Peugeot advertising 'Digital Mileage Correction,' which presumably means what I think it does, but I do admire the Red Bull style matte finish Nissan 200SX in pumped up and potent Drift specification, and there's an R32 Skyline, its flanks sporting a mosaic of Japanese script and Japanese English text. Battalion 33 anybody? Another Nissan boasts a Manga liveried dashboard (something to read on long journeys?), announces that it was "Built not Bought" and displays the quote that's often attributed to Paul Walker. The late *Fast and Furious* star has been subjected to post mortem beatification, just as Steve McQueen and Colin McRae have been, if by very different demographics. The wording reads: "If one day speed kills me, don't cry, because I was smiling." Really, do we think the unfortunate Walker was actually smiling in the passenger seat of the out of control Porsche Carrera GT as Roger Rodas smacked the car into a suburban lamppost? And what would Paul Walker have made of his family's unsuccessful law suit against Porsche, I wonder, didn't it undermine the sexy fatalism chic just a tad? At least James Dean was actually driving his Speedster when he had his fatal encounter with Donald Turnupseed's Ford Tudor back in '55.

Too much is being lost in translation here, and, frankly, that's as it should be; what sort of youth cult would it be if a superannuated baby boomer like me could get down with Time Attack's banging tune? Sanity is resumed as I talk to normal bloke Andy Hughes from Newton le Willows; he's an electrician, has a Lancashire accent you could cut up and fry, and he's driving a crazy looking Impreza with a boot mounted wing that could be a Chaparral 2F homage (as I don't actually say, as nobody likes a smartarse). "It's a two-door shell, and I had a new age Subaru before this, and transferred 80% of the components over. We've just evolved it really; we're still on a budget so we can't compete with everybody ... it's how deep your pocket is, you're not really comparing apples to apples in this series. But we dove in at the deep end and we're happy where we are. Engine's giving us between 700 and 750 horsepower." I ask about Andy's previous experience and it turns out he's done sprints and karting, and he's done well with both wins and championships. So why this, Andy? "I think ... it's just like evolved from what I've done. I found this much harder than sprints and did it as a step up. I'm bringing the car to win but there's cars here that are far, far superior to this one. I've done a 1.25.5 yesterday and I did that by following Guy Martin. I knew he was quicker, so he overtook me, I turned my boost up and I dragged on to him and stuck to him." I guess, wrongly, that with such big power the fast corners are most difficult, "no, no, it's the corner after the pit straight [Clervaux], that's hardest for me. The [Jim Clark] Esses are easy."

Umar Masood normally drives a big power Mazda RX 7 but today he's driving a Honda S2000. He's from Wolverhampton, where he has a garage business, and he tells me that the Honda "is actually stock, standard out of the box, running 200 horsepower. It's twitchy, yes, but because I'm used to a lot more power and this being stock and NA [naturally aspirated] I can handle it better. Why Time Attack, Umar? "You find, because you can develop your car, with aero and everything else. You are on the limit like in Formula 1 qualifying, it's at every turn, every second, braking and accelerating. It's good and you can go home without bumping your car when it's somebody else's fault. This is the only form of motorsport I've ever done, I've been doing it for seven years now." And Croft's challenges? "In this car the hairpin is awful!" And Umar's done well in the past, winning the Club Class championship in his 800bhp Mazda and holding various lap records. I wish him luck; he seems a nice bloke.

That Guy Martin eh? It's a mark of the man's fame that even Joanne responds when I mentioned later that I managed a brief interview – "He's that biker bloke from Grimsby with the teeth isn't he? Jayne [our biker friend] will be impressed when I post on Facebook that you've been talking to him." And I can't help thinking Joanne's interest is slightly unusual; this year I have spoken to Grand Prix drivers, including a world champion and a Le Mans winner, but the Transit driving truck mechanic with the unsettling grin is the one who sparks the most reaction. I soon find out for myself just how popular this blokiest of blokes really is as I watch him trying to walk across the paddock. He cannot manage five yards before being asked for yet another selfie and his progress is marked by elbow jabs, exclamations, and head turning. I mention to the lad I know from the local garage that I've been promised a quick word with the great man. Big grin, shoulder punch and a "Get on!"

Guy Martin is smaller than you might expect, wiry, deploys locked and loaded eye contact, and sports a haircut that is long on function and short on style. He's driving car 888, a Mitsubishi Evo IX, whose race number connotes Chinese good luck and he's driving because its owner is on honeymoon. Oh, and Martin set the fastest time of all yesterday …

Why are you doing this Guy? "Ah well, I'm sort of bored with the other stuff, I wanted a change. Yeah, I've raced here before, 2008 Superbikes, yeah." Accent unmistakably North Lincolnshire and delivery quick fire staccato. So how different an experience is four wheels to two? "Nothing like, nothing like, completely different. There's nothing you can swap from bikes to cars other than which way the track goes and that's about it, car racing is nothing like motorbike racing." Biggest challenge here Guy? "Oh … getting used to how four-wheel drive works, how the car behaves, I don't know how the car behaves. The fast stuff out the back is a bit of handful. But I'm learning … I'm learning." So why does Guy think Time Attack gets such a crowd, it's not even proper racing is it? "Nah, but it's good isn't it, it's all the stuff on the back of it, the show side of things and the cars being raced aren't run of the mill and I think that's great." Last week Martin had been working with the Williams' Formula 1 team at Spa and I ask how it had been: "Great, yeah." Biggest memory? "It's how many hours those blokes work, hard work, bloody hard working." I wonder if he's got more four-wheel plans – "Yeah, yeah, that's what I'm building to go racing, I'm building that at this minute." What is it Guy? He smiles "Top secret, top secret." And then he's away again, dodging the selfie seekers and looking really quite uncomfortable with the attention, the price of enjoying national treasure status.

I have a theory on why Guy Martin does enjoy such a high profile and it is to do with two things, the first being the fact that most Tristrams in TV commissioning live in North London, drive Audi Q5s, get the shakes if they venture north of Potters Bar, have no discernible regional accent, rarely meet tradesmen who aren't either Londoners or Poles, and have never met a truck mechanic, let alone invited one round for kitchen supper. The second reason is that Guy Martin shares a talent with Marilyn Monroe, and I am quite serious. In the flesh he seems a decent but entirely unremarkable bloke, a little intense perhaps, but otherwise indistinguishable from scores of similar men I've seen working in garages, on race cars, and on farms. But watch the same man on film and an entirely different character emerges. I suspect that it is more intuitive than learned, but in front of a camera Martin seems to effortlessly distil every likeable male trait and become the sort of tough, brave, and competent big brother that every man and woman has always wanted. And now that most of the country's working population is employed in services and not the hairy-arsed man's world of engineering and heavy industry, watching Guy Martin in his natural habitat is as alluring but as alien as the Amazonian lost tribe featured on a Discovery Channel documentary. But enough cod sociology already, what about the action?

The reality is that what happens on track is mainly unremarkable, rarely especially fast and not very dramatic to watch. A typical sprint or hillclimb not only offers a greater number of entrants and diversity of machinery but often features far quicker laps. The commentary team are voluble, excitable and enthusiastic but do get carried away when it comes to talking about lap records. The absolute lap record at Croft is 1 minute 14.8 seconds set by a 220bhp Formula 3 Dallara and it has stood for over a decade. That was set in a race, of course, as times in qualifying or practice do not count – the pole lap by Takuma Sato's Dallara a year earlier was a second quicker still. For Touring Cars, the record for the ultimate, pre-2001, Supertourers is held by Alain Menu in a Renault Laguna. That car may have been developed by Williams Grand Prix Engineering and been funded by a bottomless pit of cash but it was also hampered by being front-wheel drive, having limited aero and by having less than half the power of the claimed outputs of many Time Attack entrants, but its 1 minute 22 seconds lap is almost identical to the best Time Attack lap. Every year many cars lap Croft well under the 1 minute 20 seconds mark, including 40 year old Clubmans racers and even older single-seater cars. Does any of this matter? It does actually, quite a lot, because the impression is given by the commentators and programme that Time Attack cars somehow represent the ultimate in power and speed and whilst few 'normal' race cars can rival Time Attack entrants' claimed power figures, there are plenty that can lap faster.

Time Attack is a curious event to watch as a bevy of cars will circulate briskly, if not very quickly, until one driver goes for a time, lights ablaze and assisted by any competitors not engaged on hot laps of their own diving out of the way. There's some good driving, with lots of commitment shown and proper lines taken. Guy Martin, Andy Hughes, and Andrew Kime (in a Saxo), in particular, show how it should be done with performances that would see them comfortable in a race environment. The others? Not so much, with a handful of drivers notable for taking poor lines that rarely troubled corner apices and which resulted in pedestrian lap times around the two-minute mark. But if this is the only type of motorsport event you attend, as I suspect it is for much of the crowd, then your enjoyment won't be affected by awareness that the series is far from the quickest, and even further from the best to watch.

What I am sure many spectators do love is the hunkered down funkiness of the competing cars, which flaunt the styling cues and quirks pioneered by German Touring Cars and the BTCC from the early Nineties onwards. So there's lots of aero (some of it of dubious functionality I suspect), a riot of sponsor decals (I counted 38 different ones on a Fiesta ST), priapic exhausts, gratuitous heat shielding, an orgy of carbon fibre, and most of all, that nose down, splitter scraping body language so often deployed on Fifth and Sixth series Civics, or at least it is where I live.

I watch the afternoon runs but leave in time to watch the Italian Grand Prix highlights. At the circuit exit, I notice the evidence of much recent doughnutting and similar tomfoolery. Much high jinks then and, sneer as I am tempted to do so, this was only the sort of daftness I would have done when I was 25. Or at least it would have been if I had owned something more potent than an Escort GT at the time, many of whose claimed 75bhp were missing, presumed dead.

Verdict

1. Summary – H M Bateman drew cartoons such as *The Man Who Lit His Cigar Before The Royal Toast* and *The Man Who Crept Into The Royal Enclosure Wearing A Bowler*, which depicted the universal theme of somebody saying or doing the wrong thing at the wrong time and/or in the wrong place. A contemporary candidate for a Bateman homage could be *The Times*-reading, Radio 4-listening, 60-something, Grey-haired Retired Lawyer Who Turned Up To The Petrol And Pistons Time Attack Meeting At Croft In His Grey Skoda Yeti. But that faux pas perhaps gave me the perspective to observe an automotive subculture very different to my usual motorsport environment, and, being twice as old as everybody else, I was in stealth mode as both my car and its driver may as well have been invisible. And the fact that, at first, I could not begin to understand what attracted so many younger enthusiasts to attend Time Attack just meant I had to osmose the atmosphere of the day and then think hard about what was at its essence. What I think is that the real appeal is being part of the show, not inferior or separate to what is on track but complementary to it. There's the opportunity to display your own car in company with scores of similar, but

not identical, modified cars, and then (for only 35 quid!) to drive it briskly around the track for a few laps. The other appeal is that the competitors themselves are amateurs, easily accessible to all in the pit garages and on the pitlane walk about, and that their cars aren't the half-million quid GT3 racers you might see in GT racing, or the big budget razzmatazz BTCC cars. Instead they are pretty similar to the car you arrived in, but they are modified in ways that you might even aspire to achieve yourself.

The fact that most cars are paid for by the sweat equity of the owner rather than a sponsor's cheque only adds to the appeal ("Built not Bought" remember) as does the fact that the drivers are invariably People Like Us, or, in Guy Martin's case, somebody who isn't really like us at all but whose fame is founded principally on the fact that he is. This isn't a criticism, and it is no odder than Paul McCartney's regular bloke routine or Chris Evans' cheeky chappy, best mate schtick.

And so what happens on track is almost incidental to just being there, mixing with other members of your tribe, comparing the potency of your sound system or the efficacy of your new Turbosmart dump valve. Iconography is a key part of Time Attack, and even as you arrive you notice the seamless banners on the circuit fence for Hardrace, Takata, K-Sport, GFB Go Fast Bits, Gamegear Formula Racing and the many other brands that target this market – Ramair anybody?

2. The entry fee was £15, and the programme might have been thin but at least it was free. The commentary was breakfast DJ perky, and the information available on the live timing app and the livestreaming to Facebook added to the sense of inclusivity. The timing information was not confined to lap times either, but included sector times and maximum speed at three points, the highest being over 130mph (210km/h).

3. I've already talked about the typical attendee, and I'd guess the average age was mid/late 20s and with a much more ethnically diverse crowd than most motorsports except drag racing. Family groups, kids? Very few.

4. The Time Attack website contains up to date results, previews of future rounds and is reasonably designed. Some areas of the site are empty, such as driver profiles, but a decent effort is made in explaining what the sport is about.

5. The strapline is "It's not racing ... it's Time Attack." And I drove home wondering what the reaction would have been of a typical group of spectators at Croft today if, instead of watching yet another Evo parp and fart its way around the circuit, they had been standing with me at Deer Leap last Monday as the Chevron B37 exploded into view ...

THORNBOROUGH AUTOGRASS – 24 SEPTEMBER 2017

It says a lot about Autograss' public profile that although Thornborough is only 15 minutes from home I was unaware of its existence until 2016. Local media coverage of motorsport is patchy, at best, and is usually confined to 'local boy done good' copy about the Bedale teenager who was on the third step of the podium for a Ginetta Junior race at some place

Down South. Thornborough might have been hosting a weekend meeting for the British Autograss Series but there wasn't a word about it in the local press, nor a mention on local radio or television, before, during, or after the meeting. But the local media did go into feeding frenzy mode about the two serious crashes that had taken place during the motorbike racing at Scarborough's Oliver's Mount circuit over the same weekend. And such lazy reportage so much of it was, comprising some phone footage of the Air Ambulance (it's a yellow helicopter, who would have guessed?) and some vox pop wisdom culled from the blizzard of Facebook posts made by those who were able to play the 'I was there' trump card.

I have already written about May's York Autograss meeting and now I wanted to see a different venue and to watch the premier league of the sport. Thornborough is located a few miles to the east of lower Wensleydale, roughly midway between *All Creatures Great and Small* Thirsk and Theakston's Old Peculier Masham. Some Autograss tracks are more pop up than permanent, but Thornborough is an established presence, with rather more guard rails than Autograss newcomers might expect. Or at least until they experience a Class 7 race, which, just like the Chevron B37 I so enthused about on my Oulton Park visit, triggers our fight or flight DNA, and in quite the best of ways. The track is the usual loose surfaced short oval, has slightly higher ground to its south and offers most spectators a view over the whole course, including the splendidly named Stargate Turn and Nutters' Corner.

I was amazed at how many people were on site by 10am on Sunday; most of them looked as though they had been here for days as a whole community of caravans and motor homes encircled the track. One of the first things you notice about Autograss is the different regional enthusiasm for the sport and you are far more likely to hear the sing song of the Welsh Borders or an East Anglian twang than a Cumbrian or Lancashire accent and competing cars display not just race number but home track as well. And, far more than any other branch of motorsport I have seen this year, regional allegiance is an inherent part of the fanbase, with many spectators sporting T-shirts and hoodies logoed with their local track and/or driver. The last time I encountered this degree of tribalism was at my only visit to speedway, years ago at Alconbury. The Fen Tigers had a team mascot comprising a modestly proportioned fabric tiger, the breed of not-so-big cat that has a zip along its tummy to facilitate access to one's pyjamas and the Tigers were pitched against a team from somewhere far, far away like Leicester. The atmosphere had been febrile, border line homicidal in fact, and that was just on the part of the Tigers' many women supporters. The tribalism was feral, with each race being soundtracked by a chorus of harpies screaming abuse and Alconbury started to feel like a place where *Deliverance* met *Straw Dogs*, as scripted by MR James, and guest edited by Stephen King.

There were scores of entries but even though the programme was 50-odd pages thick I was struggling to work out the detail as entrants were only identifiable by name, race number and home track, with not a word about what was being driven nor how each class differed. Five minutes googling on the British Autograss Series website helped, but I was still surprised that the entrants for the Ladies Class 1 (Sponsor Mark Johnson Flooring,

Hartlepool) were described quite so concisely. But what's not to like about such a diversity of names – I was very taken by Ashlea Cowperthwaite and Missy Moseley and, in the men's classes there were some simply cracking forenames including Aby-Jayde, Wez, Gethin, and Jabez. I am not indulging in middle-aged smartarse sneering here, as I was the one whose infant school classmates had names as dismal as the late Fifties parsimony in which we were condemned to grow up. Janices and Patricias, Roys and Michaels, Sandras and Susans populated Little Preston Infants. I was one half of the inevitable Janet and John double act. Even Stacey was racy back then.

I walked round to the start line, past the St George's flag adorned dodgems, and I watched races at the rate of one every five minutes or so. There's none of the endless delays, green flag laps, pace car and Code 60 nonsense which can disrupt the fluency of almost every circuit race meeting. Instead, up to eight cars set off line abreast, and if there's a shunt or a stationary car there's a red flag followed by a rerun. On the infield are four marshals on quad bikes and two recovery vehicles; on the outfield the paramedics are ready to roll in their Nissan Patrol – a vehicle that probably smells like pubs used to before the smoking ban, as both uniformed occupants are enjoying a morning smoke with their coffees. The whole place has a reassuringly laissez-faire attitude, and there is none of the control-freakery and health-and-safety overkill that can make a day at some race circuits so irritating. When I arrived I had asked the young blonde on ticket duty where I should park, conditioned as I am to the complex hierarchies that apply to access to motorsport venues. She looked nonplussed for a moment, then said with a winning smile "... err ... wherever you want, love?" And whilst dogs are banned from most motorsport venues, here they are almost compulsory, with Airedales and Collies sitting contentedly with the family groups that surround the track. There's clearly a whole community of regulars, camped under gazebos, barbecues alight by 10am and fuelled by logs brought in the motor home or caravan. It is as though the organisers have resolved that they will only ever impose the absolute minimum of rules on the basis that common sense will take care of everything else.

There's lots of animation in the crowd today, with smart moves on track greeted by whoops and fist pumping. But none of them is as demonstrative as the scary guy standing next to me by the start line. He's got mad and hostile eyes, sports a 1959 specification Dirk Bogarde quiff, wears the ubiquitous Wulf leisurewear, and he is gesticulating furiously to the driver of the Micra in the middle of the eight-car grid. Friend, spouse, sibling, or child? God only knows, and I wasn't asking. Autograss races are not started by the usual green light but, in a nod towards the turf, by the abrupt raising of a wire which is strung across the track at driver eye level. As the wire lifts the Micra bogs down and Bogarde glares at me as if I am personally to blame and then bellows "Fucking shit start. Fucking shit. Jesus ..." I edge away, deciding that some homily about the taking part being the most important thing probably wouldn't cut it with the now scarily animated Dirk. His outburst would have been bad form at Cadwell and de trop down Goodwood way, but certainly added colour to my day at the races.

The racing progressed upwards through the classes, beginning with tame, but enthusiastically piloted Micras and Novas (and, bizarrely, a Peugeot 104 with Italian flag livery), then progressed through ever more powerful iterations of what had once been budget family transport until things started to get very lively indeed in the higher classes. Having watched drivers deal with understeering front-wheel drive cars it is a shock to see notionally the same type of car powering out of corners in massive oversteering slides, with rear wheels kicking up plumes of dust and debris. I twig; the cars, which had started life as front-wheel drive, are often now rear-wheel drive and, from the way they set off the line, they are packing a lot more poke than they used to on the drive to the weekly shop at Lidl.

It gets wackier still as the F600 classes appear; these are bike engined single-seaters with the driver enclosed safely within the chassis tubing, itself one big roll over bar. These are needed a lot as the cars not only pull modest wheelies off the line but also frequently crash into each other. It's notionally a non-contact sport but come on, four lap races, a single grippy line, eight cars, and a short oval are ingredients that absolutely guarantee that the plot will frequently unravel. And it does in the third F600 race as two cars touch into Nutters' Corner, get on to two wheels and then head skywards, spinning like dolphins before landing on their sides with a thud that I can hear 100 yards away. Scramble medics, remove wreckage, check Armco barrier, and the next heat is under way within five minutes. It's astonishing and had this been at a race circuit I would have had time to read half of the Observer review section before the action got under way again.

Did you watch the last Grand Prix on TV? I bet that it had featured an ultra slo-mo sequence of Hamilton or Ocon getting out of shape at turn three? It's shown again and again, as if correcting this tiny fidget of misalignment were the biggest save in the sport's history instead of just an eye blink of disruption. And my £10 says that the TV director has never seen Autograss Class 7 cars in action as I have seen few things that are more spectacular than these wild and wacky devices which join top fuel dragsters, big horsepower single-seaters and the crazier rallycross cars in my motorsport pantheon. Let me describe a typical car; it looks vaguely like a Mini Pick Up, and I am talking original Mini, not the sort of 21st Century triumph of style over substance MINI which a Hackney hipster might use to transport his artisan coffee beans. The engine isn't up front though, but in the load bay in the rear and, as often as not, the engine has brought its identical twin along for company. That's right, two engines, just like the 1935 Alfa Romeo Bi Motore but with half the cylinder count and, unlike the Alfa, here the powertrain works on the basis of one engine per rear wheel. Invariably these are big capacity, big power bike engines, meaning 200bhp per engine in something not much bigger than a ride on mower. But it doesn't have to be Minis or bike engines as the main rule in Class 7 seems to be that too many rules are a really bad thing. So Fiat 126s, Seicentos, and Cinquecentos are common sights today, there's even what had once been a Sunbeam Stiletto in 1970 and engines vary from twin-cam fours to V6s and even the odd Rover V8.

If the recipe is bonkers the finished dish is even crazier, and you know it is going to be something special from the way that, pre-race, the marshals due diligence the Armco, a John Deere tractor pulls a roller to smooth out the surface bumps and ridges and a big Case 8910 pulls a muck sprayer around to apply water to the track to reduce the dustclouding. On the line, and all eight cars are spitting venomously, stammering against their rev limiters before up goes the wire and – this I didn't expect – three cars are pulling immense wheelies, drivers enjoying a view only of any passing rooks and pigeons as the car angles up at 45 degrees before slamming back down to earth and accelerating ferociously to Nutters Corner, where, amazingly, the action gets even more spectacular. The technique is to throw the car into the apex and power through in the biggest slides I have seen in half a century of watching fast cars do daft things. The car is at least 30 degrees out of shape, the engine(s) is (are) howling and the fat rear wheels are smoking the sky with mud and soil. There's a brief respite on the next short straight but that in itself is spectacular as, standing as close as I dare, the cars howl by quickly enough to scare me, then there's another crazy lunge to the inside. But as in every form of motorsport. if you watch carefully enough, then patterns emerge, techniques become clearer and the smartest, most consistent drivers shine the brightest. The first thing I notice is that the key to staying in front is to hog the polished and grippier surface of the inside line around the curves; it doesn't really matter how slowly you go as gamesmanship enables the clever drivers to brake hard for the corner, dominate the inside line and only deploy full power in the crazy dash down to the next bend. It is the pretenders for victory who do the really bonkers stuff as they will take a much wider, and theoretically faster line into the corner, but then encounter stormier waters as they try to maintain speed on a surface coated with three inches of loose soil and dust. Result? Massive rooster tails of debris, huge slides and, if you are lucky, the unique sight of a car on full opposite lock suddenly rearing several feet skywards as the driver deploys maximum power. Overtaking is more opportunistic than tactical as overtaking happens in the blink of an eye when the man (or woman – see below) in front gets it wrong. The star driver in Class 7 has a technique that is a joy to watch – he gets his car sideways ten yards earlier than anybody else on the entry to the turn, then holds the car perfectly in a neat 50 yards slide before powering down the next straight. It's metronomic, unspectacular, and hugely effective and if Alain Prost or Jenson Button drove in Autograss they'd drive like this. And if sound and fury Gilles Villeneuve or Vittorio Brambilla were racing today they'd be the guys looking ever more desperate in their efforts to keep up. So what about strategy, undercuts and overcuts? Get out of here – this is racing, red in tooth and claw, and distilled to the pure elements of the car behind going faster than the car in front, seizing the moment and, if the move doesn't come off as planned, then trying again.

The slow cars reappear and it's time to circulate, to soak up the ambience and to identify what best distinguishes this crowd from the others I have seen this season. The biggest single identifying factor is that Autograss seems to be an almost exclusively blue collar sport whose heartland lies in the regions of the country furthest away from the gentility of the bigger conurbations, especially London and the plusher bits of the south east. If this were the USA, Autograss would be a hillbilly sport with its heart never too far from the Appalachians; our equivalents are places like Leominster, South Somerset, Gloucester and Hereford – and there must be an Autograss venue in the Forest of Dean surely? I have never been anywhere in the UK that felt more like Tennessee and the accent down Cinderford way was as impenetrable as the one in Decatur County had been.

Gender quotas and similar initiatives are possibly the sort of newspeak political nonsense this crowd wouldn't entertain but the irony is that, just like drag racing, Autograss is gender blind and has far more youngsters in the crowd than creaky old baby boomers like your correspondent. There's kids in prams, toddlers playing with dogs, young mums with two generations above them and one below and it all just works. What is clear immediately is that this really is the cliché of the good day out for all the family. But what is unique is that nearly every family group watching trackside will contain one or two people in racewear; it is utterly extraordinary to see so many kids in their early teens carrying crash helmets and kitted out in the same race suits as their big brothers, mums, dads and more than a few grandparents too. Laudably, Suzi Wolff is encouraging more women to become active in motorsport with her 'Dare to be Different' campaign. She could learn a lot from Autograss; it may be far removed from the grotesque budgets and self-importance of international motorsport but its equality of access and participation is exemplary, even if, sadly, Autograss keeps its light very firmly under the proverbial bushel. It needs to capture a wider audience, not least because there is so much to learn from it.

Verdict

1. Summary – A revelation. Spectacular, friendly and accessible, with an easy-going atmosphere and a laid-back feel. Despite its amateur feel and an absence of big budgets, Winnebagos, and sponsorship deals, the meeting was run slickly and professionally, with almost constant action. The four-strong commentary team was a study in regional accents, with Scarborough ('hope' pronounced 'herp'), Sheffield ('four' pronounced 'fower') and Kent, I suspect ('Layz and gemmun, ere's Autograss very own Sean Connery – it's Too … oo … ny Proctor!'). They were slick, fast as auctioneers at the cattle mart and clued up on who was racing what. Which was useful, as the programme was quite useless to anybody who didn't know lots about Autograss already. There was a list of previous round results (e.g. Round 2 South Wales 1 ARC 1 Lee Seagraves) but not a word about what Mr Seagraves – great surname by the way – was driving in Class 10 in South Wales, nor whether he is here today. I don't find out where ARC stands for either, nor how Class 10 might differ from Class 6 or 8. But the programme still endears and how could it not when one class is sponsored by 'K S Coles – Specialist grower and packer of fresh peas, broad beans and swedes of Chelston, Somerset'? Another class is sponsored by the local minibus firm and illustrated by a picture of – you guessed – a minibus, but so out of focus as to be nearly unrecognisable. Cheap laughs? Not really, if anything the amateurism just

reminded me of the simpler times when blokes could just turn up somewhere and mess about with cars.

It cost me £20 for a weekend ticket and, mercifully, the programme was free.

2. Nature notes – As a couple of thousand people had been corralled round a dirt track for three days all wildlife had had the good sense to get some peace and quiet elsewhere. But it is a delightful area, with a large nature reserve a mile or two west and Yorkshire's answer to Stonehenge also nearby. Obviously, this being God's own county, our henge is bigger and better than the one those southern jessies built in Wiltshire. Wherever that is.

3. Catering – The usual burger and fries, yes, but fresh baked pizza too and booze from the converted bus logoed "Look on the bright cider life," which made me smile.

4. What could be improved? – You can guess: sort the simply dire programme out so that newcomers can understand what is going on.

5. Website – The Yorkshire Dales Autograss website is a good effort, well-illustrated, but clearly aimed more at aficionados than random visitors.

RALLY YORKSHIRE – DALBY FOREST 30 SEPTEMBER 2017

Rallying culture is almost as deeply embedded in North Yorkshire as motorbike racing is on the Isle of Man. 'Killer Kielder,' a couple of hours north in Northumbria, is where the biggest and baddest special stages of them all are located, but North York Moors stages such as Cropton, Boltby, Wykeham, Wass, and Langdale still resonate with anybody who has ever been bitten by the special stage rallying bug. And Dalby Forest of course, the scene of my first RAC Rally (as described in Chapter 3) and one of the few rally venues that you might almost get away with calling 'iconic.' Only almost though, as the word is now applied to everything from brands of coffee to road bridges and has become as devalued as a Twenties Reichsmark. But, as I was soon to find out, it isn't just words and banknotes that can lose most of their value …

The day had started out so well; it was early autumn, there was high cloud in a blue sky, the chestnut trees were just turning autumn gold, and I felt that familiar tingle of anticipation as I drove north up the long hill out of Thornton le Dale before turning into the lane leading to the vast Dalby complex. I was headed for the famous Woodyard, where two tracks almost converge before one spears off up the long drag to the south west and the other heads due east on a long fast straight. In practice this layout has meant that the same car can be seen twice, and this fact alone has made the Woodyard a sacred place in rallying folklore. And this is a sport that has always had a rich heritage of legend, folklore, and storytelling. If you are at Silverstone or Santa Pod, prolonged conversations with strangers are unusual but everybody chats to each other in forest rallying. My crackpot theory is that it's a legacy from the stone age, when our forebears would stick together around the camp fire burning bright, where they would talk about hopes, fears and, especially, what horrors might be lurking in the darkness beyond the flames' reach. There is something atavistic and sombre enough about a dark forest, even in daylight, to dilute our veneer of reserve and to make the experience a communal one.

I was excited, it had been five years or more since I had watched a big league rally and if the glory days of the RAC Rally coming to town were gone for ever, the prospect of a 140 strong field of cars ranging from sophisticated World Rally Car specification Fiestas and Focuses, to Burns and McRae era Imprezas and Mitsubishi Evos, and to that immortal old warhorse, the Escort Mark II. And yes, a Mark II might just merit the adjectival accolade of icon status.

The entry fee was £15 per person, which was a lot more than the last time I had paid the Forestry Commission to watch a rally, but as I ambled down to the Woodyard at midday I still was almost bubbling with anticipation, as this place has long been my own field of dreams. In the long shadows under the silent pines and beeches, I spotted the tell-tale slots of roe and fallow deer, heard the sibilant twitter of siskins, and I planned a long walk into the woods, away from the crowds, long before the first car's arrival. My plan was then to duck and dive back through the woods over the next hour or so and then to watch the last few cars scrabbling through the Woodyard – twice. That's the appeal of stage rallying, as its anarchic character enables some ad-libbing on the spectating front and has always allowed me to find half a mile (0.8km) of track to myself where I can enjoy different views of the cars and find the time to savour the deep silence of the woods. And hell, there was always the long shot chance of a pine marten sighting, as hadn't *The Darlington & Stockton Times* reported that these little beasts were back?

I looked for the differences since my first visit here, (Christ!) 48 years ago, when my hair was black, my spine was supple, and my cynicism was still a very early work in progress. Maybe these trees are a bit taller now than back in the pre-decimal Jurassic era when the Forestry Commission didn't erect infantile, sub *Blue Peter*, interpretative signing pointing out the bleeding obvious to walkers and mountain bikers. Did anybody even ride a bike in the Seventies out of choice, rather than economic necessity? And, back in the days of *The Sweeney* and *Fawlty Towers* what would we have made of today's weapons grade carbon fibre and unobtanium mountain bikes and their lime green and pink lycra clad owners? Dismissed them as milquetoast pansies probably, before sparking up another Marlboro and getting back to moaning about petrol at 15 bob a gallon, twice what it had been only two years earlier. Bloody OPEC, we'd have mumbled into our Brew Ten bitter.

I mind mapped the stage route from previous trips and I opted to wander up the long hill to the right, as I knew that the plateau beyond had some big cojones bends punctuating the long straights. And these aren't the tight hairpins where anybody who knows how to use a handbrake can look like a hero but those high speed, flat in fifth or sixth kinks, where the tiniest mistake can explode into a huge tank-slapping moment at best or the ignominy and danger of an exit into the trees at worst. I smiled to myself at the decades of memories the forests have endowed – the resonant howl of the V6 Ferrari engined Stratos breaking up the monotony of the RS Escorts in '74, the extraordinary composure and speed of the first

Quattro in '81 and, most of all, the crazy world of Group B in '85 and '86. To watch an Audi Sport Quattro exploding out of the darkness like a bull elephant on the rampage was soul stirring, and we would have been listening to that scary monster of a car charging through the woods for at least five minutes before we saw it. We had heard the distant clang of sumpguard hitting rock, then that unmistakeable warbling bellow from the five-cylinder turbocharged engine, engine note rising and falling, punctuated by bangs and hisses, rumbles and clicks, and then we would see the white glare of spotlights flashing through the trees towards us and it was as terrifying as it was magnificent. Then the Peugeot 205 T16s, the stiletto to the Audi's sledgehammer and, if a little late to the party, the glorious error of judgement that was the Metro 6R4. The Elephant Man to the chic little Pug's Catherine Deneuve, the Metro was cursed by a normally-aspirated engine when the only way to win was to employ big boost turbo power, but its shortcomings were redeemed by the Metro being blessed with a V6 which sounded more like a Ferrari than any Ferrari ever did. And the last hurrah of Group B, the turbo and supercharged insanity called the Lancia S4, whose acceleration should have been the exclusive province of a big power single-seater racer. I will never forget how the acceleration just kept accelerating in an orgy of exponential energy as Henri Toivonen's Delta S4 disappeared into the distance, keeping on keeping on as it tore the night apart. How could we have known that we would never see him again?

As I walked on, I mused on the eras that had followed Group B, starting with the dull early Group A to the mad as a cut snake McRae era and, via sundry riffs on the World Rally Car theme, culminating in today's very fast but not especially attractive breed of 1600 turbo cars. Group B had been such a seismic disruption to rallying's status quo, following the three decades' worth of steady evolution that had preceded it, that the era still casts a long shadow over the sport. And Colin McRae, and the fevered fanbase he created, still represents the biggest thing to have happened in UK rallying since the time when Sport Quattros and 205 T16s stalked the earth. I had seen McRae driving the wheels off a Sierra Cosworth, then a Subaru Legacy, in the days when the marque was more favoured by farmers than wannabe rally stars. And then had come the growly Imprezas in trademark blue/gold livery, another car that might just scrape icon status. McRae's taciturnity was at the Kimi Raikkonen level but just like the charmless and monosyllabic Finn, the Scot created his own fanbase cult. His "If in doubt, flat out" credo made him sublime to watch, in just the same way that Gilles Villeneuve had been, but the circumstances of McRae's death, not to mention his part in the deaths of those who died with him, tarnished his legacy, and make his post mortem deification problematic. This is one occasion when the 'judge the art, not the artist' get out of jail free card doesn't work for me.

Enough musing already and what the hell is this, parked up in the forest clearing? It's a Ford Transit minibus, logoed "All Events Security" and the very fact it is here at all makes my heart sink as rallying has always been for the free spirited, where routes and viewing points are planned only by oneself, restricted only by common sense and not directed by a bloke in a hi-vis tabard. And it gets worse, because here's a burger van whose very presence infuriates me as it feels like a violation of a special place and beyond the van – no – there's only a line of portable toilets. Somebody thinks toilets are needed in 8,000 acres (3,250 hectares) of dense woodland? I struggle with that. And, as I walk into the Woodyard itself, all I can see are lines and lines of red tape and plastic mesh punctuated by warning signs announcing how very dangerous rallying could be. Who knew? With a sinking heart I realised that in 2017 any ad libbery on my part was out of the question as the spectators had been kettled into a tight enclosure as if we had been anti-capitalism protesters at the G20 Summit. And damn, I had only left my Guy Fawkes mask in the Yeti. Could it get any worse, could my spirits reach subterranean levels of despair? Oh sure they could, as I realised that only one track was being used, with the Woodyard's USP of seeing the same rally car twice remaining unexploited. The route was the slowest possible, with 100 yards (90m) of track describing two 90-degree bends, and a slow and blind entry. But at least I would know what was going on as the tired old VW Corrado beyond the stage track was being unloaded so that the public-address system could be set up. Heads turned – some amused, some less so – as I exclaimed "Oh for fuck's sake," and if you were there yourself but were not amused then look, I'm sorry, I hate swearing in public, I really do, but this, here? It was like seeing a McDonalds in York Minster.

After a succession of blaring and squawking course cars had passed to ensure that nobody was at the slightest risk of enjoying themselves, the commentator announced that the first rally car had entered the stage. Eventually, a white Fiesta WRC appeared, wheezed and popped a bit, briefly spun all four wheels and then disappeared, its progress marked by a modest bang on each up shift. More Fiestas drove through, occasionally emitting a little spit of flame from the exhaust and even getting a teensy bit sideways. But my pulse rate didn't spike, and nor was it much provoked by the WRC Focus and Fabia, but at least the warbling bark of an Impreza made me smile, if not as much as the phalanx of lairy Mark II Escorts, all snatched down shifts, opposite lock, and induction roar. But 15 seconds viewing per car, and a top speed below 40mph made this rallying-lite, and as far removed from my first experience of the sport as I could imagine. After 25 cars had passed there was a long delay, explained by the commentator as being due to the need to extract a car that had broken down. At least my thoughts weren't audible this time; when I started this game, crews would pick up the casualties after the last car had completed the stage, or the next morning if they'd opted for the solace of the New Inn back in Thornton le Dale.

Enough already, and I wasn't the only spectator wandering back to my car discontented and disappointed, as well as 15 quid lighter. We were the usual rallying crowd with family groups, girlfriend-free Impreza men living their own blokey PlayStation dreams, and also the inevitable guy from South Wales. There is always at least one guy from Cardiff or Swansea at any rally, anywhere, and we had a long chat about everything from Group B to Plaid Cymru and, yes really we did, the futility of performance indicators in the public sector. In all the excitement I have now quite forgotten how we got on to the last topic. Rallying also attracts the eccentric and today's was an aristocratic-looking woman in her late '70s wearing a leather stetson and bearing more than a passing resemblance to Dame Maggie Smith. She was sitting on the ground, leaning on her rucksack, emanating an air of frosty hauteur and (you guessed, right?) reading *The Times Literary Supplement*. That at least made me smile, but little else did apart from the mangled syntax in the event programme. Here's a sample: "Being amazed that a Colt Lancer could beat the mighty Escort." And that was the entire paragraph. Random initial capitals too: "I was only Eleven" (irritating isn't it?) and an explosion of exclamation marks!!!!!!! Nit-picking, moi? Guilty, but that's the price of being a pedant. At least there was less litter today than the three carrier bags full I had collected from the College Moor stage the last time I had watched the Riponian rally. There is a minority of rally fans who drive like idiots, constantly eff and blind at full volume, break off branches and saplings that obscure their view and generally behave badly enough to make some communities, including the one where I used to live, dread the day of the next rally. And if you're thinking I'm the hypocrite, as I'm the guy who audibly used the F-word in public only an hour ago, I was under provocation by a nanny state outrage, okay?

So why had my day been so irredeemably crap and why had this event been by far the worst of my year so far? I knew already that spectators on the snappily titled Wales Rally GB were kept in enclosures (and presumably force fed on burgers and fries by their captors), but not until today had I realised that this malaise had spread to relatively parochial events like this one. Why the fall from grace? It's easy to fall into *Daily Mail* outrage mode and complain that this health and safety thing has gone mad. I don't normally have a problem with health and safety as, actually, I don't think there is anything too unreasonable about expecting to come home alive and unscarred from a day at work. I have been to more than one inquest about people who haven't made it back home and, well, there are better ways to spend the day.

And Health and Safety law isn't anything like as prescriptive as the tabloid press imagine, as actual blame for cancelled cheese rolling and bed race bans can usually be attributed to overzealous officials and insurance companies rather than statutory provision or EU diktat. I was already aware of spectator deaths having occurred at a couple of recent events, three of them at the Jim Clark Rally, which takes place on closed public roads. I know from experience how dangerous tarmac events can be, having attended rallies that use the surfaced roads that cross the Otterburn ranges. The last time I had attended, a young spectator had been killed up the road from me and, if I was shocked, I was hardly surprised as speeds were so high and in too many places there was, quite literally, no hiding place. But tarmac rallies are very different to loose surface forest rallies, as not only are speeds much higher, as you would expect on such grippy surfaces, but, critically, the areas adjacent to public roads rarely have the natural cover of a forest stage. With only a little effort, it has always been easy to find a safe vantage point to watch forest rallies, with steep banks and mature tree trunks offering sanctuary from errant rally cars. I did some research and whilst less than exhaustive the results were surprising.

In 2015 the MSA published the Rally Future Stage Rally Safety Requirements; it's a clearly written 27-page document that sets out the safety framework within which stage rallies should operate. There is text about spectator management, the safety code, prohibited areas and so on, and who could disagree with the key message that safety must be at the heart of every rally event? The key theme is not the familiar binary one of total elimination of risk, the malaise that has caused so many egg and spoon races and village fêtes to have been banned, but the sensible management of risk instead. Rightly, it is pointed out that the duty of care means doing what is reasonable and practicable, including the designation of high risk areas as no-go areas. Nothing new there really, as for decades the areas where cars might plunge straight on in a misjudged cornering or braking manoeuvre have been taped off. But outside those no-go areas there is an imperative only to manage risk to an appropriate level, and whilst the ideal is stated as being confined to access only where specified "it is unlikely you can prevent spectators appearing at many points of the route."

Is there anything really new in any of this? Not really, the guide appears to be a consolidation of the best practice and procedure that has been applied for decades. There's certainly very little new law, as the health and safety regime has been in force for over 40 years. So what about those exclusion of liability signs that announce to spectators that "You are present at your own risk and neither organisers nor competitors are liable for any injury, however caused," are they still effective? No, even if it may surprise some to learn that such attempts at excluding liability for injury or death have been legally ineffective since the late Seventies – if you harm somebody through your own negligence then you may be liable to compensate them. It's not really 'hold the front page' news, therefore, whatever the *Mail*, *Express* or *Telegraph* might say in one of their trademark fulminations about the nanny state.

So what is going on, and why has the heart been ripped out of rallying? I think there has been a widespread misunderstanding that any accident on any rally, whether foreseeable or not, and regardless of the reasonableness of the precautions taken, is automatically actionable. I think a naïve 'one size fits all' approach may have been taken by some organisers who apply the same draconian restrictions to forest rallying on unsealed tracks as they do to the very different risk environment of tarmac rallies running on closed public or military roads. The irony is that the MSA guidance enables a far more fluid and nuanced safety regime than the absurdly prescriptive one that was in force at Dalby. There is nothing in the MSA guidance which expressly forbids the sort of ad hoc spectating arrangements that have universally applied in rallying for decades. Today I would have been in no danger whatsoever if I had been able to walk a mile or so into the woods, then selected a sensible vantage point where I was protected by high banking and tree cover and from where I could have enjoyed what the sport of rallying used to offer. But I know damned well, from both the marshal presence and the signage overkill, that the second I had stepped outside the kettled-in viewing area at the Woodyard I would have been in deep shit with officialdom.

I shall have to apply some more diligence to my Ordnance Survey maps before trying to watch my next rally. But so as to avoid future interception by rallying's well-meaning but overzealous Stasi I had better say no more.

Verdict
On today's evidence, stage rallying has become motorsport's equivalent to homeopathy. Dilute the essence to near invisibility and then pretend that it still works. Some may delude themselves that it still does. But it really doesn't ...

VSCC LAKELAND TRIAL – 11 NOVEMBER 2017
You can't help warming to a man who nearly forgets to mention that there's a Surtees TS-8B Formula 5000 car in his garage. A friend of mine had a race in such a Surtees once and he sure as hell hasn't forgotten how Oulton Park suddenly seemed to have much shorter straights. But when you're Jolyon Harrison and you have a collection of cars like his, then almost forgetting about a 500bhp single-seater is understandable. "Well, apart from this [a 1930 Ford Model A], which was built by an Irish architect who won the VSCC championship in it, there's a 1926 Bentley 3-8 [that's a 3-litre chassis with an 8-litre engine], a 1931 Bentley 8-litre (only 80 of these now exist and it's a four-seater Le Mans type car), a 1934 single seat Lagonda (two stage supercharged and running on methanol), a 1948 Bentley Mark VI Special, and a 1949 Mark VI Special but that one's got a modern engine with 530bhp. A 1948 Frazer Nash High Speed that did the Mille Miglia and the Targa Florio, a 1962 Lotus Elite with a full race engine, a Frogeye Sprite, a Healey 3000, a TR4, an Elan, and a 1965 Land Rover with a 6-litre Chevrolet engine, which is great fun. I might have missed one or two out ... oh yes, I've got a Brabham BT30 and ... oh yes, there's a Surtees Formula 5000 car as well." Jolyon is from York and he is competing in the Lakeland Trial, which consists of driving very old cars along very steep tracks leading up mountains and through forests. We are at the first stage, Drumhouse, at the top of Honister Pass; the startline is 1350 feet (410m) above sea level and the finish must be another 1000 feet (305m) higher up, somewhere on the way to Great Gable.

I have attended many Vintage Sports Car Club events before, but this is my first sporting trial, and within five minutes of arriving I have already fallen under its spell. And how could I not have done when, after the sublime drive here, all misty mountains and autumn leaves, I am welcomed into the assembly area and inch my way through the 100-odd vintage cars to the car park? There's much good-humoured badinage at the intrusion of my MX5 and one tweedy gent smiles and asks me what the Skyactiv Technology badge on the boot means. I shrug in reply: "Not a clue mate; some computer stuff they make in Hiroshima maybe?" I lose my self-consciousness once I park up my big girl's blouse of a sports car and I drink in the sights, smells, and sounds of what is to be one of the most memorable days of my motorsporting year. Sights first, and the last time I had driven up Honister Pass was 20 years ago in a biblical rainstorm, which had made working out where my Golf's bonnet ended and the big drop started a game I hadn't wanted to play. But today was flawless and if the temperature was hovering around 5 degrees then so what? I was halfway up a mountain, it wasn't even 9am and it was November in the English Lake District. Lit by the low winter sun, the view west was sublime; the light sharding the slopes above the deep shadows in the valley and, high above me, the unsurfaced and narrow track hairpinned its way up to the clouds, like an anglicised Pikes Peak, but with a much lower redneck count. I could feel the salty moisture on the breeze coming off the sea just a few miles to the west and the air was filled with the unmistakable sounds and smells that old cars and their owners make when they are being warmed up. There's the muted but insistent tuffa, stutter-pop-hiss soundtrack from ancient engines, the smell of burned oil, unburned petrol, and there's a hint of pipe smoke mingling with the irresistible morning smell of bacon sandwich and freshly brewed coffee.

The youngest car in the entry list was 80, one of the many Austin Seven Specials, and the oldest, a GN Vitesse, was 95. The odd Bugatti, Ford Model A, and Dodge apart, all of the entries were from British makes which included such gems as a Godfrey and Proctor Sports, a Morris Major (but of course), and a spidery 1925 Jowett. I have long admired Bradford's only car marque, which presaged the Alfasud recipe of a feisty flat-four, clever packaging, and a slippery shape by 30 years, but I had been unaware of earlier Jowetts like the 1925 model driven by Gavin Fielding: "It's a 900cc flat-twin and it's got no power at all really but there's lots of low down torque." My knowledge of prewar cars is so poor that, just for once, I am in the role of regular punter rather than seasoned anorak, and that fact alone makes talking to the owners as necessary as it is rewarding. They are quite astonishingly welcoming, all eager to enthuse about their cars and, even more so, about what a fantastically fun day they are having. One driver insists that I just buy a suitable car and give it a go and another almost pressgangs me into being a passenger in one of the competing cars. Oh yes, there's passengers and their role isn't entirely passive either; in addition to co-driving and push starting or cranking duties, their job is to optimise weight distribution to enable maximisation of traction opportunities. Or that's maybe how McLaren's notoriously circumlocutory Ron Dennis might have put it – you and I would say that being a passenger on a VSCC trial means bouncing up and down on the back seat like a bastard whilst waving to spectators and laughing like a hyena. Some cars (or is it more properly 'motor cars' in VSCC world?) only have space for one but others carry up to three passengers, and in the case of one svelte looking and throaty sounding Bugatti, dad is driving and teenage son and daughter are on bouncing duty – it's a family affair. Only my temperamental back prevents me from volunteering as bouncer/ ballast/organic traction controller.

Time to talk some more to Jolyon Harrison. "You really should be taking part you know; it's great fun, especially going up here, you don't really need to win anything, it's just a great day out, lots of really nice people but with challenging things to do. The car's a lot better than I am, I've had it five years and we always make one mistake that stops us getting an award. It's never easy, you might clear one or two hills but there's some you won't clear so it's a matter of how far you can get and using all your techniques. There is certainly a lot of skill involved but it's not the end of the world if you don't clear a hill and ..." he pauses "... if you'd like to read what it says on the side of my car ("there's nothing, absolutely nothing, half so much worth doing as simply messing about in cars") ... From *The Wind in the Willows*, slightly altered. I'm Ratty and my co-driver is Mole." Of course they are, and now I really can't stop smiling.

The start is just up the hill from the Sky Hi café and I enjoy an al fresco latte and a bacon sandwich as I wander amongst the cars and drivers, overhearing conversations and peering into cockpits that show decades of wear and tear. It's not the affected rat look which is such A Thing in drag racing but simply the result of years of hard usage. Cars like these belong in a community as far removed from the obsessive-compulsive world of Concours d'Elegance at Villa D'este and Pebble Beach as you can imagine. The VSCC demographic is far wider than I had imagined, with long Lancastrian vowels, bosting Black Country, and see-saw Sunderland punctuating Home Counties drawls and Welsh Marches elongations. There are some familiar names in the programme, such as Simon Blakeney Edwards (a fixture at any old car event), Dougal Cawley (boss of Longstone Tyres, who make new tyres for very old cars), and Charles Gillet (driving another Bugatti Brescia, the car that no 14-year-old could ever believe was related to the Veyron). There's a Hannah Mycock too, driving a 1930 Austin Seven.

There's time for one more driver chat before I puff and pant my way uphill – I never was an Alfred Wainwright wannabe, nor was meant to be. I talk to Stephen Fathers from Derbyshire. "This is a 1929 Austin Seven Special, made by Abbot coach-builders; it's got a pretty hot engine and I've owned it for 15 years. We came third on the Welsh Trial a few weeks ago so we're quite competitive when the driver's in a good mood. Why Trials? I've always been into them since I was a lad; it's about judging the conditions relative to the power you put on and the different routes through the stages. The key skill is not to put too much power down, when you start to skid you have to program yourself to bring your accelerator off. Not too much bouncing in this car but you need to in the bigger cars, but with these you just swivel it a little bit. Why the VSCC? They are more of an active club, they're not about turning up to shows. I want to be driving, competing in my car. And the people are great, we meet all the time; next week we're in the Cotswolds, then Prescott, there's events all year round."

The course threads its way uphill through Herdwick – grazed grass and heather, and if its width is comparable to a speed hillclimb like Shelsley Walsh, its surface is far from smooth, comprised mainly of a crazy paving chaos of loose slate. I would have thought twice about driving a traction and stability controlled 4x4 up here but none of the VSCC contestants seemed to bat an eyelid at the prospect of driving their octogenarian cars up what was little more than a sheep track hanging on to the side of a mountain. The Lakeland Trial may not involve its participants getting out of first gear too often but ancient, and possibly temperamental, cars running on rubber band size tyres, roll bar and seatbelt free, and which are occupied by people wearing every type of headgear except a crash helmet does not create an entirely risk free environment, even if nobody seemed to care over much about that. My God, but wasn't today such a refreshing counterpoint to the absurd level of safety prescription I had encountered at Dalby Forest a few weeks ago where, ironically, the speeds in the tight confines of the Woodyard hadn't been much higher than today's? Laissez-faire was the enlightened attitude to spectator attendance today, as not only did I park next to the competitors but I walked the same track as they drove up, safeguarded only by my own common sense and instructed only by the VSCC's exquisitely polite signs, which read: "When you hear a whistle, please stand to the side." That's it, no "motor racing is dangerous," no "keep out, prohibited area," and no *Blue Peter* level guff announcing that "Ari [Vatanen] says 'stay safe.'" And no oik from Ossett using his hi-vis tabard as a licence to irritate, just softly spoken old guys who treat spectators as their guests.

A Riley Special growls past, progress marked by a haze of blue smoke, whining gears and stones and slate ricocheting from its mudguards. Its bodywork might once have been green, or maybe grey, it's difficult to tell with this degree of patina (as nobody would call it today). The Riley's passenger gives a thumbs up to me and the guy in the big hat standing on the rock next to me drawls, in an accent closer to Atlanta than Ambleside – "Jeez man, don't you just love these guys? Thank Christ they use these cars – back home they'd just keep them under goddamn glass." I grin assent and climb further uphill, where the views just get better, and I am overtaken by a teenage girl wearing a Frazer Nash jumper, but looking as though she probably isn't a Xanthe or a Svetlana, but who I guess isn't a Chantelle or a Kayleigh either, so maybe she's an Emily or a Holly? A group of 20-something passengers walk down hill, which the rules require them to do after completing a run, and they are talking animatedly about the Salmson somebody's dad has just bought and this sounds like the most natural thing in the world about which to talk on a Saturday morning in Cumbria with a 500 foot (150m) drop just a spit away. And oh my word, even Sebastian Loeb never had a co-driver who looked that good ...

I have a couple of friends who do serious hill walking, who conquer Munros with insouciance and who talk of the ten-mile (16km) walk before the climb proper starts as just a wee pipe opener but I am just the plodder who usually experiences Britain's best scenery from the driving seat of a speeding sports car. My personal metric for evaluating scenery is based on 30 years living on, or near to, the North York Moors and regular trips to the North West Highlands, and I'll call the Aston metric the Suilven scale. The scenery between Ullapool and Durness scores ten, the Yorkshire Dales four, with Potters Bar and Slough a draw at minus seven. I have visited neither Yosemite nor Patagonia, except vicariously thanks to Messrs Ansel Adams and Bruce Chatwin, but on their testimony I reckon both places would get at least a 17.8 on the Suilven Scale. So, how to score Honister Pass on what, so far as I know, may be the only day it hasn't rained here since 1997? I can't give it less than a seven as nowhere in Yorkshire looks like this and I doubt anywhere else in England does. And yet for all its magnificence, it really is 'what you see is what you get' simple, with none of the nuance and mystery a more lowland setting might offer. But who cares about that when the cloud shadowed scree to the north, hour glassing down 300 feet (90m) from the gap in the high rock walls, looks like a Dürer woodcut?

It's Remembrance Day and at one minute to 11 the start line marshal asks for a two minute silence. The whole poppy thing has become so ludicrously politicised in recent years that it has become more of an opportunity to virtue signal than an occasion respectfully to commemorate. I still buy a poppy but I never wear it; I have spent more than enough time at Verdun, Vimy Ridge, Albert, and Mons to resist the move to turn remembrance into just another reality show awash with faked emotion. But here, today? Silence and reflection feel the right thing, the only thing, the proper and respectful thing to do. And, as I drive home and think about my day, the reason why becomes even clearer. What I had seen, and so loved today, was just as much a key to unlocking the English character as the humour of *I'm Sorry I Haven't a Clue*, the eeriness of *Day in the Life*, Rievaulx Abbey on a "thyme-scented … morning in May," Choral Evensong at Magdalen College chapel, and the poetry of Philip Larkin; it is an England that even I would fight for. What makes today almost unbearably poignant is that the original owners of every competing car knew the 1914-18 war only as The Great War – for how could mankind have been so stupid as ever to contemplate a second one?

THE SUMMER IS ENDED, AND WE ARE NOT YET SAVED – WINTER 2017

Motorsport embraces change cautiously and so, despite a changing climate and the advent of Gore-Tex, most motorsport in Britain still starts in March and ends as the clocks go back in October. We can have the inevitable argument about climate change causation some other time but surely no heat will be generated, even under climate change deniers' collars, if I suggest that Autumns now last longer and Springs tend to start either one month early or two months late? But our island climate has always been a fickle bastard, as even back in Seventies I had watched a Formula 1 race affected by an April blizzard (Silverstone International Trophy 1973) and had walked to RAC Rally special stages in shirtsleeves one year but thermals the next. The traditional motorsport calendar dictates that, at about the same time the first, wildly premature, Christmas themed TV advertisements appear, the emphasis changes from fast to loose. Or, in the case of rallycross, both fast and loose …

Rallycross has been on the cusp of being The Next Big Thing for decades but each time the TV deal has been clinched and the destination is almost in sight the sport sparkles for a year or two but then diverts down some back road and parks up in a lay-by, or simply loses its way and ends up on the wrong side of the tracks. Yet again. But as I write, the FIA World Rallycross Championship looks as though it might be the international success that rallycross organisers have been predicting for the sport since, oh, about 1967. The sport deserves a bigger audience as it is TV friendly, features showboating drivers in big power cars and the race format doesn't tax the attention span of even the most fickle viewer. But in Britain, it isn't too unkind to say that the domestic rallycross scene has, for far too long, involved middle aged men driving very fast cars and 20-something men driving very slow ones. Most of the older guys have been in rallycross for decades, meaning that I feel a sense of déjà vu every time I watch a round of the British Championship. But there is the occasional disruption to the old guys' hegemony and none was bigger than the shockwave created by Daniel Rooke, whom I first saw in 2015 driving a 200bhp Citroën AX and doing things with it that really should not have been possible. Such as making some drivers of big buck 600bhp cars look like amateurs. The next year Rooke moved up to a Citroën DS3 supercar and, at the age of 19, won the championship. Rooke is a driver of quite extraordinary ability whose car control and exquisite delicacy of touch, especially under braking, impressed me in the same way as Jenson Button's silky technique had many years before. Never had our little coterie of Croft regulars been more animated than when we exchanged superlatives about Daniel Rooke; we knew we had seen something remarkable and subconsciously we were already rehearsing how, in five years' time, we'd be telling our racing friends that we'd seen that Dan Rooke when he were bloody nowt. But just try googling him now; the post I made about him in 2015 on a car club website is the fifth link from the top and that tells you all you need to know about the impact of national level rallycross. Rooke's achievement didn't make the tiniest of ripples on the motorsport pond – he would have generated more column inches if he'd made the podium in a BTCC support race. We might think that popular music and motorsport should be a meritocracy, but the reality is far grubbier as well as being quite shockingly inequitable. May I give you Boo Hewerdine, one of Britain's best songwriters, but also the man of whom you almost certainly have never heard? It's hardly surprising as, your reporter apart, Hewerdine's fanbase feels as though it comprises only his mate Derek, my mate David, and their erstwhile fellow Cambridge student, Nick Hornby. And you may have heard of him.

Rallycross had a couple of hits in the late Eighties when the sudden demise of Group B rallying meant lots of big horsepower, four-wheel drive rally cars came on the market and, as rallycross was the only show in town where such cars were useable, the prices were affordable to many UK and European drivers. The spectacle of a field of Ford RS 200s, Sport Quattros, Metro 6R4s, Delta S4s, and big boosted 911 Turbos was unforgettable and the Inter Nations Cup, which was hosted by Croft in 1987 and 1990, was astonishing, like finding yourself at a Metallica gig when all you had expected was a Quo Incidence tribute act. The Cup attracted the biggest crowds the circuit had seen since the Sixties, only being surpassed by Alan Gow's TV-friendly BTCC circus in 1996. Croft had closed as a race circuit in 1981 and the site's adaptation to rallycross might have owed more to opportunism than sophisticated business planning but the result was magnificent. The track was slippery, very fast, mainly on the loose and offered the spectacle of drivers like Martin Schanche, Will Gollop and Michael Shields holding their flame-spitting cars in 200 yard (180m) slides, often in frightening proximity to the spectator enclosures. It also exposed me to what life was then like behind the Iron Curtain, as teams from Poland, Hungary, Czechoslovakia, and

Romania also entered the Cup. The UK and Scandinavian teams had state of the art cars, huge motor homes, supermodel-gorgeous hangers on, Italian coffee machines, and all the other bells and whistles that decent sponsorship makes possible. In brutal contrast, the Eastern European teams were quite pathetically poor, so much so that I found myself close to tears as I watched the Hungarians trying to raise some western currency by selling cheap trinkets and vodka from the trestle table that doubled as their national team HQ. Their baggy old Opel Rekord, having already towed the Škoda race car halfway across Europe, looked as if it was now being used as somewhere to sleep. Everybody in the impoverished team looked grey and exhausted, with sunken eyes and five-day stubble. Of course I bought a couple of bottles of vodka, had a few words with them in my crappy German and the Viel Glück I wished them was not just good manners but heartfelt, as for them to be here at all was a triumph in itself. Who'd have thought it, a first-hand lesson in global politics at a rallycross meeting?

But on 22 October 2017 Croft rallycross was more Inter-County than Inter-Nations because, the inevitable Poles apart (as it were), I doubt if any entrant was from anywhere more exotic than Eire. The event combined the final round of the British Championship and the standalone Rallycross Grand Prix, a title that was almost actionable given the sparsity of entries. And too many of them seemed to be oxymoronic Suzuki Swifts, with a small pack of Citroën C2s and Saxos, a brace of Exiges, and some retro stuff including a sonorous Porsche Turbo and a pair of TR8s that looked as though they were still bearing some unhealed scars from the Eighties. But supercars, the main act that everybody had come to see? Just a handful in this not very grand at all Prix.

I parked by the chicane at 9.30am but by 1pm I had only seen just over 20 minutes of action, despite the fact that racing was already taking place when I had arrived. At 10am, a car crashed at Clervaux, hitting the Armco barriers so hard that the rebuild took 40 minutes, but the incident did at least mobilise Croft's army of security staff, which was deployed to lay a line of blue and white cones linked by incident tape. Quite why this work was done at all must remain open to conjecture as the cones were erected in the spectator enclosure, a metre behind the catch fencing, itself five metres from the damaged Armco. "Never confuse movement with action," as Ernest Hemingway had memorably said.

Inevitably one becomes a little jaded towards the end of the season – you noticed, right? – but so lacking in excitement was most of the day that I was pleased I had bought a *Sunday Times* en route, and the distraction of reading about the deranged Trump's latest tweets, sexual shenanigans in Westminster, and the ongoing Brexit suicide mission was far more absorbing than what was happening on track. Some races featured only four cars, half the norm, few featured any meaningful competition but at least the supercar class offered the sight and sound of 600bhp four-wheel drive Citroën DS3s, and Ford Focuses and Fiestas. Even if the racing is poor, even if the cars are running two seconds apart, even if Mad Mark Watson's ex-works Citroën Xsara has expired for the 17th race running, my pulse rate still spikes, my breathing accelerates and I find myself smiling like a half-wit (can I even say that anymore?). It is the sweet alchemy of cars with far more power than grip and that are so brutally fast that, just this once, I'm thankful to be separated from their excesses by catch fencing and Recticel safety barriers. It's exactly the same rush as I felt back in May at Santa Pod, as 5000bhp was deployed to create a reeking cloud of burnout tyre smoke, the same wonder I felt as a Gould speared towards Harewood's Quarry Bend at 140mph and the same nails dug into palm buzz as the Chevron B37 induced as it thundered through Deer Leap.

There's some splendid grandstanding in a WRC-ish Fiesta from Kevin Procter, coach magnate, part-time rally driver, fulltime local hero and serial sponsor of both drivers and events. Earlier, he had been sidelined by car problems, but he was now trying to regain top dog status by exiting Clervaux in the wasteland beyond the track limits and then hurling the Fiesta into a 100 yard slide before cutting back onto the long right hander at Hawthorns. Any slicks and wings single-seater would go through this corner 20mph faster without breaking sweat but only the stopwatch would tell you. Even a Formula 3 car wouldn't look anything like as spectacular, nor anywhere near as fast, as a Rallycross supercar. Single-seaters such as the ubiquitous Dallara are set up with minimal suspension movement and the amount of pitch and roll is more apparent from its data logging than from trackside observation but big power rallycross cars offer an introductory course in vehicle dynamics, even to an arty-farty plank like me. Any decent rallycross course should include plenty of rough stuff and at least one point where cars catch air (as we say on YouTube) or yump (as we used to say in *Motoring News*). The soft, long travel suspension set ups that are needed produce the Full English of automotive party tricks – wheel waving (near compulsory in two-wheel drive cars), generous degrees of roll, and dramatic nosediving when braking. Add a gratuitous level of anti-lag banging and popping, then blend in some seismic rumbling under full boost, season with over-run flameouts, and add a drifting cloud of tyre smoke, mix in the smell of stressed metal and hot oil, and even a first timer can understand the appeal of this recipe. But, both sadly and predictably, the actual racing was low key, enlivened only by some 'me first' pushing and shoving into the chicane on the first lap of the final. Ironically, the Grand Prix was won by the same Citroën with which Dan Rooke had won last year, and it was driven by another talented young driver, Nathan Heathcote. I wonder if obscurity beckons for him as well?

I drove home feeling that whilst the title of Grand Prix had suggested a gourmet tasting menu, my hunger was reminding me that I'd had to settle for a small portion of underdone fries. But there was one consolation as, for the first time in decades, the commentary team had not perpetuated the hoary old cliché that rallycross cars out-accelerate Grand Prix cars to 100mph (160km/h). Perhaps once they did, back in the sepia tinted days of Brabhams and Tyrrells, when peaky Cosworth DFV V8s and not so sticky slicks meant the start of every Grand Prix was shrouded in a fog of burnt Dunlops and Goodyears but now, in 2017? I really don't think so. Consider the physics; a rallycross car may have four-wheel drive traction but it weighs well over 1000 kilos and won't have much more than 600bhp. A 2017 Formula 1 car may weigh a surprisingly porcine 720 kilos but it can deploy 900bhp. So, let us reflect on what 50% more power and 30% less weight might mean, let's 'do the math,' as they say across the pond. Or just watch a Verstappen or Hamilton as they hook up another killer start at Suzuka or Monza. There's seamless shifting, a shedload of volts (or is it amps?) and V6 turbo bhp to give away but there's hardly a 10th of second lost in wheel spin. Rallycross really shouldn't need to try so hard to sell itself, its bare ingredients should be enough to get a Michelin Star – fast cars, short races, sideways as you like, and plenty of argy bargy, car on car action. All UK rallycross needs now is a Rick Stein instead of the burger flipping guy from the job centre it's been lumbered with for far too long.

Two months have passed, it's 10 December, and I am listening to *Frasier*'s Kelsey Grammer's *Desert Island Discs* choice, Jimi Hendrix' spine-chilling rendition of Dylan's *All Along The Watch Tower*. I'm driving through upper Wensleydale en route to watch Le Jog pass through on its way to John O'Groats, having left – you guessed – Land's End the day before. The event is an endurance rally for cars from the mid-Fifties to the early Eighties and whilst I know that there will be neither high speeds nor sideways cornering, there is still something beguiling about this type of event. Most of all, it evokes the feeling I used to experience on RAC rallies, when a Tony Pond or Timo Mäkinen would hustle through a special stage, 'all arms and elbows' and I would marvel at the fact that they had driven 200 miles (320km) already and would be another 200 miles north before they stopped for the night, or part of it, as they would be on the road again before dawn. The Le Jog cars had come a long way already, were going even further and that fact alone was enough to add a sense of occasion to their passage.

I knew exactly where I would watch the 50-odd cars drive by – the lay-by on the B6255 with the view of Ribblehead Viaduct to my west, Whernside further beyond and Ingleborough to the south. And on a mackerel-skied day with a fresh covering of snow I doubt if many places in England could have looked better. If I had been standing here in summer there'd have been a succession of bikers screaming past the dawdling motorhomes but today it was almost deserted, with the most common vehicles being Mitsubishi L200 pick-ups and pre-Defender era Land Rovers, with a bale of hay and a hard-bitten Dales farmer on board. But hold on, here's an old boy in his pristine white Morgan 4/4, and the guy in the BMMC stickered Mondeo I've seen at Croft, both doubtless as starved of motorsport as I have been these last few weeks.

The down the road graphics of the approaching Peugeot 504Ti emphasise just how classy Peugeot was in the early Seventies, in contrast to the brand that now epitomises the PCP enabled, stack 'em high, sell 'em cheap approach. But the 504 had more than a hint of Gallic hauteur in its styling, it boasted a fuel-injection engine in a carburettor age and, without any effort, it evoked that uniquely French approach to high speed travel. An MGB GT might have had a growly twin-carbed B series, overdrive and styling that never received the credit it deserved but the frumpy old 504 would have left it hours behind on a long journey through France. The Pug wouldn't have baulked at the chaussée déformée and its long legged high-speed cruise would have left the MG gasping on the autoroutes. The 504 was in that trademark Seventies gold, now road grime streaked, and it hummed towards Hawes ten minutes before the next cars appeared, a brace of TR4s with roof mounted spotlights in period style. Both were pushing on, if not as quickly as the growling Volvo PV44, and the rowdy (and utterly lovely) Porsche 356B whose combined age might have been pushing 120 but whose pace would have humbled most moderns. As I found out on my drive home, as I ran a respectful 100 yards (90m) behind Tony Jardine's BMW 1602. I had a modern 170bhp turbo diesel Yeti, grippy wide tyres and six speed box, the little BMW had less than half the power and period narrow rubber but I don't mind admitting that both its pace and grip delighted me.

A week later and I am standing on the side of a hill above Barnard Castle on my first, and almost certainly last, visit to Barford Raceway. Today, 18 December, the raceway is holding a meeting for "unlimited bangers, banger rods, junior bangers, and open hot/stock rods" none of which I have ever seen before, although I have long thought I should sample the big stock cars that are now called V8Hotstox. But as my nearest tracks are Stoke or Belle Vue and the ambition never burned that strongly I have yet to leave harbour on that particular journey.

Crashes are an inherent part of motorsport, some contact between competitors is inevitable in disciplines like rallycross and autograss, and the British Touring Car racers are notorious for using robust 'push to pass' tactics but banger racing, obviously, is nearly all about crashing for its own sake. Five minutes' walk around the paddock and I wasn't much wiser about what cars were competing as most of them were already so battered as to be unrecognisable. But closer scrutiny and a dim recollection of the angle and design of A and B posts meant that I could work out that there were lots of early Micras (presumably coming here to die after their autograss careers had faded), Mark III Fiestas, Mark I Mondeos and some unexpected stuff like a Mark II Granada Scorpio and a pair of W210 E Class Mercedes. Yet there was something unsettling about seeing a once dignified and upmarket car crudely reinforced with scaffolding, looking as though it had already been dropped from a great height and decorated only by a hand painted "RIP Mam and Dad." But what was its alternative fate – an earlier date with a crusher? So I couldn't really object to the Merc's last moment of glory before oblivion, nor should I have found the sight of a Volvo 240 Estate, body twisted and mangled into banana proportions, quite so unsettling. But I did, and it felt almost pornographic.

The track is very short, the cars start on loosely formed grids and each race lasts for ten minutes or so. But it's as hard to follow as NASCAR and most laps are punctuated by one or more cars T-boning whatever is in front of them, regardless of whether the cars in question are impeding progress. Some cars retire hurt to the infield, spewing fluids and trailing bodywork, whilst others just keep going on, drivers oblivious to the fact that one rear wheel has 60 degrees toe out and that the nearside front wheel is now unprotected by a tyre. There's the smell of hot metal and burning rubber, overlaid with the reek of old scores being settled and new ones being created. But watch carefully and there is some classy driving going on in the mayhem, because here's the Scorpio, Cosworth fettled V6 blaring, being held in a perfect parabola around most of the lap, and here's the guy in the black and orange daubed Ka with the stoved-in boot exploiting its lift off oversteer as well as any racer.

But I left early, as whilst bangers may delight some, quite a few, judging by a healthy crowd and the 30-yard (27m) queue at the burger stand, I felt increasingly uncomfortable at what I'd just paid £12 to watch. I knew I had seen enough when I saw an 18 car field reduced to six in the first couple of minutes, with nine cars, most of them still occupied, locked together in a smoking embrace of bent metal on turn one. As I watched, two more were driven into the pile up, deliberately if not gleefully. It felt like a production of Mad Max ad-libbed by the local amateur dramatics society. The crowd may have roared but me, I just wanted not to be part of this anymore. Now wash your hands …

Every time I go to Mallory Park I am earwormed by the words 'Bay City Rollers,' not because I was a fan of the tartan trewed Scots popsters (come on, I was deeply into Genesis and Floyd back then) but because, on 18 May, 1975, I went to the Radio 1 Fun Day at Mallory. This was a big mistake, as had been clear from the five-mile queue caused by the 47,000 people who had turned up, even if only a few hundred of us were interested in the Formula Ford and saloon car racing. The rest had gone to see and hear Radio 1 DJs John Peel, David Hamilton, and Tony Blackburn, watch Showaddywaddy's retro turn, and giggle over a hunting pack of Wombles. The Rollers were the biggest draw of all and, after arriving by helicopter, Les McKeown and the rest of the feather cut crew had been ushered onto a powerboat and taken to the island on the infield lake. It was the first and only time I have seen teenage girls in hysterical fan mode and it wasn't pretty. The shrieking and tears were already tiresome enough to us frowning and grumpy racegoers but, mid-Formula Ford race, things became surreal. Packs of fans jumped over the trackside fencing, with marshals in hot pursuit, and the poptastic teens then ran across the track, racing cars jinking around them before the girls plunged into the lake and swam furiously towards Roller Island. The past being, notoriously, a different country, the race wasn't stopped and the band played on …

You'd have caught your death of cold if you'd swum in the lake today, Boxing Day 2017, when Mallory was holding its 43rd Plum Pudding Races. The temperature was hovering around three degrees (another echo of 1975 – Prince Charles' allegedly favourite girl group had also been part of the Fun Day) as the first cars took to the wet and greasy track. Short hours of daylight meant a tight programme of seven races for cars and bikes, with no qualifying as such, just untimed practice, because grid positions were determined by the order in which entries had been received. I can't tell you too much about the bikes, other than to report that some riders fell off, with no apparent harm done to either themselves or their machines, overtaking was abundant, and that wheelies were pulled. I might also add that one rider sported seasonal antlers and another wore a Batman outfit, with his Batcape waving perilously close to the rear wheel in the braking area for Shaws Hairpin.

I watched most of the action from the infield at the Esses, where I talked to *Motor Sport*'s Simon Arron, who has never lost his love of club racing despite having been Grand Prix reporter for both *The Daily Telegraph* and *Motoring News*. "It's sort of a professional commitment being here but *Motor Sport* hasn't held a gun to my head to come. I just like to be here, Brands used to have a Boxing Day meeting and it's just a nice way to spend the day. It's my 53rd or 54th event this season." We talk about the age profile of racegoers today, middle aged blokes predictably enough, but Simon points out that he's "encouraged by VSCC events where you see young kids of 18 or 19 in Austin Sevens their fathers and grandfathers had campaigned, and quite possibly their great grandfathers as well. There's evidence that the love of the sport is being passed on to new generations I think."

No spec formulae on this Boxing Day (thank God), but instead we were treated to a wonderfully eclectic mixture of cars on track; in the saloon race there was an old warrior Rover SD1, but now packing 5.7 litre heat, a Martini liveried Lancia Delta Integrale, an old shape Astra and an astonishingly fast Renault Clio whose driver showed hold-your-breath commitment between the Esses and Shaws. And, if anything, the sports cars were even better – the bevy of Caterhams and Westfields was expected but it was a surprise to see a TVR Tuscan and a Radical, let alone the lovely old Mallock Mk 16. And nothing went faster than the flame spitting Lotus Exige whose aerodynamics you could almost see working as the car found both poise and grip in the places where the big tyred, big power Sevens were lairy and loose.

I met an old friend from the Lotus Seven Club, Tony Pashley, who had edited the club magazine for many years and who had encouraged me to write about whatever I thought might interest our readers, ie whether related to our favourite daft sports car or not. Tony is a delightful man whose enthusiasm for, and knowledge of, motorsport can make me feel like a dilettante. We watched the racing together from the grass banking between Shaws and the Devil's Elbow, comparing notes on cars and drivers and agreeing that nobody was having more fun than the backmarker in the Mk 1 Toyota MR2 who seemed to be looking for the damper areas of track so he could get the little mid-engine car ever more crazily sideways. And between races we chatted – Tony mentioning casually to me, during our discussion about the aural merits of flatplane and crossplane V8s (oh yeah, we live on planet nerdy anorak when we meet up), that he had only been in one Ferrari, ever. Oh, which one was it, Tony? "It was an F40, around the Nürburgring actually ..."

As I drove home in the 4.30pm darkness I realised that, on a bleak mid-winter day like this one, nothing could have been better than chatting to old friends, drinking hot chocolate, and watching the type of club racing we had been watching for half a century and still counting. Or so I hope.

GOODWOOD MEMBERS' MEETING 17/18 MARCH 2018

You won't find it on the map, but in West Sussex there is a village called Upper Smugly and it is tucked away on the South Downs above Goodwood. You can't miss it, you just turn left after the pub in Midsomer Affluent, left again in Nether Wooster, then keep driving your motor car for a minute or so and hey presto, you have arrived in a sepia toned 1957. It's not just the etymology of the villages that distinguishes West Sussex from North Yorkshire, but the accents, the climate and the topography, so much so that the county can feel like a parallel universe, with Goodwood at its core. Goodwood is the place where all is for the best in the best of all possible worlds, thanks to the extraordinary conjuring trick that the Duke of Richmond and Gordon has been perfecting since the first Revival Meeting in 1998. Plain old Lord March, as he then was, created a template for historic motor racing by not only ensuring that la crème de la crème of cars and drivers would attend but also by conjuring a soft-focus vision of what motor racing had been like in the decades that followed the Second World War. Don't let on, but it's actually Never Land sleight of hand, as the Sixties' motor racing I attended bore not even a passing resemblance to Goodwood's recreation, but in whatever capacity we attend Goodwood's Revival, whether driver, hanger on or punter, we are all complicit in creating a pastiche which, thanks to dress codes and public school japery, can veer a little too close to pantomime.

I once created what I would call a shitstorm, but what the Duke might call a furore, by having a letter published in *Motor Sport* after the first Revival in which I raised an eyebrow at the uncritical adulation it had received. I wanted to know where this great gushing legion of born again motor racing fans had been during the rest of the racing season. Goodwood's excellence wasn't in question, but it was, even back then, a long way from being the only show in town, and so how come I never saw you guys at Cadwell or Oulton? Or was it the dressing up bit that was the real appeal, as nobody ever underestimated the British public's love of looking stupid in public? The then editor, Andrew Frankel, devoted most of his monthly editorial to pointing out how very wrong I was, although he did have the grace to thank me for creating the platform for some serious Goodwood fandom on next month's letters page. Although I still believed I was the only one who had spotted that this particular Emperor's new clothes were of the see-through variety (so very 1966), pragmatism overcame iconoclasm and I joined his Lordship's Goodwood Road Racing Club, exhumed my tweed jacket, sweet talked Joanne into sporting blazer and cravat and attended the '99 Revival.

And it was bloody brilliant. No matter that the inner class warrior that lurks inside every Yorkshireman thought the dress code absurd, the prices eye-watering, and the Hooray count as high as the plum trouser score, the Revival's unique quality made any such cavils sound petty and mean spirited. And the best bit of all happened even before the meeting started, when Joanne and I had walked casually into the moonlit paddock on Friday evening. It was near deserted, and no one challenged us as we explored the ranks of priceless racing cars slumbering under the timber-built paddock shelters. We paused (okay, I paused) to admire the unmistakeable snouts of a Lotus 49, an ERA and a Cobra and then I found myself in that worrying territory that lies between joy and tears as I saw a whole line of jut-jawed Ferrari 250 GTOs and – no! – only the divine 330LMB, the car that combines the 250 GTO's brutish fitness for purpose with the Lusso's poster girl chic. I had worshipped at the Ferrari church since the teenage encounter with a 275 GTB I described in Chapter 9 and that velvet night at Goodwood felt like a foretaste of heaven.

But fast forward 20 years and the Revival has become inaccessible, transformed from homage to the past to an homage to itself, and I had let my GRRC membership slip years ago, intending to re-join as and when needed. As if, as there is now a waiting list for the waiting list and I don't even get the classy Christmas card signed simply "March" any more. Some fair-weather friend he turned out to be ... But there was still hope, as the Members' Meeting was relaunched in 2014 and its egalitarian 'access all areas' policy and, deep joy, optional dress code meant that chippy buggers like me could now avoid the hierarchical tosh of the Revival but still savour the taste of a world class event. The 75th Members' Meeting in March 2017 was to have been the first event I featured in this book but, thanks to my back problems that year, the 76th Meeting, a year later, became the last event the book features. But that is a good thing as, despite the freezing temperatures that produced heavy snow flurries, grew eight inch icicles on the tea hut and froze racers' methanol, despite the £120 weekend ticket price and the £18 programme, no other event gave me as much sheer enjoyment as did this one, no venue tried harder to make my day unforgettable and hardly ever have I enjoyed myself more at a race circuit.

Let me start with the circuit itself. It may once have been unremarkable, just another of the many race circuits that used the peripheral track of wartime airfields, but after the bowdlerisation of Silverstone (and the rest) by the creation of huge run off areas and the interruption of the flow of long, fast corners Goodwood is now unique. To stand at the double apexed Madgwick, almost within touching distance of the track, is a stark reminder of how involving it had been to look down into the cockpits of Formula 1 cars as they exited Silverstone's Club Corner at 130mph, the cars giving an impromptu lesson in the dark art of downforce as they did so. Only Cadwell Park can eclipse Goodwood, thanks to even closer proximity to the track and the double trump cards of elevation and mature woodland. Goodwood has its views of the South Downs and, whilst it's lovely in a Home Counties sort of way, if you can see the Pennines from your back bedroom and the North York Moors from your front room, as I can, Goodwood's location might not impress you so much.

But geography apart, Goodwood is pre-eminent. Just consider its extraordinary attention to detail, including the pastel blue colour coding of everything from the tea huts to the enamelled entrance badge, even the free pencil inside the programme. The art deco themed Great Hall might rely on trompe l'oeil bookshelves and candelabras for its gravitas but its long tables and benches remind me of the privileged glimpse I once had of Magdalen College Oxford's dining hall. It didn't resemble Leeds University's refectory too closely ... Surmounting the long tables are replicas of the four house shields – Torbolton, Methuen, Aubigny, and Darnly – and that is where things get a little too Harry Potter for me. Having attended a fee-paying grammar school that tried way too hard to pretend that it was a public school (Founder's Day services and more Latin than you could shake a stick (lignum?) at) I don't welcome reminders. And the sight of House Captain (spare me ...) Anthony Reid in his broad blue striped race overalls, as well as mortarboard and gown-clad facsimile teachers, was a reminder of my long-held wish that Lindsay Anderson's 1968 film, *If*, had been a documentary. Maybe that's why there was a sniffer dog on duty at the main entrance? But if I ignore the showbiz, I will admit that nowhere have I met more helpful and polite race circuit staff who, even in the most appalling weather conditions, went the proverbial extra mile. Come on, where else would you find log filled fire pits to keep you warm, where else would you find freshly made vegan porridge with right-on fruit and ethically sourced coffee, and where else would you be told: "I'm so sorry if the car park is rather muddy today, sir, but if you do get stuck just put your hazards on and we'll rescue you"? You can even buy a Goodwood-branded hot water bottles but at £18 a pop, I'd rather shiver …

But it's the cars, and the people who are driving them that really entrance and the Members' Meeting offers a cornucopia of delight to someone like me. The first car that makes my heart skip a beat is the exquisite Porsche 910, the racer that had won so much, so often in the Sixties, usually in the hands of a crew-cutted Gerhard, Hans, or Udo, the car that epitomises the industrial genius of Porsche. There's none of the showboating exuberance of a Sixties' Ferrari, with its sexy swoops, gratuitous curves and a trademark whooping and howling from the V12 prima donna in the engine room. The 910 is just a very low, almost all white racing car, every feature of whose tiny proportions is there for a logical and researched reason and tell me, should I be worried that I find those little pantograph wipers quite so sexy? I wait for the 910 to start-up, and like nearly every Porsche road and race car I have ever seen, it starts instantly, without drama or tantrum, before settling into an even flat-six drone. It's tiny, and if the 935 is called *Moby Dick* then, in cetacean terms, this little guy must be a bottlenose dolphin. Later that morning I stand by Nick Mason's enormous Ferrari 512 BB LM as his crew try to coax it into life and what a diva that thing was. Coughing, spitting, popping, and banging, rarely running on more than a handful of its twelve cylinders and as guilty of gross attention seeking behaviour as an eight-year-old child in mid-tantrum.

Lured by the sound of V8s breathing in the cold air I speak to Stephen Hepworth, who is driving his late father David's Formula 5000 Hepworth-Ferguson, the same car that, long ago, I had pushed to the Harewood start line so many times. It's reassuring to hear Stephen's Brighouse accent and, despite the snow, it's clear that he's just brimming with excitement. "It's based loosely on a Brabham BT 11; the gearbox was originally in the Felday sports car and it raced in three Formula 5000 races before four-wheel drive got banned. Then it went on to the hills and won the championship in '69 and '71. No, I've never driven it round a circuit, but we did Carfest North, and the Festival of Speed, and some demos at Shelsley and Harewood, but otherwise it hasn't run since the early Seventies. It's unpredictable to drive and the steering … oh yes, very heavy." It's obvious, and deeply touching, that running his dad's car, half a century on from its glory days, while surrounded by his whole family is such a privilege for Stephen. It was for me too, and I smile as I remember his burly dad, open-face pudding-basin helmet and yeoman forearms wrestling this very car away in a blur of acceleration as I stood a foot away from the fat rear wheel. No wonder I'm bloody deaf, and standing by Scott O'Donnell's Begg Chevy as it chunters, and coughs, and bellows, from unsilenced exhausts doesn't help. But the Begg had been flown 12,000 miles to be here today, and I feel it's only polite to snuggle up so close to it.

Here's Patrick Watts, who, despite his practice session starting in ten minutes time, is laid back and happy to talk. He's driving a Capri that "raced in Holland and Denmark in the Eighties and round here it's just a big Ford Escort, but with a lovely sounding V6, the car's so well balanced. The fun part? Oh, it's St Mary's down to Lavant; the chicane is a corner where you can never be very quick … if you try too hard you come out very slow, so I attack it with caution. Easy to lose time there but hard to gain it. Patrick points out the appeal of historic racing to him: "I'm putting my money into an appreciating asset. Modern racers are out of date in a year – throw it away and get another one." Perhaps ironically, Patrick's favourite car "has got to be the Supertouring Peugeot 406 in 1998; those cars were just the ultimate."

I admire the Daytona inspired shape of a Rover SD1 and spot Tiff Needell; he's in his default cheeky chappy mode: "It goes sideways occasionally and is a lot of fun. Through No Name is good, the car's so well balanced. Historic racing works because the cars are enjoyable to drive and good to watch; my rule of thumb is that if one car goes through a corner and it isn't exciting, then it's not a good formula." I wouldn't disagree, but sadly the Rover ended its race on lap one by being squeezed into the tyre wall at Madgwick. The pictures of the shunt went viral, resulting in the long dead Rover marque getting more publicity than at any time since it was still trying to sell its often terrible cars. Rover Streetwise anybody?

Resisting the siren call of beefy Chevy Camaros and beefier still Lister Jaguars, I had intended to walk down towards Madgwick, but find that escape from the paddock is impossible when I am confronted with the car that has haunted me for 50 years: the Ferrari 275GTB. I know, I know, I mentioned it earlier and (another spoiler alert) I'll mention it again, but the sight of Vincent Gaye's ice blue 275GTB/C makes me tingle like a moonstruck kid. The "C?" Competizione, and try rolling that around your tongue. It's tiny by the standard of any modern Ferrari, but it is so achingly lovely that, if I did find the necessary £10 million down the back of the settee, I'd keep the GTB in my front room; or maybe it would be even better upstairs, as, with the possible exception of the Lamborghini Miura, no road car's styling has ever come as close to pornography as the GTB. I had watched Vincent Gaye wring the car's neck in practice, and as svelte and sweet the chasing Porsche 904s may have been, nobody had eyes or ears for anything other than the catwalk queen Ferrari. I would swap a year of my life to have been Vincent for the 15 minutes he spent on track but, racing drivers being what they are, he's laid back and calm as he tells me about the car's long life. "My car is an American one. It's a Chinetti car, which lived in the United States for 30 years, had many races there, and then came to a German collection. The car's good, I'm enjoying myself, yes, and the track is good. But you know, the car is too heavy after the 904 …" I have to ask if the car sounds as good from the inside as it does from the outside; well, does it Vincent? He laughs "… Oh yes, yes it does."

Sunday morning and not only are many of the cars in the paddock dusted with snow but there are people sledging and skiing down Trundle Hill, a mile north. Goodwood has always felt surreal, but its trademark has been lazy late summer days, warm beer, straw boaters, and more than a hint of Spitfire fuelled Battle of Britain nostalgia. But today feels like having a walk-on part in Pieter Bruegel's *Hunters in the Snow*, meaning it is still bloody parky, but a big improvement on yesterday's Siege of Stalingrad re-enactment. Flat white fuelled, I walk to the top of the paddock after the Formula 3 race finishes and congratulate Jon Milicevic on another race win. He won this race at a canter, as had seemed inevitable when you translated the body language of the blue 'John's Motors' Brabham BT21 through Woodcote and the Chicane. And this most quietly spoken of drivers has even kept himself warm: "It took two laps to get the tyres working but you've got to go on it from the start – you've got to work the car here. Getting the exit from Saint Mary's right is important but it's all pretty daunting. No, I'm not cold – I've got heating!" I feel the warmth from the tubes running back from the front-mounted radiator and wonder if Jon would notice if I just sat in the car and simmered for a few minutes. But how many Sixties Formula 3 drivers had my build?

The meeting passes in a hazy blur of sound, colour and smell; I savour the hammering bully-boy engine note of the big-block Daytona Cobra, revs spiking with wheelspin, I let my eyes linger almost lasciviously over the Martini-liveried Lancia Beta Montecarlo, and I breathe in the warm, organic perfume of a Bugatti Type 35 as it warms up. There's a tang of old leather, hot metal, petrol, and the reek of the old school oil that would choke a Ford Mondeo. The owner blips the throttle, Bugatti straight-eight barking and snorting, and he looks up, makes eye contact, and grins – and so do I. Forget the house points and the amateur dramatics, we are all part of this magic, and, stealthily but inexorably, historic motorsport seems to have stopped being parenthetical to the main motorsport narrative, but is now a central part. And as long as its progress stops there, and we avoid being drowned in nostalgia, I won't complain.

Late Sunday afternoon, people already drifting back to the car park, and I am leaning on the fence at the start line, watching the prewar Bolster Cup drivers slide their steampunk chic confections out of the chicane. I had seen Jolyon Harrison in the Lakeland Trial four months ago, but instead of a Ford Model A, today it is his monstrous Bentley 3/8 Special that is running wild, with driver Patrick Blakeney-Edwards in charge of taming the brute. Like most other Bentleys in the race, it's sideways out of the chicane, smokes its tyres under acceleration, and it speaks in a gruff baritone several octaves deeper than the aristocratic tenor of Bugattis. A Bentley wins, but who cares? Because this race, this weekend, and this place aren't really about winners and losers, but about creating new memories that evoke a past that only ever existed in our imaginations. And that's a good enough reason to love it.

Verdict

1. Summary – A confession. Joanne and I used to have a minor opera habit and, like some more illicit habits, what had once been a minor indulgence risked becoming a ruinously expensive addiction. Opera tickets for shows in Leeds or Gateshead are affordable enough

but once you move on to scoring your hits at Covent Garden, then you start wondering if there might be a market for one of your kidneys. But it would almost have been worth it, as not only were the performances sublime, the sound perfect, and the players world class, but the setting was so glorious that the sense of occasion (and yes, privilege too) made the price we paid seem irrelevant. Goodwood is like that, and my ticket may have cost as much as a season pass for my local circuit, but the Members' Meeting weekend created more memories than a dozen days spent almost anywhere else. The programme cost six times more than the one I'd buy at a typical club race meeting, but the price included an ear piece radio, and the 100 page text was beautifully designed and illustrated, printed on quality paper, error free, and included features by respected motorsport historians Rob Widdows and Doug Nye, as well as the Duke himself.

The catering, a lukewarm breakfast in the Great Hall aside, was excellent and only slightly more expensive than my usual habitat. And Hallelujah, the catering did not include chicken nuggets, greasy burgers, and the rest of the dross that still infects so many UK motorsport venues.

People? Goodwood is high on Rupert Bear tweeds, Le Chameau wellingtons, and big cigars, but it's low on tattoos and regional accents – I heard more conversations in French, German, and Italian than at any other event – and as for Americans? Well, hell yeah. More women, and rather more black and brown faces than I'd expected, too.

And you do get to meet the most extraordinary people in the Goodwood bubble, such as Steve Pilkington, the quietly spoken man who started a conversation with me after we had watched a Ferrari 250SWB scythe past us. He was maybe ten years older than me and as he commented on how much the circuit had changed since his last visit, I caught a trace of Lancashire in his accent – Steve was from Ormskirk. He asked me what my favourite car of the meeting had been, and, of course, it was the 275GTB/C; he twinkled and said "I've two GTBs, and you wouldn't believe the difference between the two-cam and the four-cam, you know." He gestured to his daughter, "show him that film of me driving the 250 GTO at Donington." Then says to me "it's free, you know, that err ... what is it called?"

"YouTube, Dad." Steve told me how he had been driven round Goodwood once by Moss in a 250SWB "years ago now," and how he'd reduced his Ferrari collection down to "13 or 14, is it?" A lovely man, and only at Goodwood would I encounter someone like him and not fear that he was an automotive 'Walter Mitty.'

Only a few days before the Members' Meeting, Henry Hope-Frost died in a motorbike accident near the circuit. He was a superb colour commentator, his motorsport knowledge was encyclopaedic and, for many, he was the voice of Goodwood. I had spoken to Henry at the Silverstone Classic, and I warmed instantly to his good humour, charm, and simply rampant enthusiasm – or 'fever' as he notoriously called it. His loss was keenly felt by everybody at Goodwood, especially by the commentary team who, understandably, sounded much less ebullient than their normal selves. I was touched to find a #HHF Fever sticker in the programme and many competing cars displayed similar logos.

2. Nature notes – Had it not been for the intermittent snow showers being carried on the biting wind dubbed 'The Beast from the East,' I would have expected to have seen my first swallows and skylarks of the Spring. Instead, I saw a couple of blackbirds, some chaffinches ferreting around the food outlets, a pissed-off looking robin, and some distant rooks. It wasn't a *Springwatch* sort of weekend.

3. What could be improved? – Damn and blast you, Your Grace, you've nailed it and I wouldn't ask you to change a thing. But, if you insist, drop the house system, okay?

4. Website – You guessed already, it is yet another benchmark.

AND FINALLY

This is my last event report and it feels appropriate that I end on a high note. Goodwood really is extraordinary, but it is so unlike any other event that comparisons will not reflect well on either. But there is one common theme, and if it isn't the first, or last, time I will mention it, it's still worth repeating – live motorsport is incomparably better than anything you will ever see on television. I watched the TV highlights of the Members' Meeting and enjoyed them, but I didn't choose what I saw of the event, it was chosen for me by ITV4. Nothing illustrated the shortcomings of TV more than its coverage of the Bolster Cup because, in time honoured TV style, the cameras focussed on the so-called battle for the lead. It was entertaining enough, and how could it fail to have been when contested so furiously by a Bentley Special, an Amilcar Hispano-Suiza, and a GN Parker Special with a combined age of 287? But if you were standing next to the start finish line, hot chocolate in hand, and east wind on your back, air full of the blat and bluster of ancient machinery, you might have smiled as you watched the leading trio squirm out of the chicane, but first you held your breath, then cheered out loud as Mark Walker held his GN Thunderbug in a 100 yard slide every single lap. In practice, in the snow, the slides had been half as long again. I have no idea where he finished, but it was somewhere near the back, and yet who cares when the nonagenarian GN was so emphatically the best show in town?

The chain drive GN has a 4.2-litre Vee Twin, is geared for 65mph per 1000rpm in top gear, lacks seatbelts and roll over bar, and its driver has neither HANS nor Halo protection. Lewis Hamilton has all four items in his 2018 Mercedes W0 9, and, even if Mr Walker is lucky enough to be one of the 2% of the UK population who earns more than £100,000 per annum, then Lewis can match that, but does so on every single day of the year. But judging by Hamilton's expression on the 2018 Australian Grand Prix podium, I know which driver had the more fun, and I also know which driver didn't induce a premature mid-afternoon nap. So, what was Lewis' problem, by the way? Oh, it was a software bug, apparently, and it had robbed him of victory. The bug wasn't in the 'power unit,' you understand, but in his team's race strategy software. We used to have Grands Prix but in 2018 it's Robot Wars, and I think that really ain't so Grand at all.

14
THE WAY IT WAS

*Unfortunately, the clock is ticking, the hours are
going by. The past increases, the future recedes.
Possibilities decreasing, regrets mounting.*

Haruki Murakami, *Dance, Dance, Dance*

I drove 5000 miles and spent about 120 hours behind the wheel of Focus, Caterham, Yeti, and MX5 over the 12 months it took me to experience 20 different motorsport events at almost as many different venues. I spent at least 30 days watching cars, talking to people and, well, just enjoying venues as different as flat-as-a-board Silverstone, and half-way-up-a-mountain Honister Pass. I watched racing contested by cars ancient and modern, I saw speed hillclimbs, drag racing, rallycross, time attack, autograss, a sporting trial, and a stage rally. Of course, I expected that watching so many events would give me an insight into the state of the motorsport nation, but, once I had digested the season with the perfect vision that hindsight enables, I actually learned far more than I had anticipated, and in this chapter I will explain why.

But, let me consider first, just how much an appetite the British public might have for motorsport. Because there is saturation television coverage of Formula 1, ITV 4 dedicates whole days to the British Touring Car Championship, and YouTube and specialist TV channels enable access to a huge range of motorsport events, you might think that the public's appetite must be insatiable, yes? But I don't think it is at all, I just think that far too many people enjoy grazing on whatever visual pap their remote controls can find them on their smart TVs. Television may feature more celebrity chefs, cooking competitions, and healthy eating consumer shows than ever before, but my local Tescos is not over troubled by avocado riots or by fights breaking out over the last sourdough loaf. So the fact that millions watch Jamie Oliver bish-boshing his way through his diamond geezer cuisine, and that millions more watch Jason Plato getting into a finger waving row after yet another touring car shunt doesn't mean that we are a nation of calorie counting, cholesterol angsting, wannabe chefs with such an addiction to motorsport that they really care whether the Subaru Levorg crashes into the MG6, or vice versa. It's not because the BTCC is the only place you'll ever see either model, it's just means that lots of people watch far too much telly.

But apart from the Croft BTCC meeting, the Silverstone Classic, and the Goodwood Members' Meeting, hardly any of the events I attended received any TV coverage on mainstream channels, nor did they get any publicity in the non-specialist press. My local paper might cover the minutiae of village cricket, trail racing, and pony club events but, rallycross and stage rallying apart, it rarely features four wheeled motorsport. And this, despite the fact that within an hour's drive of the paper's office, there's a race circuit (where I have watched Messrs Button, Raikkonen, Hunt, and Hamilton), three hillclimbs, a drag strip, a banger racing track, and three Autograss sites. And whilst Google can be your friend (in the odd moment when it isn't tracking your every move and thought) it does help your searching to have some leads on what you suspect may be out there. Just now, I searched for 'Yorkshire motorsport' and all I found were lots of car dealers, a surprising number of race preparation businesses and a solitary reference to Croft race circuit. Motorsport can operate under the radar of even the most diligent enthusiast, which explains why, until 2017, I was completely unaware of Thornborough Autograss track, just 15 minutes from home. We may live in the age of information but since the demise of *Cars and Car Conversions*, which covered every amateur and most professional motorsport disciplines, *Motorsport News* (née *Motoring News*) slide into oblivion, and *Autosport*'s transformation into an F1 fanzine, there is actually very little in print, and not much more online, about the branches of motorsport that haven't been turned into soap operas, pantomimes, or reality TV.

But enough of the grumpy old git stuff already, because I loved my year of travelling to so many different venues, seeing such a diversity of machinery, and talking to so many different people. In this chapter I want to reflect on the different qualities of the places I visited, the people I met, and the cars I watched compete – from the saggy old Ford Ka in the banger race in County Durham, to the 20 million-dollar Ferrari 250 GT 'Breadvan' at Silverstone. And then, if you'll forgive the management speak, I'd like to drill down into the reasons why some events, the venues where they took place, and the facilities and experience they offered were so much better than the others. It's the confessions of a mystery shopper; a motorsport Michelin Guide, covering every dish from the Menu Gastronomique at Goodwood to the bellybuster breakfast at the banger racing.

Places first, and if nowhere was more spectacular than the venue for the VSCC Lakeland Trial, that shouldn't be too much of a surprise, as the majesty of Honister Pass under a faultless blue sky was never going to be threatened by any permanent motorsport venue. Had the weather been more characteristically Lake District though, I would have had to have riffed some words on a Race to the Clouds theme, shamelessly ripping off some Pike Peak myths and legends, and then I'd have worked in something about the pathetic fallacy (weather matching mood, as employed in everything from *Macbeth* to *A Hard Rain's A-Gonna Fall*) before buggering off back home to the Vale of Mowbray, which basks in the benign rain shadow of the Pennines.

Where I live, we can even go out some days 'baht'at,' tha' knows, and as Ilkley Moor is in sight of Harewood hillclimb, now might be the time to confess that, despite my 50-year relationship with Harewood, I lost my heart to Shelsley Walsh. The hill may be shorter, the viewing far more restricted, and the top speeds lower, but how I could not fall for the place that will feel forever 1949? It's not just those brooding Teme valley hills that surround Shelsley, but the half-timbered buildings, the rustic paddock and, perhaps most of all, the languid commentary from Vox Villa and the sight, sound, and smell of six decades' worth of racing cars. Shelsley represents a gentle evolution of its own long past, and every meeting adds another chapter to its story, and not only did I feel I was osmosing its heritage from the moment I arrived, it felt as though everybody else was feeling the same way, as if we had all learned the same script. Only Cadwell Park manages to engender that tangible sense of wellbeing I felt at Shelsley, as only at Cadwell does nearly everybody fail to suppress the smile that betrays the sharing of a secret pleasure. There's magic at work at both places, and you are steeped in it from arrival until departure, but even then the magic remains, becoming the dream you replay to get through those black dog days of winter.

Obviously, it won't now come as the remotest of surprises that Cadwell Park, for the 43rd year running, is comfortably the best race circuit I visited in 2017. Its parkland setting means that, unlike former airfield circuits such as Silverstone and Croft, there are not only changes in elevation, but there are mature trees and buildings that weren't hastily erected by the Air Ministry in 1942. Cadwell's advantage over every other circuit is the startling proximity of race track to spectator, and only Oulton's Deer Leap and the inside of Mallory's John Cooper Esses even begin to compare. Looking back at old photographs, it is a shock to be reminded just how close to the action you could also stand at Brands Hatch, Donington, and even Silverstone, where despite the blinding speeds enabled by the latter's original layout, I once stood only ten or 15 yards away from drivers like Hunt, Andretti, and Peterson, protected only by a horizontal length of scaffolding pole.

The biggest event of my year was the Silverstone Classic, boasting not only by far the largest entry, but also the biggest crowd and the longest circuit. In spite of the fact that it is possible to watch cars racing in east Buckinghamshire from a grandstand located in west Northamptonshire, and that only Village Corner even hints at the proximity I used to enjoy at Club, Woodcote, and Bridge, the organisers' enlightened policy of access to all, everywhere, makes the Classic unmissable. And so what if the action on track is distant, when there is the opportunity to stand on the edge of the pit lane as 40 Historic Formula 1 cars blitz their way on to the circuit?

The least attractive venues? Neither Santa Pod nor the York Raceway will ever be confused with Florence, but when the air is being ripped apart by the heavy metal thunder of a big-block V8, the scenery hardly matters. The nadir of my year was banger racing at the Barford Stadium, as the sight of old cars being driven into one another may appeal to some, but it didn't to me, and, on a cold grey day in December on a windswept hillside in County Durham, poor old Barford was never going to be any kind of highlight.

And Goodwood? There's some voodoo going on down West Sussex way, there's some black cat bone and maybe a mojo too, because nowhere else looks or feels like the Duke's Never-Never Land. The entry of cars and drivers at the 76th Members' Meeting was world class, the choice of races as eclectic as it was delightful, the circuit staff's customer care was exemplary, and the track itself made me feel like a time traveller. But all this magic does not come cheap, and a Goodwood weekend can cost more than a season anywhere else. So comparisons are largely pointless, and it's best to think of Goodwood as the motorsport equivalent of the tasting menu at Belmond Le Manoir aux Quat'Saisons. It is the annual treat that is as ruinously expensive as it is unforgettable, but it is also likely to induce indigestion if it forms part of your regular motorsport diet.

So what about the people? Lawyers often said that magistrates were "middle aged, middle minded, and middle class," and those words could also be applied to many of the people who attend motorsport events, except the words 'white' and 'male' also need including. Looking around the paddock at Shelsley, the pits at Silverstone or the grandstand at Oulton Park can feel like finding myself in a hall of mirrors, as nearly everybody looks, sounds, and talks just like me. Superficially that may feel both attractive and welcoming, as random conversations with strangers are made so much easier when your back story is the same and you're old enough to remember both The Bomb and The Beatles. But the downside is confirmation bias, the fact that similar backgrounds often mean similar views and as long as divisive stuff like Brexit is avoided (not all of us baby boomers fell into the Leave camp, okay?) it's far too easy to fall into a rambling lament that Fings Ain't Wot They Used To Be. Or arriving at the consensus that Vittorio Brambilla wouldn't have put up with any of this 2018 Formula 1 halo shit, even if one fewer bang on the head might have meant that the Monza Gorilla was still with us in body as well as in spirit.

But every yin needs a yang, and I wanted to experience events where the grumpy old white man hegemony was disrupted by something more diverse. I found the most disruption in Autograss and drag racing, and discovered that both disciplines are far more gender blind than any other branch of motorsport I witnessed. From the feisty young women I met at Santa Pod who were racing in junior dragsters, to the teenagers, young mums, and grandmothers who were battling it out on the Autograss tracks, there was clearly something about the subculture of their sport that had made them take the opportunity to compete. Only in the VSCC trial did I encounter so much female participation, but only in Autograss did I hear female race commentators.

So that's age and sex taken care of, so what about ethnicity? Although 13% of the UK population identify as Black, Asian, or Minority Ethnic ('BAME') you would never guess this from watching most motorsport. But not all of it, as on the evidence of my not remotely scientific survey, drag racing (yes, them again) has a higher BAME attendance and participation than either racing or speed events. But not as high as Time Attack, which is possibly the only event I attended where the BAME percentage came even close to reflecting the national picture. Why? Because the average age of both attenders and drivers in Time

Attack is half, or possibly even less than that, of the average at club racing and speed events. Too many older people don't like change and find that accepting racial diversity isn't easy, and that's putting it kindly. But most young people aren't bothered about ethnicity or social change, just like they're not too fussed about homosexuality, immigration, transsexuality, the EU, and all the other stuff that gives some oldsters night sweats and panic attacks. So ... if far more young people attend Time Attack than traditional motor racing, it seems to follow that their numbers will include far more representatives of ethnic minorities. There's another, if more mundane reason for Time Attack's appeal to da kidz, and it's the combination of tribalism and involvement that comes from the fact that the car you drove to the circuit can look and sound pretty much like some of the cars on track, and if you drove to the circuit with your mates in a convoy of dump-valve-hissing, Japanese-script-emblazoned Skylines and Civic Rs, then you are half way to bridging the gap between watcher and player.

Class? Time for some gross over-simplifications. Historic racing and speed events appear predominantly middle class, and the older the car the more likely it is that the driver and/or owner will be found in *Burke's Peerage* or *Country Life*. Autograss, rallycross, and stage rallying are predominantly blue collar – the term middle class people like me use because we fear 'working class' is offensive, and God only knows my tribe already has enough apology and guilt to handle, unlike those above and below us in the social hierarchy. Sorry ...

No subculture of motorsport I sampled was unfriendly or hostile, and if the welcome was more muted at some events than others, I never felt remotely uneasy or discomfited. And if you are thinking "why the hell should you have been?" then consider some other sports. I have never been to a football match, but I have been caught up in the mayhem of a crowd of pumped up football fans, and I loathed everything about it, from the bellowed effs and blinds, to the banter that feels only a heartbeat away from a lynch mob. And, as I live ten minutes' walk away from Thirsk Racecourse, I am also no stranger to race days' collateral damage of sobbing girls in snapped high heels and shiny suited feral drunks, eight pints down and the 50 quid win on the 1.15 already a hazy memory. But motorsport isn't like that, and the only police I have ever seen at events had only dropped in to watch the action. There's some joshing at Touring Car races, and I've heard some Hooray Henry braying at the Goodwood Revival, but it's good natured stuff. Only once have I experienced what might be termed 'an unpleasantness' at a race circuit, and that happened two years ago as I watched qualifying at the entrance to the Mountain at Cadwell. I'd been aware of a bored kid of maybe ten or 11 behind me, who was amusing himself by rolling down the grassy bank. But then the little bugger rolled right over my bag, which contained breakables like camera and stop watch, and I asked him to go and play somewhere else. Grandad, clearly a stranger to both underarm protection and dental hygiene, then threatened to "beat my f***ing head in" if I carried on abusing his grandson. I pointed out that Cadwell was a racetrack, not a playground and that maybe grandad should look after the kid rather than shouting at me. After more pointless accusation from him and counter accusation from me, halitosis man left, still swearing and muttering threats. Not your typical BRSCC race day visitor and

I remain as bemused about the incident now as I was then. That sort of unpleasantness would never happen at a VSCC meeting, as nowhere hosts a more friendly, engaging and utterly charming bunch of eccentrics. The eccentricity even extends to the format of VSCC events, with the long-established Pomeroy Trophy, ostensibly designed to select the best touring car (as long as it's a Frazer Nash), but in reality, motorsport's answer to 'Mornington Crescent' on Radio 4's *I'm Sorry I Haven't a Clue*.

And what of the scores of people whose words punctuate my event reports in the previous chapter? I don't belong to the foot in door school of journalism, and I was slightly uneasy about the task of not only asking busy people to talk to me, but also to consent to being recorded whilst doing so. And, because I wanted any conversation to be spontaneous, that also meant that not only did I not know to whom I would be speaking, or when, but I also had no time to prepare questions except during the interview itself. But I need not have worried, as with only one exception (ironically, a member of the media), everybody, from Le Mans winner to Grand Prix driver, and from Touring Car superstar to weekend hill climber, was happy to talk, and nobody was remotely precious about copy approval or similar nonsense. Almost everybody had a story to tell, and I encountered only one instance of blood-out-of-stone taciturnity. The most important thing I learned is that motorsport is a fundamentally friendly community, and that even those drivers who have achieved international success are accessible and remain enthusiasts at heart.

That's enough of the people, what about the real reasons I love the sport so much – its spectacle, sound, and fury. There's a pattern emerging in this commentary as, yet again, drag racing and autograss stand out. Because nothing in any branch of motorsport comes even close to the sight and sound of a Top Fuel dragster or a Funny Car. Your every sense is consumed, leaving you incapable of cogent thought or intelligible conversation, because you've just been reduced to a quivering bunch of burned out nerve endings. Team crews may get used to it, but I bet the drivers don't, and I haven't even tried. Drag racing is not only the fastest, but the loudest, the most accelerative, the smokiest, the smelliest, and the shortest duration motorsport of all, and its spectacle is in inverse proportion to its duration. The standard of preparation of machinery is the equal of anything in circuit racing, and drag racing's sheer showmanship and chutzpah is unrivalled. But does the pure competition live up to the spectacle? Not so much actually, and I suspect only drivers and their crews really give much of a damn about who wins most drag races. Just look at the tiny number of fans watching at the finish line, where you might see a dragster snatching victory from the jaws of defeat as it moves that crucial yard ahead of its rival at 220mph (355km/h). But few of us bother with all that, because what we really crave is an overdose of burnout action, the countdown drama of the Christmas Tree, the hope of a holeshot, and the chance of a wheelie. I love drag racing, and if you enjoy feeling like an awestruck kid again then so will you.

And Autograss can thrill too, because nobody will ever forget the first time they watch the utterly compelling spectacle of a Class 7 race. It's not just the sky-clawing wheelies at the start, it's all the other wheelies that happen every time full power from both – both! –

engines is deployed. And it's never better than when one car is in a broadsiding opposite lock slide, spitting mud and soil 20 feet high, but at the same time it's also shoulder charging the car alongside.

But neither drag racing nor Autograss could ever be the best, as my first love is circuit racing. I love it all, from the ad hoc moves at the start to the thrill of one driver chasing another down, gaining half a second here, and a tenth there, then running too close to call, and finally consummating the move in a late braking climax. And really powerful cars don't even have to run closely together, as something big, fast, and noisy will always make me tingle, but the purest racing of all must feature single seater racing cars running close and tight together, and whilst overtaking must never be the formality it can be in DRS enabled Formula 1, it must be frequent and at least as dependent upon the skill of the driver as the superiority of his car.

One Formula has been delivering this quality of racing better than anything else for half a century – Formula Ford 1600. Once it was the key training ground for aspiring Grand Prix drivers, and in Seventies and Eighties FF1600 I saw everybody from Mansell to Hill, via Senna, Irvine, Moreno, Byrne, and Herbert. Latterly, Formula Ford lost its way, with wider cars and Zetec engines being adopted in the early Nineties, and its closest modern equivalent is Formula 4. This series supports the BTCC and features small grids of ugly sounding cars which, as often as not, all lap two seconds apart and don't overtake each other very much. Thanks to turbocharged power, aerodynamic downforce, and young and ambitious drivers, Formula 4 cars lap quickly but they don't enthral. Unlike FF1600, which attracts enormous support from drivers young and old in the Historic Sports Car Club championship. The entry is oversubscribed, meaning heats and finals and full capacity grids; at Silverstone this means 50 plus cars, and even at shorter circuits such as Donington and Croft entries of 26–32 cars are common. Every race enthralled.

Formula Ford's recipe is its simplicity, from which stems its affordability and popularity, and it helps that its cars don't become obsolete at the send of the season and therefore hold their value. But its most important attribute is what it lacks, as Formula Ford cars don't have big tyres, big power, paddle shift gearboxes, and, most importantly of all, they don't have any meaningful level of aerodynamic downforce. A Crosslé, Van Diemen, Swift, Mygale, Reynard, Dulon, Hawke, or Lola racer (to name only a few of the scores of firms who have made FF1600 cars) may only have the Ford Crossflow engine that was first seen in Sixties' Cortinas, its power may be less than a 1-litre hatchback's, and its tyres narrower than a driving school Micra's, but a tiny frontal area and a flyweight sub 450kg mean that a good FF1600 racer will lap Silverstone Grand Prix circuit faster than a D Type Jaguar, which you might half expect, but it will also outpace most mid-Sixties Formula 1 cars, which maybe you wouldn't. Road cars? Pah ... a good FF1600 will lap Cadwell Park ten seconds faster than a banzai spec Nissan GT-R, which is none too shabby at all.

Formula Ford races feature lots of slipstreaming, with tightly bunched groups of up to eight or even more cars fighting over the same position. There's locked wheels and outbraking manoeuvres at every corner, and even though the soundtrack may be the blue-collar bark of a Dagenham four, the chorus of four-star backfires, pops, and bangs that punctuates every race adds to the spectacle. Thankfully, it's now not just older drivers who compete, as Formula Ford's affordability and competitiveness has attracted increasing numbers of young drivers who have graduated from karting, and in how many other sports can you watch a 50-something battle on equal terms with a teenager?

The only thing that rivals Formula Ford as a single seater spectacle is the slightly older and more expensive Formula Junior, whose key attributes echo its younger rival – lightweight, no aero grip, and not much power. A few years ago, I interviewed repeat Formula Junior champion, Jon Milicevic, after watching him win race after race in his 55-year-old, 1100cc Cooper T59. The car always looked quick in his hands, but even Jon was surprised to be told that he had lapped Silverstone in the same time as Adrian Newey's no expense spared Ford GT40 with 4.7 litres of V8 power. And I doubt if the little Cooper had spent as much (or indeed, any) time in the Red Bull wind tunnel as the GT40 had – allegedly ...

Don't think I am enthusing about Formula Ford and Formula Junior racing because the cars are nearly as old as I am, I am doing it because they are good. I would far rather be able to report on a vibrant single seater racing scene featuring modern cars but not only is Formula 4 both under-supported and tedious to watch, the once thriving Formula Renault is dead as a meaningful UK championship, its spiritual predecessor Formula Ford 2000 died decades ago and Formula 3 has been in and out of intensive care for nearly a decade. For many years you could make a strong argument for the British Formula 3 championship being one of the three or four most important racing series in the world, as it was responsible for producing scores of Grand Prix drivers in its 60-year history. Overtaking in Formula 3 has never been as easy as in the lower Formulae, and this was especially the case in the Senna/Brundle era when the cars had ground effect grip but strangled engine power, and yet the jewel-like chassis, very fast lap times, and sheer driver quality of the series made it the highlight of many seasons. A modest British championship is scheduled for 2018 featuring eight rounds at seven circuits, each hosting three races. And in 1970-74, British Formula 3 (despite fuel crises, inflation, 3-day weeks, and political mayhem) was healthy enough to support three separate championships ...

Away from historic racing there is no opportunity to watch really fast, big horsepower, and spectacular single seaters apart from during the British Grand Prix weekend at Silverstone, when both Formula 1 and 2 race, but there's almost nothing else, that is your lot. I am reminded that the opportunity I had in the Seventies to watch non-championship Formula 1, Formula 2, Formula 3000, and 5000 races was an extraordinary privilege that I am unlikely to enjoy ever again. Sometimes, it really was the good old days ...

But racing is a long way from all bad now, and personal highlights ranged from the diversity of series like the Northern Saloons and Sports Cars championship (where anything from a World Touring car to a bike engined Suzuki Whizzkid can feature), to the big grids of affordable cars promoted by the 750MC, the good place in which British GT racing is living and the stirring spectacle of a big grid of pumped BTCC cars. The touring car phenomenon has been motorsport's populist favourite for the last 25 years, and your elitist reporter had expected to indulge in some enjoyable sneering, at both the cars and the fans, but he ended up admiring the drivers, enjoying the cars, and remained only slightly puzzled by the fans (guys, just where are you the rest of the year?).

Thin grids can ruin a day's motor racing and last season there were times when I despaired at the prospect of a 40-minute race contested by a dozen cars, or even fewer as, whilst it only takes two cars to make a race, that solace is no help when every car in a thin grid is separated by five seconds. The worst offenders for thin grids are often the single make series, which are designed to promote affordable and close competition by featuring identical cars, often in very close to road trim, and with very few modifications allowed except for safety reasons. One make racing is an institution that goes back to the days of Ford Mexico racing in the early Seventies, and it has featured everything from Citroën 2CVs to Fiestas, Marcos Mantises to Renault Clios, as well as forgotten cars such as Volkswagen Vento VR6s and MGFs. There has also been a host of championships for various iterations of Caterham Sevens and Mazda MX 5s which are hugely popular, and deservedly so, as both cars are rear-wheel drive, handle well, slipstream each other beautifully, and are affordable. But some one make series are woefully under supported, and few were worse than the Chevron GR8 (get it?) Challenge that ran in 2010. The one round I dozed through had a dozen entries, with drivers of wildly mixed ability, and hired gun Mark Hales lapped 20 seconds faster than the guy at the back, and I only bothered to time the backmarker to stop myself dozing off. And, sadly, it was little better in the Britcar and Porsche GT3 series I have watched recently.

But one make racing can be terrific, never more so than in the BMW M1 Procar series of 1979/80, which starred mid-engined 470bhp sports cars driven by Grand Prix drivers. It wasn't cheap, but it was wonderful, as was the far cheaper, and almost as spectacular, TVR Tuscan series which ran in the UK for over a decade from 1989. Big power, little grip, iffy brakes, and some big name drivers made the Tuscan Challenge the highlight of the UK racing scene for many. It still stumbles on, in emasculated and rebranded form, but its heydays are now long in the past. No national one make series has ever come close to rivalling the Tuscan Challenge, and that is a tragedy.

But if there's one thing even worse than a sparse grid of one-make cars it is the oxymoron called a celebrity race. This involves C and D list celebrities driving slowly in dull races in even duller cars, whilst the poor commentator tries desperately to inject some excitement into the non-spectacle, which may have only started ten minutes ago but already feels like half a lifetime. It doesn't help that many of the celebrities tend to be unknown, except to keen devotees of daytime TV and those *Holby City fans* who can recall the name of the actor who once played a stroke victim. A non-speaking part, obviously. I saw one celebrity race in 2017, it took place on a cold and wet Silverstone evening, the cars were race-prepared Austin A35s and I can't now recall a single thing about either the race or most of its contestants – was that *Dragon's Den* guy there? For some, peak celebrity might involve a Shergar-mounted

Kim Kardashian in hot pursuit of Lord Lucan, or any combination of the same. Me? I'd rather watch paint dry.

Let's leave that image behind and consider speed hill climbing instead, the sport that has changed little in decades and that still uses venues that look just like they did when Ted Heath was at Number 10. It also includes some drivers who are still competing in the same cars they were using before decimalisation, and marshals who have been officiating since I was at school. But it also features some of the fastest, most spectacular and most innovative cars in all motorsport. Speed hillclimbing is a delightful backwater and still perpetuates that delightful Garden Party With Racing Cars vibe I fell for in 1969. There might be fewer road-going cars entered than there used to be, and maybe track days are to blame, but there's even more ballsy single-seaters than there used to be and the view from Harewood across Wharfedale on a spring Sunday is still a joy.

I only wish I could say something positive about rallying; single venue events at circuits and disused airfields are, at best, okay to watch, but that damning with faint praise is as nothing compared to my take on current forest stage rallying. A once addictive spectacle has been diluted to a tame parody.

And finally – what could be done better, what could make a visit to a race meeting more enjoyable for a regular, or more welcoming for a newcomer, and how can race circuits best coexist with the rest of the communities where they are located? Is a Millwall style "no-one likes us and we don't care" approach even sustainable anymore?

A lot might have changed since I first went to a race meeting, and a lot of it is for the better. MotorSport Vision ('MSV') own most of the UK's race circuits and have improved them immeasurably since taking them over in 2004. Back then, venues like Oulton and Cadwell suffered from chronic under-investment and were badly maintained, shabby, and felt as though their glory days were ancient history. But not any more, as both circuits, along with the others in the MSV portfolio, have benefitted from investment in infrastructure and staff. Customer care is at MSV's heart as I found when I had a serious back problem in Spring 2017, meaning that I was well placed to judge different venues' approach to disabled access. MSV's was exemplary, responding to emails immediately, and their staff literally went out of their way to welcome me and to help me park as close to the track as possible. What a contrast this was to the shabby treatment I had from the British Automobile Racing Club ('BARC') who manage Harewood Hillclimb. It left me seething, and here's why:

Harewood features a hilltop car park from which almost the whole course can be seen. I had arrived at 8am for the April championship round as my mobility was limited to a few yards and I was keen to secure a good view. I was told by the guy in the tabard that on this, one of Harewood's biggest meetings of the year, the hilltop car park was closed "to prepare it for the supercar show on Sunday." I told tabard guy that I would drive down to the start line car park instead, by the route shown on the event programme, one that I had taken many times before. That wasn't possible either, I was told, and I was redirected to the disabled car park, which was as unfit for purpose as the disabled access in the notorious court case (where it had been signed as being located "at the top of the stairs"). Harewood's disabled car park was located a long way further from the track than I could walk. So, channelling my inner Liam Gallagher, I told tabard guy that I wasn't having it, and suggested that he called his boss. He was no help either, but I wasn't budging (by this time I was in a heroic strop) and eventually the MSA steward became involved and told me that, of course, I could drive down to the start line, but not on the next day. I left at 4pm, and guess what? The hilltop car park was still deserted, with no sign of any preparation work at all. I emailed the BARC secretary that evening and asked how I could get access the following day, given my mobility problem. And I am still waiting for his reply ...

Hill climbs and race circuits need to think about making their venues more accessible, and not just for the disabled either. In the Eighties it wasn't unusual for circuits to offer spectators the opportunity to ride around the track in a coach or minibus. The small charge was worth it, as feeling the bus roll and heave as it went through Copse Corner at 40mph gave a whole new perspective on watching Piquet or Senna go through the same corner at more than three times the speed. There will be a reason, possibly even scores of them, why this is no longer possible at a Grand Prix, but at a touring car or club race meeting, why not? Charge passengers a fiver, with some of the fee going to a local charity, and arrange for one of the competing drivers to talk through the lap. Wouldn't that add something, wouldn't a teenage fan's day be made by Gordon Shedden or Matt Neal hyping up just how quickly he'll be taking the next corner in his pumped-up Honda race car, and how that bastard Plato nearly had him in the Armco here last year? I have already mentioned that hill climbs could do something similar, not only giving punters the opportunity to experience the track but also offering them transport up or down the hill to the viewing areas that might be inaccessible to the older or disabled, or indeed to the plain lazy. I might be able to climb Shelsley at a breathless canter now, but I couldn't get beyond The Crossing last July and I would have loved to have seen the view from the top.

And what about the information given to the public? I didn't hear a single bad commentator and some, such as Ian Titchmarsh, Marcus Pye, the late Henry Hope Frost, and Graham Beckwith, were outstanding; they informed, entertained, enthused, and amused. Applying the maxim that those who can, do, and those who can't, criticise, and confessing that I would struggle to give an informed commentary on a one lap, two horse race, I will say no more. Programmes won't get off so lightly, as too many are sloppily written and tell you too much you don't need to know, and miss out on the stuff that you do. Programme format hasn't changed in the half century since I bought my first one, and so there's lots of spurious text about the names of officials (which is only interesting if you are one of them and like seeing your name in print), there are often long winded summaries of technical regulations, or, worse still, verbatim extracts from them, there are "you attend at your own risk" disclaimers that haven't been legally effective since the late Seventies and there is often some tired copy about what happened at the previous round of the championship you had never heard of until today. Throw in a few typos, stir in some clichés, add some press release guff from the race sponsor's chairman, and that's your fiver's worth. Except it isn't, not when you can get so much information already on your phone.

So what might a good programme look like? This is getting monotonous, because, once again, Santa Pod shows how it can be done. At smaller events there's a free programme, listing and illustrating each car and driver in their respective classes and, unlike many race programmes, it isn't even printed in black and white. Wow. At bigger events the Pod programme is in glossy magazine format with in-depth features and interviews and, critically, useful details of cars' expected performance. I think race programmes should either be free sheets with details of entries and timetable or, if paid for, they should have content that is actually worth reading. It might be about the competing cars – how powerful are they, how quickly will they lap (and including lap records for other types of car would help), how fast will they take that scary looking corner after the chicane, and what speed will they be doing on the back straight? I mentioned earlier how, even 35 years ago, Brands Hatch had a dot matrix display showing top speeds before Paddock Hill Bend in Grand Prix qualifying and so, with the gigantic leaps in information systems, data logging, and communication since those dark ages why is it still only drag racing, speed hill climbing and, to a limited extent, Time Attack that gives the spectator any idea of the speeds they are witnessing? And what about the people on track? Instead of boilerplate stuff about championship rankings, dropped scores and similar tedium why not just focus on two or three names to watch instead, with some biography of each, preferably spiced with some wit? God only knows that there can be enough delays, pace car tedium, and dead air at some race meetings that a good read isn't just desirable, but essential. VSCC programmes are often excellent, with erudite and informed copy, and I liked the Classic Sports Car Club's decision to feature in-depth interviews with well-known racing figures in their programmes. The rest? Goodwood excepted, they could try harder …

Websites are obviously a key source of information, and I would single out the HSCC and Harewood Hillclimb for special praise, as, not only are full details of entry and timetable published well before each event, but results are posted soon after the event itself. In the case of the HSCC the amount of information is quite astonishing and includes full qualifying and race results, lap times (and sectors), and maximum speeds for every single contestant on every single lap completed. No surprise, but the Santa Pod website is excellent, in contrast to a sizeable minority of club and venue websites – some are members-only access, and others feature little, if any, advance information about their events. It's important stuff to know, as I once drove two hours to a circuit, only to find that the day's main attraction was a four hour race for the VW Fun Cup (or was it a two hour race that just felt like four?), and the only thing I can remember was that if anybody was having fun, it sure wasn't those of us who'd paid a tenner to watch …

Catering is one facet of race circuit life seems condemned forever to live in a Seventies' theme park, because it can be every bit as bad as back in the days when people thought that

DRIVEN – An Elegy To Cars, Roads & Motorsport

Top Deck Shandy, Brew Ten Bitter, Angel Delight, and Vesta Curries were actually products fit for human consumption. Too many motorsport venues still only offer grease laden pasties, burgers of iffy provenance, hot dogs (which are anything but), and coffee the colour of mud and the temperature of bath water. Little has changed in 50 years and I am at a loss to understand why, because none of us go to the work canteen any more, preferring a wrap or sandwich 'al desko,' and few of us drink instant coffee when every high street has a Costa and a Starbucks, and the office tea lady disappeared years ago, to be replaced by a far sexier coffee machine that never talks back. So why is it impossible to buy (even) a Shell Station quality sandwich or (especially) a Caffè Nero quality coffee when we go motor racing? Only Silverstone Classic, Oulton Park Gold Cup Sunday Market, and Goodwood were able to offer consistently decent food and drink, but my gold star is awarded to Harewood, as its catering is a model of how it can and should be done.

You can't drive very far in rural Britain before you come across a sign for a farmers' market or farm shop and you can't visit a country town without seeing at least one new microbrewery or mini distillery. Oulton Park successfully featured a food market at the Gold Cup, but why don't more venues offer visitors not only a day's motorsport but the chance to eat and drink some local produce, for which there is clearly a huge public appetite? Isn't there an opportunity for some synergy here, with farm shops benefitting from a captive audience and circuits not only offering a better ... umm ... customer experience (sorry) but also cementing a relationship with other local businesses and communities?

And that brings me to the last issue I want to discuss, and it's possibly the most important. From my perspective, many motorsport venues, and their supporters, behave as if they are under constant siege from enemies both real and imagined. A few minutes spent trawling through threads on websites such as *PistonHeads* and *Ten Tenths* will reveal the usual canards of local authorities pursuing their secret agendas of closing down race tracks, and the ever-popular scapegoat of the family who moved near a racetrack and then complained about the noise. There may be the odd instance of the latter, but I suspect it's actually far from common and – Brighton Council's persecution of the Madeira Drive speed trials apart – I have yet to see much hard evidence of the former. The local authority I used to work for had a chairman who drove a Porsche Carrera 4S, one of his predecessors owned a Group C race team and turned up to meetings in a Ferrari, and nobody seemed bothered about me using my very noisy Caterham to commute to work on summer mornings. The simple fact, which some motorsport followers fail to grasp, is that motorsport venues, exactly like everywhere else, are subject to the same regime of the law relating to planning and nuisance as everywhere else. Britain is a small country, people need to rub along together, and local authorities and legislators need to balance conflicting interests by not only insisting on upholding rights but also making concessions. I quoted the Millwall mantra earlier – "No one likes us and we don't care" – and it seems to epitomise an increasingly paranoid mindset in some, such as the guy who launched the Parliamentary Petition seeking the enactment of legislation that would have removed any legal rights of some local residents to complain about, or seek legal redress, for noise and nuisance caused by a motorsport venue. At least I think that's what was intended, as the petition was written by someone who hadn't been paying too much attention during GCSE English. It was risible, and didn't stand up to even a moment's scrutiny, let alone the big question of who was going to pay the compensation bill for those residents who had had their legal rights removed. But the petition was good enough clickbait to get 40,000 signatories, and in what now passes for an online debate (which is typically just a torrent of abuse from opposing sides) mention was made of both Croft and Mallory Park, both circuits that had encountered legal problems.

But unlike some, I had actually read the Croft court judgment and I had also researched the Mallory dispute in as much depth as I could, as well as talking to one local resident who was also a motorsport enthusiast. In both cases the problem was neither arbitrarily enforced rules, nor overzealous officialdom but a substantial increase in usage, especially for resting and track days. And even though a family vendetta had allegedly triggered the complaint leading to the Croft case, a domestic dispute per se doesn't create any right to prevent an activity unless there are also planning or nuisance grounds. Motorsport is subject to exactly the same rules as every other business and activity, and I have yet to see a convincing reason why it shouldn't be. It was clear from the Croft case that the complainants had no issue with the existing calendar of race meetings, but they did with the 200 days a year the circuit was being used for other purposes. The Mallory Park case was eventually resolved and, when the good news was announced, the circuit invited its supporters to an open day to celebrate. I read in *Motor Sport* that so mature and supportive of the circuit's renaissance were some of the celebrants that they pointed the race can exhausts of their superbikes towards Kirkby Mallory and held the throttles wide open. And you have to wonder, with friends like that, who the hell needs enemies?

You might remember that, for nearly every event report, I included 'nature notes' as part of the conclusion? But please don't think that I did so to be ironic, as if even admitting the possibility of wildlife coexisting with motorsport is misplaced. I do think that the environment is important, that being in denial of environmental concerns is stupid, and that professing interest in the environment and loving motorsport are not and should not be mutually exclusive. Race circuits, especially, are missing a trick, not only to make their venues more attractive, but to foster better relations with their local communities and to do something positive for the environment. And this is why. When I was a kid, the only time I ever saw most wildflowers and birds of prey was beside or over a motorway, because their verges were one of the few places in the English countryside that weren't under perpetual assault by herbicides and pesticides. Things might have improved, with red kites and buzzards now hardly worth remarking upon, but we still have major problems, such as the effects of neonicotinoids, loss of habitat, and climate change. In respect of the latter, by the way, unlike some of my fellow motorsport fans, I don't write it off as a global conspiracy perpetuated by a tree hugging liberal elite. Race tracks can be an ideal environment for insects, birds, and plants, as circuits are rarely intensively farmed and large areas are free of human traffic, offering the potential for undisturbed habitat. Cadwell has its nature conservation areas, Goodwood has its daffodils and cornfields, but too many venues seem happy to leave the no man's land between spectator areas and Armco barrier as ad hoc landfill, with discarded plastic cups competing for space with Red Bull cans and glass fibre shards amongst the thistles and nettles. It looks ghastly and I shudder to imagine the impression it gives to first time visitors. There's a missed opportunity here, and that is for venues to talk to local schools and conservation groups and to encourage them to get involved in habitat improvement, maybe even sponsoring a conservation area. Give them somewhere to manage and the results could so easily be havens for wild flowers, and good habitat for both birds and insects. I can't be the only one who'd rather watch a Classic Touring car race through a haze of red admirals hovering over sorrel and wild grasses, with skylarks arcing above me on a lazy afternoon in June – or can I?

I can almost hear the chorus of "No, we can't," "That won't work," and "The insurance won't allow it" to some of my suggestions. It's the usual response to anything new or to any departure from custom and practice, and the chorus is never louder than when it's being sung by those who can play the volunteer trump card. Which works like this: "We're nearly all volunteers, working hard in our own time, it's a thankless task and if you're so smart why don't you do it instead?" It may sound reasonable enough, but the toxic subtext is that some seem to think that being a volunteer means an exemption from criticism and that the very fact of something being said or done by a volunteer validates it. Which is utter bollocks of course, and I speak as a serial volunteer for decades. The truth is that most of us can't accept criticism, are hostile to new ideas, and resistant to any change because they are an affront to our innate conservatism. And, when a race circuit official or motor club volunteer has been working in his or her one area of specialism for decades, that may be laudable, merit a long service award and a lapel badge, but where is the objectivity, where's the exposure to different approaches and new ideas? As Kipling said: "And what should they know of England who only England know?"

Formula 1 has given us the mantra that if you are not constantly moving forward, you're not even static, but actually you're going backwards. And there are some facets of motorsport where it feels as though the sport is stuck in reverse. Wake up ...

15
A READER WRITES

These books will leave you reamed, steamed and dry cleaned,
tie-dyed, swept to the side, true-blued, tattooed and bah fangooed
James Ellroy, The Hilliker Curse

If only I hadn't spent all that money on buying car magazines there'd be a Ferrari in my garage. Trouble is, if I hadn't bought all those magazines I wouldn't have known which one to buy, would I? The 7000-odd magazines I've bought since 1967 still mean the Ferrari would be secondhand (or is 'preloved' the preferred term?) but, without having read them all, there'd be the risk of a runt of the litter Mondiale outside, instead of the manual F355 which, I know from all those Buy Your First Ferrari articles, would have been the really smart buy. Or it would have been, if I'd bought at the right time, which was before everybody else cottoned on to the fact that the understated Ferrari with the open gate gear shift was the last hurrah worth preserving. I've been doing my Ferrari and Porsche 911 homework for decades, and set books have included *Autocar*, *Autocar & Motor*, *Automobile*, *Autosport*, *Car*, *Car and Driver*, *Cars and Car Conversions*, *Classic & Sports Car*, *Evo*, *Fast Car*, *Motor*, *Motor Sport*, *Motoring News*, *Octane*, *Performance Car*, *Road & Track*, and *Supercar Classics*. And the lack of Ferrari content in *Custom Car* didn't matter, as I pretended to buy it for the drag racing coverage, but spent more time looking at the hot chicks draped across Camaro 396s. And *Hot Car* might have lacked Maranello pornography, but it did help me to fantasise that a rorty Mini Marcos really was affordable on a £1700 salary. That's per annum, younger readers ...

I still have the *Autocar* I bought on Thursday 1 June, 1967; it cost two shillings, the equivalent of £1.70 in 2018, and its 132 pages are an extraordinary contrast to the 90 pages of the *Autocar* I bought last Wednesday for an inflation busting £3.80. Sixties' *Autocar* content applied to every single facet of the motoring scene, and the 'Racing Car' edition featured four closely typed pages on the new BRM H-16 engine, illustrated reports of a Formula 2 meeting at Crystal Palace, the Tourist Trophy at Oulton Park, and the Nürburgring 1000km. The report of the latter runs to more than 2000 words, and the results were sufficiently detailed for me to learn not only that the winning Porsche 910 averaged 90.41mph, but also that the fastest lap in the up to 1000cc GT class was the 12 minutes, 1.2 seconds, 70.9mph set by a Honda (I'd guess an S800?). And amongst the new car prices for white goods – like the Vauxhall Victor 101 Super, surely an early example of ironic nomenclature and yours for £771 including purchase tax – are to be found prices for a Lola T70 at £3800 (with gearbox, but without engine) and a Lotus 41 Formula 3 car for £2255.

What amazes me now is the sheer breadth of coverage because, apart from the sexy stuff about racing cars, and the five page Lotus Elan S3 S/E road test, there's the not so riveting copy on Opel's renaissance and the downright tedious industry news, which included the revelation that Barbet Engineering, of Leigh-on-Sea were handling the distribution of Autogroom products in Essex and Hertfordshire, and I bet the church bells were ringing out in celebration at that news. There's no colour, apart from on the glossy cover, and there is relatively little advertising until the classified ads. Spoiler alert, just look away now if you are of a sensitive disposition, and if you know where I can hire a time machine do get in touch because with a 2018 proportioned wallet those '67 prices are heartbreakingly affordable. Because here's a Ferrari 275GTS for under four grand, a '57 Porsche Speedster for – no! – £499 and an Aston Martin DB 4 Convertible for £1500. Or, if your budget is small-saver size, why not a '59 VW Beetle for £245, or a '58 Land Rover for £250? And even the wet blanket of inflation isn't going to spoil our time travel because the 275GTS's inflation adjusted price now would be about £65k, which is just the £1.5 m short of its typical auction value. And don't even ask about the Speedster, with 356 values going even crazier than old 911 prices, and that's before the James Dean fairy dust gets sprinkled. And yes, I know that Dean was in a Spyder when he checked out but you've heard of the halo effect, right?

My 2018 *Autocar* does not feature even one classified ad because the only place now to find a secondhand, pre-owned, or pre-loved car is online in *Autotrader* or eBay. Instead, issue 6296 has a few glossy advertisements, including several for itself, and an uninspiring selection of ads for sundry Volkswagen-Audi Group hatchbacks, a Hyundai hybrid I had never heard of and, on a similar theme, an ad for an MG SUV that nobody will ever buy. Why would you, when nobody under 50 really knows what MG is, and those over 50 will look at the cheesy Chinese tribute act to the brand and weep? The USPs that are trumpeted the loudest in the ads aren't the sexy stuff like go or grip, but connectivity and the dead hand of cheap finance instead. As for editorial content, the road test (of a bland Subaru SUV nobody will buy either) is in broadly the same format as its '67 counterpart but there the similarity ends. Motorsport is confined to a back-page comment piece, there's lots of desktop illustrated speculation about forthcoming models from the usual German premium brands – does the world really need yet another overpowered RS Audi or AMG Mercedes? – and a generic comparison test between (and you're right with me) even more SUVs. For the obligatory supercar content there's a slightly breathless piece about driving an Aston Martin Vantage in the snow, just like the owners don't. I also learn that, as with all Astons since the DB5-aping DB7, every new model is a tribute act to its predecessor, meaning that, even after half a century, the DB5's ghost is still haunting the drawing office down Gaydon way. The only piece I didn't skim read is editor-in-chief Steve Cropley's musings, and that's mainly habit as I have been enjoying Cropley's writing since his days with *Car* in the Eighties. His prose may now suggest a benign 'best of all possible worlds' dotage, but anybody who has owned a Lotus Six, a Ferrari 308, an Ariel Atom, and a turbocharged 2CV is someone I'd be happy to have as my neighbour.

Autosport was compulsory reading for everybody who was as interested in motor racing as I was in the Sixties and Seventies, and, if your fashion sense inclined to the bobble-hatted end of the spectrum, you also had to buy *Motoring News* for its rallying coverage. I was mainly a tarmac sort of guy (except at RAC Rally time), and that's why I still have my 11 April, 1974 copy of *Autosport*, and you would have kept it too if you had been at the *Daily Express* International Trophy pictured on the cover, the first Formula 1 victory for both James Hunt and the Hesketh team, which felt like, and proved to be, the start of something big. Forgive another ancient and modern comparison, but it's worth doing to demonstrate the seismic shift in motorsport and its coverage. I paid 17p (equivalent to £1.96 in 2018) for 64 large format pages and, 44 years later, *Autosport*'s real price has more than doubled to £3.99, for 74 slightly smaller pages. Price up, size about the same but what about content? I wrote in an earlier chapter about how Formula 1 was no longer at the peak of the motorsport pyramid, but had become a big pointy building all of its very own, and the 2018 *Autosport* illustrates this point perfectly as Formula 1 dominates on no fewer than 62 of its 74 pages. And in 1974? Despite the opportunity for some jingoistic tub-thumping afforded by the win of a former public schoolboy for a team owned by a Lord, only nine out of 64 pages featured Formula 1, with the remainder revealing, not only the extraordinarily diverse motorsport scene in the Seventies, but also the importance attached by the specialist press to them. There were reports on club racing at Cadwell, drag racing at Blackbushe, autotests, sprints, trials, a long preview of the Scottish Rally, and even a paragraph on the Castrol Motor Club Quiz Championship, which I will own up to not having followed closely. And in 2018? You might still get a fleeting reference to a Cadwell club meeting, but years have passed since *Autosport* devoted any space to the other grassroots motorsport covered in '74, as it is now F1 or bust. That's been the direction of travel (as we say in our marketing meetings) for years, but in 2017 the magazine was even bought by an F1 guy, Zak Brown of post Ron Dennis McLaren. A cynic might fear that news bodes even worse for editorial independence than it does for future coverage of Prescott hillclimbs …

And on the independence theme, I now want to talk about the car magazine that, at its best, was as stylish as *The Face*, as influential as *NME*, as subversive as *International Times* and as iconoclastic as *Oz*: *Car*. The postwar British motoring press was buttoned down, humourless, equivocal, conformist, jingoistic, xenophobic, took itself much too seriously, and had a worryingly cosy relationship with the manufacturers whose advertisements had become their weekly cash cow. Readers of most car magazines were made to feel that they didn't really deserve to learn about a Lotus, let alone a Lamborghini, until they had served their time ploughing through humourless prose detailing the minutiae of the DAF Variomatic transmission, or the enhancement of the Ford Anglias by the introduction of a four-speed gearbox and a heater. As a kid, I read everything, every classified ad and every road test chart and graph, but even I knew that most of the copy would have bored the journalist who had written it even more than the poor sap who was now reading it on the 4.15 bus from Wakefield to Castleford. I was that sap, and in 1967 I may have been listening to Pink Floyd's *Piper at the Gates of Dawn* and Cream's *Disraeli Gears* but in the pages of *Autocar* and *Motor* it was forever a sleety monochrome day in 1957. And in *Motor Sport* it was forever 1934, as every copy would feature some esoteric piece from editor Bill Boddy about the place he always called The Track: Brooklands. Rock 'n' Roll it wasn't.

Car's iconoclasm created a whole new narrative about what it meant to be a car guy, even the teenage one who was two years away from a provisional driving licence, and longer still from getting the real key to the highway. You didn't just read *Car*, you savoured every feature, osmosing what they thought was cool and rejecting what wasn't by reading *The Good, The Bad and The Ugly* and sneering at every word the mainstream motoring press printed. The establishment was going to be challenged, every orthodoxy was to be binned, and nobody ever seemed to care too much about the collateral damage to the advertising revenue. In one story, entitled 'We Start the 3rd World War,' Rolls-Royce's emperor was exposed as a clay-footed impostor who couldn't hold the proverbial candle to a Mercedes 600. In another, the Ferrari 250GTO was pitched against its Pontiac namesake, which in the mid-Sixties was as sacrilegious as comparing a Da Vinci with a Warhol, or a Mozart with a Beach Boy. And neither mink coat nor silk knickers was ever compulsory wear at *Car*, with the scantily clad girls draped over a cover-starring Daytona Cobra, and a motor show TVR adding even more sexiness to the already hot copy.

Car's style owed much to the cooler than cool US magazine, *Car and Driver*, which had taken on the old money establishment *Road & Track* with writers who were younger, hipper, never short of an opinion, and unafraid of poking fun, nor of having it either. Writers like Leon Mandel and Brock Yates riffed as effortlessly and entertainingly about a Saab V-4 or Fiat Dino as they did about a Chevy Corvette or a Dodge Charger, and David E Davis (of whom more later) could make reading about even a humdrum Fiat 850 a lot more fun than reading an *Autocar* test of a Ferrari ("we found the handbrake disappointing" announced their 365GTB Daytona test – wasn't the 4.4-litre quad cam V12 enough?). It wasn't just how *Car and Driver* read, but how it looked, because instead of *Motor*'s austere black and white ads for Cleveland Discol petrol, *Car and Driver* would hit you with double-page Technicolor spreads advertising a Dodge Coronet with a 426 cubic inch Hemi and "a sway bar Charles Atlas couldn't bend." Hoo yah …

Car's irreverence, its willingness to pick fights, and its refusal to be pushed around by anybody, came from its succession of Australian editors; the men like Doug Blain who patently Did Not Give a Shit about Old Worlde tradition, respect, and deference and who were smart enough to employ writers whose prose would light up the page. LJK Setright was the star in the early years and Russell Bulgin in the later ones, and there's more about both of them later on in this chapter. Add in the borderline purple prose of Mel Nichols, balance it with Roger Bell's driving expertise and faultless reportage, season with Henry Manney's mischief, illustrate with pop art flair and zeitgeist cool, stir in some Stan Mott cartoon surrealism, illuminate with Phil Llewellin's travelogues, wash down with George Bishop's Lunchtime O'Booze conviviality, and you had the magazine that compelled me to scurry from newsagent to newsagent in the hope that this month's edition might have arrived, just this once, one day early.

In *1971 – Never a Dull Moment: Rock's Golden Year*, rock journalist David Hepworth argues, you've guessed, that 1971 was the best-ever year for music and cites *Who's Next*, *Led Zeppelin IV*, *Tapestry*, *Blue*, and *Hunky Dory* in his evidence. And I can buy that, because by '71 the Sixties high voltage current of innovation hadn't yet shorted out and been replaced by the low spark of progressive rock and its devil spawn, glam. I think that the glory years of motoring journalism peaked in the mid-Eighties, and that's unsettling, if not downright spooky, as there's a good case for saying the same about both Formula 1 and rallying. The mid-Eighties represented another point in time where the stars moved into perfect alignment, enabling the motoring media and some of the cars it featured to be not only better than they ever had been before, but in some respects as good as they ever could, or would be. Think about it; following years of unrest and instability, the "greed is good" credo of the Eighties had become a new religion, stock markets' Big Bangs were echoing around the world, marketing budgets were huge, pre-millennial angst was still a decade away, safety was more important than it had been but was still no big deal, all eyes were focussed on the future, and nobody was investing in nostalgia stocks. There were still only four TV channels in the UK, and, over at the CERN labs, the internet was only the tiniest twinkle in Tim Berners-Lee's eyes. Thanks to the fights that Margaret Thatcher and her chums chose to pick, the Eighties was the worst of times for coal mining and much else that involved real blokes doing real work in real communities, but it pains me to admit that, for us limp-wristed white-collar guys with a car habit, it came close to being the best of times. There was a huge appetite for fast and expensive cars, and manufacturers were squaring up to each other to get bigger market shares in an unprecedented display of corporate willy-waving. It was in that febrile climate that the first great hot hatch war was fought, primarily between Volkswagen, Ford, and Peugeot, but with occasional skirmishes involving Fiat, Lancia Vauxhall, Honda, and Toyota. Turbocharging had become the new rock 'n' roll, and race tracks and rally stages were being torn apart by insanely fast cars with telephone number horsepower. There was fighting going on between Porsche and Ferrari as well, as they reignited their Sixties grudge match, but instead of punch ups at Le Mans and Daytona, the fight venues were Europe's autoroutes and autostrada and America's freeways and interstates. Enter the Porsche 959 and the Ferrari 288 GTO, make some space for Lamborghini's bonkers Countach, allow Aston's Vantage to sit with the BMW M1 at the bar, cue a feeding frenzy in the motoring press and savour *Car*'s finest hour.

Until the Eighties, even *Car* offered a slightly balanced diet and whilst there might not have been the roughage that *Autocar* 'Industry News' might offer (let alone the thin gruel of *Motor Sport*'s interminable 'Wartime Diary of an RFC Officer') the reader still often had to chomp through a Ford Corsair or Fiat 132, or chew on some Volvo 145 hard tack before getting down to some supercar action. But not anymore, as the menu offered in the mid-to-late Eighties became ever richer, meaning you could skip the starters and mains, and truffle your way through an endless indulgence of the sweet stuff. I loved it before the indigestion kicked in sometime in the Nineties, and nobody did it better than *Car* as they had invented not only the supercar story but even the word itself.

That man Setright was to blame but he would have turned in his long and elegant grave if he had been around to witness how the term 'supercar' eventually became so devalued by overuse that it was superseded by 'hypercar,' a term that some might say would benefit from the removal of the first letter 'r.' Setright applied the term to the Lamborghini Miura that he helped drive to the UK from Sant'Agata in the autumn of 1967. In the 21st century a motoring journalist might take the early morning Ryanair from Stansted to Milan, thrash a Punto down to Maranello, get his 30-minute Fiorano slot with yet another variation of a mid-engined Ferrari V8, lunch at the Cavallino, and be back home to his new town semi in time for *Newsnight*, having written his copy on a laptop on the way home. Hadn't the editor said 750 words max, as the pictures – smoky sideways stuff, right? – would take up the other four pages? But back in '67 LJK Setright was getting in tune with the Miura's song on the 1000-mile drive home:

… a steady, mechanical mezzoforte made up of all the mumbling, thrashing, whining whirring, groaning and grumbling metallic obbligati that a race-bred engine furnishes to fill the octaves left unoccupied by that exuberant exhaust. It is a lovely noise, an expensive noise, but I suppose when all is said and done it is a noise.

I would expect nothing less from Setright's erudite pen, for wasn't he also responsible for describing the exhaust note of the Jaguar E-type he had taken for a dawn drive as "… a great vortex of acoustic spume?" I will talk some more about the message soon but a final thought first on the motoring press medium. To put it bluntly, it's fucked. Few of us buy magazines, and those of us who still do, grizzle about content and price because, like everything else in our lives, the internet and the smartphone have changed our habits forever. But I will concede that the classic car press will prosper for a few years yet, as each successive generation of 40 or 50-somethings with money to spend now wants to buy what they couldn't afford as 20-year-olds. And, unlike the girl with the big brown eyes you yearned for when you were 22, that 1991 Porsche 911, or "964" if you must, has neither crows' feet, nor a husband, nor a massive backside. It was somehow inevitable, that the original bench mark for classic car coverage came in the *Car* spinoff, *Supercar Classics*, which started off gloriously in the early Eighties before tailspinning to an ignominious demise a decade later. The title that had started by covering Ferrari 250 GTOs and D-Type Jaguars ended up, like all the rest, wittering on about tragic MGBs.

Autocar seems immortal, so on it stumbles, whilst Car took the decision years ago to bag the market of readers with attention spans of ants and it therefore peppers nearly every page with bite size factoids and trivia. Its spiritual successor, Evo, features meatier text and majors on hooning about in hot hatchbacks, extolling yet another iteration of Porsche 911 and getting very moist about six-figure supercars. And why not, because since the National Lottery arrived in 1994 aren't we all just the drop of a lucky ball away from a Lambo? There's a host of single make and budget classic titles too, targeted at the sort of guy whose Triumph Stag has been rotting under a tarpaulin at the bottom of the garden for a decade but who has told his wife that it's an investment. And, tragically, he even believes this crap himself. And finally there's Motor Sport, and if that ever ceases to be published then old men like me will be wearing black armbands because, since we all hit 50, it has become the only magazine for People Like Us.

In spite of the financial austerity we civilians have had to endure since 2008, the classic car press has moved seriously upmarket since the time when "classic" meant that unloved, rusty Triumph Stag, whose owner has been putting of restoring since 1981. Now it's tales of barn-find Maseratis and Bugattis, not buggered old Triumphs, which get us feverish with excitement. Correspondingly, the house style of some of the classic titles has ascended to the same rarefied altitude inhabited by the high net worth (aka stinking rich) folk who are now the only people who can afford the sort of old Ferrari that was worth Mondeo money a few years ago. Not only is much coverage given to market trends and what was hot (and what was only lukewarm) at Pebble Beach but some of the copy has moved firmly into self-parody, with the ghost of Alan Partridge stalking the more ludicrously portentous pieces. Autocar journalist Matt Prior memorably described some of the exclusive events attended by the classic car glitterati as "Concours des Pantalons Rouge," which was enough to make me smile in recognition. But you cannot deny that the classic magazines know their market, and my how they adore a Steve McQueen themed cover, because just one reference to the Bullitt and Le Mans star is all it takes to spike the sales of this month's issue. McQueen has undergone post-mortem beatification amongst a certain demographic of middle aged men, many of whom are eager to flaunt their Gulf Petroleum liveried accessories at classic race meetings and revivals. One of these guys even spent $984,000 (count 'em) on McQueen's Michael Delaney race overalls – a sum that would buy an Eighties Formula 1 car, with enough change left over for a race transporter. And a new Ferrari. The classified advertisements in the leading publications, Octane and Classic & Sports Car, are an especial joy – I read of a Mercedes 600 Landaulet (price on application, natch) having been owned by "Infamous Yugoslavian Revolutionary and President, Josip Broz Tito," transforming it into "A Very Significant and Historical Car with Documented Provenance." Love those gratuitous initial caps, guys but – help me with this – am I meant to stand up when reading this overblown tosh? Another, and very special, delight was the advertisement in Octane that referred, breathlessly, to the "now unbelievably for sale Porsche 997 Rothmans Slantnose," which was "comparable to a Stinger." I was then left gasping at the immortal words "Derick Bell this should be yours." I only hope that restoration was more accurate than the English, as I will confess to admiring both Singer Porsches and Derek Bell, and I will admit to being partial to a well-placed comma as well. Now read this carefully please:

It helps that you're sat carb side on the engine too … it's just the inside wheel that spins disappointingly … I'm anxious of the R500's box, but at the first tug of the lever they all evaporate …

For once, I won't name and shame, as this sort of mangled prose is almost ubiquitous in the motoring press. The present participle has become an endangered species, and so nobody is sitting in the "vicelike grip of the Recaros" while they savour the "riflebolt gearchange" – they're bloody "sat." And I die a little every bloody time, even though I should be used to it, being a wounded veteran from the great 'railway station' war. You remember the one, when we lost after a rearguard action against the 'train station' jihadis? And I know that language is an evolving thing, that nobody ever died from a split infinitive, or even a dangling participle, that the rules were never set in stone, yadda, but please can I be spared from "inside of," "met with," "likely" instead of "probably?" And why is it necessary to describe anything or anybody of the slightest merit as being the best "of all time" (the phrase described by *The Times Style Guide* as being "meaningless and not to be used in any circumstances")? There's worse too – "kudos to" (guys, you can't award kudos, only earn it), an obsessive compulsion to use the word "rotate" (or "turn" as we used to say in Earth language) and expressions like "mechanical grip" (as if road cars, at road speeds, ever had any other sort of grip). And don't ever say "iconic" in my presence, as things could get ugly.

Motoring journalism has never had its equivalent to journalists who can write like A A Gill, Caitlin Moran, George Orwell, Bernard Levin, Matthew Parris, Jonathan Raban, Martin Amis, Jonathan Meades, Clive James, Tom Wolfe (pace "Kandy-kolored Tangerine-flake Streamline Baby"), or Ernest Hemingway. Yes, Meades might have written excoriatingly about Downton Engineering's Daniel Richmond ("whose milieu was upper bohemian oddballs, bolters and bankrupts") and his wife Bunty (whose "Palaeolithic cruelty was … much more than difficult. This was clinical.") and James was the man responsible for the mother of all quotes about Murray Walker ("like a man whose trousers are on fire") but very few have written about our favourite subject with the wit, passion, and insight of Nick Hornby when he wrote about football in *Fever Pitch*. But hold on, what about that big guy in the corner, that's right, the one with the loud voice, "the fashion sense of a market trader," and the tragically bad hair, he's sounding like his third glass of rosé has kicked in and look, now both of his index fingers are jabbing for attention just like they used to do on *Top Gear*. Jeremy Clarkson (for it is he) trained as a journalist on the *Rotherham Advertiser*, learning how to cover courts and council meetings, before finding a springboard to fame at *Performance Car*, where he alchemised the leaden road test format into pure gold. He is astonishingly productive, writes with a discipline few can match, can rant for his country, pokes fun at anything and anybody (but especially himself), and who has become almost beatified by those men (and they are nearly always men) who feel victimised by what they invariably term as "political correctness gone mad." Clarkson writes almost, but not quite, as well as his late friend Adrian Gill, and if he ever returns to motoring journalism, Clarkson will have no rival. For the meantime though, he will continue to earn his living by doing what he has elevated to an art form, which is talking and writing about cars and driving for an audience primarily made up of those who have no interest in, or knowledge of, either.

There are three journalists whose prose on cars and driving transcended the genre and they are Setright, of course, David E Davis, and Russell Bulgin. Just like Clarkson, you didn't need an interest in the subject matter to enjoy their work but unlike Clarkson, it really helps if you do. It may be a tad meta (bloke who is writing about cars writing about blokes who write about cars, but better), but hell, it's the last chapter …

Setright, yes. The journalist who was also an engineer, concert standard clarinettist, and lawyer, and who can claim the unique distinction of having written car reviews in both rhyming couplet and sonnet form, and who made not the slightest concession to his readership. As you might do when faced with an inspirational teacher, you either kept up or slunk off to the back of the class and moaned that Long John Kickstart was as pretentious as he was arrogant. Lazy jibes, as of course he was neither, but Setright never did 'just my humble opinion' equivocation, his prose was forged with iron conviction and it really did not matter that you didn't agree that Honda and Bristol were the only jewels in a sea of automotive mediocrity, or that all speed limits were "… a tool of oppression, a codification of yesterday's prejudices." But who couldn't smile at his description of the 1.5-litre Formula – "… their tiny jewelled engines sang a pure high strain, a clear clarion with six scales and a tiny polished woodtipped gear shift to pluck each in turn from the coils of exhaust pipes ecstatic in their mating." You aren't going to read that about the new Red Bull in this week's *Autosport* …

And you really must read *Thus Spake David E*, an anthology of over 100 articles that David E Davis wrote for *Car and Driver* and *The Automobile* between 1962 and 1999. The range of subjects can be gauged from titles including *Henry Ford – The Windmills of His Mind*, *I Drove a Ferrari 275LM from Philadelphia to New York and Found Truth (graunch)*, and *God is my Unindicted Co-Conspirator*, the latter about Ayrton Senna's bible habit, obviously.

Davis's love of fast cars, even faster women, and good wine is complemented by trenchant opinions on just about every other subject that creeps into his prose. Charming and abrasive in equal measure, he worked at a time when the US motoring press had massive influence and huge circulation. Davis's stories range from accounts of fast drives in BMWs across Europe to gossip about the movers and shakers in Detroit, the legendary big beasts such as Ford and Chrysler boss Lee Iacocca and Corvette grandfather Zora Arkus Duntov. The author adored light and manoeuvrable European cars but this was tempered by his affection for forgotten US cars like the *Unsafe At Any Speed* Corvair and his enduring love of good ol' boy Jeeps. Motorsport was important to Davis, his friends included Bruce McLaren, Jo Siffert, and Pedro Rodriguez, and his own distinctively lopsided appearance was the legacy of the accident in an MG TD that nearly killed him in a 1955 Sacramento race. Davis wrote in that uniquely punchy, laconic, and wry style that the best American writers have made their trademark. Stuff like this:

Well. We have a new president (Clinton) who drives a 1966 Mustang, smokes very large cigars and is widely rumoured to chase women. This is not a bad prescription for winning the hearts and minds of us disaffected Americans.

Or this:

On the Ferrari 330GT's dash to the airport, it was hitting on eleven cylinders and one of the exhaust manifolds was cracked. Today it sits in its garage, listing slightly and looking for all the world like some terrific girl with whom you went to high school and found, thirty years later, slumped on a barstool in Calumet City. I want to save that old harridan from further deterioration ... I also want to buy her cheap.

And this too:

The Fiat X1/9 has now taken the place of the Chevy Vega as the car in which most Americans like to be marooned at the roadside. These poor, benighted little cars, evidently conceived as transport for midget clowns in Italian circuses, have now rusted to the point that one can usually see through them ... and are coughing their insides out miles from home, all over the Republic.

Davis' finest work of all was *The Freedom of Wild Ducks*, a long piece he wrote on the simple, elemental joy of driving, the passion that came to define the man:

In an open car we enjoy the heightened freedom of the coursing hound, racing across the land with only the wind for clothing, it is the freedom of wild ducks shining in their colorful plumage, flying at impossible speeds through the treetops to impress the duck-women they love.

There's more:

Sometimes I drove for miles without lights, just following the road by its contour and by the march of the utility poles stretching away towards the ends of the earth in the moonlight. Going where? ... Going to the end of the road because I'd never been there before. Going to ... I don't know where. Perhaps going to the future, to the rest of my life.

And sorry, but if you don't love this we can never be friends:

Our service manager was something of a loner ... from what I knew of this guy he loved four things – three were tatty BMW 328s ... and the fourth was any woman who would go home with him. But the mind boggles when she saw that they'd be sharing a single bed with a cylinder head and a bouquet of pushrods.

The slim white book I'm looking at cost me £20, but it is now worth £300, maybe more. Because few were printed, nobody wants to be parted from their own copy and that's why copies of this slim 130-page work are so sought after, and just FYI, mine's not for sale. The book is simply called *Bulgin* and contains the best work of the best motoring journalist of them all, Russell Bulgin. He died in 2002 but had few rivals then or now. If you want to know about Ayrton Senna's day out in the Welsh Mountains driving rally cars, then Russell's your man. He's also your man if you want to know just what it feels like to try to Vmax a Lotus Carlton on the Autobahn, or what it was like getting down with the cool kids on the Chelsea Cruise in a Mercedes 190E Evo homologation special.

Of course, Bulgin loved cars but he painted on a much broader canvas than most journalists; his greatest ability was effortlessly to grasp what was cool, what wasn't, and then to tell us exactly why this was so. Only the excellent Stephen Bayley has that insight and the skill to transform it into text whose every word you can savour. Bulgin had a unique style, often conversational, but knowing and wry too, effortlessly funny and piercingly insightful. Bulgin would find it both ironic and absurd that his biggest legacy is that too many motoring journalists are still trying, and failing, to ape the Bulgin style. This tendency has been exquisitely satirised by Richard Porter on his Sniff Petrol website; just read a couple of spoof reviews by Porter's Troy Queef, road tester extraordinaire and no stranger to cliché. Me? I avoid them like the plague, natch.

Bulgin wrote for *Motor*, *Autocar*, *Car*, *Evo*, *Cars and Car Conversions*, *Supercar Classics* and, curiously, the *Daily Telegraph*, but he was never the guy who drew the short straw of road testing duty, not for him the agony of writing 1000 words of calm objectivity about yet another dull new hatchback from Ford or VW. He wrote instead about subjects such as a car's body language, its societal subtext, and its capacity for irony. He loved motorsport and I still regret not saying hello to Bulgin at a Donington race meeting in the Nineties where both his height and his loping air of cool made him instantly recognisable. He was *Motor*'s Grand Prix reporter and had been at Estoril in '85 to see Senna win his first Grand Prix:

A short sharp shower preceded the Portuguese Grand Prix and a short sharp shock disappeared into the rain lashed middle distance as the lights blinked green. The shock's name was Ayrton Senna and he thought the race should have been stopped.

It's temptingly easy to sneer at Elvis Presley's grisly taste in cars and clothes but Bulgin, ever the iconoclast, dug deeper, and thought deeper still than his peers. He went to Graceland and tracked down Percy Kidd, the man who sold the King his Cadillacs and his De Tomaso Pantera, the car that was punished by its owner for its misbehaviour, "... So he took out his pistol and shot it fulla holes," reported Mr Kidd. Driving south east from Memphis to Tupelo, Mississippi, Bulgin stopped at the shack that Vernon Presley had built and wrote:

Two room-simple: Elvis was born there. One glance at 306 Old Saltillo Road explains the gold-plated seatbelt buckles and plumped-cushion excess of Graceland.

Bulgin paddled up some of the less explored backwaters of the automotive world, it wasn't all getting moist about supercars and WRC Sierra Cosworths, and this is his take on the stealth machine, which was the fastest car of all on Britain's motorways in 1990:

The fast lane ... is where you get blitzed by a Bedford Astra Van at 95 and explaining just why they are so quick – Because there is an unspoken code surrounding every move made by a serious van user: don't give a shit. That, blunt as it seems, is the Zen of van driving.

Bulgin on the 190 Evo and the Dodge Viper:

This was going to be the perfect evening. What more could a man desire? Had everything I needed: two South London girls with minds like razors, a stash of Ribena, a cassette of T Rex's finest work and a £55,000 Mercedes Benz styled by people to whom the phrase "creative drugs" was, quite patently, far from oxymoronic.
Just one look. That's all it takes now. Just one look. And instantly you are either a believer, a convert or even – just maybe – an evangelist. Or perhaps you don't get it at all. Don't care. Want to continue your monochrome life locked in a turbo diesel world. Don't dare to dream ... Look once, look twice, drool. That's the core of the Viper GTS.

And finally, unimprovably and perfectly:

Last Thursday morning I had a huge shunt on the M4 westbound. Early morning, lightly trafficked, perfect visibility: the clean crew had to be called. In the restaurant at Heston Services, that tricky cafetiere/damp tray interface finally got the better of me. I'd been eking out grip on dry sections of the tray but the cafetiere suddenly understeered. I couldn't hold the slide – it hit the carpet like an IndyCar tagging the wall at Turn Four.

There were many affectionate obituaries after Bulgin died but this coolest of journalists had that base covered too, with these words:

... when I finally croak, a line in my obituary will read 'In 1993 (he) was the first journalist to ponder the precise facial hair rationale of Williams' Grand Prix driver Damon Hill.' But then I guess you usually get the obituary you deserve.

And that is not only the best way to finish my tribute to Russell Bulgin, but also to finish this book. I hope you have enjoyed the trip.

Afterword
THE SCOTTISH PLAYLIST
The North Coast 500

The serious stuff first – unlike Route 66 or the Route Napoleon, the North Coast 500 (NC500) has no official status, nor is it a recognised route between A and B. Instead, it is the title given by Visit Scotland to a tourism initiative it wished to promote. As such, it deserves to succeed, but the recommended route has some flaws, not least its inclusion of some of the east coast, and the starting point of Inverness. The route has become popular with keen drivers, but risks becoming the victim of its own success, thanks to the selfishness of a minority.

The route? Try this:
▶ Travel clockwise from the southwest, heading north and west to the north coast, then drive east, turning south before Thurso.

▶ Start in, or near, Fort William or Invergarry, and head for the Kyle of Lochalsh. After the obligatory photo stop at Eilean Donan, a good route might take in Strathcarron, Applecross (via Bealach na Bà), Torridon, Gairloch, Ullapool, Loch Assynt, Kylesku Bridge, Scourie, Durness, Tongue, and Altnaharra. But there are many variations on the route and I would recommend including Achnasheen and Loch Maree instead of Bealach na Bà, later diverting through Inverpolly and Lochinver north of Ullapool and, after, driving round Loch Eriboll on the north coast, then turning south on to the single-track road leading past Loch Hope to Altnaharra.

▶ You won't need sat nav – ten minutes with a map will show you virtually the whole road network north of the Great Glen.

Here's how to enjoy yourself:
▶ Don't drive in convoys. They look crass, encourage bad driving and annoy other road users. The NC500 is best enjoyed alone, but if travelling in a group, split into pairs and drive five minutes apart.

▶ Many Highland settlements don't have a 30mph speed limit. That doesn't mean it is actually compulsory to drive through a village or past an isolated croft at high speed .

▶ Beware of hazards you don't get at home. Sheep can spoil your day, but Highland cattle and Red Deer can spoil your life. And take special care early and late. You can be a very, very long way from help.

▶ The journey is about far more than the road; it helps to know what you're looking at. Such as the Five Sisters of Kintail, Quinag, Ben Loyal, Foinaven and the weird, fish-tailed mountain called Suilven.

▶ Talk to the locals; they are friendly, often eccentric, and sometimes borderline bonkers.

▶ Even if you are pressing on, don't assume that the lights in your mirror must belong to a hard charging Ferrari F40 with a Franchitti at the wheel. The fastest vehicle in the north west highlands is typically a Citroën Nemo van driven by a Kinlochbervie plumber who is running late for his tea.

▶ Don't drive like a plank, don't assume that you are doing anybody a favour by sharing your exhaust noise and bear in mind that people come to the far north for many reasons – walking, climbing, cycling, birdwatching, angling – so do try not to ruin their day. Press on by all means, but be discreet.

And just remember, if your car displays a sticker announcing "Bad Boys Hoon – NC500" everyone, me included, will think you are an adolescent jerk.

Soundtracking your trip

If the engine in your car was born in Maranello, Sant'Agata, Stuttgart, and possibly even Blackpool then you don't need much help from me in deciding what to listen to, but if your car isn't too shouty then here's some music for the places you will see on the NC500 and the emotions they will trigger.

▶ The Byrds, *Wasn't Born To Follow*: Day one, and you're climbing north out of Invergarry with a 250 mile drive ahead. Want to know what immortality feels like, even for only 124 seconds?

▶ Skeewiff, *Man Of Constant Sorrow*: The cheapest power increase you'll ever buy. But things could get ugly if you're driving a 911 GT2.

▶ The National, *Anyone's Ghost*: The clouds are smoking Glen Torridon, and now it's just you and the road.

▶ Jimi Hendrix, *All Along The Watchtower*: Ardvreck Castle with an angry Loch Assynt beyond; savour that shiver down your spine.

▶ Captain Beefheart, *Same Old Blues*: For when you just need to keep on keepin' on.

▶ Joni Mitchell, *Shades Of Scarlett Conquering*: Bealach na Bà, after the rush, when you come back down.

▶ Massive Attack, *Eurochild*: Kylesku Bridge, and now you're starring in your own road movie.

▶ Scott Walker, *Seventh Seal*: Hear this in Strath Dionard and you've got a walk on part in a Bergman film. Just don't look in the mirror, okay?

▶ Johnny Cash, *Further On Up The Road*: Ullapool's behind you, the scenery is out of Tolkien but The Man in Black will see you through. Hell yeah!

▶ Public Service Broadcasting, *Spitfire*: You're flying even if there isn't a V12 Merlin under the bonnet.

► Talking Heads, *Listening Wind*: You're east of Altnaharra in the Flow Country; "the time is surely now or never." And if you want to be really with the zeitgeist, check out Angelique Kidya's 2018 version.

► Fatoumata Diawara, *Kanou*: Is it 'dreich' or 'drookit,' are you frowning in a 'fret' or harried in a 'haar?' Then here comes the sun ...

► MC Solaar, *Le Nouveau Western*: Loch Eriboll is sparkling and you're feeling good.

► Bruce Springsteen, *All That Heaven Will Allow*: "Rain and storm and dark skies, well now they don't mean a thing;" as usual, the Boss is right.

And, when you are back at home, planning next year's trip whilst reliving this year's, you really need to be listening to Mary Gauthier singing *Our Lady of the Shooting Stars*. It works for me, and I hope it does for you.

MORE FROM VELOCE ...

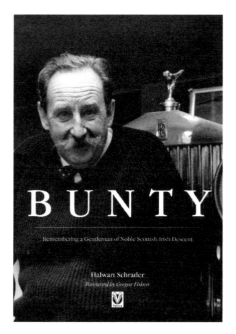

The biography of a larger-than-life character in the world of motoring, especially among classic car collectors. David Scott-Moncrieff, aka 'Bunty,' claimed to be the Number 1 in the Rolls-Royce second-hand car trade. He was a colourful personality, an experienced car expert, a charming entertainer and a passionate vintage race car addict.

ISBN: 978-1-787113-48-0
Paperback • 21x14.8cm
216 pages • 81 pictures

A veteran motoring journalist's extraordinary life, told through delightfully eccentric stories and charming diary extract. This unique book is packed with fascinating stories about classic cars and motorcycles, set in a bygone world, and properly fixed in time. (Fiction)

ISBN: 978-1-845848-44-6
Paperback • 21x14.8cm
288 pages • 5 pictures

For more information and price details, visit our website at:
www.veloce.co.uk • email: info@veloce.co.uk • Tel: +44(0)1305 260068

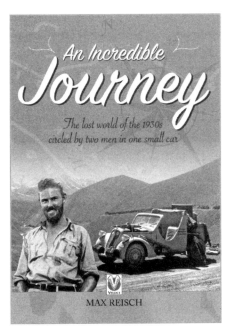

MAX REISCH

The compelling story of Max Reisch and Helmuth Hahmann's journey across Asia in 1935 in a Steyr 100.
It is a story of adventure and discovery, revealing the countries, people and problems that they encountered along the way. With stunning period photographs, this book provides a historic and fascinating insight into a pre-WW2 world.

ISBN: 978-1-787111-65-3
Paperback • 21x14.8cm
288 pages • 231 pictures

This book recalls the golden age (in the author's view) of motoring journalism, during the last two decades of the 20th century, with additional material from before and after. Although the book is about cars it should amuse, irritate or even inform people who are not interested in cars at all.

ISBN: 978-1-787111-84-4
Paperback • 21x14.8cm
256 pages • 30 pictures

THE GOOD
THE MAD
&THE
UGLY

... not to mention
Jeremy Clarkson

The GOLDEN years of motoring journalism?

Peter Dron

For more information and price details, visit our website at:
www.veloce.co.uk • email: info@veloce.co.uk • Tel: +44(0)1305 260068

INDEX

AC
Cobra 21, 184
Willment Ghia Cobra 188
Alesi, Jean 85
Alfa Romeo 44, 45, 89
1750GS Zagato 192
2600 Sprint 20, 196
Alfasud 45, 46
Spider 88, 89
Allerton Bywater 10, 18
Andretti, Michael 162
Another Small Fortune 171
Arron, Simon 8, 133, 228
Aston, Dr Clifford 12, 13, 34, 35, 38
Aston, Joanne 8, 63
Aston, Squadron Leader Frederick 13, 20
Aston Martin
DB6 17, 19, 81
DB-SC 19
Attwood, Richard 163-164
Audi Sport Quattro 213
Austin
A40 34
Seven Special 219
Austin, Rob 161
Autocar 16, 17, 20, 32, 35, 51, 252, 253, 255, 258
Autograss 206, 211, 240, 242
Class 7 208, 209

F600 208
Thornborough 206-211
York 152-153
Autosport 22, 51, 114, 238, 254
Avro Vulcan 10, 12, 14

BARC 26, 143, 246
Banger racing 226, 227
Barbon Manor 174, 175
Barford Stadium 226, 227, 239
Bateman, HM 204
Beckwith, Graham 144, 145, 247
Bell, Roger 255
Beltoise, Jean-Pierre 114
Beuttler, Mike 112, 113
Binbrook 64
Bishop, George 256
Bizzarrini Strada 19
Blain, Doug 255
Blankstone, Margaret and Peter 27
BMRMC 23
BMW
M1 Pro Car 178, 245
M4 7
V12 LMR 197
Brabham
BT36X 30
BT49C 190
Jack 114
Bracewell, Melvyn 34

Bradford, Charlotte 171
Brain, Martin 26
Brambilla, Vittorio 240
Bramhall, David 177
Brancatelli, Gianfranco 198
Brands Hatch 93, 95, 98, 248
Brawn, Ross 120
Bristol 401 19
British Scooter Organisation 200
BRM
P83 57
P153 189
P160 29, 92
Brown, Zak 191
BTCC 157-162, 237
Bugatti T40 155, 156
Bulgin, Russell 103, 255, 262, 263
Buxton, Roger 192
Byrne, David 70, 108

Cadwell Park 56, 62-64, 105, 148, 152, 163-168, 239, 241
Campbell, Donald 183
Campbell, Gina 184-186
Cape Wrath 76
CAR 35, 254, 255, 257, 258
Car and Driver 82, 255
Carlin Motorsport 64
Cars and Car Conversions 51, 238
Castleford 11, 22, 37

Castrol R 21
Castle Howard 26
Chapman, Colin 6, 39, 51, 54,
    120, 188
Charlotte, NC 122, 123
Citroën
    2CV 42, 141
    Visa Super E 69
Chevron
    B37 194
    GR8 245
Clan Crusader 50-52
Clark, Alan 78
Clark, Jim 114
Clarke, James 140
Clarke, Bill 155, 156
Clarkson, Jeremy 250-260
Classic & Sports Car 258
Cleland, John 189
Code 60 150, 151
Cooper
    T59 165, 244
    T81 26
    T86 21
Cranage, David 154
Croft 59, 65, 137-143, 157-162,
    176-177, 222-224, 250
    Inter Nations Cup 222, 223
Crombac, Jabby 72
Cropley, Steve 254

Dalby Forest 211-217
Datsun 120 Y 44
Davis, David E 123, 255, 260-262
Dean, Tony 90
Dennis, Ron 83

Diniz, Pedro 28, 100
Dixon, Dick and Jane 166
Donington Park 137, 177-182
Duffy, Tony 158, 159
Ecclestone, Bernie 109, 112, 124
Eklund, Per 26
Elf Petroleum 199
Epps, Michael 160
ERA R4 40, 72, 111, 183
Ethnicity 210, 240
Evo 258

Facel Vega HK500 19
Fathers, Stephen 219
Fen Tigers 206
Ferrari 80-89
    246 F1 81
    250 GTO 86, 87, 229
    250 LM 27
    250 Lusso 85
    275 GTB 81, 232
    312 B2 82, 94
    330 GT 81
    330 LMB 229
    365 GTC 81
    512 BBLM 231
    512 M 81, 88
    640 117
    Dino 206S 88
    Enzo 86, 99
    F40 83, 84
    F430 Scuderia 83
    P4 15
    SEFAC 82
Fiat 89
    Uno Turbo 46, 47

Fielding, Gavin 218
Fletcher, John 149
Folch, Joaquin 190
Ford
    Corsair 17
    Escort MkI/II 25, 26, 214
    Focus 39, 40
    GT40 5, 15, 16, 27, 93, 244
    Lotus Cortina 21
    Model A 217
    Mustang 18, 37, 129
    Popular E93A 24
    Sierra Cosworth 198
Forestry Commission 212
Forghieri, Mauro 120
Formula 1 90-106, 107-121
    penalties 118
    rules 120
    turbocharged 97, 98
    tyres 117
Formula 2 91
Formula 3 244
Formula 5000 90
Formula E 120
Formula Ford 1600 165, 166, 243
Fox, Steve 52
Frankel, Andrew 229

Gallagher, Noel 7
Ganley, Howden 189, 190
Gascoigne, Rodney 34
Gaye, Vincent 232, 233
Gierach, John 26
Gilbert and George 106
Glenton, Robert 17
Glob, Lotte 78

GN Thunderbug 235
Good, David 28
Goodwood 239, 240
    Houses 230, 231
    Members' Meeting 228, 236
Gordon Keeble GK1 20
Goring, Roger 145, 146
Grande, Ariana 157
Grand Prix
    Azerbaijan 108, 109, 112
    Bahrain 108, 112
    British 109
    French 108
    Monaco 114
    Russian 112
    South African 111
Group C 178
Gurney, Dan 123

Hamilton, Lewis 83, 105, 109, 139
Hanson, Patrick (Paddy) 21, 23, 25
Hardy, Steve 43
Harewood 26, 30, 65, 133-137,
    153-157, 177, 246-247
Harrison, Jolyon 217-219, 233
Haussauer, Paul 50, 51
Hedges, Matthew 112
Henn, Preston 84
Henney, Marc 170, 171
Hepworth, David (driver) 30
Hepworth, David (journalist)
    256
Hepworth, Stephen 231
Hepworth-Ferguson 231
Hewerdine, Boo 222
Hildyard, Nick 155

Hill, Damon 183
Hill, Graham 94
Honister Pass 217-221
Hooker, John Lee 81, 82
Hope-Frost, Henry 191, 234, 235, 247
Hornby, Nick 259
HSCC 163-164, 243-244, 248
Hughes, Andy 201
Humber Hawk 12, 34
Hunt, James 95, 96, 112, 113, 195, 196

Ickx, Jacky 21, 94-95

Jaguar
    D-Type 72, 80
    E-Type 17, 18, 30, 40, 42, 257
    Mk II 14
    XJ 220 191
James, Clive 259
JDM 200
Jenkinson, Denis 132
Jess the Cadwell Cat 151
Jones, Martyn 172
Jowett 7hp 221

Kahne, Kesey 128
Keselowski, Brad 127
Keys, John 13
Kubota, Katsu 196

Larson, Kyle 128
Lamborghini Miura 88, 257
Lancia Delta S4 213
Larkin, Philip 11

La Vache Qui Rit 86
Lauda, Niki 6, 96, 101, 102
Lee, Richard 179
Le Jog 225, 226
Lehto, JJ 104
Llewellin, Phil 75, 257
Lola-Aston Martin 15, 16
Lord Lorne Jacobs 186
Lotus
    Eclat 52
    Elan 6, 18, 42, 49, 187, 188
    Elite 42, 52
    Esprit 52
    Six 189
    Seven (Caterham) 6, 8, 9,
        39, 47, 49-58, 59-68, 69-79,
        154, 166, 178, 179, 180, 181
    56B 92
    72 82, 102
    78 117
    98T 117
Lovett, Andrew 184
Low Flying magazine 71
Lyons, Pete 119

MacDowell, Mike 30, 190
MacKrill, Nigel 51
MacNish, Allan 182
Mallory Park 36, 91, 250
    Plum Pudding Races 227,
        228
Manney, Henry 256
Mansell, Nigel 98, 102-104
Maranello 80, 83-84
March
    711 82

712 **195**
Martin, Guy **202-203**
Masood, Umar **202**
Matra MS 120C **189**
Mazda MX5 **6, 43, 149**
Mays, Raymond **183**
McDonnell Douglas F4
   Phantom **14, 81**
McLaren
   M10A/B **28, 30, 90**
   MP4 **117**
McQueen, Steve **164, 258**
McRae, Colin **213**
Meaden, Richard **192, 193**
Meades, Jonathan **259**
Memphis, TN **128, 129**
Mercedes F1 **111**
Merzario, Arturo **94**
MG
   Midget **41**
   Metro 6R4 **213**
Miles, Jon **196**
Milicevic, Jon **165, 233, 244**
Mikkola, Hannu **22, 25**
Mitchell, Joni **7, 69, 88**
Montoya, Juan Pablo **128**
Moore, Alan **15**
Moores, Derek (Classic
   Carriage Company) **52**
Morgan, Lee **150**
Morris Marina **44, 51**
Mosley, Max **118**
Motor **16, 17**
Motor Sport **115, 229, 255, 258**
Motoring News **23, 114, 238**
Mott, Stan **256**

Mr Whoppit **185-186**
MSA **216**
MSV (MotorSport Vision) **149,
   246**
Murray, Gordon **6, 104, 120**

NASCAR **122-129**
Needell, Tiff **232**
Nelson Ledges **52**
Newey, Adrian **6, 120**
Newton, John **184, 185**
Nichols, Mel **256**
Nicholson, Viv **18**
Nominative determinism **89**
North Coast 500 **79, 264**
NSU Ro80 **47, 48**

Octane **258**
Olivers Mount **26**
Oulton Park **21, 23, 90, 92, 93, 249**
   Gold Cup **194-199**

Panis, Olivier **114**
Pashley, Tony **228**
Pateman, Brian **169**
Patrick, Danica **126**
Pescarolo, Henri **91**
Peugeot
   205GTi **46**
   205T16 **213**
   306GTi6 **61**
   504Ti **225**
Peterson, Ronnie **91, 102**
Pilkington, Stephen **234**
Piquet, Nelson **66**
Pontiac Firebird **169**

Porsche
   910 **231**
   911 **25, 32, 62, 64**
Posey, Sam **132, 133**
Postlethwaite, Harvey **117**
Presley, Elvis **184**
Prior, Matt **258**
Procter, Kevin **224**
Prost, Alain **102**
Pye, Marcus **167, 199, 247**

RAC Rally **23, 24-26**
Radio 270 **11**
Raikkonen, Kimi **133, 139**
Rally Yorkshire **211- 217**
Rallycross **221-224**
Regazzoni, Clay **82, 123**
Reid, Anthony **231**
Reliant Scimitar **18**
Remembrance Day **221**
Reynolds, Trevor **92**
Ribeiro, Alex **112, 113**
Richmond, Duke of **229**
Riley Kestrel **40, 59**
Rindt, Jochen **114**
Road & Track **255**
Rockingham **125, 126**
Rodriguez, Pedro **29, 92, 93**
Roebuck, Nigel **118**
Rooke, Daniel **222, 224**
Rosberg, Keke **30, 102**
Rover
   2000 **12**
   3-Litre **12**
Rufforth **20**
   750MC **244**

Santa Pod 168-174, 240, 248
Sato, Takuma 104, 196, 203
Savile, Jimmy 19
Scourie 76
Senna, Ayrton 60, 62, 104, 105, 178
Scotland 69-79
Setright, LJK 51, 93, 255, 257, 258, 260
Shelsley Walsh 182-187, 239
Siffert, Jo 91
Silverstone 59, 82, 93, 95, 99, 100, 102
Classic 187-194, 239
Smales, David 140, 151
Snetterton 20, 31
Sofa Man 125
Somervail, Jimmy 72
Soper, Steve 197
Stevens, Jon 76
Stewart, Jackie 92, 105
Strand cigarettes 53
Stringfellow, Scott 60
Sunbeam Tiger 16, 20
Supercar Classics 257
Surtees, John 94, 217
Suzuki SC 100 40, 43, 44

Tauranac, Ron 177
Taylor, PM 22
Taylor, Simon 115, 168
Tesla Model S 48
The Prisoner (TV series) 50
The Wind in the Willows 219
Theophile Schneider 155
Thwaites, Richard 30
Tilley, Ben 166
Time Attack 199-205, 240, 241
Titchmarsh, Ian 167, 199, 247
Toivonen, Henri 213
Tomdoun 74
Trickle, Dick 12
Triumph
Dolomite 44
Herald 12, 18, 32, 34
Vitesse 35-38, 44
Tyrrell
001 92
003 82
019 117

Vettel, Sebastian 112, 171
Vivian, David 55
Volkswagen Golf GTi 45, 46
Voodoo Hemi 172

Vox Villa 183
VSCC 153, 238, 242
Lakeland Trial 117-221
Volvo 144 37

Waldegaard, Bjorn 25
Walker, Mark 235
Walker, Murray 259
Walker, Paul 201
Warner Medical Diary 22
Watts, Patrick 232
Webber, Mark 112
Webster, Dave 158
Welch, Denis 193
Westfield 52
Wheatcroft, Kevin 179
Wheatcroft, Tom 177
Williamson, Roger 180
Wilson, Morgan and Caitlin 171

York Raceway 66, 67, 143-148, 239
Young, Eoin 17

Zandvoort 101